3/23

D1308187

THE MAKING OF BRYCE HARPER

PHENOM

ROB MIECH

THOMAS DUNNE BOOKS

ST. MARTIN'S GRIFFIN

NEW YORK

THOMAS DUNNE BOOKS.
An imprint of St. Martin's Press.

PHENOM. Copyright © 2012 by Rob Miech. All rights reserved. Printed in the United States of America. For information, address St. Martin's Press, 175 Fifth Avenue, New York, N.Y. 10010.

www.thomasdunnebooks.com
www.stmartins.com

The Library of Congress has cataloged the hardcover edition as follows:

Miech, Rob.
    The last natural : Bryce Harper's big gamble in sin city and the greatest amateur season ever / Rob Miech.
        p. cm.
    ISBN 978-1-250-00145-0 (hardcover)
    ISBN 978-1-250-01241-8 (e-book)
 1. Harper, Bryce, 1992–   2. Baseball players—United States—Biography.   I. Title.
    GV865.H268M54 2012
    796.357092—dc23
    [B]

                                                                2012009369

ISBN 978-1-250-03202-7 (trade paperback)

Originally published under the title *The Last Natural*

First St. Martin's Griffin Edition: March 2013

10 9 8 7 6 5 4 3 2 1

For Allen and Rebecca Miech
My saints

PHENOM

PROLOGUE

HE'S *SKINNY*, TIM CHAMBERS thought as Bryce Harper inched into the snug confines of the College of Southern Nevada baseball coach's office. From behind his simple and orderly pine desk, Chambers scanned from his young slugger's furrowed brow and hollow cheeks to the obvious void between his stomach and white T-shirt. Harper looked as if he would need a jersey one size smaller than usual, a tighter belt, and some hefty portions of his mother Sheri's succulent macaroni and cheese, and savory spaghetti.

Chambers instantly knew that an arduous annual schedule of at least 160 to 170 baseball games, for years, had caught up with Harper. It seemed the games, for his high school, junior national squads, and club teams in Las Vegas, Southern California, Arizona, the Midwest, and other side of the country, had been nonstop. Harper had just led the US eighteen-and-under national team to a Pan American Junior gold medal. Mighty Cuba, which had won the tournament's previous seven titles, had fallen to Harper and his fellow Americans in the championship game at Daniel Canonico Stadium in Barquisimeto, Venezuela.

But when Harper came back to CSN in October 2009, four months after *Sports Illustrated* had splashed the sixteen-year-old prodigy on its cover and tagged him as the game's CHOSEN ONE and WONDER BOY, he weighed 185 pounds, twenty-five less than his normal playing weight.

The constant games were part of that exhaustion, as was the barrage of hype, interest, speculation, and venom aimed at Harper's maverick maneuver from Las Vegas High School after his sophomore year to CSN, a junior college in Henderson, Nevada, on the outskirts of Las Vegas. His burgeoning star's fragile constitution shocked Chambers.

"You're stressed-out," Chambers told Harper. "We need to get you away from it." Harper shrugged but didn't disagree. Chambers gazed at a young man about to implode from all the pressure, from the blizzard of criticism and scrutiny. Harper couldn't disguise that the cameras and writers and questions had worn him out. And he's so young, Chambers thought, it would be difficult for Harper to accurately express the turmoil swirling inside him.

Chambers told Harper he was shutting him down. "You need to rest and watch." He instructed Harper to sit next to him on the dugout bench for the next ten days of practices.

The series of events that had led to the country's top amateur player reporting for duty inside Tim Chambers's office had initially been triggered by the removal of Bryan Harper, Bryce's older brother, from a game almost six months earlier.

A six-foot-six, left-handed pitcher, Bryan Harper had spent an eminently forgettable freshman 2009 baseball season at California State University, Northridge. When he'd got wrongly plucked, Bryan believed, by coach Steve Rousey from a late-April 2009 game at UNLV—in Bryan's own backyard, no less, to add to the indignity—the elder Harper had hit rock bottom.

That night, Bryan called Chambers and inquired about spending his sophomore season at CSN. Chambers quickly hung up. Talking to the coach of another team during a season is verboten, but it reflected how desperately Bryan Harper had wanted to get out of Southern California.

In the ensuing days, Sheri Harper, a paralegal, found a blog on an Internet site that raised questions of great interest to her family. Why don't American baseball players have the same options as Dominicans, say, or others in the Caribbean and the rest of the world? Those talented youngsters can sign professional contracts at sixteen years of age and begin polishing their skills in major league academies, hastening their paths to the big leagues. Why are US players not afforded that same avenue and are only eligible to be drafted after their senior season in high school or, unknown to the average fan, a year after they leave high school? UNLV hadn't been an option, either, because those who played at a four-year university were not eligible for the draft until they had completed their junior season.

What's more, the Collective Bargaining Agreement between Major League Baseball owners and players was set to expire after the 2011 season. It was widely believed that major changes with a new deal would include slotted draft picks—players would be paid rigid, and much lower, salaries according to where in the draft they were chosen, and bonuses were expected to be scaled back. The quicker a raw talent such as Bryce Harper could get drafted, before such changes were enacted, the better.

Sheri showed the Internet story to her husband, Ron, and they began to formulate a plan. Once they took their information to Chambers, a close family friend for years, the circumvention of the system was truly under way.

Ron Harper and Chambers had first crossed paths in high school, when Chambers's Utah prep team played Harper's Rancho High School squad in an Easter tournament in Las Vegas in the early 1980s. About ten years later, their rec-league teams played softball against each other. They talked more frequently. That friendship became fortified when the Harper boys started working out at CSN soon after Chambers had started the program in 1999.

Bryce, his parents, and Chambers devised a bold idea: Bryce would leave Las Vegas High after his sophomore year, earn his GED, and enroll at CSN, with Bryan, to play for Chambers for the 2010 season. With Bryce using a real stick in one of the rare wooden-bat collegiate conferences, professional scouts would be able to accurately gauge his hitting ability. This improvised plan placed Bryce on an accelerated schedule, in an environment that in some ways resembled a low minor league. If it worked, Bryce could be drafted a year ahead of his high school graduation class. And if all went according to the master design, the Washington Nationals, with the number one draft pick, would make history by nabbing a junior college player—Bryce Harper—with the first selection of the June 2010 draft.

But many of Bryce Harper's new CSN teammates didn't know what to make of the arrival of the most dynamic young baseball player to come along in ages. They welcomed his powerful bat in the lineup. Harper hit an impressive .599 as a freshman at Las Vegas High and a staggering .626 as a sophomore, when he became the first nonsenior to be honored as the national high school player of the year by *Baseball America*. That's heady stuff, but Harper wanted more. He always wanted more, always wanted to get better. He always pressed.

With more than two hundred two- and four-year collegiate baseball conferences in the country, CSN competed in one of only four that used wooden bats—the Scenic West Athletic Conference (SWAC). Harper planned to show scores of professional scouts that he was a powerhouse hitting with wood, which he'd be using if he reached the major leagues. If he continued to excel, the rest of the Coyotes figured they would soar to a Junior College World Series championship and capitalize on playing with Bryce Harper. He would get an abundance of attention, the Coyotes thought, and the increased exposure would benefit them, too.

Still, some were curious how he would fit in, how he would act and carry himself, and how he would respond to tough stretches. Fail at the plate 60 percent of the time and, well, that's grounds for immediate enshrinement in the Hall of Fame, a postage stamp, and an inevitable spike in babies name Bryce. Enter a wunderkind accustomed to succeeding 60 percent of the time. How would he react when the game threw him its many curves? That would provide the true measure of whether he would have what it takes to thrive in the cauldron of professional baseball and the major leagues.

Several Coyotes who did not have offers or even looks from Division I recruiters worried that 2010 would be their last competitive season. And along comes the $10 million kid. A host of Coyotes had concocted that moniker for Harper relative to his first pro contract they figured he'd sign as the presumptive top draft pick.

Some were in awe just to call him a teammate. They were not from Nevada, so they hadn't seen him play in high school; they didn't know about Harper's arsenal of skills. Ryan Thomas, the blond-haired lumberjack of a first baseman from Utah, set out to watch Harper's every move. Thomas had always wondered how big leaguers operated, how they handled their immense adulation, and how they reacted to failure. Even though Harper was younger, Thomas knew he would learn plenty from him. Thomas assumed Harper would display some big league ability and behavior.

Others wondered if a Junior College World Series championship truly mattered to someone using the season as a springboard to *real* World Series games, endorsement deals worth tens of millions of dollars, and a nine-digit contract or two. They even figured he was headed, ultimately, to immortality in the National Baseball Hall of Fame in Cooperstown, New York. Those feelings simmered until the end of the season and were answered in stunning fashion. Further clues as to Harper's likely fate were also strewn throughout the year.

A few Coyotes knew him well since they had competed against him in high school and on the club circuit. They didn't have fond memories. No doubt Harper could crush the ball. Other scenes had disturbed them, fans, and parents. Bryce would bunt on a third baseman, who had been playing way back in shallow left field, and laugh boisterously upon reaching first base without a throw. Or he would sneak extra feet down the third-base line to coax a throw from the catcher after a pitch, and he'd sprint toward home as soon as the catcher had fired the ball to the third baseman. Was that competitive cockiness or an outright lack of respect for all foes, an arrogance in which everyone else was just a pawn in his personal chess game?

Then there was the gear. Because of Bryce Harper's presence at CSN, the All-Star sports-equipment manufacturer supplied the Coyotes with masks, chest protectors, and leg guards, among other accessories. Many catchers favored that brand because it's durable and comfortable. Even with such prime equipment, Harper's stood out; MONDO, one of his nicknames, had been etched in dark blue against the yellow padded top of his chest protector. This was special stuff, but his was just that extra bit of special. Other Coyotes noticed.

The CSN cocoon thickened, becoming even more familiar to Bryce Harper, when local products Donnie Roach (a savvy starting pitcher who had toiled at the University of Arizona) and Aaron Kurcz (a hard-throwing reliever who had disliked and left the rigid lifestyle of the Air Force Academy) joined Bryan in coming back home to play for Chambers. Trent Cook, a steady and quiet lefty first baseman with a keen eye and powerful stroke, and—like Bryce Harper—a devoted Mormon, would be another influential addition to the avant-garde season.

Bryce Harper had played some ball that summer for the Westmoore High School squad in Oklahoma City, where two coaches from another prominent collegiate program had queried Ron Harper about his two boys' playing for them in Texas. At the time, Bryan was throwing in a wooden-bat summer league in Alaska.

J. Bob Thomas, who coached the Howard College catchers out on the West Texas plains, had fielded calls from several friends who said they had heard Bryce Harper tell a national ESPN radio audience that he was going to play for a national-championship junior college program in 2010. "They were saying, 'Good job on Harper! He said he's gonna play for *the* national champions . . . that's fucking awesome! Congrats! How'd you pull that off?' " Thomas said. "I said, 'Huh?' " None of those friends knew each other, so Thomas figured this wasn't a hoax. Howard had lost only one game in 2009, winning a record fifty-seven in a row en route to the Junior College World Series championship in Grand Junction, Colorado.

That's impressive, but it wasn't about to lure Bryce Harper to West Texas. Harper had said on the air that he was going to play at a *former* national junior college champion; CSN had won its crown in 2003. Thomas didn't yet know that part of the story. He and Hawks pitchers coach Pat Leach found out where Harper was playing, and they drove five hours to Oklahoma City to talk with Ron Harper and see Bryce play. Ron told the two coaches it had been an honor to meet them and appreciated their interest, but his older boy, Bryan, was already going to CSN and Bryce would be joining him. Thomas and Leach stayed for the game, watched Bryce hit a couple out of the yard, then drove back to Big Spring, Texas, about forty miles east of Midland.

"Did we have a legitimate chance? Shit, I don't know," the twenty-eight-year-old J. Bob Thomas drawled. "But we had enough bullets in the gun to not back down from anyone. We thought, 'Let's go get him.' We probably have the best hitter's park in the country, and it's probably the best hitter's conference. Hell, I'd bite on that."

Ron Harper didn't even nibble on what Thomas tried to feed him. Ron wasn't about to move to Texas. He had his ironworking job and his wife, two boys, and a daughter to support in Las Vegas. He knew this experiment would only work under the vigilance and guidance of Tim Chambers, and in a setting familiar enough to sometimes seem almost too cozy, despite the high stakes. With so much on the line, the combustible Ron Harper nearly extinguished his relationship with Chambers in a volatile exchange of words one night on the road; but that took months to fester.

Back in late-July 2009, Bryce had been in the middle of another hectic stretch. He was still basking in the afterglow of his *Sports Illustrated* cover when he left Oklahoma for home, went to Yankee Stadium for a function, returned to Las Vegas to enroll at CSN, traveled to North Carolina for US U18 training, then flew to Venezuela for the Pan Am junior tournament. Finally, Harper returned to the desert and the disbelieving eyes of Chambers over his slimmer physique.

In Carson City, up at the other end of the state near Lake Tahoe, Western Nevada coach D. J. Whittemore thought it was the craziest baseball scheme he'd ever heard of. A kid who should be a junior in high school was going to swing a wooden bat against a battery of superb pitchers in the SWAC, a league with extreme travel demands and a tight, relentless schedule of Friday-Saturday doubleheaders? The usually reserved Whittemore was certain that would be way too much for any seventeen-year-old player.

"I thought swinging a wood bat was not the best thing for him, in terms of his draft stock. I really felt like it would hurt his ability to prove that he was, and to remain, the number one pick." Whittemore believed a better option for Harper would have been playing junior college ball in an aluminum-bat conference in Southern California.

Had the sample size only been Harper's first couple of practice games against his own teammates, Whittemore would have been proven entirely correct. Harper's first hiccup arrived way before the first pitch of the regular season. After eight days of October practices, he much more than budged next to Chambers on the dugout bench. Remember, Chambers had given Harper an edict to sit, stock-still, next to him for ten days of those October practices. Chambers told him to watch and learn.

But Harper squirmed. It looked as if he had contracted a lethal dose of poison oak as he itched and scratched to get out on the diamond. Chambers finally relented, letting Harper play in an intrasquad scrimmage. With longtime Chambers pal Ronnie Simmers—a diminutive man with a pit bull's stare, infectious enthusiasm, and a bark that a Marine Corps sergeant would have envied—calling the balls and strikes across Heather Drive at Foothill High School, Harper struck out four times.

This had been dubbed the golden sombrero over the ages by those in the game. It's a takeoff on the hockey term *hat trick,* when a player scores three goals. Fans would toss hats onto the ice after the third goal. Four is bigger than three . . . and what's a big hat?

At Foothill High, Bryce Harper didn't even come close to making contact. Worse, his right arm nearly popped out of its socket when the left-handed-hitting slugger wildly stabbed at six-foot-five, 215-pound, lefty Taylor Jones's wicked curveball with the count three balls and two strikes. "Awwww, a three-two curve?" Harper said. "They do that in college," catcher Ryan Scott shot back to Harper.

Scott had had a mediocre freshman season at CSN but aimed to be in top form and shape as a sophomore, to earn a Division I scholarship. Harper's favorite position? Catcher. "I bust my ass and here comes Babe fucking Ruth," Scott had told his father, Dick, when he first heard that Harper was coming to CSN. Well, the Babe just struck out four times. Scott was not unhappy. He had wanted to prove he still deserved to catch the majority of the games.

A six-foot-two, two-hundred-pound sophomore from Scottsdale, Arizona, Scott was known as Evil Genius around the CSN clubhouse for his clever and dastardly acts of revenge on anyone who messed with him. He kept his dark brown hair short. He had green eyes, angular features on a narrow face, and a quick wit. Scott had known what he was doing when he called for that devilish three-two delivery from Taylor Jones. He had wanted to push Harper. He also knew Jones had excellent command of that pitch.

"So I called for a curveball," Scott said with a sly grin. "It was a funny moment. I was a little trickster back there."

The presence of a superstar kid who should have been playing his junior season in high school compounded with the usual challenges of the game, and a desire to advance his thoughts about the sport, compelled Scott to consult with a prominent sports psychologist during the season.

Bryce Harper had some adjusting of his own to address after whiffing three more times a day after he had earned the golden sombrero.

Seven strikeouts in two games. He sank. He wanted to quit. That wasn't just a case of thinking out loud after a poor plate appearance or two, either. Bryce believed he might have made a big mistake, as did Ron Harper. Ron had watched from the Foothill High stands as his son, the phenom who was going to have so much riding on the season, struggled.

That night, Ron Harper called Coach Chambers and said this might be too much, that Ron and Sheri were thinking about pulling Bryce out of CSN and sending him back to Las Vegas High. They believed he was potentially on his way from *Sports Illustrated* cover boy to a poster boy for ill-fated moves, buried by an avalanche of expectations.

Chambers told Ron that Bryce had to stay at CSN. Chambers had sent a stipend check for $1,000 to the family, as part of Bryce's scholarship to cover incidental expenses such as gas, but Ron said he had not cashed it. Didn't matter, Chambers said. He had cut the check, so Bryce was committed. "You can't go back," said Chambers, who then tried to comfort Ron by telling him this slippage out of the gate would be just a blip and a fantastic learning situation—exactly why Bryce had attempted this unorthodox move to begin with, to cope with and conquer failure, to adjust his body language accordingly so he would be more composed and seasoned when he started playing minor league ball.

"[Chambers] knew he could do it. I knew he could do it. Of course, you have second thoughts. You think about it," Ron Harper admitted many months later. "He was sixteen, turning seventeen. You want to see him happy. That's all I can say. It's not that I've ever shied away from anything in life or he's shied away from anything. You want to make sure he's always working hard. Nothing is going to come easy in this life. We knew you have to go take it if you want it."

Long after he had thrown it, Taylor Jones recalled the three-two curve and smiled. When he was twelve, Jones had visited CSN with his parents to watch older brother Tyler play for the College of Eastern

Utah against the Coyotes. Taylor fell in love with everything about the CSN program: the stadium, the facilities, the coaches, and the intensity with which the players competed. Jones didn't grow up wanting to play at Louisiana State or Texas or Stanford, or any other premier collegiate program. He grew up wanting to throw for Chambers at CSN. Jones did not know there had been serious discussions about Bryce's returning to Las Vegas High. "Really? That's crazy," Jones said. "But he grew up and took off."

After Bryce had fanned so many times in two practice games, Chambers saw the fog that had enshrouded the prodigy. The next day Chambers called the dazed and confused Harper into his office—a big, white beanbaglike baseball chair and a short couch covered in blue canvas competed for the tight space in front of his desk—for a somber forty-minute chat. Possibly for the first time in his life, Bryce had a crisis about his immediate future in baseball. Questions laced his thoughts. Had he overextended himself? "Maybe I'm not good enough?" he told Chambers, who saw tears. "Maybe I should have stayed in high school?"

Chambers chose his words carefully. Here's the deal. You are good enough. You're the most talented player I will ever coach. The bonus is you have great players around you. You don't have to carry us. We don't need you to carry us. When you go oh for four, guess what? You'll be in the lineup the next day. You don't have to hit .600. "You should thank the Lord you're having a slump right now because we can figure out how to deal with failure, accept it, find a way out of it, and move on. This is the first slump of a hundred. You're going to see pitchers three or four times a week that you maybe saw once all last season. The more you see them, the better you'll get."

Perhaps Harper didn't have to carry the full-time load at this level, but these were his first competitive games. Sure, they were in practice, just simple tune-ups to determine which players stood out from their teammates. Chambers needed to establish his starters, his leaders. Still, this was a player with no lower or middle gears. Harper attacked every pitch as if it were the last he would ever see. He always played as if he were carrying the whole load. Why change? From the start, with all of his new peers watching, he had wanted to prove himself, to live up to his incredible reputation. Not producing had made him miserable.

Chambers asked Bryan Harper and Marvin Campbell, the closest players to Bryce Harper, to help settle Bryce, to convince him he belonged in junior college and that he would find his groove sooner rather than later. Bryan and Marvin talked. Bryan, being the older brother, knew he could only say so much to Bryce and have his words matter. "He's his *brother,*" Campbell said. So Campbell took it upon himself to soothe Bryce.

Campbell had seen Harper go one for five at the plate in a high school game. Harper mishit some fat pitches and steamed, but he had reverted to his normal playful self the following day. After the fiasco at Foothill, Bryce Harper was nearly disconsolate. Campbell saw doubt and pain all over Harper's face. In particular, that three-two curve had stung.

"He hated that, *hated* it," Campbell said. "I mean I'm talking about strikeouts where you've never seen him get blown away, and now he's getting blown away. He didn't even smell a pitch. He's never had that feeling before."

Campbell paused. You have to realize, he told Bryce, that CSN hitters faced some top-notch pitchers—their own teammates—in practice and scrimmages. During the season an Internet report speculated that the Coyotes' pitching staff—Donnie Roach, Joe Robinson, Bryan Harper, Tyler Hanks, Tyler Iodence, Taylor Jones, Taylor Larsen, Chasen Shreve, Aaron Kurcz, and Kenny McDowall—might be the best in all of college baseball; the June draft would validate that statement.

"If we can hit our staff," Campbell pointed out to Harper, "we can hit anyone."

That was a key point Campbell reinforced to Harper. Uh, Bryce, *these* pitchers are *good*. Also, don't expect a three-two fastball all the time. "Everybody, they'll come after you," Campbell said. "This isn't high school anymore. You won't walk sixty-two times. Guys want to get you out. It'll be a battle. You can't go ten for ten."

Campbell groped to prop up Harper. Campbell saw someone who was wondering what he had gotten himself into.

"Hey, everyone goes through it," Campbell told Harper. "Let's see how you bounce back. Challenge yourself."

"I told him, 'We all believe in you . . . Tim does . . . I do,'" Ron Harper said. "Tim called him into that meeting and [Bryce] decided, 'I can do this. It will be all right.'"

Chambers further eased Harper's transition by shutting off almost all media contact to him. *Oprah, 60 Minutes,* and *This Week in Baseball* were some of the many requests, begging to feature Harper, that Chambers would rebuff throughout the season. Only scant inquiries were approved. "Blame it on me," Chambers told Ron and Sheri Harper if anyone in the media had an issue with the access shutdown.

"Bryce was relieved," Chambers said. "So was his daddy."

In the next scrimmage, Bryce Harper homered in his first at bat. Pounded the ball clear into the middle of the Foothill High soccer pitch. He also doubled twice and tripled, driving in seven runs. On November 8, 2009, with Washington Nationals executives in Morse Stadium, Harper tripled in two with a shot off the center-field wall, cleared the loaded bases with a liner off the wall in left, cracked an opposite-field homer over the oak trees in left, and laid down a bunt for a hit to complete the cycle. He had driven in seven more runs.

"Once he got his confidence, the game was no different," Marvin Campbell said. "I think a lot of it, too, was the media. It was kind of a big whirlwind. I don't even know how you can constantly handle that."

A bit later, CSN scrimmaged against Fullerton College at Cashman Field, the home of the Triple-A Las Vegas 51s, just north of the downtown hotels and casinos. Before the Coyotes ran to the outfield to shag flies in a pregame routine that reinforced hitting the correct cutoff man, they had huddled along the first-base line. They glared out at the imposing twenty-foot, blue left-field wall, which was marked 364 feet to the power alley. The huge wall and distance shocked many of them. One of them wondered aloud if a ball could be thrown over the wall from where they stood. No way, had been the consensus.

"I can," Bryce said flatly. Some quickly disagreed with him. *Riiiiiight,* they said. Bryce grabbed a baseball, reversed a few steps, roared back, skipped forward, and gave it a chuck without touching the dirt in the base path to first with either cleat; the ball cleared the fence, over the 364 sign.

Four hundred fans showed for the exhibition, triple the high of any previous CSN fall scrimmage. Harper belted a solo homer that just cleared the fence in right. "Shoulda walked me!" he yelled at the Fullerton dugout as he rounded third base. Players jawed at each other and it appeared that the verbal test might turn physical, but CSN catchers coach Cooper Fouts grabbed Harper and guided him back to his dugout. It didn't escalate. Harper also sliced a liner over the shortstop's head that he stretched into a double, and he singled. He had driven in three runs in the Coyotes' 9–0 victory.

However, Harper did something else in that game that Coyotes pitchers coach Glen Evans did not miss. Harper etched a line in the dirt with his black Marucci bat on the other side of home plate after the umpire caught him looking at strike three. Harper thought the pitch had been wide, and he traced its path for the ump. The umpire did not eject Harper, and Chambers did not discipline his young player for one of the game's most egregious acts of insubordination to one of its officials. The emotional sombrero fallout seemed to have occurred in the way-distant past. Cockiness was again coursing through the prodigy's veins.

Long after the season had ended, Campbell recalled the way Chambers had addressed the Coyotes before the start of the regular season. You will have to pick him up, Chambers said. He will need you guys. You guys will come together, and you'll need each other like he needs you. "It's ironic thinking of it now," Campbell said. "That's how it was. Everyone needed everyone."

After months had passed, when Harper had sufficiently reflected upon his experiences of the unique season, he admitted that it had been the most stressful time of his life. All the anticipation and exposure had been extraordinary, he acknowledged, an incredible burden for a seventeen-year-old trying to prove he was the best player in the land—trying to prove he was worthy of being picked first in the draft. He had felt tremendous weight in every game and every at bat, as if his next twenty years if not his place among the sport's all-time giants had depended upon how he handled each pitch.

Others were there to pick up the slack, to provide offense and push across runs if he was riding a cold streak. But he wanted the burden of everything resting on his shoulders. He begged for it. He courted controversy. He could not dodge the consequences, or the poorly placed concrete foundation of a brick toolshed that would threaten a splendid career before it had a chance to begin. Even in such cozy surroundings with so many familiar faces around him, he had been tested from the moment he saw his first pitch in a practice game to the last one that was delivered to him as a junior college player.

Bryce Harper had one word for it all.

"Insane."

THE LAST PRESEASON PRACTICE of Bryce Harper's amateur life started on Thursday, January 28, 2010, with a meeting of all the College of Southern Nevada coaches and players in center field at Morse Stadium. The verdant diamond sat in the southeast nook of the vast Las Vegas valley, which was more of a bowl. Envision a large, square table, roughly tilted from Summerlin in the northwest to Morse Stadium, in Henderson, at the southeast. Rainwater generally flowed toward Henderson, toward Morse. That is also where the eyes of the baseball world gushed in 2010.

The square, white steeple and narrow spire atop a Church of Jesus Christ of Latter-day Saints, a wide, dull-brown-brick edifice off to the right beyond a swath of desert brush, marked the long I-515 off-ramp Harper descended every morning to College Drive.

After he turned left on College and zipped through the freeway underpass, to Harper's left a football field, soccer pitch, and baseball diamond were nudged between the freeway and Foothill High. Basketball and tennis courts were wedged between the street and the far left of three buildings, wide and white, with a red-tiled, low-arching roof. The middle one was low and white, too, with a flat, red-tiled roof. The main building on the right looked like a prison, with a tall wall of red-sandstone blocks topped by a thin layer of gray-sandstone bricks. Between the street and the two right-side structures was the school's sprawling parking lot. Black Mountain loomed behind the campus to the west.

As Harper turned left onto Heather Drive, just past the high school, to the right stood the main CSN building, its tall, beige corner square topped by a light blue ribbon. That corner was cut off to form a flat, inviting entrance, with a seven-pointed window tilted at the top that bathed those inside with the morning sun.

Heading west on Heather, newcomers could easily miss the short, S-curved, downhill asphalt drive, whose three well-camouflaged speed bumps destroyed innocent shock absorbers. At the bottom, on the other side of the fifteen-foot-tall ashen-sandstone clubhouse with the tilted metal roof to the left and the three batting cages to the right, Morse Stadium and the Lied Baseball Complex—the new home for the local baseball hero whose fame had been increasing by the day—awaited.

Out in center field, Coach Tim Chambers told the Coyotes to be prepared for the four games they would play over the next three days. Chambers confidant Jim Schwanke, a former assistant coach at Oklahoma State and Louisiana State, talked about the importance of bonding and selflessness. But Chambers held court. He shooed the seventeen-year-old Harper away in his white pants and gray practice jersey. CSN catchers coach Cooper Fouts stuck by Harper's left as they strolled toward the right-field foul line. This is about you being successful, Fouts said as he looked up at Harper, and us being successful. Chambers shifted his tack to the supporting cast when Harper had slipped out of earshot.

"You all know that guy's the shit. None of you know what he's going through, what he's thinking, or what he's feeling. He's why we have that new scoreboard. Why we have those new seats. Why we have that new parking lot. Protect him. Watch out for him. If we have no jealousies, we'll be fine."

Thirty professional baseball scouts, taking notes and enjoying the sun and wasting their employers' money, peered out at the practice. Some sat on shiny blue plastic seats on the red-boulder bleachers behind home plate. Some stood behind the protective black netting, surrounding the plate area, in clumps of two or three. The black cord of his stopwatch, in his right pocket, that wrapped around his right wrist gave away a scout from twenty paces. Logos of the St. Louis Cardinals, New York Mets, Arizona Diamondbacks, and Washington Nationals, especially the Nationals, advertised on Windbreakers, sweaters, and visors.

In the ten previous CSN seasons, maybe a dozen scouts had watched the Coyotes at any particular practice. Twenty-four hours after this practice, Morse would burst at its seams with a record crowd of nearly two thousand. In three weekends, CSN would surpass its gate revenue from the entire 2009 season. They all were eager to see what the Rook, what Chambers called his burgeoning star, would do with a wooden bat in junior college.

The scouts swarmed that Thursday practice to see Harper, who had graced the June 8, 2009, cover of *Sports Illustrated* wearing his red Las Vegas High jersey and gaudy wrestlerlike eye black, at the tail end of his powerful left-handed swing, squinting as if he were watching the Rawlings he had just poked turn into a pea and plop into the Pacific Ocean, with the setting sun glowing orange against the base of Frenchman Mountain behind him.

"Looks a little lean," a scout said to Fouts.

"He's at 208 pounds," said Fouts, glancing at the six-foot-three Harper. "Don't worry. He's eatin' Mama's cookin'."

Harper towered over Chambers, Fouts, and just about everyone else in the stadium that afternoon. Indeed, when infielder Casey Sato first saw Harper enter the CSN clubhouse, he thought the slugger looked more like a twenty-two-year-old man—a pro seasoned by a rapid rise in the minor leagues who carried himself like John Wayne, just as his old man had taught him—than a kid who was halfway through high school. Harper's hair was jet-black, thanks to dye, and closely cropped and blocked off in back. He wore his sideburns like Montgomery Clift and the bottoms of his jeans turned up, like Marlon Brando. All he needed was a woolen uniform to complete his throwback appearance. His matinee-idol good looks, those almost phosphorescent green eyes and strong chin, and the tiny birthmark just below the outside of his left eye, just might convince *Gentlemen's Quarterly* scouts to slap Harper on their own cover.

The *Sports Illustrated* cover cemented Harper, targeted for baseball stardom at an early age, as a public figure. It brought him an added measure of celebrity in major league clubhouses, too.

Soon after that edition had hit the newsstands and mailboxes, Harper attended a game at Dodger Stadium. His name served as carte blanche at clubhouse doors. He sat in stadium front rows or luxury suites. Harper knew Orlando Hudson well. As they chatted in the Dodgers' clubhouse before the game, Hudson, in the only season he played second base in Los Angeles, told Harper to go sit on the bench in front of first baseman James Loney's cubicle. Loney, who had Harper's *Sports Illustrated* cover taped on the inside of his locker, screeched to a stop, eyes wide and mouth agape. The cover boy was sitting right there in front of him. "What the hell you doin' sittin' there?" Loney said. "That's the Kid!" responded Hudson, laughing and nearly falling onto the Dodger-blue carpet. Loney found a black Sharpie and had Harper sign the magazine cover. "I love LA," Harper said, "and I love those guys."

The *Sports Illustrated* fame had convinced Aaron Marcus, an investment banker who lives on Long Island, New York, to pay $12,500 for a one-of-a-kind Bowman 2010 SuperFractor Bryce Harper baseball card. After seeing the magazine cover and reading about Harper, Marcus became enthralled with the prodigy and began buying his cards. Marcus was awed by Harper's physical ability, work ethic, and potential. After splurging for that card, Marcus said, "For all we know, in a few years he could be hitting six-hundred-foot home runs regularly."

Harper's celebrity was circumnavigating the globe. When Las

Vegas businessman Jan Landy, who visited Rio de Janeiro so frequently he bought an apartment in the South American playground, was introduced to someone on Ipanema Beach in January 2010 and the Brazilian learned where Landy called home, he asked Landy, *Entao voce conhece Bryce Harper?* (So you know Bryce Harper?) Landy, who spoke fluent Portuguese but had never met Harper, was astounded by the young star's far-reaching popularity.

Harper had created his own end around to the draft. He'd pummeled the preppies with an aluminum bat. Now he'd jumped to a new level of competition, and attention, in the Scenic West Athletic Conference. The only other collegiate leagues in America whose hitters employed wooden bats were the Empire Conference, Arizona Community College Athletic Association, and the Division II Mon-Dak Conference, all in junior college.

Typically viewed as a last-chance refuge for athletes who couldn't make the grade on the field or in the classroom at four-year institutions, junior college baseball took on a whole new diamond-studded dimension in 2010. Professional-talent evaluators and college recruiters would flock to Morse Stadium. Harper would swing his black Marucci CU26 maple Pro Models, even a few pink ones, with vigor . . . when umpires weren't examining his every move with a magnifying glass, or Harper wasn't imploding over striking out, popping up to an infielder, dueling with his coach, or melting down from his own expectations.

At that last preseason practice session, as the Coyotes stretched along the right-field foul line, they made fun of Cooper Fouts, who had settled on a day and venue with his bride-to-be for their midsummer wedding. Already lost one nut by getting engaged, they roared at Fouts as they lay on their backs with their left legs way out right. They stretched their right legs way out left. "In July," they said, "you lose the other one." They talked about girls and clowned on each other. Harper's teammates mimicked his walk, the way his weight instantly shifted forward to the balls of his feet when he took a step. He always seemed to be leaning forward. Perpetual aggression.

Harper showed that on the diamond by always looking to stretch a single into a double, rounding first base hard, or trying to turn a double into a triple. Walk him and he could easily be on third a minute later, having stolen second, then third. Stealing home plate was always on his mind, too. He lived on forcing the issue. That intensity would be his worst enemy and cost him dearly.

But in January, bliss filled Morse Stadium. Laughter grew louder as each copycat stride of Harper's gait by a teammate bettered the previous one. Harper looked most comfortable standing with his right size fourteen, at ten o'clock, just in front of his left size fourteen, at two o'clock. An odd stance, to be sure, but it seemed as if he could fall asleep, like Secretariat, while standing up.

Sixty thousand feet above Harper, contrails from F-22 Raptors, F-15C Eagles, and F-16 Fighting Falcon Aggressors, developing tactics out of Nellis Air Force Base to the north of Las Vegas, crisscrossed and ran parallel to each other. The jet vapor widened and broke up the farther each one stretched. Those pilots looked as if they were attempting to arrange a giant game of tic-tac-toe. A light breeze drifted in from Lake Mead over the River Mountains and into Morse from right field. Yellow, four-inch, heavy-duty corrugated plastic tubing topped the outfield walls and four-foot-high chain-link fence just beyond the foul lines and dugouts.

The Longhorn Casino & Hotel, attorney Michael T. Schulman, LaDuca's Italian Deli, and good luck wishes from Bob and Nancy Joslin were some of the sixteen banners that advertised on those dull-green outfield walls. The biggest, with large, white block letters against a black background, celebrated the Coyotes' NJCAA World Series championship in 2003. All were bleaching from the harsh desert environment.

Low mountains and sandy hills almost completely ringed the

valley, whose rough base of alkaline and caliche—surface deposits of sodium nitrate, calcium, and other carbonates—formed a harsh moon-scape that shifted from shades of coffee grounds, to maple bars, to manila folders, and cinnamon. The unforgiving Mojave Desert terrain had a base of volcanic ash and molten lava from massive eruptions 30 million years ago. "Bleak, stark and often beautiful," wrote Russell Elliott in his book *History of Nevada*.

At dusk, the view from Morse Stadium, which pointed northeast from home plate to center field, captivated its audience. At different times during the season, CSN players Casey Sato and Gabe Weidenaar stood on the right side of the dugout and stared out to the left, contem-plating the sunset melding of yellow and orange and red, blotches of amethyst, puffs of crimson, and streaks of magenta that seemed to drift out of a giant genie's bottle on the other side of the Spring Mountains. "Like a field of dreams," Weidenaar said softly.

At night, the Las Vegas Strip glistened twenty miles beyond the left-field foul pole to the northwest. Planes from all over the world, ev-ery minute or so, descended into McCarran International Airport at the height of the lights in left-center field and then in the middle of the light stanchion in left. Wide-eyed passengers on the right side of those cab-ins could see a half-size Eiffel Tower, the come-hither emerald-green glow of the world's largest hotel, a mini Statue of Liberty and Empire State Building, and a concentrated white light beaming to the heavens from the point of a dark pyramid behind a fake Sphinx—this one with a full beak—all beckoning to their purses and wallets.

Those tourists also viewed the 1,149-foot Stratosphere—the tall-est freestanding observation tower in the country—piercing the eve-ning sky. Unlike its brethren, such as Canton Tower in China, Tokyo Sky Tree in Japan, and CN Tower in Canada, the Stratosphere re-flected the city in which it was rooted by not just giving its visitors a neat view as they sat in its rotating restaurant; it offered adrenaline junkies thrill rides, including the Big Shot—a favorite of Lisa Marie

Presley, Elvis's lone progeny—that propelled its victims in a capsule to the top of the needle.

At that Thursday practice, CSN's big shot prepared for his special season. The lush Bermuda grass had scattered brown pockmarks, but rye overseed would soon wipe out those blemishes. The jet contrails drifted behind a few feathery cirrus clouds against a wild blue canvas on the sixty-degree afternoon at the stadium named for the late William R. Morse. The longtime area legal figure and former Las Vegas High star quarterback flew bomber missions in World War II and had been CSN assistant coach Marc Morse's grandfather. MORSE STADIUM was highlighted in yellow against the blue-painted wood press box behind home plate. A dozen Mexican fan palm trees, six to a side, stood sentry behind the press box and red-rock stands.

Harper bounced around like, well, a junior in high school. He tapped the left shoulder of teammates and slipped away right. He tapped the right shoulder of others and feigned landing haymakers. He tossed a softball-size, green plastic ball at unwitting bystanders, unleashing a giddy cackle when it landed on his target's chest fifty feet away.

"Just having fun out here," said sophomore Scott Dysinger, a lean, five-foot-eleven second baseman and leadoff hitter whose high cheekbones and genuine black hair came from his Taiwan-born father. His eyes looked like butterscotch Life Savers. Every teammate called him Dice. He had been born in London to a Scottish mother, Elly, who was an accomplished dancer. She had relocated to Southern California after a divorce from Scott's father, Bob, when Scott was a junior at Bishop Gorman High School.

Silverado High School product Trevor Kirk, an outfielder, came from a splintered family, too, and lived with his maternal grandfather. During the season, Kirk dyed his short brown hair black, giving him the uncanny countenance of Portuguese and Real Madrid soccer superstar Cristiano Ronaldo. Kirk was the team jester. He always looked to smack the groin of an unaware teammate, or wandering writer, with the back of his right hand. Some of his more serious teammates tried avoiding him. Some chided him when they became the object of his tomfoolery.

Kirk had also been gifted with a knack, almost as fine as Harper's, for connecting his bat with the ball. The Milwaukee Brewers had spotted that talent and picked Kirk in the forty-seventh round of the draft after his freshman season at CSN, but he opted to continue his education and polish his skills. Dysinger and Kirk would often hit first and second, respectively, in the batting order; that also represented their positions in the team hierarchy.

Trevor Kirk had a connection with Bryce Harper, too, since Kirk's father, Rich, had played on the same Rancho High baseball team as Ron Harper when the Rams had faced Tim Chambers's squad in that Easter tournament almost thirty years earlier.

Rich Kirk had vivid memories of pitcher Greg Maddux, the sure-fire Hall of Famer who was all arms and legs when he threw for Valley High School. Maddux, whose father, Dave, served in the air force, was born in Texas and grew up in Madrid, Spain, before moving to Las Vegas at a young age with his family. It had not surprised Rich Kirk and many in the valley when Maddux, at the age of twenty, made his major league debut in September 1986 for the Chicago Cubs.

Sam Thomas, who had coached Bryce Harper in his two seasons at Las Vegas High, caught Maddux's games in 1983. Thomas was a senior and Maddux, who won eight of nine decisions, was a junior. Valley won the state championship that season, not a shock considering its sterling roster that included Michael Greer, Steve Chitren, and Dan Opperman, who were all drafted by major league teams.

Mike Morgan, however, had first attracted major league scouts to Las Vegas. Within one week in 1978, Morgan had graduated from Valley High, been selected with the fourth overall pick in the June draft by Oakland, and started for the Athletics in a game against Baltimore. Morgan went the distance, but Orioles pitcher Scott McGregor beat him by shutting out the A's. Morgan had a 141-186 record in twenty-two major league seasons, and he expressed caution about how it had all started.

Jumping from high school to a big league mound in a week had brought him much recognition, but he spent most of his first four seasons in the minors. He told *Sports Illustrated* that the rush to see what he could do at the game's top level had *crushed* his development.

Maddux's development had been paced; he threw two complete seasons in the minors before being called up at the end of his second year, and after four Triple-A starts in 1987 he was called up to the Cubs for good. Maddux won 355 major league games, became the first pitcher to win Cy Young Awards in four consecutive seasons, and earned eighteen Gold Glove trophies in a sterling career that ended after the 2008 season. Go ahead, Maddux told me when I visited him in his luxurious home behind two gates in the exclusive Spanish Trail development in Las Vegas after he had won his thirteenth Gold Glove in 2002, try one on. Huh? "They're actual gloves," he said. I removed one from its stand and was surprised at how comfortably it fit on my left hand.

The start of what Bryce Harper hoped to be a Hall of Fame career would depend upon what he did at Morse Stadium. But Scott Dysinger and Trevor Kirk were the Coyotes who spent most of their waking hours at the diamond, raking its dirt and trimming its fringes, praying that their careers wouldn't end there.

Nearly cut from the squad during fall workouts in 2008, they rallied to become pillars of the CSN program. They were the first players Coach Chambers consulted when he first learned that Bryce Harper was seriously considering CSN. Dysinger didn't hesitate. Great idea, he said. Bryce is a superplayer and he'll be good for the team. Dysinger believed every Coyote would benefit from all the recruiters and scouts who would come to watch Harper. Dysinger had first seen Bryce play when he was eight; Harper had hit a home run over the two-hundred-foot fence that day. At that time, Harper would sleep with his favorite bats and dress up in his Little League uniform days before games, to get properly psyched.

Having gone the Southern California route out of high school, an arm injury and high out-of-state tuition at Saddleback College pulled Dysinger back home before he played a game for the Gauchos. He marveled at how expectations of Harper had soared, how so many believed he would hit one out every time he stepped to the plate. Harper never satisfied everyone . . . especially himself, every Coyote quickly learned. "He just needs to relax, calm down, do his thing, and he'll be fine," Dysinger said. "There are a lot of people who will see us play, a lot to see him. That's a lot for someone that age."

The only son of Bob Dysinger, the head of props for the Cirque du Soleil musical *The Lion King* at Mandalay Bay on the south end of the Strip, Scott knew the line between the real world and make-believe, how the glitter and glitz of a million white-hot watts of klieg lights made some larger-than-life and withered others. Scott had seen his dad's show four times. The elder Dysinger had acted a bit, too; most prominently as a "punk at car" in the 1985 Charles Bronson movie *Death Wish 3,* which had been filmed in London.

Not exactly Shakespearean stuff, the fifty-two-year-old Bob Dysinger admitted. He had preferred participating in musical plays, such as *West Side Story* and *Starlight Express,* in which he could show off his dancing steps. Those moves had helped him excel on the fencing team at San Diego State, where as a male cheerleader he was once nearly goaded into a fight with Ted Giannoulas, or the Famous San Diego Chicken mascot, during an Aztecs football game. In London, when a show had kept Elly Moir Dysinger busy and a babysitter couldn't be found for Scott, then an infant, Bob took his baby boy to a theater aboard a red double-decker bus. As Bob worked in *Starlight Express,* a few people in the wardrobe department kept Scott laughing.

"Stuff happens," Bob Dysinger said. "You improvise."

Other Coyotes, including Harper, had Las Vegas ties that stretched for generations, to when the gaming and entertainment mecca had been an outpost with only a railroad depot, a resting spot between Los Angeles and Salt Lake City, where tumbleweeds and trains passed in the night.

Now the fantasy playground—the city where so many visitors hoped to make fortunes with a roll of the dice, where Rakeman plumbers proclaimed A FLUSH BEATS A FULL HOUSE on their van panels, where video-poker machines enticed customers upon checkout at the front of every grocery store—served as an appropriate backdrop for Bryce Harper's big gamble. It was also where an Elvis impersonator twirled a yellow, cardboard, cutout guitar advertising COLONICS to attract business on suburban street corners and where seventy-foot-tall artificial palm trees badly camouflaged cell-phone towers—cell palms, they had been dubbed.

Harper's grandfather and father were ironworkers who had laid most of the very foundation of the Strip, turning the former horizontal cow town, whose casinos housed a few craps tables and slot machines, into an actual city with a bona fide skyline.

Bryce Harper had yearned to establish Las Vegas as a place that could sprout its own sports stars, too. No Las Vegas native had ever been the top draft pick of a major sports league. In addition, since the Major League Baseball draft had been altered to its current form in 1961, no junior college player had been picked with the first overall selection.

Among those number one draft picks since 1965, only Tim Foli (seventeen years, six months, in 1968) and Ken Griffey Jr. (seventeen years, seven months, in 1987) were younger when they were drafted than Harper would be, at seventeen years and eight months, come June 2010. It took both Foli and Griffey two years to reach the major leagues. Foli, known as Crazy Horse, played sixteen seasons, from 1970 to 1985, for six big league teams. Foli has worked for the Washington Nationals since 2005 and had been elevated to general manager Mike Rizzo's special assistant. In a career that lasted twenty-two years and ended with his retirement during the 2010 season and would no doubt land him in Cooperstown, Griffey played for three teams and hit 630 home runs.

That fifty-seven-year-old superagent Scott Boras, with cool and calm lieutenant Kurt Stillwell at the constant beck and call of Ron and Sheri Harper, served as the Harper family's adviser should not have surprised anybody. Coach Chambers believed Boras first became aware of Bryce in 2003, when the ten-year-old competed in a tournament with one of Boras's three sons.

Widely regarded as the most powerful man in baseball, Boras started out as a player. He is still in the top ten of several offensive categories at the University of the Pacific, and he played four seasons of Single-A ball in the St. Louis Cardinals and Chicago Cubs organizations. Knee injuries shortened his career, and Boras earned a law degree just as baseball's reserve clause, which forced players into a kind of indentured servitude, was eliminated. He hooked on with a Chicago law firm, but former teammates pestered him for legal advice in dealing with owners. When he got reliever Bill Caudill a deal worth $7 million, just eight minutes before a salary-arbitration deadline in February 1985, a star agent with savvy resolve was born.

Boras had wrangled Alex Rodriguez's ten-year, $252 million deal with the Texas Rangers, and the record $15.1 million pact that Stephen Strasburg, the top pick by the Washington Nationals in the 2009 draft, had inked just seventy-seven seconds before the signing deadline. Boras told Nationals owner Ted Lerner that Strasburg was a fifty-year pitcher—a prospect so rare, he came along once every fifty years—and Harper was a fifty-year player.

Industry experts believed Harper's first professional pact would break the record $9.5 million signing package Mark Teixeira, another Boras client, had received from Texas as a position player in 2001. That year, the Philadelphia Phillies picked right-handed pitcher Gavin Floyd at the fourth slot and signed him for $4.2 million. Josh Karp, another right-handed pitcher, went to the Montreal Expos with the sixth selection and signed for $2.65 million. Teixeira, a third baseman from Georgia Tech tabbed fifth, had somehow defied logic and mathematics with his package. *The New Yorker* headlined a 2007 feature on Boras THE EXTORTIONIST.

"Boras was famous for extracting more money than other agents for amateur players," Michael Lewis wrote in his bestselling book *Moneyball*. "If the team didn't pay whatever Boras asked, Boras would encourage his client to take a year off baseball and reenter the draft the following year, when he might be selected by a team with real money. The effects of Boras's tactics on rich teams were astonishing . . . by finding the highest bidders for his players before the draft and scaring everyone else away from them, Boras was transforming the draft into a pure auction."

In 1991, the Yankees picked high school pitcher Brien Taylor with the first overall draft selection. His mother balked at an initial $300,000 offer and again when the Bronx Bombers went to $650,000. A year earlier, Boras got $1.2 million for pitcher Todd Van Poppel, the fourteenth pick in that draft. Mama Taylor, who had Boras's counsel, wanted Van Poppel money. She was shrewd and knew about business, much like Ron and Sheri Harper. Bettie Taylor could reduce her son's value to a simple evaluation, about buying and selling. She told *Sports Illustrated,* "Look at it that way, and Brien's a commodity. It's not a very pretty picture."

Hours before Brien Taylor planned to attend his first class at Louisburg College, a junior college near Raleigh, North Carolina, and become off-limits until the next draft, the Yankees bumped their offer to $1.55 million. Taylor couldn't get home quick enough to sign the contract. He injured his left shoulder in a trailer-park fight and never reached the majors, which might have tagged Taylor as the game's biggest draft flop. But the Taylor case showed that Boras knew how to use a junior college to his and his clients' advantage, as leverage if not a springboard, long before he discovered a pudgy, blond-haired, left-handed-slugging kid out in, of all places, Las Vegas.

Players under Boras's management were the first to sign contracts worth more than $50 million (Greg Maddux's $57.5 million deal for five years with the Atlanta Braves in 1997), $100 million (Los Angeles Dodgers pitcher Kevin Brown, $105 million for seven years in 1998), and $200 million (Alex Rodriguez's $252 million deal with Texas in 2000). Rodriguez's current deal with the New York Yankees could be the first to bust $300 million if he hits certain incentives.

B-listers weren't on Boras's agenda, but his clairvoyance wasn't absolute. In 2000, catcher Landon Powell, a highly rated high school prospect from Apex, North Carolina, followed Boras's advice and obtained his GED after his junior year. That had made him eligible for the draft, but nobody knew, so he didn't get selected; Boras and everyone around the player did not announce his status. Boras succeeded in having Powell declared a free agent. However, it was a sordid situation and no major league teams wanted to deal with Boras for Powell.

The ploy forced Major League Baseball to change the interpretation of its rules regarding high school juniors. Powell went back to high school, and he pitched for four years at the University of South Carolina. He was drafted, having signed with the SFX agency, in the first round in 2004. In 2009 and 2010, he hit .222 and belted nine home runs in eighty-seven games for the Athletics.

"It's kinda like being a goalie," wrote Kevin Goldstein of base-ballprosepctus.com. "You're staying in the same place, and Boras shoots from eight million angles. You never know where he's gonna shoot from next."

The Washington Nationals were tight with Boras, especially when compared to his relationships with other franchises, such as the Chicago White Sox, Baltimore Orioles, and Philadelphia Phillies. Washington had several of his clients, including Strasburg and catcher Pudge Rodriguez. Boras often spoke highly of owner Ted Lerner, with whom Boras could deal directly rather than through channels. Boras and Nats manager Jim Riggleman once were minor league roommates; Riggleman lent his car to Boras so he could attend church.

Although his cocoon of servants thwarted my many requests to interview Boras, he was on occasion effusive about his star Las Vegas–based client. He told the *Washington Post* that, over ten years, fewer than ten players will come along and play at a high level for fifteen to twenty years. If you're in a position to get one, he summed up, "You have something that you normally don't have a chance to get." Bryce was one of those, Boras insisted. In another chat with the *Post*, Boras said Ken Griffey Jr. and Alex Rodriguez "were not close" to Harper, in terms of hitting power, when they were seventeen.

Boras hadn't seen Mickey Mantle hit at such a young age, but Boras—sounding like George Clooney's character Danny Ocean in *Ocean's Eleven*—knew a guy who knew a guy. "I found a scout who once talked to a scout who saw Mantle at seventeen," Boras told the *Post*, "and he said Harper has more opposite-field power than Mickey."

New York Yankees scouting director Damon Oppenheimer es-timated that Bryce Harper became a household name within major league scouting departments when he was fourteen, so Boras had been four years ahead of the curve. Boras never came around the CSN grounds, whose Henderson campus was one of three in the CSN system, which served about forty thousand students. The association between Boras and the Harpers was informal and unofficial, however; signing a legal agreement with an agent, for representation, would strip Bryce Harper of his amateur status. Thus, in Major League Baseball's ver-nacular, Boras and deputy Kurt Stillwell were mere advisers to the Harpers.

Reviewing the Coyotes baseball program was left to Stillwell, who popped into Morse Stadium in the summer of 2009 to inspect its ame-nities. Sorry, Stillwell told Coach Chambers after getting a tour of the place, "I don't want to come in and step on anyone's toes. Just wanted to see what's going on. You guys get it. You'll never hear from me the rest of the way." When the two talked during the season, it was always when Chambers visited with Stillwell in the stands, and those were just a few small-talk exchanges. "Kurt trusted me," Chambers said.

Before seeing his first pitch in a junior college game, Harper had received stacks of autograph requests in the mail at CSN. Chambers piled it all up in a corner of his cramped office. Could he please sign this magazine cover? These baseballs? These cards? Coach, if it's not too much trouble . . . "It's ridiculous," said Scott Dysinger. That attention only swelled, putting Harper, Chambers, and the rest of the Coyotes in uncomfortable situations all year. Dysinger discounted the possibility that he and his teammates would hold Harper's immense popularity against him.

"I don't think anyone on this team is jealous," said Dysinger, who sort of smiled when he talked. "Honestly, who would want all that pressure? I know I wouldn't. I feel for the kid sometimes, with all the pressure that's on him. Some people, I guess, want him to fail. I don't know why. But he's a good kid. He doesn't need all that added pressure."

In an August 2009 installment of ESPN's *E:60* show, *Oakland Tribune* columnist Monte Poole said he believed Harper was setting himself up for something other than a fat contract and rich endorsement deals. Poole probably echoed the sentiments of many when he questioned Harper's leaving high school, and its invaluable lessons and maturation process, at such a young age.

Harper often said he didn't mind the attention, criticism, and taunts that came with his notoriety, that he thrived in this kiln that he'd created with his bold gambit to dodge his final two years of high school and get to the draft a year early. However, as much as CSN coaches, and the many teammates he grew up competing with and against, tried shielding Harper from the mania, they couldn't protect him all the time. Most of all, they couldn't protect him from himself.

Once he reached the big time, maybe Harper would hit more major league homers as a teenager than the sixteen Ken Griffey Jr. smacked, or Mickey Mantle's thirteen, or Robin Yount's eleven? Maybe he'll come close to the record twenty-four that Tony Conigliaro belted before he turned twenty?

Atlanta Braves slugger Jason Heyward had been twenty years

and eight months old when he hit his first major league homer, a three-run shot, in his first big league game on opening day of the 2010 season. He had spent three years in the minors. In 2009, Heyward hit ten homers for a high Single-A team and seven in Double-A. He went four for eleven, all singles, in three Triple-A games, but the big club saw enough in Heyward in the spring of 2010 to promote him.

Harper and criticism were twins. That's what came with being a *Sports Illustrated* cover boy at sixteen, when you laid the bat down by the plate, took two steps, bent over, rubbed dirt between your hands, smeared the eye black all over your cheeks, and touched the other side of the plate, in the dirt, with the business end of your bat before tapping the tip of your right shoe, as Harper did in high school. When you said you played to take an opponent's head off, that and the rest of your routine could make more than a few want you to fail.

"I love the way people talk crap," he told *Sports Illustrated*. "I hear it all the time. Overrated. You suck. I'll just do something to shut them up. Like, I'll show you. It's like in regular pregame work. I like to show off my arm. Just so it's like, 'There you go. Don't even think about trying to run.'" Asked about his goals, he told the magazine, "Be in the Hall of Fame, definitely. Play in Yankee Stadium. Play in the pinstripes. Be considered the greatest baseball player who ever lived. I can't wait."

Chambers had looked out for the kid since Harper started showing up in the CSN batting cages when he was seven. Yup, Chambers said, Harper carried himself a certain way. He's got the confidence, the arrogance that all the good ones possessed.

"But the question about his goals, to be in the Hall of Fame, and to be the greatest player to ever play the game . . . if you didn't want the answer, why ask the question? He doesn't walk around and tell you that. I've never heard him say that. But if you ask him, he won't say, 'I hope to be an Average Joe and make the big leagues.'"

Chambers lit up like the Strip on New Year's Eve when critics aimed their malice at Harper. Chambers would become the front line of defense in protecting Bryce. Chambers believed nobody had the right to criticize Bryce's parents' and his decision to test himself in junior college.

"My thought is, leave him alone. He's a *junior in high school* doing something that's never been done, right here in Southern Nevada. He likes criticism. He feeds off it. He likes to prove people wrong. But me? I'm a little different. As a coach, I care about my guys. Someone says something about him, it pisses me off."

Baseball America writer Dave Perkin, a former major league scout, had penned a not-so-glowing review of Harper going oh for five, with three whiffs, in an Alcoa All-Star game in San Diego during the summer of 2009. Off his game, Perkin wrote. Couldn't catch up to a decent fastball. Badly fooled by every curve. His swing has gone backward. Far too long in the back end. Lunging. Diving. "He has a major hole, outside corner at the knees. Unless he proves he can hit that stuff, he's going to be a bust."

Chambers called Perkin with some of his own opinions. You realize he's sixteen? You realize everyone he's playing with is eighteen? Well, Perkin said, it can't all be positive. Chambers's faced burned as if he had just chomped on a handful of habaneros. "I'm fine with that. But don't say he's regressed. How about the competition is stiffer? He didn't have the success he's used to having? Nobody has ever left high school early to do this. He did, and he did it with confidence."

In the middle of January, when a national cross-checker for the Boston Red Sox dropped by Morse Stadium to see Harper in another practice game, that golden sombrero episode had long faded from memory. After Harper fired a bullet, from his knees, to second base, the Red Sox scout whose job it was to confirm colleagues' information ran to Chambers to show off his stopwatch—1.84 seconds from glove to glove, or nearly two-tenths of a second better than the major league average.

"What do you think of that?" the scout said.

"Are you serious, Danny?" Chambers said. "That's pretty good!"

"Yeah, for a second I thought my watch was fast. But it isn't."

"If you're doing that in less than two seconds at our level, you're blowing runners up. You won't run on us."

He's only seventeen, Chambers told that Red Sox employee. Chambers would constantly repeat those three words throughout the season. Harper's girlfriend at the time attended Green Valley High School, and Chambers told him to continue doing high school stuff. In the second inning of a Friday fall scrimmage, Harper sheepishly approached Chambers in the dugout.

"Coach," Harper said.

"What's up?" Chambers said.

"I gotta leave early."

"Why?"

"I got homecoming tonight."

"Why didn't you tell me?"

"It's stupid. I don't want to leave."

"Bryce, I told you already. You have to go do those things. At two fifteen or two thirty, just roll outta here. Don't say good-bye to anyone. Go do your thing."

Chambers flashed back more than ten years, when he coached at Bishop Gorman. He had never dealt with such raw adolescence here, in junior college. All of this will be new, Chambers thought. Harper was embarrassed about leaving the practice game. He had wanted to play. It's so easy for outsiders, Chambers thought, who did not know Bryce and had no idea what he or his parents were about, to pop off.

"I told his dad, 'Ronnie, all that matters is Ron, Sheri, and the three B's—Bryce, Bryan, and [daughter] Brittany,'" Chambers said of his advice to Ron Harper about all those outside opinions.

The awful economy had affected Ron Harper and played a role in Bryan Harper's coming home from Cal State Northridge, since the downturn that had punched Las Vegas in its nose with an unemployment rate that would hit 15 percent caused Ron to lose workdays. Four unfinished buildings, visible from Interstate 15 through the core of the city, showed that something had been slipping. The eyesores hadn't been touched in many months, more than two years in a few cases, by the end of 2010 and started giving Vegas the grubby, half-assed feel of Tijuana.

The bleakest example stood northwest of Flamingo and I-15, sticking out amid a vast expanse of single-story residential and commercial buildings. An eight-story, curved concrete carcass with metal wall wrappings, and bundles of exposed vertical steel rebar looking like stacks of dried spaghetti noodles, resembled a giant air conditioner that had been discarded in the desert. Cranes at both sides of the Wyndham Desert Blue project cantilevered out, away from the building, like a drawbridge, from nothing to nowhere. It was designed to soar nineteen stories and had been scheduled to open in early 2010.

Las Vegas Sands chose to cover its bare-steel St. Regis condo eyesore, in between its high-end Palazzo and Venetian properties, with huge cloth strips that resembled a finished building. David Baird, the director of UNLV's School of Architecture, dubbed that tactic "urban camouflage." About $3 billion in construction activity had been lost in 2008 and 2009. The *Las Vegas Review-Journal* speculated about those unfinished buildings remaining untouched, preserved as is in the arid environment, for twenty years.

Ron Harper and father-in-law Jim Brooks, the other steelworker in the family, endured those economic doldrums. Plus, out-of-state tuition had only been increasing. Those fiscal realities combined with Bryan Harper's disenchantment at Cal State Northridge led him to CSN, which enhanced Bryce's decision to become a Coyote.

When Bryan pitched, Sheri Harper knew not to bring a camera, and Ron Harper crept down the right-field line, took a seat on a little metal bench, and didn't say a peep to anyone. When Bryce hit, Ron sat behind home plate, but Sheri took a walk. Long ago, the superstitious baseball family figured out the game within the game when the boys were on a diamond.

Chambers was figuring something else out in attempting to coach a precocious talent in uncharted waters, to help guide him through a maze of hope and hype that even Chambers couldn't fathom. But he was certain that Bryce Harper couldn't return to high school. Those pitchers would be scared to throw to him. If they did, he would gain nothing by hitting with aluminum for another season. And those hurlers would become targets. Someone might get hurt.

"He could hit .700 in high school and regress," Chambers said. "He'd get bored with the game being so easy. He needed a challenge. This was his only option."

Bryan, as a senior, had stood on first base the day Bryce, as a Las Vegas High freshman, slammed the 570-foot home run that *Sports Illustrated* had documented. For ESPN's *E:60,* in which sportswriter Monte Poole criticized Harper, Bryce Harper wore his black Southern Nevada uniform when he guided reporter Rachel Nichols out past a street and into the desert to show her where his mammoth homer had landed.

"A grand slam," Bryan told me in recalling that prodigious blast. "I turned and looked, and it just kept going. Wow. That's when I *knew.*" That was the moment Bryan knew his younger brother was bound for stardom. "That one was pretty crazy. That same game he hit an opposite-field bomb [*oppo boppo,* in Bryce Harper vernacular] off the scoreboard. That was a fun game for him."

Marvin Campbell, the former prep teammate of the Harper boys, had hit cleanup behind Bryce, who batted third, at Las Vegas High. So Campbell was in the on-deck circle the day Bryce belted that homer into the desert.

"As soon as he hit it, there was no doubt," Campbell said. "I started walking toward home plate [to greet Harper]. Everyone was going, 'Ooooooh.' I look up and it's bouncing on the other side of the street. It's great hitting behind him because they'll probably pitch the same way to me. You pick your poison."

Pitch to Bryce Harper or intentionally walk him to throw to Campbell, another left-handed-hitting slugger? When Bryce was a freshman at Las Vegas High, that had been the dilemma, which Campbell relished, for opposing coaches and pitchers. Campbell cherished a photograph from that 2008 season. He's looking off into the distance, as is Bryce, whose dome Campbell had just given a Mohawk cut. Bryan sits on a watercooler. The three close friends, together again. The Reunion, Campbell called it.

Reunion II took place in 2010, when Morse Stadium transformed into a Bermuda-covered petri dish, under baseball's unforgiving microscope, out in the Mojave Desert. A high school junior planned to test himself on a junior college team stacked with veterans, with the added benefit of being able to sleep in his own bed and eat breakfast and dinner each day with his family.

Bryce Harper started almost every day, before sunrise, by glancing at the vintage Mickey Mantle poster on his bedroom wall before trudging downstairs. It's a photo of the Mick surrounded by all of his baseball cards with his signature. Harper's grandfather Jim Brooks had paid a buddy eight hundred bucks for it and given it to Bryce.

His first few years in the game, Harper wore number seven, as a tribute to Mantle. When he was ten, someone else on his Desert Storm club team had that number and wouldn't yield it. Harper settled on number thirty-four. Add the two figures and it still honored Mantle. "Pinstripes are in his blood," Brooks said. No wonder Harper had such affinity for the Sooner State and so enjoyed playing with the Oklahoma Elite Baseball club and the Westmoore High summer teams in Oklahoma City; where Harper would be roughly a ninety-minute drive from Spavinaw, where Mantle was born, and less than three hours from Commerce, in whose high school Mantle starred in three sports and was good enough in football to get a scholarship offer from the Oklahoma Sooners.

A die-cast model of a yellow 1955 Chevrolet Bel Air, what Harper saw as he left his room, sat on a shelf. Brooks had owned a candy-apple 1957 two-door Bel Air hardtop back in the day. Bryce had seen it in photographs and adored it. Brooks once asked him what he wanted.

Bryce said a Bel Air. Soon enough, Bryce unwrapped a small box that contained the yellow model. "The little car," said Bryce Harper, smiling. "That's grandpa."

Harper always gave Harley, his eight-year-old, yellow Lab, a few brisk pats before trekking the 9.7 miles from the modest two-story home at the end of quiet Cantelope Court at the foot of Frenchman Mountain to the College of Southern Nevada campus in his ten-year-old, black Toyota Tacoma pickup truck that had logged more than 120,000 miles.

"What was I doing when I was a junior in high school, besides weighing 132 pounds and being a moron?" Chambers said during that last preseason practice. "I hear critics say he's making a mistake. I don't agree. Who can judge what's better for him than him and his family? Let him enjoy it. He's a special kid and this is a special circumstance. And everything you hear is going to happen. I guarantee it."

JIM BROOKS AND HIS four companions eagerly left San Diego for Las Vegas in June 1962, but they didn't make it out of Southern California before crapping out. The primer-gray Volkswagen Beetle sputtered and jerked as it attempted to scale Cajon Pass, just past Rancho Cucamonga. After they'd vaulted that steady fifteen-mile incline, the high desert awaited, but the quintet had barely started the ascent when the Bug halted. Ten hands pushed it, with all the suitcases on the rooftop luggage rack, to a service station. Soon the vehicle was repaired and rolling toward its occupants' new chapters.

Of all the backgrounds and connections that intertwined to make Bryce Harper's 2010 season so rich in Las Vegas lore, none was more critical than the trek James Wesley Brooks Jr. embarked upon to lay the foundation of his family.

Jim Brooks eventually cruised into Las Vegas, which had about seventy thousand residents, at dusk on US Route 91. Brooks and his crew passed the Hacienda on the left, the Tropicana on the right, the Dunes and its thirty-foot fiberglass Arabian sultan on the left, the Aladdin and Flamingo on the right, the Castaways on the left, the Sands—in whose Copa Room Frank Sinatra, Dean Martin, and the rest of the Rat Pack would perform in three months—and Desert Inn on the right, and the Stardust on the left. They passed the original Las Vegas

High and found the popular Blue Onion drive-in restaurant, where a complete charbroiled Eastern-steer steak dinner cost $2.40, on East Main.

The city's bright web seduced the gray, four-wheeled moth.

"The surprise was all those lights, the tremendous amount of lights," said sixty-six-year-old Jim Brooks while overlooking Morse Stadium on a postcard spring afternoon. "It was such a wide-open country back then. What a great town. The people were great. But the lights . . . the lights were just amazing."

Junior became an ironworker and helped build almost every major property that has been erected on the Strip, starting with Caesars Palace and Circus Circus in 1966, first for the Century Steel Structural Division and then Pacific Coast Steel, Inc., for which he occasionally still worked.

Brooks's daughter, Sheri, met Ron Harper at a young age. Brooks and his wife, Joan, just about became instant surrogate parents to Ron, who compared his childhood to Coach Chambers's hardscrabble youth. Comparing pasts tightened the bond between Ron Harper and Chambers.

Ron started eating meals at the Brooks home when he was twelve. Ron and Sheri didn't go out on a date, with a chaperone, until they were sixteen. They were not alone together until they were eighteen, when the Rancho High sweethearts graduated with the class of 1983. Ron obtained his Reinforcing Ironworkers Local 416 union card, followed his father-in-law in the steel trade, and became a foreman for Jim Brooks at Century. Ron Harper also embraced the Mormon religion practiced by Jim and Joan Brooks, and their daughter.

The Church of Jesus Christ of Latter-day Saints (LDS) movement first set foot in the Las Vegas area in 1855, when thirty followers of LDS leader Brigham Young built a fort whose remnants stand two Bryce Harper home runs, perpendicular from the left-field foul line, from home plate at Cashman Field, where Harper had led CSN in its winter scrimmage pasting of Fullerton College. It's the beginning of a rough patch of the city, in between the north edge of downtown and North Las Vegas. If Harper could have hit a thirty-seven-hundred-foot homer over the Fullerton center fielder's head at Cashman, the ball would have landed on the Rancho High diamond, where Ron Harper had played center field for the Rams.

Ron and Sheri Harper were married, when both were twenty-one, in the grand Mormon temple, whose six signature narrow, white, 110-foot spires oversaw the valley, to the west, from its Frenchman Mountain perch.

Jim Brooks said the family's faith was tested when Sheri Harper delivered Bryce Aron Harper as a blue baby on October 16, 1992. *Cyanosis*—derived from the Greek word *cyanos,* which means "dark blue"—is the medical term for the condition that can allow blood that is not fully oxygenated to enter arterial circulation via a heart malformation, which Bryce described.

"I don't know if I'm a miracle baby. But I was really sick with pneumonia. I had a hole in my heart. My lungs were really small and filled up with fluid. I was about twenty-four hours away from dying. I was fine when I came out. I was put in a room and I turned gray, really gray. There was drama. I was in an incubator. I spent probably three months in the hospital. It was pretty rough on my parents and family. I don't know if I'm a miracle baby. It just happened."

Jim Brooks, whose grandfatherly smile turned somber in a second, claimed otherwise. "We almost lost Bryce. Joan and I felt he was saved for something. There is something waiting for him. In the church, missions are common. Well, Bryce's mission is right out there."

Brooks pointed to the outfield.

"He's going to do more for young people and young kids than any of us would ever think of doing, because of how he does things . . . pictures he takes with his head bowed. That, to me, will be more of a help to young kids than anything in the world, because of his religious background. Religion is a funny thing to talk about. You have to *have* something. If you don't *have* something, you don't have anything your whole life."

At the end of ESPN's *E:60* piece on Harper, host Jeremy Schaap speculated about Harper and steroids to reporter Rachel Nichols, who said Harper had never even thought about using illicit drugs. That wasn't the first time that topic had been broached, either, to the family. When Bryce was in high school, *Las Vegas Sun* sportswriter Ron Kantowski had raised the issue with Ron Harper, who told Kantowski that his son would pass any drug test, anytime.

In fact, a few Coyotes remembered that nothing made Bryce angrier in his youth than when a teammate or foe ribbed him about being so big for his age; they'd ask him if that was because of the steroids they had heard he was given to combat his ailments when he was born. Having battled since he took his first breath, repeatedly hearing something like that as a kid could figure into the genesis of a vicious swing.

Harper also hit with his faith. He had Marucci print LUKE 1:37—*Nothing is impossible with God*—where his name belonged on his black maple bats. Scott Dysinger, the second baseman, had a large tattoo of a cross, formed by two baseball bats, on his back with a baseball in the middle and LUKE 1:37 written above the horizontal bat. That artwork inspired Harper to adopt that New Testament Bible passage for himself. Dysinger also inscribed it under the bill of his cap and batting helmet.

However, Harper never preached. If I asked about his faith or the passage on his bat, he would talk about it. To tap into the heart of his convictions, Harper had to be pressed. Only after weeks of getting to know him, and his getting comfortable with me, did I ask him about his faith. By many accounts, Harper regularly attended Sunday church services with his mother and sister. He agreed with his grandfather that baseball would serve as his mission, unlike the two-year commitments, highly encouraged but not required by Church elders, that many Mormons undertook in their late teens to early twenties.

"I feel I can be a walking Book of Mormon and help people on the baseball field and off it," Bryce Harper quietly explained. "Like my inscription on my cards and bat—LUKE 1:37. 'With God, nothing shall be impossible.' Even if I can't help people like that, I'll be able to touch people by just signing things. I think that's incredible. I'm second to everything. He is first. Even with my family, He is first and always will be. That makes things a lot easier, when you have something else on your side besides friends and family."

Bryan Harper knew Luke 1:37 meant the world to his younger brother, a motto of how to live every day, how to compete, and how to inspire others. "That's his way of life. He loves the gospel and everything that comes with his faith. We wouldn't be where we are without God and His blessing us with the talent we have. That's really important to us."

The list of the Mormon baseball luminaries includes Danny Ainge, Roy Halladay, Bruce Hurst, Wally Joyner, Jeff Kent, Harmon Killebrew, Jack Morris, and Dale Murphy. In statistics and stature, Bryce Harper might eclipse all of them.

All that neon that so wooed Jim Brooks to the city as he drove into Las Vegas in 1962 glowed from signs built by the Young Electric Sign Co., or YESCO. In 1945, Mormon businessman Thomas Young built the tall, narrow BOULDER CLUB neon sign, the first in Las Vegas, and the company took off. It constructed the seventy-five-foot-tall Vegas Vic cowboy, the largest mechanical neon sign in the world, which stood outside the Pioneer Club. The famous diamond-shaped WELCOME TO FABULOUS LAS VEGAS sign at the south end of the Strip, and elaborate symbols and logos in front of the Golden Nugget and Caesars Palace, as well as the two giant, yellow-and-red-flashing guitars outside the Hard Rock Cafe and Hotel, are some of YESCO's many bright creations that now lure visitors into Las Vegas.

Bryce Harper remembered taking to the Church and its teachings at an early age. He attended seminary every morning at five and hit early-bird weight-room sessions at six. That, he said, started his day off "great."

"It's amazing having that with you all day. Nothing like that. You could have a terrible morning or wake up and be tired, lagging . . . you don't want to go. But you need to get there and you feel great the rest of the day. That's how it was for me."

Harper teammates Trent Cook and Casey Sato took the more traditional two-year Church missions that are so critical to spreading the Mormon faith. The twenty-two-year-old Utah natives were bedrocks of stability for the Coyotes. Cook, a six-foot-two, 190-pound lefty, had short blond hair and aquamarine eyes, and his fair skin developed a tinge of pink within two innings of a day game. Big-numbered sunblock was his best friend. The most even-keeled Coyote, Cook wore the same quietly confident expression whether CSN led by a dozen or trailed by double digits.

Cook took comfort every time he saw his red Mizuno maple bat, Big Red, angled on the bench at my right side. He had started that for good luck and kept doing it. Every player would, at least once during the season, do something to irritate Chambers or make him pause. Missing a class. Failing to fulfill field-maintenance duties. Yapping at an umpire's call. Every player, that is, except Cook, whom Chambers called Cookie.

Sato, a five-foot-ten, 175-pound infielder, was often positive despite constantly battling for playing time. An S-curved scar, visible through his short black hair, ran from the crown of his head to his right ear; a three-hour surgery had been required to alleviate brain swelling after he had been smacked with a baseball when he was twelve. He had just pitched the ball to a buddy twenty feet away, in a game of home-run derby. Thirteen staples closed the wound.

Sato's smile had filled his round face when the Red Sox fan received word from the Church that he'd serve his mission in Boston.

Cook was sent to Finland, where he had to learn one of the most difficult languages for native English speakers. A year into his sojourn, Cook hit a comfort zone when his parents spoke to him in Finnish in his dreams.

They typically canvassed their areas, with a companion, for nine or ten hours. They often dispelled myths about or explained early practices, such as polygamy, of the Church. Studying scripture dominated their personal time. Neither Cook nor Sato experienced violence, but both knew of missionaries who had been killed or seriously injured during their journeys. Sato didn't believe the true number of threats or injuries to missionaries was accurately reported because they never wanted anything to interrupt their work. "It's such an important aspect of our lives, something we want to do for the whole two years. My brother [Nate] didn't tell the story of having a knife pulled on him until six months after his mission. No way he wanted to worry our mom."

In a predominantly Lutheran land with scant sunshine, Cook had been tested daily in Finland. Staying positive had never been so important. Strangers would reject Cook's advances, telling him there isn't a God or that they didn't want to hear what he had to say. It would have been easy to take those words personally, but he didn't. He would politely depart, retaining his smile, and move on. Cook believed Harper would learn how to brush off all the heckling and fan abuse he would receive as a Coyote, which would temper him. "Those are experiences Bryce could only have here at the junior college level. He'll realize how important it is not to show defeat to anyone, that he can overcome all that and go get 'em next time. The best thing to do is keep competing."

Chambers had a newspaper photograph of his 2006 baseball camp that had included San Francisco Giants outfielder and Las Vegas resident Aaron Rowand in the foreground and a young Trent Cook, identified as "Brent" in the caption, in the background. Cook had been in his doctor's office, about to undergo a physical exam in Utah to get cleared to play for Chambers, when he saw the *Sports Illustrated* with Harper on the cover on a table in the waiting room.

Sato—who had played for the same high school coach, Jon Hoover, at Cottonwood High School, who had tutored Chambers at Pleasant Grove High School in Utah—heard some rumors about Harper playing for CSN. Then Sato saw the magazine cover when it was delivered to his home in Salt Lake City. "I thought, 'Holy shit!' I pop it open and it talks about him being baseball's LeBron James. I'm really going to play with this kid? What a huge opportunity. Crazy. I was in shock. I couldn't even imagine being on the cover."

Sato figured CSN would have a solid nucleus in 2010, that it would be one of the best teams in the country. When he heard about Harper's addition, Sato knew the Coyotes had all the ingredients to do "something special." The team had so many leaders that Chambers, for the first time in his twenty-one seasons as a baseball coach, did not find it necessary to have his players choose captains; there were too many candidates, so Chambers left it to nature.

In the last half of the season, Harper inscribed 2 SAMUEL 22:33–34, from the Old Testament, on the tape around his left wrist.

God is my strength and power, and He makes my way perfect. He makes my feet like the feet of a deer and sets me on my high places.

Did Harper often feel like he has the feet of a deer?

"That's a pretty good one. When I run . . . I don't feel like a deer. I wish I ran like a deer. But I thought that was a pretty good one. Having the Lord on my side, that's always good. I always put that kind of stuff on my wrists. It's a lot of power."

Cook believed the passages on Harper's wrist, bat, and the underside of his cap reflected his humility. Harper knew he was blessed with extraordinary abilities and skills, which he would show fans and foes throughout the season.

"But in the end, he's still human," Cook said. "We all make mistakes. We all aren't perfect. And you can't do everything on your own. You need extra inspiration, whether it's from good parents that set good examples or from scripture or praying to that God you believe in, or whatever it may be. I think that says a lot about a person. When they have a sense of humility like that, they're coachable and approachable in all aspects of life."

Sato attributed Bryce Harper's maturity and poise to Ron and Sheri Harper. Not that reading the Bible makes you a better person, Sato said, but it is grounding and it shows respect to his parents.

"He has a desire to learn what they know. He does study the scriptures. He does pray. He wants that relationship with God. Those 'antics,' yeah, a lot of them are showboating, but he's a grounded individual. He knows who he is. Those scriptures, they're not a lie. He doesn't put them on there because that's what Tim Tebow does. . . . Bryce does that because he actually knows it."

Watching Harper experience such highs and lows, and witnessing him breaking his bat in half on home plate or throwing his batting helmet around the dugout, Sato suggested another passage to Harper. In Section 122 of the Doctrine and Covenants of the Church, there's scripture that Sato felt appropriate for Harper.

And if thou shouldst be cast into the pit, or into the hands of murderers, and the sentence of death passed upon thee; if thou be cast into the deep; if the billowing surge conspire against thee; if fierce winds become thine enemy; if the heavens gather blackness, and all the elements combine to hedge up the way; and above all, if the very jaws of hell shall gape open the mouth wide after thee, know thou, my son, that all these things shall give thee experience, and shall be for thy good.

It's about learning from experiences, Sato said. He admitted that he leaned on those lines often when he ran into so many challenges, frustrations, and self-doubt during his mission in Massachusetts. He bluntly elaborated, "Our missions sucked. But they're the best two years of your life. Baseball was completely eliminated from my life . . . everything normal in my life was gone for two years. I put myself into a situation where I knew I would struggle and face adversity. I think everyone has to go through trying experiences and hard times, to come out the best they can be . . . if that makes sense. We all knew Bryce would struggle this year, maybe. That's where Trent and I come into the picture. Having us older guys brings its advantages. We know what it's like to struggle. We know what it's like to be in pure frustration for weeks and months. The growth I experienced and the mental toughness I have in my life completely stem from those two years."

Cook confirmed that at times on his mission he wanted to quit. He did not want to be in Finland. He missed his family and his country, and baseball, but he vowed to keep going, to stay positive. He kept thinking of the quote about how you don't learn from situations in which you're given something.

"It's best when we learn and grow. When we have challenges, we need to find ourselves and overcome things, to learn. In the end we get the reward. That's the way it's been with Bryce. He's had to work at everything. He's had to overcome challenges. He's gotten so many rewards, but he'll only keep getting rewarded because he keeps working at it and he keeps facing challenges, and he keeps overcoming them."

The Las Vegas population had tripled, to about twenty-five thousand, in the post–World War II boom. Mormons had become pivotal players, primarily in banking, in the city's expansion. The valley, with a population around 2 million when Bryce Harper donned a CSN uniform, had 178 LDS churches or wards, six times more than the number of Roman Catholic or Southern Baptist buildings of worship.

Jim Brooks and Ron Harper have left their indelible fingerprints on many of the corners, properties, and outlying structures that have spurred the area's incredible growth. Even though he later worked at other commercial jobs to better accommodate his sons' schedules, Ron admitted he had a measure of pride every time he saw the Strip or drove down one of the world's most-recognized avenues.

"He always raised us to be hard workers on teams, to lead through work, not vocally. To show people that you work hard . . . and they'll work hard," Bryan Harper said of his father. "It's good that we were raised that way. You can tell we're pretty gifted, and Bryce and I think it's the hard work my dad put in with us when we were younger. We've worked our butts off to get where we want to be, and Bryce and I are exactly where we want to be right now."

Outside the CSN clubhouse, against a wall of jagged, red-speckled ashen-sandstone blocks, players could find a thick, three-foot piece of iron with a spiraling exterior. Many Coyotes carried the thirty-pound hunk of metal around as an inspirational weight-lifting tool. Swinging it like a baseball bat took two seconds. They were common at Las Vegas High. Jim Brooks and Ron Harper carried sixty-foot versions of them, weighing a few hundred pounds, around for eight- to fourteen-hour shifts to put food on the table and pay the bills.

Brooks called them elevens, as in eleven-eighths of an inch, the diameter of the piece of rebar. They were also made in fourteens and eighteens, and Brooks had seen them as long as 100 and 120 feet. Bundles of those were what stuck out of that unfinished eight-story eyesore on the west side of I-15. Handling them required a new pair of leather gloves every week. "Shoot, every couple days," Ron said. In less than a month, thick calluses developed on shoulder surfaces that contacted the steel.

The exteriors of elevens, fourteens, and eighteens were twisted so they bonded to cement. Jim Brooks called that deformation. "You cannot imagine the jobs. These were hardworking kids [such as Ron Harper]. You don't see anything now like these kids were. Work hard or go home. That was the attitude."

Brooks and his crew usually started at four in the morning and went until four or six at night. On a job in Laughlin, by the Colorado River, they once worked until midnight, when it was 110 degrees. Hefty college football players would join the crew in the summer and boast about the easy work, and they wouldn't last three hours. They would hitchhike home and not care about getting paid. Brooks has shoulder, back, and knee issues from the hard labor. Ron has three disks in his back that give him serious problems. A monthly painkiller shot in his neck helped.

I delicately asked Bryan how his parents produced a six-foot-six, 200-pound pitcher such as himself and a six-foot-three, 210-pound masher, a wannabe middle linebacker in the mold of Dick Butkus, such as Bryce? The five-foot-eleven Ron Harper stood eye to eye with Jim Brooks; their wives, Sheri and Joan, are not tall. A photo from that famous *Sports Illustrated* issue showed Sheri and Brittany, a beautician, sitting, with Bryce and Bryan standing behind them. In the middle, up top, is Ron, looking seven feet tall; he's standing on a ledge. Jim Brooks said Ron's father or brother cracked six feet. Bryan smiled and nodded halfway through the question. He told me four or five generations back there had been a six-foot-eight or six-foot-nine relative.

"There's a photograph of him in a cornfield, with the corn up to his eyes. He's pretty tall and he looked a lot like me. The same long face, same droopy eyes. It was really weird, like looking in a mirror. I think I'm a direct descendant of that great-great-great-uncle."

Ron Harper didn't hesitate in naming another Chicago Bears middle linebacker when I asked him what kind of football player Bryce would have become. "Great!" Ron said. "I think he would have been outstanding, a Brian Urlacher type." YouTube video mostly showed a young Bryce barreling and twisting his way for chunks of yardage, and touchdowns, as a bruising fullback.

Bryan and Bryce acquired their competitive drives from their father. Ron Harper, whose bushy goatee offset his shaved head, had a giant persona. His stare was as steely as a sixty-foot rod of rebar. He had been better at football than baseball at Rancho High, and he ran a 4.4-second forty-yard dash on the track. He also excelled on the BMX circuit. "Good genes," Bryan said with a big smile.

The Harper boys might idolize certain athletes, but for both there was only one hero—that guy with the bulging disks who rose so early to get to job sites so he could work with them at their baseball, soccer, or football practices in the afternoon and leave town all those weekends so they could travel with club teams all over the country. On occasion Ron was grubby from goatee to work boots in soot and grime after a long shift as he threw batting practice or hit fungoes with his boys in the afternoon at Sunset Park. Other times, he took them for cherry Slurpees and they talked about school or sports. Bryce and Bryan also spent some time on their dad's work site, carrying rebar or helping with other side jobs.

"They understood," Ron said. "They know what it takes." He ran a tight and efficient crew. His quick reflexes once saved a fellow worker from falling down an elevator shaft at the Lady Luck. The details weren't significant to Ron; all that mattered was that he had reached the guy in time. "I jumped down and grabbed him. He was okay, thank God. I just showed up every day, tried to keep everything safe, and worked hard. I kept a good eye on my guys."

And his boys. Bryan called his father Superman.

"By far, he's the toughest man I know. He'd bust his butt all the time, trying to get us to tournaments. He worked his butt off carrying that rebar with three torn disks in his back. Even tying rebar, he wanted to be in and out, doing it as fast as possible but doing it right. My brother and I learned a lot from him."

Parental aspirations were reflected in the gold pendants Ron and Sheri designed for their boys to wear around their necks. The 220 on the front meant "second to none," and their uniform numbers were on the back.

"I don't think anyone should accept failure," said Bryan, who wore number thirty-three. "We've always been raised to be the best, to go out there and win. Who wants to be a loser? I don't. I hate losing. Being in the sport of baseball teaches you how to lose and win at the same time. You can fail as an individual but win as a team. That's one thing I love about baseball. You can have a bad outing on the mound or go oh for four at the plate, but the guys behind you pick you up and you move on."

That would prove to be a tough lesson for Bryan's younger brother to learn.

The Harpers' comfortable, two-story, frame, stucco home on Cantelope Court had five bedrooms, three bathrooms, and a concrete-tile roof. It did not have a pool, a summertime desert staple, or a year-round spa to soothe sore muscles that had lugged three-hundred-pound bars of steel for ten or twelve hours. Those luxuries could be found at Grandpa's house.

So much of the male side of the family worked with iron, Bryan and Bryce figured when they were young, at least a few times, that they might be fated to the daily hauling of elevens, fourteens, and eighteens around Las Vegas on 115-degree summer days.

"[But] growing up and seeing how much pain he was in all the time, not being able to sit down or relax, coming out and throwing to us, and not moving for three days . . . that instilled in us to get our education, to get a job we love," Bryan said. "He didn't want us to deal with what he was dealing with. He'd do anything for us to get our education. Anytime a dad doesn't want to put his kids through the same pain he went through for twenty-five years is really special."

Bryce Harper wasn't just a magnet for all of those recruiters and scouts to expose his CSN teammates to more opportunities. The *Sports Illustrated* cover and the rest of the constant media attention aimed at him also shone a spotlight on Las Vegas, the fantasy city for so many visitors from all over the world. Continuing his career past high school in his hometown thrilled Bryce.

"Having the support of my hometown and playing for a hometown team is awesome. I get to support my hometown and say I'm from Vegas. They say, 'What? Vegas? There's no baseball in Vegas!' All the top talent is usually from Texas, California, and Florida. It's all about football and baseball there. For people to say, 'Wow, you're from Vegas? You must have done something well.' I didn't want to be one of those guys from Vegas that didn't do anything with their lives, just stayed here and worked at a 7-Eleven. I want to do something with my life."

THE ROCK GROUP SUPERTRAMP blared on the Morse Stadium loud-speakers as CSN players prepped their diamond for the last of three Coyote Classic tournament games, their season opener, on the crisp night of Friday, January 29, 2010. *When I was young, it seemed that life was so wonderful* . . . "The Logical Song," more than thirty years after hitting the airwaves, echoed around the stadium and served as a poetic anthem to a game, maybe even a season. A career?

Scores of camera bulbs flashed when Bryce Harper strolled to the on-deck circle, half a dozen steps from the home dugout on the first-base side, in the bottom of the first inning. He wore his white uniform with the dark blue pinstripes and dark blue number thirty-four trimmed in yellow. "Is that Bryce Harper on deck?" a squinting fifteen-year-old high school player said to another as they stood by the fence along the left-field foul line. "Don't you see *God* above his head?" said his buddy.

Harper hadn't been so heavenly in the batting cages in recent weeks, however. Coach Chambers and assistant Cooper Fouts had worked overtime to correct a right knee that turned inward and a left knee that sprang from a dramatic bend with every swing. That would soon be addressed in a major way.

At 8:44, Harper loped to the plate for the first time as a junior college player. His face was plain. He did not drop his bat in the box or grab handfuls of dirt. "Brrrrrrrryce Harrrrrrrper!" screamed announcer Mike "Bulldog" Carroll. That triggered a cascade of flashes, a mini Barry Bonds–like moment from when that lefty basher chased down and overtook Hank Aaron for the all-time home-run record. In ten previous CSN seasons, Chambers had never seen such starbursts in his park. In the dugout, Bryan Harper glared at the theatrics. He had seen many of those games as a fan but had never witnessed such pomp or seen nearly two thousand bodies in the quaint park.

In another first, two campus police officials guarded the low, black wrought-iron gate several steps from CSN's on-deck circle. As many as a half dozen security personnel would stand guard, keeping the public away from both sides of the dugout and Bryce Harper, during the season.

On the night of his junior college debut, an eager crowd greeted Harper's arrival. A wolf moon, the biggest and brightest full moon of the year, so named by some Native Americans as it related to hungry wolves howling at the moon on cold winter nights, seemed to offer a cartoonlike, faint-blue target to Harper just beyond the right-field wall. He would soon clear that fence, but not tonight. That didn't mean the evening passed without note.

In his first at bat, with those camera flashes twinkling around him, Harper, hitting third, looked at a low pitch. Ball one. The next two also flew out of the strike zone. Arizona Western's five-foot-eight pitcher Raul Vazquez threw one over the plate, but his fifth pitch was low and Harper walked to first base, moving Trevor Kirk to third and Scott Dysinger to second.

Washington executive Bob Boone and several other members of the Nationals' front office, and the rest of the record Morse Stadium crowd, saw their breath in the chill. A wise fan behind home plate had brought two portable, bulky heaters to comfort him and his wife. Bo Bochetti, the corpulent concessions supervisor from Brooklyn whose relatives still sulked about the Dodgers having left the borough for

Los Angeles after the 1957 season, toasted big, salty sourdough pretzels on his wide, black grill. Each came with a little plastic cup of warm nacho cheese sauce, an elixir in the brisk conditions.

The last of the 150 new parking spaces, a solid walk up the short hill from the stadium and on black tar that still looked wet, went two and a half hours earlier. The 120 gleaming blue stadium seats had long been filled. The rest of the visitors had either sat on blankets or beach chairs on the boulders behind home plate, or stood on the big red rocks, or tried finding a view in between or over all the caps and hats in the aisles, walkways, and food area. Jim Brooks scored, too, that night when he won $102 in the fifty-fifty raffle. Nobody could recall anyone ever pocketing triple figures in winnings from the drawing before.

After drawing that walk in the first inning, Bryce Harper darted to second on Marvin Campbell's infield groundout and scored on Ryan Scott's double down the right-field line. Harper singled to right on a three-two fastball from Raul Vazquez in the second inning for his first collegiate hit. It scored Trevor Kirk from second base to give the Coyotes a 6–0 advantage.

On defense, Harper double-pumped a throw from third base in the fifth, allowing a two-out hit and, eventually, two runs to score. He liked to boast that he could play defense anywhere on a baseball diamond, but that hesitation showed why the hot corner might not have been the best position for him. One teammate had seethed inside the dugout since he'd first seen Harper's name at third base on the lineup card hours earlier.

In the eighth, when Vazquez's first pitch to Harper sailed wide to standing catcher Adrian Gutierrez, a scout behind the CSN dugout said, "Intentional walk . . . time to walk." As he sloughed out of the stadium, another scout stood still, glanced at his departing colleague, and said, "You never know . . ."

At that very moment, Bryce Harper leaned in to home-plate umpire Glenn Ballangao to ask how far up he could toe the plate. Bryan

Harper, leaning on the far left side of the yellow-padded dugout rail, smiled and said to anyone within earshot, "He hates this. He absolutely *hates* this. He's going to do anything he can to not get walked."

Trent Cook, waiting in the hole by the edge of the dugout to hit after Marvin Campbell, in the on-deck circle, heard Bryan Harper. "I've seen him hit an intentional [pitch] before," said the elder Harper, "so they should watch out." This is new, Cook thought. This will be exciting. Cook meant this at bat, then he thought how it just might apply to the next four months.

Two wide pitches later, Bryce reached out over the plate and belted the shoulder-high ball to deep left-center field for a sacrifice fly, caught just before the warning track by Arizona centerfielder Josh Young; Trevor Kirk scored. Chambers had never seen that in his yard, either. It was the final run of CSN's 11–4 victory.

Thirty-six-year-old Glenn Ballangao had moved to Las Vegas from Hawaii with his family when he was eighteen. He had started umpiring in area Little Leagues and moved up through the ranks. He had worked Las Vegas High games the two seasons Bryce was a Wildcat. Ballangao ran a landscape crew when he wasn't on a diamond pursuing his passion. "That was pretty cool," Ballangao said of Harper's sacrifice fly off an intentional ball. "From an umpire's perspective, I felt honored to do that first game. I knew what the hype was going to be about. It was quite unique."

Kirk, at third, had been talking with Chambers, in the third-base coach's box. Neither had been paying much attention to what had been unfolding at the plate, and they were stunned to hear the bat connect with the ball. Kirk easily scored on the long fly. Dysinger, on second base, saw the third wide pitch and the bat move, but somehow, it didn't make sense. He ran to third base the moment the deep fly ball was hauled in by Young.

"That was the very beginning of all those wow moments," Casey Sato said. "The list goes on and on. Are you kidding me? I'd never seen that done before."

Bryce was eleven or twelve when Bryan first saw him pull off that feat. Bryce had been playing with the Southern California Red Wings club team when the opponent tried giving him first base for free. Bryce snarled. He asked the umpire how close to the plate he could stand and lurched right on top of it. Bryce toed that line, and if any of the pitches missed, well, the ball and the pitcher would pay the price. That's just what he did for the Red Wings. "He did it again," Bryan said on opening night. "Pretty funny."

Bryce Harper often downplayed what he did on the diamond, and his sacrifice fly didn't represent anything special to him. "I've been doing that for a while. Pitchouts . . . I hate when they walk me. But, yeah, I poked out and got a little sacrifice there. So it's okay, as long as it scored a run."

Trent Cook wouldn't see Morse Stadium bursting at its seams with an overflow crowd again. "Incredible," he said. "That weekend there was so much hype about him, and he definitely fulfilled those expectations."

Joe Robinson, who resembled a young George Harrison of Beatles fame, started on the hill that night for Chambers. Bryan Harper won the game in relief. All was not completely well among the Coyotes, though. Infielder Tomo Delp, whose given name was Robert but who went by an abridged version of his middle name, Tomotaka, had the habit of twirling his bat twice in the air, 720 degrees, high above his head like a blade of a helicopter, before settling in to take a pitch at the plate. It had become so ingrained he never realized he did it. Delp, like teammate Gabe Weidenaar, could also dunk a basketball. The most athletic Coyote? That was arguable.

But on opening night, Delp, a graduate of Bonanza High who had short, dark hair, dark eyes, and a dark complexion, was on the bench, stunned to see Bryce Harper starting at third base.

"I was pissed off about that," said Delp, who had played third all through fall ball and thought he owned the position. Delp did not talk much, and he had a nervous habit of saying "Huh?" before someone had completely finished asking him a question. But he did not hide his opening-night feelings. "It sucked. I couldn't believe it. I thought it was crazy." He talked with Chambers after the game and was assured that he would get plenty of time at the hot corner, just as Chambers had to convince Ryan Scott that Bryce wasn't going to catch every game.

Harper caught the first game of the next day's doubleheader and played center field in the nightcap, both victories against Yavapai College. He had gone oh for eight in the twin bill, and he hadn't collected a hit in twelve consecutive trips to the plate. After a dismal at bat against Yavapai, Harper tossed his helmet at the dugout foundation as he returned to the dugout.

Late that Saturday night, CSN equipment manager Sean Larimer, who watered the infield, cut the grass, washed the uniforms, and tended to anything else the team or Chambers needed, had been locking up the place when he heard the unmistakable *foomp-thwack, foomp-thwack, foomp-thwack* of Bryce Harper's bat. He was tattooing pitch after pitch in the far right of the three batting cages, in the area beyond the clubhouse and right-field foul line, against a pitching machine. Harper thought nobody else had been on the premises.

Larimer strolled up to Harper, encased in a long tunnel of loose nylon netting on all sides and above him, in the glow of two bulbs sixteen feet above whose soft yellow light barely covered the area. With a chaw of Copenhagen long cut in his lower lip, Larimer told Harper that taking sixty or seventy-five "angry" hacks right now wasn't going to solve anything. "It won't change your swing or help your swing. You won't get better right now. Go home. Clear your head."

Larimer and Harper had a special relationship. The twenty-two-year-old former Green Valley High School baseball player covered in the outfield in Tuesday scrimmages if the team was shorthanded. Larimer, whose lofty recommendation of Green Valley pitcher Joe Robinson to Chambers had turned Robinson into a Coyote, punched singles up the middle if the CSN pitchers didn't respect the slim hitter's bat.

The Coyotes only knew Larimer as Showtime. In his youth, Showtime had earned his nickname because of his penchant for slowing down on easy fly balls and timing a dive perfectly to turn a routine catch into a spectacular achievement. He empathized with some of Harper's struggles because of the immense criticism Larimer had received in his life. Many of the Coyotes also knew Larimer's story, that he had a piece of titanium in his right cheek, where his face required reconstruction, from the night he drove drunk and caused a crash that killed three of his close friends.

When he was sixteen, Larimer had had his driver's license for nine weeks when he ran his blue 1995 Pontiac Grand Am, carrying four passengers, into a fortress of a wall. Larimer twirled spaghetti, stabbing at the meatball on top, as he recalled the events that led to the horrific accident and the aftermath of the tragedy.

On the evening of November 9, 2003, Larimer drove himself and friends to a party, but they soon left because it had been mostly an older crowd. They went to another gathering in the upscale Seven Hills area, where a few dozen kids were partying. Larimer slammed eight cans of beer within an hour. When the homeowners complained of noise and ended the festivities, Larimer and his group went to a Vons grocery store to buy two cartons of eggs and toilet paper. They were going to retaliate at a classmate who had TP'd a friend's house a week earlier. After the store, they were en route to drop off Kyle Poff, but at the last moment Poff decided to go with the crew and sleep over at Travis Dunning's home. When they dropped off Ryan Olson, there were five in the Pontiac. They never made it to the Henderson house, two minutes away, that they had targeted for the eggs and toilet paper.

At 12:29 the morning of November 10, Larimer turned right, or east, from the northbound Green Valley Parkway onto Silver Springs Parkway, which bent into a long, gradual right curve. The speed limit was twenty-five miles an hour. Larimer gunned his Pontiac above eighty. His friends yelled for Larimer to slow down. When the road finally straightened and began bending left, Larimer didn't compensate or hit the brakes. Most were not wearing seat belts. The car crashed into a wall of thick, jagged-faced, black-speckled sandstone blocks, at the entrance of the Creekside neighborhood just before the parking lot of a community center.

Neighbors said the ultra-sturdy, seven-foot, curved wall had been reinforced with titanium rods and massive amounts of cement. At three and five feet, rows of ribbed, or fluted, red bricks stuck out. It was foreboding. Maybe a locomotive could have smashed through it, but the Grand Am had been no match. The right side of the vehicle had been obliterated. Kyle Poff, Josh Parry, and Travis Dunning were killed. Larimer and Cody Fredericks were hospitalized with critical injuries; the quick response of a Nevada Highway Patrol trooper who had been half a mile away and heard the loud crash helped save them. All were high school sophomores.

Larimer required several facial reconstructive surgeries and had the T-shaped piece of titanium, as long and wide as the nail of a pinkie, inserted in the right side of his cheek to replace a crushed bone. It set off metal detectors in airport security systems. The wall had barely been scraped, belying the severe nature of some of the fatal injuries. The blood-alcohol limit for drivers under twenty-one in Nevada was 0.02. Larimer's reportedly registered at 0.19.

James Dunning, father of the late Travis Dunning, predicted that Larimer would have "a huge cross to bear for the rest of his life." Larimer was arrested on December 31, 2003, and charged with drunken driving and involuntary manslaughter. Under a plea agreement that included probation until Larimer turned twenty-one, he wouldn't be released from the Clark County Juvenile Detention Center until February 2006. His mother, Susan, visited once a week, for ninety minutes. He was allowed two weekly five-minute phone calls. Susan Larimer played a significant role in getting Nevada to enact stricter teen driving laws that have helped reduce teen driving deaths. The case was featured in a *Time* magazine report.

Sean Larimer's six hundred hours of community service required him to speak about the perils of drinking and driving to area middle and high schools. Coyotes outfielder Trevor Kirk remembered being in the eighth grade when Larimer spoke at his middle school before hundreds of students. Left fielder Marvin Campbell recalled the somber speech Larimer gave in the Las Vegas High gym when Campbell and Bryan Harper were freshmen. Larimer had walked to the podium wearing an orange jumpsuit. His hands were cuffed and ankles were shackled. Police removed the handcuffs when Larimer addressed the crowds. He always spoke with his head bowed.

In the fall of 2009, an officer had been giving the never-drive-drunk speech to a Bishop Gorman auditorium of about two hundred students, which included CSN coach Tim Chambers's daughter McKenzie, when the officer flippantly talked about Larimer getting off easy, "on a cakewalk." McKenzie Chambers yelled at the cop, "You don't know anything! He thinks about that every day of his life! That ruined his life!" The officer changed topics. Larimer continues to speak at schools and other groups. He appeared nervous talking about his past at the Italian café, but he was stern when he said he never wanted anyone to have sympathy for him about the talks he conducted for kids.

"Like 'poor Sean.' I've never taken that approach and I never will. My friends' families have it a lot worse. The biggest message I try to get across is that I don't want people to forget them. As time goes on, people move on with their lives. I never will. I'll always miss my friends. I also realize I have to take a positive approach to life, be happy, and smile, and know in my heart what my friends would want me to do. I'm doing the speeches for my friends and to try to help kids."

On a nightstand next to his bed, Larimer had a photograph of Josh Parry, Kyle Poff, and Travis Dunning in a wood frame. Today is for you guys, Larimer says to his three friends every morning. In the middle of the rear window on Larimer's silver Dodge Ram pickup truck was a black SF logo, for his beloved San Francisco Giants. At the bottom right, a C for "Coyotes." In the lower left corner, a white oval sticker with Parry, Poff, and Dunning, each pictured in a tuxedo, with their names below their photographs. Above, it read JUST KEEP THINKING SAFETY.

Today, the full branches and leaves of two thirty-foot oak trees reach over the curved Creekside wall. A six-foot Mexican bird-of-paradise with red, vinelike stems and the tentacles of a chest-high Mondale pine shrub, both just left of the CREEKSIDE sign on the street side, frame a serene scene.

Larimer tried to impart some knowledge of how to cope with intense scrutiny to Harper. Larimer told Harper that he should only focus on playing for his teammates, friends, and family, not for members of the media or scouts of major league teams who might be in the stands.

"At the end of the day, they can talk shit about you but you're still going to be drafted high," Larimer said to Harper. "Your at bats will speak for themselves." Larimer had recognized that Harper's many antagonists, critics, and doubters had been affecting him, and then he went hitless in those two games. "Just because you're struggling doesn't mean you'll struggle forever," Larimer said.

As much as Chambers had done and would do for Harper, Chambers always endured stretches in which he searched for answers or ways to help the prodigy. There's no blueprint, Chambers repeated, on how to handle a high school junior playing college ball. This has never been done before, Chambers repeated to himself and others. Some teammates didn't know how to address or handle Harper. Others were tough on him in certain situations.

That's where Larimer filled in when appropriate. When Larimer was sixteen, his brain was in the midst of its second and final stage of development as he made a series of fatal decisions. The prefrontal cortex, behind the forehead, governed logical, sound decision-making and gauged potential risks. It isn't fully developed until roughly the early twenties. Throw in peer pressure and an emotional current, and alcohol, and even the smartest of teens can make the dumbest decisions.

Harper's prefrontal cortex was at a similar stage of development during the 2010 season. Larimer tried to help Harper by mellowing him and telling him to only worry about what he could control.

"I was trying to get across the mental side of it," Larimer explained. "I learned a long time ago, as hard as it is to close off certain people, you have to. If you forget about the big picture and dwell on bad things or people . . . Bryce knows what truly matters. So who gives a fucking shit what Joe Blow, or an area scout for the Angels, has to say? His opinion doesn't matter. His boss will make the decision. If a GM comes out and says, 'I love Bryce,' that's all that matters. Who cares what Clown Boy, or whoever, has to say?"

Coyotes who had heard Larimer's speech didn't broach the topic with him. They were surprised Larimer talked about it so deeply with me, but Larimer said he didn't want to forget the worst decision he had ever made. He tried to honor his deceased friends' memories by talking about what can happen, how many lives might be affected, when a terrible decision is made to drive drunk.

Every speech upset Larimer. He got emotional. The speeches stirred up such tragic memories, but he never turned down a request. Maybe only one out of fifty kids listened to him, but letters and phone calls he has received from kids who had altered their or a parent's lifestyle because of his words reinforced the importance of his speeches.

"Most high school kids, like I did, think they're invincible," said Larimer, his hazel eyes fragile but determined. "They think they can make decisions and they don't think of the consequences. I miss my friends dearly, every day. At times it's too sad. I cry. I also know baseball is a release for me. I'm grateful for opportunities I've had and I hope to coach."

Harper thanked Larimer. They hugged. As Larimer picked up the bucket of baseballs and turned to store it in an equipment locker, to close up the shop for the evening and turn off the lights, Harper stopped him.

"Can I hit just ten more balls?"

"Yeah." Larimer shrugged and gave Harper a half smile. "Hit ten, then get out of here."

Harper met Chambers in the clubhouse Sunday morning at ten. They reviewed videotape of his previous day's swings, in which Harper had taken the doubleheader collar against Yavapai. Again, he had been turning his right knee in and dipping his left knee. They trudged to a batting cage. Chambers, with a camera rolling, tried convincing Harper how to iron out his mechanics. They went back to the clubhouse and Chambers showed him the glaring difference between the two stances, swings, and torque, on the flat-screen.

Nobody can hit like that, Chambers told Harper. It was a marvel that Harper could even connect with the ball to foul it off, with so many moving parts. Fans, scouts, parents, or just plain loudmouths had yelled from the stands about Harper's springy lurches at pitches. *He's jumping at the ball! Why does he keep jumping at the ball? He's jumping at the ball! Every time he makes an out, he jumps more!*

"Nobody wants to say *why* he's jumping," Chambers said. "So we showed him why. He was turning his right leg and sitting down on his backside about a foot and a half. There's only one way to go from there. *He* saw it. That's what mattered."

Hit it to left field, Chambers told Harper. "I don't care where it goes or what happens, hit it to left in your first at bat and you'll get a home run today." Harper sliced his third pitch out there to handcuff Arizona Western left fielder Erick Martinez and eased into second base. In the second inning he walked. In the fifth Harper drilled an oh-two pitch for a home run, his first in junior college, over the 335-foot fence in right field.

In the dugout Harper hugged Chambers, who moments later showed Harper video footage on a small camera, taken by a fan, that revealed his rear leg as still for the home-run swing, as it had been earlier that morning in the batting cage. What a difference, Chambers said after the 8–5 victory.

At practice two days later, no scouts were at Morse Stadium. Harper walked onto the field with a bat completely wrapped in white tape. Everyone is doing it, he told Marvin Campbell. It gives you more pop. He laughed to himself and admired his artistry. "It's the Mummy, bro."

Harper rarely strayed from Campbell. Harper reserved his biggest hugs for his six-foot-four buddy who resembled a young Vladimir Guerrero, especially if Vlad the Impaler had swung from the left side. In one of the more punchy scenes, in the middle of the season, Harper and Campbell spent a few giddy minutes busting already-broken bats on their thighs and helmets in the clubhouse entryway. When the Coyotes stretched before practice, Campbell always was one of six who faced the rest of the team, as a de facto captain, and paced its regimen. Harper always stood opposite Campbell, who was so close to Ron Harper he called him Dad. Campbell called Jim Brooks, the grandfather of Bryan and Bryce Harper, Grandpa. Many times Campbell was the lone black player, in both dugouts, during the season.

At the age of twenty, in 1974, Campbell's namesake father left Hodge, Louisiana, for Las Vegas and played two seasons of football at UNLV. Compact and sturdy, the senior Campbell had worked for the Clark County Fire Department for thirty-two years when he retired in the fall of 2009. He had battled the notorious blazes at the MGM Grand, which killed eighty-five people in November 1980, and the Las Vegas Hilton, where eight died in February 1981. He recalled seeing corpses of those who had died from smoke inhalation in the MGM Grand stairwells, but he didn't care to relive those gruesome memories.

The Florida Marlins had picked the junior Marvin Campbell in the thirty-first round of the 2008 amateur draft, but that was too low and he went to CSN. He often returned to Hodge, in the upper part of

Louisiana near Ruston, to play summertime basketball with his father's friends, reminisce, and reconnect with his family's roots.

Due to the low numbers of black baseball players in area high schools, Chambers had recruited maybe half a dozen to CSN in his eleven seasons running the program. Campbell remembered playing well at baseball camps but not being such a high priority for recruiters or scouts; he felt they believed he'd be leaning toward basketball or football, so they concentrated on other players. Campbell grew up watching tapes of the basketball legend Julius Erving, and marveled at Michael Jordan and Kobe Bryant. Many friends wanted to be like those stars. Campbell recalled only a few of his pals wanting to be like Hank Aaron or Ken Griffey Jr.

"That has a lot to do with race," he said. Growing up, when his parents took Marvin to baseball tournaments in Utah, and many other places, he had been the only African-American on the field; his parents were the only African-Americans in the stands. "That can easily make someone from an urban area uncomfortable. They're out of their element. And many view baseball as boring."

Campbell had vivid memories of watching sports on television. "When you turn on the TV as an African-American kid and watch a baseball game, and you only see a couple of African-Americans . . . well, that doesn't look fun. Am I even supposed to be playing this game? You turn on a basketball or football game, and it looks comfortable. I can relate to that. That's what it becomes. I like to turn on the TV and see somebody like me playing the game."

He had seen the *USA Today* headline about the percentage of blacks in the majors declining, after its first rise in fifteen years in 2009. But Campbell liked what he had been seeing in the Futures Game, the part of the annual All-Star festivities that featured a contest among the young, upcoming stars of baseball. "There are *a lot* of African-Americans in that game the past couple of years. I think a lot of kids are starting to put in the extra work. The RBI program, that helps."

Major League Baseball started its grassroots Reviving Baseball in Inner Cities (RBI) program in 1989. Professional teams had donated more than $30 million to fuel the effort. In 2010, three hundred RBI leagues in more than two hundred cities worldwide had more than 175,000 participants. C. C. Sabathia, Carl Crawford, Jimmy Rollins, and James Loney were some of the many black major league players who had matriculated through the RBI system.

Campbell's comfort level at CSN soared in 2010, with Bryce again hitting in front of him and Bryan Harper around for more familiarity. Campbell laughed at his first memories of Bryan, the tall, thin lefty with the clean-cut Mormon image. Now, there wasn't a more ardent fan of Lil Wayne in all of Nevada if not the West Coast than Bryan Harper.

There might have been too much comfort among the Coyotes. Any outsider would have been astonished to hear *nigger,* most often as *niggy,* so frequently. Every day, in practice or games, on the bus or in a convenience store far from home, it had been tossed around as often as baseballs. Malice didn't figure into the usage, though, as the prevalence of it in rap music and movies, and other outlets, had seemingly mitigated its connotation. And Campbell always seemed to be cool with it.

Which wasn't entirely accurate. In the wrong situation, with the wrong tone or over-the-top usage, Campbell paused. Okay, Campbell thought, and he would pause some more. In so many words or with a gesture, even by walking away, he'd signal that that was enough. Real or imagined, and it often appeared to be the former, Campbell had issues with umpires and race throughout the season, too.

But he quickly dismissed the arc of the conversation to say that he wanted to be a role model for all kids, whether they're black, white, purple, or green. He also enjoyed the diversity in baseball, the Latinos, the blacks, the whites, and the Asians, and all the different styles with which they added flair and flavor to the game. Dominicans started the current fad of wearing their pant legs down to their cleats. They are hemmed heavy to stay down.

"When they started playing, maybe they didn't have the right size pants?" Campbell said. "They hung over the shoes. Now, everyone wants those. And Ichiro Suzuki and Kosuke Fukudome have their own styles. It's how they were taught, and I love it."

After the Coyotes had stretched and arranged teams for a scrimmage, Chambers leaned on the short fence between the diamond and the clubhouse. He had conducted seven or eight phone interviews earlier that day. I'm doing your job, he said to Bryce Harper as the phenom jogged from right field to the dugout like a carefree Saint Bernard puppy. Over a few days, Chambers had unsuccessfully tried to deflect all baseball inquiries to the school's office of public information. He had tried to shut down access to himself, but too many had his cell phone number and he didn't want to go through the hassle of changing it.

"It's wearing *me* out," a deflated Chambers said as he looked at Bryce, taking warm-up swings with his Marucci and laughing with Campbell. "Imagine if he had to do it."

The top-ranked and 4-0 Coyotes gathered at the stadium the following morning at six for a six-hour bus trek to the Phoenix area to play GateWay College. Harper singled three times, scored once, and drove in a run in a 12–0 rout. Bryan Harper—with his left knee and shin often scraping the mound dirt as he uncoiled, like a praying mantis lurching at lunch, his six-foot-six frame upon delivery—won his first start as a Coyote.

Bryce Harper filled in at third base and had made Marc Morse, who coached the CSN infielders, cringe when he moved to his left to field a grounder, blocked it with his chest—like a catcher—and threw the batter out at first base.

"That's one way to do it," Morse told Harper with a grin after the inning. Morse would have liked to see that intensity in some other infielders, who would have bailed out of the way of such a mean chopper in between hops. Morse told Harper, we'll work on it more so you don't do that again. "It was a great play, but we can make that with our glove. Those [scouts] in the stands, they're watching you do that, and they'll throw third base out of the window on you, know what I mean? That won't necessarily work in the big leagues." They worked on Harper's sliding to his left in subsequent practices, but he did not play much at third the rest of the season. The hot corner was left to Tomo Delp and Gabe Weidenaar.

CSN followed that long travel day with a Thursday-night game that had been attended by far fewer fans than opening night. There were no camera flashes, but a star appeared. Former Los Angeles Dodgers first baseman Steve Garvey, who had befriended the Harpers a few years earlier and had made the three-hour trek from his home in the Palm Springs area, watched with keen interest next to Ron Harper, not far from the CSN dugout.

At the age of twenty, Garvey had played his first game for the Dodgers in September 1969. In his nineteen-year career, he had jacked 272 home runs, hit .294, participated in ten All-Star Games, and helped the Dodgers win the World Series in 1981.

Bryce Harper was fourteen when he went to Southern California to play for a Riverside Reds club team on which Garvey's son also played. Ron and Sheri Harper had chatted with Garvey, who met Bryce, and the families have been tight since. Bryce Harper raved about Garvey, his wife, Candace, and their kids.

"What a great guy. Everything about him is class. He took me in and treated me like I was one of his own. Anytime I need advice, he talks to me from that big-league mentality. He told me I'd struggle at the beginning of the season, maybe until the middle of the season. Learn from one-for-twenty-two stretches, he told me. Do what I can to progress and keep my mind off it, play the game how I know to play it, and help the team other ways, by catching and throwing, stealing bases . . . you don't always have to do it at the plate. He played hard every day. He didn't take one day off. He told me to make sure I play every game like it's my last. He loved the game, that's for sure."

The Harpers also had a special relationship with Kurt Stillwell, a former major league infielder who had played on the San Diego Padres with CSN assistant coach Kevin Higgins. When Stillwell played for the Cincinnati Reds, manager Pete Rose called him Opie because of his wholesome, all-American manner. Chambers believed superagent Scott Boras's pairing of Stillwell with the Harper family for any questions Ron or Sheri might have about the business side of the game was Boras's most savvy move.

In accordance with baseball rules, Boras never came around. Stillwell, in his capacity as an adviser, could watch games and lurk, but with restrictions on his involvement; for instance, he could dine with Ron and Bryce and the family, but Stillwell was only allowed to pay for his own meals in a restaurant.

Chambers pointed to me as an example of how the mellow Stillwell, Stilly to friends, meshed with the sometimes-volatile Ron Harper. You're laid-back, Chambers told me. "And I'm uptight, always moving. That's why we get along so well." Opposites attract, or something like that. That's why the easygoing Stillwell, who always wore a beige floppy hat to games to protect his nearly bald dome, fit so well with the intense Ron Harper, who could be as quick with a handshake and smile as he was with an icy stare or comment if he felt a loved one or a friend had been wronged or threatened.

When the elder Harper needed a sounding board, Chambers was always there. The slightest criticism of Bryce made Ron clench his teeth, so he most often watched games alone, down on that metal bench along the short fence that ran alongside the right-field foul line.

"Ronnie gets wound up like a two-day clock, like Chambers," said Jim Brooks, Ron Harper's father-in-law. "Ronnie and Chambers are a good group, but I don't see how one can calm the other one down. Both are so hyper."

Ron Harper managed a laugh when he acknowledged Chambers's

comparison of Chambers's relationship with me as being similar to Ron's dynamic with Stillwell. "More fiery," Ron said of himself and Chambers. Ron got along well with Stillwell, whom Ron respected as an even-keeled family man. "I'm a little more hot-tempered," Ron admitted in one of our few conversations. "He kind of cooled me down if I was getting excited or upset about something."

That frigid Thursday night, Steve Garvey, Kurt Stillwell, Tim Chambers, and Ron Harper all saw Bryce begin to morph into the guy who had graced that *Sports Illustrated* cover. He wore his socks high, with his white pants tucked in below the knees. Every other CSN player, except Marvin Campbell, wore his pants down to his cleats. When Bryce reached the plate, he dropped his black bat to the ground and rubbed dirt between his hands. It was the first time he had gone back to that part of his colorful high school shtick.

Harper went hitless in four at bats, which again landed him in the cages Friday morning after a chat with pitching coach Glen Evans. Two years earlier, Evans had coached at Calvary Christian High School. In a game against Las Vegas High, Evans watched Harper hit with absolute authority. Harper had just returned from a stint with the national sixteen-and-under team. What did you do then? Evans asked Harper. Unbeknownst to Harper, Evans had told Chambers how confident Harper had looked, and swung, that season. Bring that up to him, Chambers said, "in a matter-of-fact way, as if you're just talking and it just came to you."

To Evans, Harper recalled that he had spread his feet out a bit more in the box, nullifying any knee jerks. So he did that that Friday and hammered, just pounded, five or six pitches in the cage. Harper's eyes were wide when he strolled into Chambers's office.

"Been a while since I felt like that," Harper said.

Good, Chambers said. "Let's finish it off. I saw how you put the bat down in the box last night. I saw how you spit in your hands and rubbed dirt in them. Now put the war paint back on. It's all a routine when you're hitting. Everyone is talking shit anyway. Why not be you? That's who you are."

When Harper signed with CSN, he had asked Chambers about the signature eye black that he wore so infamously on that *Sports Illustrated* cover. Can I still wear it? Absolutely, Chambers said. "We are not going to change who you are." After the game against GateWay in Arizona, Marvin Campbell sent text messages to Harper about that very topic. Before Harper's iPhone died, they had agreed to go back to the face paint, Campbell with big blocks under his eyes and Harper looking as if he belonged in the middle of a National Football League team's defense. In high school, they had tried Easton eye black. But it wasn't *black* enough. It didn't smear on *thick* enough. They discovered a Franklin tube and their search was over.

Ryan Scott walked by Harper in the clubhouse bathroom as Harper applied the Franklin eye black in the lipsticklike case under his eyes before that Friday-night game. "He's baaaaaack," said a giddy Scott. Harper laughed. Campbell applied big blocks under each eye.

Harper had been seven years old when he watched Louisiana State beat Texas in a College World Series game on June 10, 2000. Some of those players had splattered the grease on their cheeks. That looked cool to Harper. When he was ten or eleven, Harper watched a few Gaels, such as Jon Berger, doing it at Bishop Gorman. Berger went on to pitch for CSN and San Diego State, and he spent the 2010 season in the San Diego Padres' minor league system. Harper wanted to be just like them.

He added his personal touch by bringing the grease down, with two fingers, on the outside of each cheek. "Everyone was saying, 'Holy crap! What is he doing? Idiot!' I said, 'Whatever. Screw you guys.' Then I saw others doing it a few years later. I guess I just had that effect on people."

Little Leaguers had been watching him. In their 2010 World Series, in Williamsport, Pennsylvania, the American tykes used plenty of the stuff. Once Harper completed his routine by slapping it on both cheeks for a doubleheader against Yavapai College on Friday, February 5, the results weren't surprising.

Yavapai coach Sky Smeltzer had already watched his Roughriders lose to CSN three times in the young season. However, Smeltzer had also seen Harper go oh for twelve against his club. He saw Harper, wearing his stirrups high, walk into the CSN clubhouse via a door three steps from the parking lot and said something to Chambers about Harper being a lone wolf, that no other CSN player had been wearing his pants high. Not so, Chambers said, Marvin Campbell will be wearing them that way, too.

No matter, Smeltzer said, Harper hasn't gotten a hit off us. Chambers quietly boiled.

With that wider and sturdier stance, and the war paint, Harper slammed a triple to the wall in right-center to score two runs in the first inning. "Make that one for thirteen!" Chambers yelled from the third-base coach's box to Smeltzer, fifty feet away in the visitors' dugout. In the sixth, Harper creamed a two-run homer over the fence in dead center field, a shot of at least 450 feet, and one more feat that Chambers had never seen in his park. "Make that two for fifteen!" Chambers yelled at Smeltzer.

"Something happened. It was electric," Harper said of how the eye black had affected him. "Putting that on and being ready, I look in the mirror, that's on, and it's 'Let's go!' It's a total transformation. When I put the eye black on and walk between those lines, nothing else matters. I just want to rip your head off. I'm such a different person on the baseball field than I am off it. I'm totally different. I'm pretty much a dick on the baseball field. I will respect you, but I want to rip your head off. I want to do everything I can to beat you and your team."

"I think he just got part of himself back," Ryan Scott said. "He's confident, there's no arrogance. He's not a guy where it rubs you the wrong way. Every day, you like him more."

Harper drew a late intentional walk in that first game, then went one for three, with an RBI double, in the second. Marvin Campbell hit a home run in the second game, a 5–0 victory. With the eye black, both were back in their comfort zones. After his one for eleven start, Harper ended his first full week in junior college hitting .323. The top-ranked Coyotes were poised atop the JC polls at 8-0. "What a team! What a team!" Chambers exclaimed to the ceiling rafters as the team high-fived after a postgame chat in the clubhouse.

A lifelong Los Angeles Dodgers fan, Chambers relished those three words and repeated them frequently throughout the 2010 season in tribute to Kirk Gibson, who said them often during the Dodgers' World Series championship season of 1988. Chambers believed 2010 would be just as memorable for him and his Coyotes.

THE OFFER, TO SIT in the CSN dugout and experience, up close, the sights and sounds of an incomparable baseball season, to dodge a laser-like foul ball or two, to smell the musky liquid pine tar—tougher to shake from fingertips than maple syrup—and whiff the brain-freezing fusion of Rust-Oleum inverted striping paint, and to ingest a few granules of dirt along the way, came from Coach Chambers's heart. Between his brain and his mouth there are no synapses. He says what he thinks. If you're on his bad side, you will know it; his nose will touch yours.

As genuine as the invitation was, though, I weighed consequences like a first-time runner in Pamplona. First and foremost, that's the sanctuary of coaches and players who had earned their stations. Anyone else was trespassing, or so I thought. Come on in, Chambers said. Players know you and recognize you, he said. You've been to every practice. You're always here, he said. They'll welcome you.

How I had detailed Chambers's dark history with his father, for a 2003 profile before he led the Coyotes to the Junior College World Series championship, had forged a strong connection between us. That story depicted *exactly* what had happened, he said. It was *perfect,* he said. That trust is what enticed him to open his program to me, to chronicle every day of Bryce Harper's quest, to witness the stories behind the statistics, to portray the players who had merged to form this dynamic team.

Ultimately, declining the offer would have insulted Chambers. The opportunity was extraordinary. Chambers had never made such a proposal or heard of a manager, at any level, allowing a writer into his inner sanctum for games. None of his assistants—including Kevin Higgins, who had played in the majors—knew of an outsider being granted such incredible access. David Segui, who had spent fifteen seasons in the big leagues, laughed when I asked him if he ever knew of a writer being able to hang in the dugout during the action. Absolutely no way, he said. Longtime Los Angeles Dodgers pitcher Jerry Reuss, now a broadcaster, reacted to my query as if he had just bitten into a lemon. He shook his head.

Chambers had wanted me to witness history. Chambers knew it would be a special season. He knew Harper would dominate. He knew every day had to be chronicled. He knew the makeup and inter- actions of the rest of his players would be compelling; they were the ones who would protect Harper, and they would be the ones who would correct, guide, and temper him, to prep him for his next level.

Plus, something of a guidebook would now be available for fu- ture coaches who would have the task of managing such a prodigious young talent, although Chambers believed this would never happen again. What's more, for better or for worse, as a cautionary tale or a road map, future wunderkinds would get an idea of what to expect if they chose to test themselves against such older and more experi- enced competition.

I had to get in there.

But what would the club's luck be with the bunker addition of a six-foot-five writer, old enough to be the father of any of these Coyotes, with the invisible trifocals, whose baseball claim to fame had been striking out three times in a media game at Dodger Stadium? My bat had touched a pitch, barely, only once. That crafty lefty hurler, a Dodgers batting-practice pitcher, was throwing split-fingered fastballs, maybe even a spitter or two, and slurves, only at me, right? Baseball is one of mankind's most superstitious games. What if CSN lost after winning its first eight games, and when I turned forty-six on February 12? Get in there Big Bird, Chambers said. Endearingly, he had nicknamed me on the spot the day I had showed up at practice wearing an orange, long-sleeved San Francisco Giants T-shirt. It wasn't yellow, but for Chambers it was close enough. Players mostly called me by my last name, which rhymed with *wish*. Get in the middle of them, Chambers said. Make yourself at home. They will love it. And come to the yard early.

As instructed, I arrived at Morse Stadium a few hours early that Friday. Chambers called me into his office. Happy birthday, Big Bird, he said as he tossed white, blue, and black fitted CSN caps at me. If you're gonna sit in there, he said, you have to look the part. Yup, I said.

If you were part of the Coyotes, it wasn't *yes, yeah,* or *yep.* It was *yup,* with an emphasis on the *Y. Yyyyyyyyup!* Frozen ropes into the dugout were *ugly finders.* A bat broken on a hit *died a hero.* Batters hit by a pitch never rubbed the area that had been wounded. "Don't touch it!" implored teammates. When a blooper was headed over infielders' heads and in front of outfielders, Coyotes raised their voices. "Nestle. . . . *Nestle!*" *Nose goes* was the saying, as players touched their noses, when more food or chewing tobacco was needed; the last one to do so carried out the task. And CSN caps were worn—always with hair tucked inside, not hanging down on the forehead—only during games. Away from the diamond, anything else was fine. Bryce Harper favored a dark Florida Marlins cap away from diamonds and parks and stadiums.

Chambers's pal Ronnie Simmers, the small but gritty umpire who had overseen Harper's four strikeouts in the fall scrimmage at Foothill High, once wore his white cap with the dark blue *C* to a nightclub in the Orleans, just off the Strip. Word quickly spread to Chambers, who was out of town. He called Simmers on his cell phone as

Simmers showed off his latest John Travolta moves on the dance floor. "Sorry, Coach," Simmers said over the Top 40 throb as he removed the cap.

Simmers had the strongest lungs in the West. At times, Scott Dysinger and other players beckoned him to cool it at the edge of the dugout. Then, as if by magic or a crane or marionette strings, that shrill voice rained down from above; Simmers had climbed to the roof of the clubhouse, more than twenty feet high behind the dugout, in a flash to cheer on CSN and howl at foes.

I had tried to sneak into the dugout like a church mouse, immediately hanging a left by the eye-level, orange Gatorade jug. Didn't make eye contact. Then shifted my rear atop the bench. Did anyone notice? Bryce Harper bounded into the dugout and chest-bumped Ryan Scott, who was among the first curious players, with Scott Dysinger and Trevor Kirk, to greet me and say hello on their hallowed turf minutes before an actual game. Assistant coaches Cooper Fouts, Steve Chatham, Jay Guest, and Glen Evans welcomed me at various points in the game.

The stout and soft-spoken Evans and Chambers had been tight since they met in high school in Utah. They played football together at Dixie College, where Evans was involved in a tragic accident. On October 6, 1984, after catching a screen pass on the left side in the first quarter, Evans barreled into Snow College defender Ray Billingsley. The helmet-on-helmet hit flattened the six-foot, 220-pound Billingsley, who was shuttled by ambulance to the emergency room of a local hospital. He escaped and returned to the game in the second half. He collapsed on the sideline, slipped into a coma during surgery to alleviate a subdural hematoma, and died ten days later.

At five feet nine, Evans weighed 215 pounds, about a hundred under his current figure, that day. He had been a gifted athlete. His father, James, was a prolific prep basketball player in Georgia, and Glen Evans, despite his squat stature, could dunk a basketball on a regulation hoop in his youth. More recently, he broke the spring on the diving board of the pool in Chambers's backyard. Evans took some solace in that he had heard that Ray Billingsley had sustained previous head injuries while boxing or playing football. Still, Evans admitted that he thought about the episode when he saw kids playing football or a player lying on the ground.

"It flashes through my head," Evans said with no emotion. "But I don't say it haunts me, not at all. It was an unfortunate incident."

Evans became glassy-eyed when he recalled how Bryce and Bryan Harper had arrived at his house just before Christmas 2009. Evans's wife, Nikki, had been battling cancer, and the Harper boys wanted to brighten her holiday with a substantial gift certificate. "It was no fifty-dollar gift card," Evans said.

Steve Chatham, much to Chambers lieutenant Kevin Higgins's chagrin, was the lone CSN assistant who had won a College World Series. In 1995, Chatham played on a Cal State Fullerton team loaded with talent. Its rudder was Mark Kotsay, whom *Baseball America* had tabbed as its player of the 1990s. The Titans defeated Southern California, 11–5, for the title.

The next three years, Chatham, who hit .339 in his collegiate career and belted twelve home runs, played with Aaron Rowand at Fullerton. At Rowand's wedding, Chatham met and eventually married Lisa Griffen, the sister of Rowand's bride, Marianne Griffen. Both families called Las Vegas home. Aaron Rowand was a familiar face in the CSN batting cages and diamond every winter. Chatham, Chatty to all, was particularly adept at stealing pitching signals from opposing coaches, in their dugouts, to their catchers.

Jay Guest and Cooper Fouts were bald and wore their baseball caps military-style, like Joe Torre or a state trooper down South, almost higher in the back than in the front. Fouts had played catcher at CSN and moved on to Texas Tech, where he became accustomed to shaving his head after merciless *Ro-Gaine* chants about his receding hairline in a game in College Station against Texas A&M. Marc Morse, the infielders' coach, tossed me a couple of gray dry-fit shirts bearing the CSN paw logo the following week and said, "Welcome to the family."

It took some Coyotes weeks to get comfortable with me, so I just tried to blend in and keep an eye on the Rook, and his surroundings and teammates, and how they interacted.

Cochise College caught the Coyotes' attention when it was announced, pregame, that the Apaches were 6-0. With good reason, CSN players were more focused on themselves, being in top condition and executing properly, than any opponent. A three-run Cochise homer caught more of CSN's attention in the third. When Bryce Harper swung and missed at strike three, with one out and the bases full in the sixth, he banged his helmet to the bench when he returned to the dugout and splintered his black Marucci bat as he slammed it into the ground. It was my introduction to Harper's volatility.

In a 6–3 defeat, their first of the season, the Coyotes never led. Harper went three for five, which included a ninth-inning double. He eventually scored. Chambers blasted his players in a thirty-minute clubhouse meeting about going to class and taking care of responsibilities, about "not thinking you could just show up and win."

Do I return to the dugout Saturday afternoon in the first game of a doubleheader? Chambers fluffed it off. Why wouldn't you, Big Bird? Sounds simple, I thought, but if the Coyotes lost again, I told myself I'd leave the sacred grounds for good. Another defeat with me in there? There would be no way at least a few Coyotes, as cool as they had initially been to the outsider, wouldn't connect their first two losses with my presence.

Central Arizona took a 3–1 lead, but the CSN mood was light going into the top of the third. "Won't you take me to Funky Town?" blared over the speakers, and freshman catcher Kyle "Kaz" Smith juked and jived and had many fans clapping as he shot his right index finger from his hip to the sky, and back to his hip, at the edge of the dugout. When the song ended, Smith and Chambers exchanged fist bumps and smiles. Dancin' Kaz would be a familiar sight, even to rave reviews outside road dugouts, the rest of the season.

Central Arizona padded its lead to 7–1. The discomfort thickened. But Bryce Harper saved the day . . . or, at least, kept me from exiting the dugout for good. He doubled in two and scored in the third. He knocked in two more, with another double, by hitting the base of the center-field wall in the fourth. Standing on second, he smacked his helmet. That close, he said, to another home run. Scott Dysinger yelled at Harper for home-run-trotting to first. Had he been running, Harper might have wound up on third. He then stole third but didn't score.

Harper atoned by swatting a two-run homer, his third of the season, which cleared the right-field fence in two heartbeats in the sixth. Mine was the last fist he bumped when he returned to the dugout. CSN won, 10–7. Harper's uprising had allowed me to keep watching the special season unfold from this perch among the Coyotes.

In between games, just Harper and I sat in the dugout. He chomped on a cheeseburger as I uttered, "Way to hit the ball in the first game."

"Thank you, sir," he said.

Josh Demello, the Honolulu-born outfielder who often sang the national anthem before games in a mock baritone, serenaded along to "Everybody Plays the Fool." He said his dad, Monte, loved the oldies. "Classics are always the best," Demello said. He played a key role with his singing, island lingo, and lightness as much as with anything he did with a bat or a glove, although Chambers considered him to be one of the finest defensive outfielders he'd ever coached.

If the team was sluggish, it was often because Demello, with his surfer's smile and inviting almond eyes, had not been talking with his Hawaiian humor and slang, such as *Howzit* or *leenyar,* a takeoff on the Spanish word *linea,* which means "line," or "hit a liner" or "frozen rope" in player vernacular. If Demello was down or quiet, a coach would talk to him to boost his spirits. A buoyant Demello often meant the Coyotes were up, talking, positive, and ready to roll. He was always quick with a *shaka,* the hang-loose aloha wave of a hand with the middle fingers curled and the thumb and the pinkie out. During one game, Demello had convinced Casey Sato that coaches from Dixie College, a two-hour drive from Las Vegas in the southwest corner of Utah, were flying down from Utah in a helicopter the following day to whisk him back to their campus for an elaborate official recruiting visit. Wasn't true, but Demello had Sato convinced of the ruse for about thirty seconds.

Demello would stroll through the dugout and sing, "I wanna love ya, love ya, girrrrrrl," by the popular Oahu band the Green. Demello's given name was Joshua Tamatoa Kealii Demello. *Tamatoa* translated as "son of a hero" in Tahitian. James Michener wrote about a King Tamatoa of Bora-Bora in his epic novel *Hawaii*. Most teammates called him Tama.

Shortstop Danny Higa was the other half of CSN's exotic Oahu connection. The reserved, five-foot-nine, 175-pound Higa wasn't nearly as animated as Demello. However, Higa wore his heart on his left calf, where part of an elaborate tattoo that had cost $300 featured a family shield and the flag of Hawaii—the British flag in the upper-left quadrant, in recognition of its period as a British protectorate, and red and blue stripes representing each of the eight islands. With more than twelve thousand Hawaiians in Clark County, Las Vegas had unofficially been dubbed the ninth island for its influx of Hawaiians and Pacific Islanders. For two hours every Saturday, a local radio station aired *The Little Grass Shack* show, which played island music for Polynesian transplants.

Higa had the epicanthic folds, a skin fold of the upper eyelids covering the inner corner of the eye, common among people of certain Asian, Native American, Inuit, and Oceanic—including Tongan, Samoan, and Hawaiian—descent. His paternal grandparents had been born in Japan.

Both Demello and Higa had attended the prestigious Saint Louis

School, an all-boys, Catholic, college-preparatory institution that had been established in 1846, in Honolulu. It shared property with Chaminade University, a tiny NAIA school whose basketball team made big mainland headlines in 1982 when it upended the powerful Virginia Cavaliers and center Ralph Sampson in a Thanksgiving tournament on Maui. NFL center Olin Kreutz was the most famous athletic graduate of Saint Louis. In 2011, Saint Louis alum Brandon League pitched in the major leagues for an eighth consecutive season.

Demello also played football at Saint Louis and started in consecutive state championship games as a junior quarterback and a senior receiver. He had to fill in behind center in a semifinal game his junior season, when the starting quarterback got hurt, and called the signals before thirty thousand fans for the title game in the Aloha Bowl. Saint Louis, 12-0 before both championships, lost both. Playing before so many people, however, would serve Tama well at the end of the 2010 baseball season.

Demello often wore a red Philadelphia Phillies cap, as a nod to Shane "the Flyin' Hawaiian" Victorino, a twenty-nine-year-old outfielder from Maui who had played Triple-A ball in Las Vegas and had cracked the big leagues for good in 2006. Thirty-six Hawaiian natives had played in the majors, a short list of names that Demello and Higa envied. After Higa had accepted Chambers's scholarship offer, Demello turned down some lower-level collegiate football opportunities to follow Higa and walk on, with no financial assistance, at CSN in 2008.

Demello had been raised in the Kuliouou Valley area of Honolulu, near the southeastern tip of Oahu at Koko Head. A bit farther inland and closer to Saint Louis, Higa's home was nestled in the Pauoa Valley. His father, Danny Sr., was a bartender at the Kahala, a luxury resort just east of Diamond Head that featured saltwater pools in which guests could frolic with dolphins. When the Coyotes participated in a Las Vegas run to raise funds for cancer research in the fall of 2008, Higa had randomly been picked by a television reporter to talk about the event. Higa revealed that, when he was eleven, breast cancer had claimed his mother, Leslie.

Whenever Higa did something well on the diamond, Chambers paid tribute to Higa's Japanese ancestry by honoring him with a formal bow. Higa always bowed back and smiled. When Higa strode to the plate, smacked a hit, or made a fine defensive play at shortstop, assistant coach Cooper Fouts barked, "A ja Boo" or "Boo Boo"; Higa's half brother Mark Ancog always called Higa "Boo" when he watched Higa play as a freshman, and Fouts quickly adopted the moniker.

Higa neither lived in a hut on the beach nor surfed every day in his youth. That mainland image of how most Hawaiians lived amused him. The Pauoa Valley was so far from water he and his friends would never have considered biking to the beach. When Higa did get to the ocean, he enjoyed bodysurfing more than the difficult stand-up version. It also amused him when friends and acquaintances in Las Vegas told him that they believed Hawaiians generally disliked white, or haole, visitors to their islands. Not the case, Higa always responded. "It's about respect," he said. "Simple respect."

Respect on the diamond, too. "Everyone from Hawaii looks up to us, and they know we're playing with Bryce Harper," Demello said. "Everybody checks up on us to see how we're doing. They expect us to do well. But everyone wants to find out how he's doing, too. A lot of people like to hear that Bryce is doing well."

The Coyotes took the nightcap, 12–4, thanks to a nine-run first inning filled with four walks and three batters hit by Central Arizona pitchers. Very likely, it contained more history as Harper committed two outs in the same inning—groundouts to second for the second and third outs in the first.

Early on, with Central defenders on the diamond, sprinklers had inexplicably popped up and spit all over the infield. Here, said catcher Ryan Scott, we have a seventh-inning stretch and a third-inning shower.

Throughout the game, as in most, the Coyotes hid their tins of long-cut and wintergreen Copenhagen, and peach Skoal, out of the view of the umpires and Chambers. If caught, a player and Chambers could be ejected and suspended. The tins were kept well out of sight, up in the back of the sturdy black-metal shelf over the dugout bench. I became an accomplice, looking out for nosy umpires, as Coyotes turned their backs to the diamond and pulled down their tins between them and me. *Psst. Miech.* They would quickly slip a pinch, not so chunky as to alert any ump sixty or ninety feet away from them on the diamond, inside their lower front lip.

CSN took the doubleheader from Central Arizona, but it would not be the last time the Coyotes played the Vaqueros. They would meet again, months later, with everything on the line, in a tempest that would defy all logic, reason, and strategy.

Late Sunday morning, the Coyotes gathered for some revenge. Cochise, Friday's victor, was the opponent again. Half of CSN's players chimed in on "Ain't No Sunshine When She's Gone" . . . *I know, I know, I know, I know, I know, I know, I know, I knoooooooow* . . . and Bryce Harper led a chorus when Jimmy Buffett took over the speakers. *Wastin' away again in Margaritaville.*

The Coyotes wasted away, again, to Cochise in a 6–5 defeat. The stinger was having the bases loaded, with nobody out, in the sixth and not scoring. Danny Higa and Gabe Weidenaar struck out, and Ryan Scott flew out to right field. Veteran Apaches coach Todd Inglehart had been impressed by Harper, who played third base, center field, caught twice, and switched late to catcher in another game. He went eight for seventeen at the plate.

"You lose sight of the fact that he's seventeen," Inglehart said while wearing dark sunglasses. "I've never heard of this being done. You have to keep everything in perspective. He already looks the part, physically. He's a tremendous athlete. He can do a lot of things. I think it's definitely right. I've seen a lot of kids that you hear this and that about, then you go play them and a lot of times it isn't quite what you expect. He is very gifted. He has a lot of tools. I was impressed. It takes a lot of courage for him and his family to put themselves on the line like that. There's a lot of notoriety that goes along with it. Obviously, in the end, you have to be able to earn what you get. But, obviously, he's ready. Hopefully we'll see them again [at the district tournament] in May. It'll be interesting to see how much better he gets. I'm sure he gets a lot better."

The Cochise coach hadn't been bothered by Harper's tossing his wood in the batter's box, spitting in his hands, bending over, and rubbing dirt between his palms, or by the eye black. Players in the other dugout were always spotted talking among themselves and pointing. They were either in awe, astonished, or amused at Harper's routine.

"He's a pretty confident kid. I don't mind it. Whether or not he produces that day, he knows he's good. I want players like that. I want players who don't know any better, to play with arrogance. It's different playing with arrogance and being a bad kid . . . if it's a kid who didn't produce and wasn't a good teammate, he's embarrassing himself. I like kids who don't know any better. 'I'm better than this guy and I'm going to walk with a swagger.' I find nothing wrong with that. I admire that."

The third week of the season started with Chipola, the third-ranked team in the national junior college poll, visiting from Florida to participate in the Coyote Slugout. Chipola squeezed in a late-afternoon practice on Wednesday, February 17, at Morse Stadium, and the Indians arrived early enough to watch Bryce Harper swat several home runs in the twilight over the right-field fence.

Before Thursday's opener, Chipola players dashed out of their dugout and ran to shallow left field, where they jumped and screamed as if they had just won a national lottery worth hundreds of millions of dollars. A dozen CSN players froze in their tracks in their dugout and stared at the Chipola players. The passing seconds seemed like hours.

"I remember my first beer," said Bryce Harper, finally cutting through the stunned silence and drawing a round of laughter and applause from teammates.

Ryan Scott saw me spitting sunflower seeds into an empty Burger King cup—I didn't want to sully their home—and softly shook his head and waved his hands parallel to the ground. No, he said. Do what we do. Spit the shells on the ground. No problem. Harper tapped the left ear of pitcher Kiel Harmon, to his left. He tapped the right ear of pitcher Donnie Roach, to his right. I don't know, Harper said, raising his palms and walking away. Might be a bug?

Harper drove in a run with a two-out single in the first, but the game was a testament to Chambers's belief that the prodigy did not need to power the Coyotes in every game. Harper was not part of a four-run rally in the fifth, which he ended after walking but getting caught trying to steal second.

"Fudge! Fudge! Fudge! Fudge!" Harper yelled as he walked through the dugout, dumped his helmet and bat, and grabbed his catcher's mitt, mask, and shin guards.

Baseball is the land of F-bombs, of which Harper was keenly aware. In one of his first team meetings in the fall, he had counted thirty-seven from Chambers. Soon enough, that was brought to the coach's attention. Chambers steamed. He wanted to know who had been counting. Nobody fessed up. A week later, Harper was incredulous when he laughingly told Chambers, "Thirty-seven F-bombs?" Chambers walked away blushing and trying to hide a smile.

In the opener against Chipola, Demello provided CSN with a cushion run in the seventh, leading off with a wall-denting triple to left-center and scoring, in the Coyotes' 6–4 victory.

"I should have hit the weight room," said a laughing Demello about missing a home run by maybe five feet as he high-fived teammates after scoring. One more push-up, a teammate told him. Tyler Hanks came on in relief and hit ninety-seven miles an hour on the radar gun. He had snuffed out a Chipola rally with his heat and admitted to feeling nerves on the mound.

"I love getting jitters," Hanks told Trevor Kirk in the dugout. "Jitters are the best part. If you don't get jitters, you don't belong being a baseball player."

CSN defeated Chipola, 9–1, in the first game of a Friday doubleheader. Harper singled but got caught stealing in the fifth—"Even the fuckin' shortstop said I was safe," he said—and doubled and scored in a seven-run sixth. As Coyotes shuffled into the dugout and three prepared to bat, several sang along with Smokey Robinson to "My Girl." *What can make me feel this way?* . . . During a pitching change, Kaz Smith again kept the dugout upbeat and drew a few claps and whistles from girls in the stands, with his swinging steps to "Y.M.C.A." He had started dugout dancing at Cimarron-Memorial High School in Las Vegas and hadn't stopped.

During the game, several Coyotes took interest in LeVon Washington, the Chipola player who had turned down $1.1 million from Tampa Bay after the Rays had picked him near the bottom of the first round in the 2009 draft. The Coyotes had been stumped that Washington had declined seven figures, and that became a pattern. CSN players were always quite familiar with a few foes who had been picked high in the previous draft but chose not to sign, and the Coyotes knew the exact financial terms those players had declined.

This guy, they said in the dugout of Washington, turned down a million dollars? Washington went two for five, with three walks and a run, in the first two games, and he didn't play in the third game against CSN.

(Washington would hit .327 during the 2010 season, belting eight home runs and driving in twenty-five runs. In the June 2010 draft, the Cleveland Indians would pick Washington high in the second round and sign him for $1.55 million. Scott Boras, Bryce Harper's agent, represented Washington.)

Chambers had felt his own jitters about the nightcap on February 19, which would be played with those Looney Tunes aluminum bats against Cypress, from Southern California. Cypress wouldn't have played unless Chambers had agreed to the metal stipulation in his own yard. "Welcome back to Little League," said Ryan Scott.

Chambers wasn't concerned about his team's hitting, but he knew his players didn't get a chance to acclimate on defense in a round or two of fielding against aluminum bats in practice. Worse, Chambers and his coaches had shrugged when the three umpires walked in before the game. Chambers had a bad track record with one, going back to his high school coaching days at Bishop Gorman. "When he was young," said CSN assistant coach Steve Chatham of Chambers.

All of which proved prescient, although Harper jumped out of his shoes when he hit with the tin in the cage before the game. I'm so excited, he told freshman Burke Seifrit. This should be illegal.

"If I had gone back to high school, I would have petitioned to use wood," Harper told me when he returned to the dugout.

What followed was a menagerie of kangaroo hops to the outfield for Cypress, and baserunning blunders, fielding errors, and liners hit directly at fielders for CSN. The Coyotes' deficit was 11–0 in the bottom of the fourth when Chambers blew a fuse, getting tossed by the home-plate umpire after blaring his short rendition of "Three Blind Mice" at him and his two colleagues. Chambers tossed a gray, rubber trash can, six feet to my right, almost out to right field.

It had been building. Nice hit, Chambers said when another six-hopper had made it 10–0. "It's the second quarter, we have lots of licks left! Someone start us up! Let's play softball! If we get a touchdown, we'll go for two!" Cypress—a 24–12 loser here two years earlier after pinging its way to a 9–0 lead—had extended its advantage to 12–0 when CSN, and especially Harper, woke up.

On another frigid night, he smacked an inside and low pitch from right-handed sidewinder Dylan Kuhn over the left-center wall for a two-out, two-run homer to cut CSN's deficit to 12–3.

"Nine ain't shit now! Let's go! We can get nine!" Harper yelled upon returning to the dugout. "Let's go! We're fucking winning! It's just nine! Let's go here, baby! Let's go!" It was Harper's first outburst in junior college. He knew how aluminum bats made a mockery of the game, and he knew what he could do with one. There was no stunning comeback, although CSN tallied three in the eighth and Harper scored in the ninth, after drawing a leadoff walk. The Coyotes won the final four innings, and they beamed about Chambers's sticking up for them.

"That was pretty tight, coach getting run like that. That got me so excited," Josh Demello said. "You saw we started hitting after that."

Chambers couldn't direct the Saturday-afternoon game against Chipola, due to the one-game suspension from the previous night's ejection, but Chambers peeked at it through the blinds of his office window, in the clubhouse fifteen steps from the fence along the first-base foul line. Jeff Johnson, the Chipola coach, popped into Chambers's office during the game and shared a pepperoni pizza with Chambers for a few innings.

When Chipola had advanced to the Junior College World Series in 2007, Chambers had been among the few coaches Johnson rang for advice. Don't be fazed by the surroundings, Chambers told him. Play your game. Let your guys have fun. Sign every autograph request. The Indians won the championship, Chambers and Johnson struck up a friendship, and Chipola and CSN started playing each other regularly.

CSN swept the three games against the Indians by winning, 11–5, on Saturday, February 20. Harper walked twice and scored both times. He flew out to center and lined out to first base. And he got caught looking at a called third strike; once in the dugout, he kicked the bench with his right foot, then his left.

With the victory secured, the Coyotes started the name game. Say a name, anyone who played in the majors, and the next guy must use the first letter in the last name you used for the first letter in the first name he uses. Repeat a name, you're out.

Honus Wagner, Whitey Ford, Fred Lynn, and so on . . . the Coyotes were rolling in the hazy yellow light of their dugout. Dustin Pedroia. Pedro Borbón. More were joining. . . . Reggie Jackson . . . Joe

Mauer . . . Harper jumped on the back of the bench and claimed a spot in the rotation after watching that third strike sail by him.

"Mickey Mantle," he said.

"Already been used," several teammates barked in unison. "Fuck you guys," said Harper, walking away with a sullen expression as his teammates burst out in laughter.

5

TIM CHAMBERS NEEDED TO know that the body inside the cherrywood box was his old man. The director of the funeral parlor resisted. Chambers insisted. No way would he leave the building in Bartlesville, Oklahoma, without absolute proof that he would never see Connie Chambers, his biological father, again; that he and his mother, Rena, would never again hear that shrill voice.

The director and the preacher still didn't yield to Chambers. Okay, Chambers told them, you are making a grave mistake. He would open it himself, in front of the small gathering if need be. Making a scene? Chambers did not care. That did it. The preacher told the attendees to please leave the room for five minutes, a small matter had to be addressed but it would not take long. Thank you.

Two minutes later, Chambers lifted the top section of the casket. He saw Connie, with a square piece of chocolate cake on a napkin and a soft pack of Marlboro Lights on his chest, lying there, the chain-smoker with the sweet tooth in eternal peace. Chambers felt a wave of peace.

Fine, Chambers told the preacher, that's all I need to see. There was not a hint of emotion. Chambers, whose lineage was mostly German and Cherokee, knew it had been a dramatic scene, but he had to know that that part of his life was gone forever. Rena Chambers did

ROB MIECH

not attend her former husband's funeral; he had been dead to her a long time. She would never forgive him for the way he had treated her and for not being there for their three kids.

Thirty years earlier, the family had moved from Oklahoma to Ontario, California, outside Los Angeles. Connie kept drinking and physically abusing Rena; Tim had conked an iron skillet on Connie's skull when Tim found him standing on his mother's stomach when she was pregnant with Tim's sister. Connie went back to Oklahoma. Rena juggled several jobs to support her two young boys and infant daughter. She took welfare at times.

With her so busy, Tim turned into a hellion. He attended thirteen grade schools in the San Gabriel Valley. He'd fight. His mom would move him to another school. He'd fight again. Chambers figured he had been in 150 scuffles. Fisticuffs were how he justified his anger for not having a dad. He would spot the bullies who had picked on someone smaller than them or had slapped the lunch lady. "I would thump them. I wasn't a good kid. I was wild," said the forty-five-year-old Chambers. So wild, Rena packed up her sons and their little sister and bolted to Pleasant Grove, Utah, when Tim was fourteen, to settle them. It was the most propitious move of Chambers's life.

His brown hair ran down to the middle of his back, befitting his delinquent, skateboarding, California-cool nature. As a freshman at Pleasant Grove High, Chambers had run into baseball coach Jon Hoover. Hoover grabbed the smart aleck by his nape and asked him what he wanted. Chambers said he might like to be a professional baseball player or to forge some kind of career in the game. "You are not going to do anything like that, not even close, if you keep being the person you are today," Hoover told him. If you want that, Hoover continued, you had better do everything I tell you to do for the next four years. Then you'll achieve what you want to do. First, cut your hair. Chambers sprinted to the nearest barber.

At his first baseball practice, Chambers, a lefty, ran out to third base. Hoover scratched his head. Lefties, kid, don't play third. Hoover sent him to the outfield and hoped to soon send him home for good. But Hoover's every word about baseball, school, and life registered with Chambers. He became the hardest worker Hoover had ever tutored in his thirty years at Pleasant Grove. The coach would hit countless summertime fly balls to the kid, from foul line to foul line, and the kid never tired or wanted to go home.

"He hung in there, man, and made himself into an unbelievable player. I don't know what he would have done without baseball. He was going down the wrong path," Hoover said. Jail or digging ditches, Chambers said of his probable alternatives.

It took attending four colleges, but Chambers eventually earned his bachelor's degree. After sustaining a shoulder injury in a Toughman boxing tournament, which featured locals battling in a knockout format in bouts of three one-minute rounds, Chambers ended his baseball career on a low independent minor-league team in Salt Lake City and moved to Las Vegas to be with Kim Turley. They married in 1990 and Chambers was hired as an assistant coach at the private Bishop Gorman High School

A year later, ninety minutes after he had accepted the Valley High School baseball coach's position, Gorman offered Chambers its top baseball post. Chambers called Larry McKay, the athletic director at Rancho High who was taking over in the same capacity at Valley High and from whom Chambers had accepted the Valley job, to apologize and inform him that he had to take the Gorman gig. Chambers guided the Bishop Gorman Gaels into national prominence, via the *USA Today* rankings.

Chambers resembled actor Robert Conrad—the actor who did the old commercial with a battery on his shoulder . . . go ahead, try to knock it off, I dare ya—with a Cary Grant–like cleft chin. Cleft chin, devil within. When I told him that line, Chambers closed his eyes, smiled, and slowly nodded. He took an Adderall pill in the morning and a time-release, blue-and-white capsule in the afternoon to treat his attention-deficit/hyperactivity disorder (ADHD). He got so wound up when he was ten, his aunt Bea would take a deep breath and say, "Slooooow down. I can't . . . understand . . . what . . . you're . . . saying," as he chatted away.

Every three months, he visits his doctor to renew a prescription. Two-year-old Chase Chambers exhibited her father's traits, showing some obsessive-compulsiveness, too. She opened the refrigerator door, picked up everything in the side compartment she could reach—the mustard, the ketchup, the chocolate syrup, the two types of relish, the capers, the mayo—and slammed them back in their places. She closed the door, opened it, and repeated the pattern.

Tim Chambers slept three hours a night. Visit him at noon on a Saturday in his comfortable Red Rock Country Club home and he will already have done four loads of laundry, cleaned the pool, swept and mopped the floors, and peeled and sliced carrots, potatoes, celery, and other ingredients into a Crock-Pot, with a hunk of roast beef, to slow-cook a concoction he called the Last Supper for dinner.

Chef Chambers. He had taught himself how to cook when he was in grade school. Had to, he said, or he and his two siblings didn't eat, with his mother working so many jobs. Glen Evans had suggested they open a restaurant called the Coach's Kitchen in 2005. Didn't happen. That's when the five-foot-ten Chambers weighed 225 pounds. He took his family to Italy for a rare vacation and was embarrassed at the photos of him with his shirt off. He hit the treadmill and weights, and he watched what he ate. During the 2010 season he tipped his scale at 178.

The eighteenth green of the country-club golf course lay on the other side of the low, iron-and-stone wall in his spectacular-mountain-view backyard. He had his own cart in his garage. Like Rodney Dangerfield, he always cranked his tunes, most often country, as he tooled around the course. The old fogies cringed, but nobody challenged him. Garth Brooks, Brooks & Dunn, Brad Paisley, and Tim McGraw most frequently echoed around Morse Stadium, too, during practice, to the delight of Bryce Harper, Cooper Fouts, and many other Coyotes.

The home in the cul-de-sac at the end of long, quiet Turtle Head

Peak Drive, behind the armed guards at the entry station and double set of gates, symbolized how Chambers protected his wife and two daughters.

Chambers spoke at Jon Hoover's Pleasant Grove High retirement banquet in the summer of 2003—Hoover would return to coaching at Cottonwood High School in Salt Lake City—and did not mention baseball. Chambers had talked about relationships. He had talked about influencing young players to be productive and responsible citizens, and good people. He had talked about his success being reflected in what his kids did when they left him. What did they do with their college opportunity? Did they get their degrees? Were they dependable husbands and fathers?

Four seventysomething coaches from Oregon recognized how much Chambers cared about his players when they spent a couple of hours with him talking about baseball and touring the CSN facilities. They had watched Sean Kazmar, an infielder from Las Vegas High who had been a leader on the Coyotes' 2003 national title team, play for the San Diego Padres' Triple-A affiliate in Portland in 2009, and they were curious about his background.

San Diego had picked Kazmar in the fifth round of the 2004 draft. In 2008, Kazmar became the first CSN product to play in the majors. In his first game, on the first pitch he saw from Milwaukee Brewers starter C. C. Sabathia, Kazmar hit a single into left field at Petco Park. At Kazmar's wedding in August 2009, as he stood next to his pop, Kazmar called Chambers "Dad." Kazmar's biological father leaned in and gave Chambers a little nod, signifying *It's okay*.

Yup, Chambers told the four coaches from Oregon, come on by. Situations like these were why Chambers, a clean freak, insisted that his players keep a spotless clubhouse and dugout. When volunteer aid Don Cooper found Chambers cleaning the nooks and crannies of his stadium before a game, Chambers told Cooper, "I'm just a simple Okie boy."

During a long discussion about how he had started the program,

Chambers guided his four Oregon visitors on a walk around Morse Stadium. It culminated beyond foul territory in left, by a large red-stone barbecue that fans used during games. The quintet hadn't been standing there for a minute when, in a drizzle, a dazzling rainbow appeared way beyond center field and stretched to the right-field foul pole, against a backdrop of charcoal-colored clouds. Chambers could not have choreographed a more dramatic climax to the tour. Those four coaches left wearing new dark blue CSN caps.

They had watched Chambers closely during their visit. Your guys all come back, they said, don't they? Chambers was stumped; they had witnessed how every Coyote who passed Chambers not only addressed him as Coach before saying good-bye, but they *touched* him. A simple send-off wasn't sufficient. Chambers might not have had a son, but every season for twenty years he had played that paternal role for about thirty ballplayers.

"That's what matters," one of the coaches told Chambers. "If you never win another ring, it doesn't matter. What matters is you're changing lives."

Chambers nodded. He had left Bishop Gorman to become the athletic director and baseball coach at CSN, then called the Community College of Southern Nevada, in 1999, and he had promised—for the record—to shape the new program into a national powerhouse within five years. In 2003, in their fourth season, the Coyotes won the NJCAA national championship in Grand Junction, Colorado. Jon Hoover had been in the stands for every World Series game. He had talked frequently with Chambers's former teammates and friends.

"All of them say, 'Can you believe what that guy's done, knowing his roots?'" Hoover said. "He's done it all by himself. He hasn't had anything given to him. He's worked his fanny off. He's done it the hard way. The right way."

Chambers knew whose fatherly footsteps he did not want to emulate. He hadn't seen Connie for more than ten years when Rena pressed nineteen-year-old Tim to meet with Connie.

"He was shaking," said Tim Chambers. "I'm 185 pounds, a college athlete. He's five feet six and a drunk. He was shaking in fear that I'd beat him up. He tried to get involved in my life, but Jon Hoover's my father. Not him. Connie had a heart attack and died at fifty-two. He'd sit on a barstool sometimes for seven or eight days straight without getting up. Ultimately, that ended his life."

Chambers, who calls Hoover "Pops," doesn't have time for sentimentality or tears, although he did pause, and quickly turned his head to compose himself, when he spoke about how Hoover influenced and shaped him. Hoover knew of the bitterness and hatred Chambers harbored toward his biological father.

"It didn't surprise me a bit. If you treat [Chambers] right, he's a friend for life. If you treat him wrong, you don't want to be his enemy." At a former Coyote's wedding, Chambers shook another ex-player against a wall, out of sight. The guy had just started a family but had been dabbling in drugs. Chambers found out. He always finds out. He knew what most everyone who had ever played for him was up to, all the time. The confrontation at the wedding, Chambers heard from others, scared the kid straight; he was now a solid husband and father.

Ron Harper had told me how his youth had so mirrored Chambers's, which helped cement their friendship. However, Ron only hinted at that part of his past with me. He told the *Washington Post* that he only occasionally saw his father.

"He has some problems, some inner demons he has to deal with. The stuff I've been through, and my sister and my brother and my mom, it's amazing. It's amazing we've survived some—some stuff. But what I took from that was—you can rise from the ashes and say, 'You know what? I'm not going to be like that, and I'm not going to raise my kids like that.'"

Chambers developed his toughness all on his own. He also wrestled in high school. And, well, there were all of those fights. Chambers's football career at Dixie ended when someone spit on a black teammate at a party. Chambers left with the player, gathered many of the rest of his black teammates, and returned (with a baseball bat) to the party, starting a brawl. Authorities gave Chambers a choice: spend thirty-two days in jail and pay a $380 fine, or leave school. He departed for Utah Valley State.

When I asked him if he had ever lost a brawl, Chambers shook his head. Are you kidding? If it got down and dirty, if he had been on the verge of defeat, that's when he poked eyes and kicked groins. There were no rules in fighting, he said, and that's why Chambers believed he would have made a fantastic mixed-martial-arts fighter had that discipline been around in his time.

He found a healthier outlet in baseball and had learned well. During the second inning of a CSN game, out of nowhere, he yelled at Gabe Weidenaar at third base, "Gabe! Don't fall asleep!" Weidenaar shook his head, as if he had been jostled awake from a deep slumber by a glass of water that had been dumped on his face. He nodded toward Chambers. Composed, Weidenaar settled in. The next pitch was hit to his left, a two-bouncer that Weidenaar smoothly fielded and zipped to first base.

The twenty-four-year-old Marine Corps corporal with the closely cropped red hair had jogged out to shallow center field in his camouflage pants and jacket. He tossed a baseball back and forth with Chambers on a clear winter afternoon. Soon enough, with the no-nonsense demeanor of someone who had served two tours in Iraq, Wes Johnson had shed his jacket in foul territory. He stepped backward every minute to lengthen the distance between him and his former baseball coach.

He's out there in boots, a CSN player said of the newcomer's tan footwear, which covered his ankles. His well-developed pecs and arms stretched an olive T-shirt and impressed every Coyote. Johnson said he was in "weight-lifting shape." Man, one player said, "that guy's yoked." The former pitcher had been accurate with his throws, too. For an initial workout, Chambers had been pleased with what Johnson showed him.

Not everyone who had played for Chambers would want to throw a ball around with him today. He didn't profess to be a saint. He had made mistakes with players, misjudging their character or talent, or both. He had aimed to recruit team players. Some weren't. They were *I guys*. They were in it for themselves. Scott Dysinger shrugged that the 2009 team had several of those selfish players. During a blowout defeat, they were happy to get a hit. In tight games, it hadn't been a priority for them to simply move a runner ahead with a groundout to the right side—a staple of the game. Dysinger said *I guys* with utter disdain.

Chambers was not universally adored or respected by his 2010 team. One player left the team before the real fun, the play-offs, had started. The mother of another player, in a letter to her son's agent, blistered Chambers for how Chambers had used the pitcher during the season. Of course, she only knew what was on the surface, like an iceberg. Not everyone on that 2003 championship team had fond memories of that season or Chambers, either.

However, the many visitors—such as Wes Johnson, Jino Gonzalez, or Jonathan Slack, a long list that included some people who had never even played for CSN—who regularly showed at Morse Stadium to work out or just say hello showed how fond many were of Chambers.

A former Silverado High star who once had Arizona State and Southern California looking at him, Johnson had read about Bryce Harper during his second deployment in Iraq when he had picked up that issue of *Sports Illustrated*. Johnson had seen the picture of the kid, in a red and black jersey, swinging a bat. He had recognized the uniform and the sloping desert terrain at the foot of Frenchman Mountain in the background. Immediately, he knew it was about Las Vegas High. He read about the phenom's 570-foot home run and thought, No way. Johnson's mouth gaped. He had been pretty good in high school. He had gotten some attention from big-time colleges. But this was something else.

"This guy's getting ridiculous exposure," Johnson said to himself in his bunk. Johnson bolted to a computer to search for videos and found the ESPN *E:60* report on Harper, saw some footage from the area-code all-star games on YouTube, and watched the mammoth shots Harper hit at Tropicana Field in Tampa.

"Just amazing," Johnson, covered in cool sweat, said at the stadium after working out with Chambers. "I couldn't believe a kid that age was having the success he was experiencing. You never hear of anything like that. A-Rod in the pros at eighteen? Those guys are few and far between, especially here in Las Vegas. I was intrigued."

Alex Rodriguez had made his major league debut with the Seattle Mariners in 1994, a few weeks before his nineteenth birthday. In 1996, he became an everyday player in the big leagues.

In his research, Johnson had found many critics who blasted Harper about taking such a premature path to the draft, potentially risking such public humiliation. Johnson was just as critical. He had figured the best route would be college, to be mentally developed and prepared for professional baseball.

"He could get to the pros and the media could get to him. That's one of the big aspects of creating so much attention for yourself. He'll obviously go in the first round. If he does, they'll rush him through the minors to get to the majors. And if he doesn't produce like everyone says he will, he'll have a bunch of critics bashing him, which could be a real big load for him being so young. It all comes down to his decision. Ten million dollars to sign? That's hard to turn down when you're seventeen or eighteen years old. I hope he makes the best decision for him and his family."

Johnson had made some poor decisions. He had committed to then-UNLV baseball coach Jim Schlossnagle early, turning down ASU and USC. However, by the time Johnson became a Rebel, Schlossnagle had gone to TCU in Fort Worth, Texas. Buddy Gouldsmith, who had recruited for Schlossnagle at UNLV, became the Rebels' boss. He and Johnson frequently clashed.

Johnson reversed the usual path of going to a junior college and then to a four-year institution; he left UNLV, where he needed arm surgery, for the College of Southern Nevada. Like others who played for Chambers at CSN but had only known him as an opposing skipper in high school, when Chambers ran Bishop Gorman, Johnson grew to admire the guy whom he had first viewed as that arrogant figure in the other dugout.

That day Johnson and Chambers tossed the ball around wasn't just an impromptu, hey-how-are you reunion, either. Johnson had showed that he could throw the ball without pain, and with accuracy and zip, with Chambers. Johnson wanted to jump-start his career in the fall of 2010 and play for Chambers in the 2011 season.

"He gives everyone a shot until they show otherwise," Johnson said of Chambers. "I'm glad I'm back here now. I'm older and more mature than I was. I made a lot of stupid mistakes."

Johnson joined the Marines after he ran into a friend who had just gotten out of Marine Corps boot camp. His buddy had a new car and money in his pocket. Johnson had a fiancée who had wanted him to settle down, buy a home, and start a family. Soon afterward, at a CSN practice, Johnson looked at a teammate next to him and told him if the next ball he threw hurt his arm, he would sign up for the Marine Corps. "He kind of laughed," Johnson said. "I threw it and it hurt. I went down and signed up, and two weeks later I was in boot camp."

On October 15, 2004, Johnson signed his papers. On November 14, he arrived at the Marine Corps Recruit Depot in San Diego. He graduated from boot camp on February 11, 2005. "You *know* those dates," Johnson said. He entered weighing 195 pounds and left, in the best shape of his life, at 167.

In early November 2009, from Baghdad, Johnson finally contacted Chambers via a secured telephone line. What's Iraq like? Chambers said. Have you been scared? Johnson detailed his first deployment, how he and his unit provided security for convoys from one forward operating base to another FOB, and how they were training Iraqis to protect their own people and country. Johnson's second eight-month deployment was much tamer than his first.

"The [second] one was a successful deployment," said Johnson, who manned a fifty-caliber machine gun from a Humvee turret. "I'm home. I'm alive. I have all my faculties."

His unit had remained in Ramadi one night after leaving Fallujah for Baghdad. Late the next afternoon on Long Island Road, a two-lane highway strewn with potholes from improvised-explosive-device blasts, a Humvee at the front of the convoy had rolled over into the desert. The gunner had been crushed, pinched from the top of the left side of his rib cage to his waist, by the lip of the turret.

"His ribs were disintegrated," Johnson said as he sat on the metal bench between the CSN diamond and the clubhouse and stared at the dirt below him. "There was chaos everywhere, people running around trying to figure out what to do and calling for support. They set up security and tried to clean it up. They put this guy in my vehicle as ground medevac back to Ramadi. I'm up there on the gun in the turret and look down, and we made eye contact. My first instinct was 'This guy is going to die.' As bad as he was fighting . . . I couldn't help but think he will die.

"We rush him back to Ramadi within the golden hour. That's the rule with life-threatening injuries. If you get him to safety and into treatment within an hour, the chances of saving his life are very great. We got him there within the golden hour, but five hours later he died in surgery. That kinda sucked a lot of us down and out for a couple days. But the mission tempo back then was so high. You had maybe thirty minutes to mourn. You had to get ready for the next convoy three hours later, okay? Life sucks out there."

The shooting of a ten-year-old girl during his first deployment had affected Johnson the most. When a civilian vehicle neared an operations post or military vehicle, a series of signals warned it that it was in danger if it got closer. First, shots were fired straight up. Last on the list, shots were aimed directly at the vehicle. This one had not stopped, forcing marines to open fire. The driver and front-seat passenger ducked. Two rounds were sent into the vehicle. The car rolled to a stop.

"I saw it right after it happened," Johnson said. "The mother was freaking out, smacking everybody. The rear door opens and out comes the body of this girl with brain matter everywhere. That was the most disturbing. A child. They were innocent. There's nothing you can really do. Collateral damage happens."

When he returned to Las Vegas from his first deployment, Johnson had been prescribed antidepressants, to treat his post-traumatic stress syndrome, and sleeping pills. He said he now slept well, only occasionally needing help. Back then, he had found work as a carpenter at CityCenter, the mammoth project in the heart of the Strip, but he lost that job due to the poor economy. Nicole, Johnson's wife, lost her job, too. Needing money, Johnson shipped out for his second tour of Iraq almost two years after his first one.

"To keep our heads above water," he said. "I've seen some stuff, a long list of things. But we'd be here forever. It's almost surreal to be here. I've been away from the game for so long. I see guys I played with and against, like B. J. Upton and Delmon Young, in the pros now. For a while, it made me sick. I could probably be there if I didn't join the Marines."

Johnson turned and stared at the pitcher's mound. "I'm hoping everything works out. I have visions of me right out there, throwing the ball."

An altar on that mound had created quite a vision on a spectacular afternoon in October 2008. Pastor Greg Massanari, who had coached Jino Gonzalez when he was twelve years old and whose son, Bryce, had played at CSN, signaled to Chambers for a right-handed reliever. Chambers shook his head. Before the wedding party of about two hundred, Chambers yelled, "Give me a lefty!"

Gonzalez, in black tux and tails, dashed out to the mound to a round of applause. His wedding had been magnificent. That scene was a stark contrast to what Gonzalez had thought of Chambers when Gonzalez had pitched for Cimarron-Memorial High and Chambers was coaching at Gorman. More than thirty high schools were in the valley. Every one always relished beating Bishop Gorman, the elite private institution where many of the area's top young athletes matriculated.

"I hated him all through my high school career," Gonzalez said. "But just to have an opportunity to even throw a bullpen session today is a beautiful thing."

Beautiful is Gonzalez's favorite word. By the end of his high school career he had badly wanted to play college ball, but there were no takers. UNLV didn't call back. Dixie College, which had just moved from the Scenic West Athletic Conference to four-year status, didn't ring. Nobody called just to tell him he wasn't good enough. He felt worthless. His vocabulary did not include *beautiful*.

Then Rodger Fairless, a longtime Las Vegas–area coach who had agreed to start the CSN program, suffered a heart attack. The junior college turned to Chambers, and he and pitching coach Glen Evans watched Gonzalez throw eighty-four and eighty-five miles an hour against Bonanza High. Chambers asked him about becoming a Coyote.

"I was glowing," Gonzalez said.

Evans designed a weight-training program for Gonzalez, who grew two inches, to six feet two, and increased his weight to 195 pounds. In his first season as a Coyote he had hit ninety-two on the radar gun, but Gonzalez felt something give in his left shoulder. Subsequent surgery to clean out the labrum had shrunk the capsule. Few pitchers returned from such damage. Gonzalez wept in Chambers's cramped office when he was told of the outcome.

"I thought my life was over. I was nineteen, and I thought I was going to be one of his giants, his number one starter. It just crushed me. Guys don't come back from that. I've talked to so many pitchers who had it and never came back. They don't do that surgery anymore, either. I thought I'd never pitch again."

Chambers aimed to turn Gonzalez into a hitter even though it had been years since he had stepped into the batter's box. I don't care what the doctor said, Chambers told Gonzalez, come out here, bust your butt, and we'll get through it. Years of tears from many sources had soaked into the faded blue carpet in front of Chambers's desk. "It's just amazing to have a coach take all the doubt out of my mind," Gonzalez said. "It was huge. Doing rehab on the arm with doubt [would have been] tough."

As he prepared to become a hitter, and maybe play first base, a minor miracle took place as Gonzalez's left shoulder socket started feeling better during his strenuous rehabilitation regimen in 2002. That October, he hit ninety-three miles an hour throwing in a junior college all-star game in Salt Lake City.

He played a crucial role, as a starting pitcher, during the Coyotes' run to the national championship in 2003. Two days after winning the title, Tampa Bay officials negotiated with Chambers to sign Gonzalez. For a signing bonus, they said $300,000. No, $350,000, Chambers countered. They said, $320,000. No, $350,000. The check ended up being for slightly more than $350,000. In the 2002 draft, the Rays had drafted Gonzalez in the forty-sixth round—1,356 players had been selected before him. They had a year to follow and sign him and liked what Gonzalez did in the Junior College World Series.

Before 2010, Gonzalez had a career minor-league record of 34-38, with a 4.50 earned run average. While he was working out at CSN, Tampa Bay released Gonzalez. But he found a spot on an independent league team in Victoria, BC, where he would lead the Victoria Seals' pitching staff in 2010 by logging 106⅔ innings, and he went 7-6 with a 4.05 earned run average.

With Bryce Harper on the CSN roster, Gonzalez believed 2010 would be a most unusual season. Tampa Bay had always been a bottom-feeder, so Gonzalez got to play with pitchers Wade Townsend and David Price, infielders B. J. Upton and Evan Longoria, and outfielder Delmon Young, all high first-round draft selections who had spent time coming up through the Rays' minor league system.

"Year after year, I'd see these guys . . . they're freaks," Gonzalez said. "But this guy [Harper] is on another level. The way he handles himself is amazing, but he's still a kid. I wasn't that mature at that age. There's a lot on his shoulders. He's handling it all well."

Gonzalez hadn't made much money in the game and only got one or two days off a month during a season, but he still couldn't believe his good fortune. Leathery lines gave him the brown visage of an Indian chief, but Gonzalez looked as if he was about to cry when he leaned forward and, just above a whisper, said, "I'd still do it for free."

Like Gonzalez, Jonathan Slack got paid to wear a uniform, too. He had played on Chambers's first two CSN teams, in 2000 and 2001. As a valet at the Rio, Slack had a quintessential Las Vegas gig. He parked cars for hotel and casino guests, which enabled him to drive some exotic wheels: a black Lamborghini Diablo, a Ferrari, an Aston Martin. His most common challenges were all those babes who had tried to shed their vehicles during busy weekends when valet service had only been available to hotel guests. They couldn't produce room keys, but they did flash certain body parts at Slack to try to curry a favor. Kudos to your surgeon, he would say, but I still can't park your car.

Fellow valets with degrees had not been employing them because they were earning annual salaries of about $80,000, which stretched even further considering Nevada had no state income tax. Even if those friends could find a job in their chosen field, they wouldn't be able to make such a good living.

The New York Mets had picked Slack in the fifth round of the 2002 draft, after he had played a season at Texas Tech. But to jump to his professional career would be doing Slack's time as a Coyote an injustice.

Chambers, who didn't even have a diamond yet at CSN, had held his first tryouts at Basic High School in Henderson in the fall of 1999. There were no offices or a clubhouse. "We used portable trailers," said Slack. When the Coyotes finally had a yard to call their own, it was simple. A chain-link fence served as the backstop. The bleachers were high school metal. The small scoreboard barely had enough room for nine innings, runs, hits, and errors. HOME and VISITOR were the only designations for the teams.

"Like playing in a litter box," said Slack, who had short brown hair, long sideburns, and some chin whiskers. "When you start a program with nothing, that's what you get. We had no expectations and we played that way; and we were good, really good."

Chambers nearly won one hundred games those first two seasons combined. Like Wes Johnson and Jino Gonzalez, Jon Slack had viewed that guy coaching the Bishop Gorman baseball team—Chambers—as the cocky manager full of himself in the other dugout. Aren't winners always despised? Slack had played at Green Valley High. But like Johnson and Gonzalez, Slack learned that it was much different playing for Chambers.

Pacific and the University of San Francisco had shown some interest in Slack out of high school, but he chose to stay home and help start the new junior college program. He had wanted to play for Chambers. The Coyotes went 48-10 in their debut 2000 season. Slack hit .446, which still stands as a single-season school record. In 2001, CSN won its first twenty-nine games and finished 50-8.

"Chambers's mojo was like no coach I've ever played for," Slack said. "It's like he has a golden horseshoe up his butt . . . you felt honored to play for him. You tucked your ego in and it was all about team."

Slack was partial because Chambers had played a crucial dual role in his life. When Slack was eleven, his mother, Debbie, moved him and his younger brother, Chris, from the Boston area to Las Vegas, where she took a job in the human resources department at the Riviera on the Strip. The boys' father and Debbie's ex-husband said he would never talk to her again if she took the boys to Las Vegas. Indeed, they never talked again. Her former husband never gave Debbie a dime for child support. Jonathan said his dad died of liver failure.

"We could have turned to shitbags in this city," Slack said of the round-the-clock hedonistic nature of Sin City. At eighteen, it was possible to obtain one of those sweet valet jobs. Slack believed earning good money at such a young age, in this city, could be detrimental to most teens. At twenty-one, with certain connections, a six-figure bartending position could be had. Other cities had last calls on weekends at 1:00 a.m. The words *last call* do not exist in Las Vegas.

"It's the entertainment capital of the world and comes with all the distractions you can think of," Slack said. "We were lucky to have the love of a good mother and family, to give us direction. That's also the beauty of sports: the camaraderie and friendship."

In 2004, Slack had just finished playing the outfield for the Mets' Single-A squad in Port St. Lucie, Florida, when he was packing up his belongings. A hurricane had been brewing, so he was hustling to get out of town. His manager called him into his office. What did I do now? Slack wondered. He was told to report to the Triple-A Norfolk Tides. Slack would never play in the major leagues, but he had felt as if that's where he landed when he got to Norfolk.

"You put that uniform on and stepped out onto that field, and you're right there; you could smell the big leagues. I thought, 'It gets better than this?' "

Those six weeks represented the zenith of Slack's athletic life. He only played in six Triple-A games, and he had three hits in fifteen trips to the plate. All were singles. To Slack, though, it was the big time. Gary Carter and Brett Butler, who had played for the Mets, were roving instructors who had dropped into Norfolk to tutor the hopefuls. Slack's playing career ended in 2006. In five minor league seasons, he hit .248, with thirteen home runs, in 437 games. He stole thirty-eight bases one year, and he swiped thirty another season. He only made three errors as a pro. Slack didn't fully appreciate or comprehend his relationship with Chambers until he had finished playing ball.

"There was nothing you couldn't talk to him about. His door was, and is, always open. If you lost or let him down, you felt like shit. You never wanted to feel like that. He gave us the attitude and motivation . . . he'd get the best out of your ability in baseball, and it made you ready for life. The experience of playing for Chambers makes you a better person."

SINISTER, SOOTY CLOUDS JOUSTING along the eastern horizon had prevented the sun from peeking over the River Mountains the morning of Thursday, March 4. That meant everyone along the right side of Kenny's Grand Canyon Skywalk coach would get his necessary beauty sleep, undisturbed by rising rays, as we headed north to Twin Falls, Idaho, for the start of the conference schedule.

The black-netted shades remained furled at the top of the windows. Veteran road-tripping sophomores usually yanked those all the way down the second they boarded. Two hours outside Las Vegas, snow started falling. A few more miles up skinny State Route 318 and a blanket of white covered the rough desert terrain.

The bus resembled a boxcar of loose mannequins, limbs wantonly tossed around from the disjointed side-to-side action of a freight car on rails. Players had sought every inch of comfort and space. Coach Chambers always sat in the first seat on the right side. The large window in front of him both comforted Chambers and drove him crazy; any ledge or cliff sent him scurrying to the other side of the bus. He tapped out messages on his iPhone or read the paper or talked with assistant coach Marc Morse or Kenny, to the left, whose hands grappled the flat steering wheel. Chambers's feet dangled, as usual, on a metal rail. When someone made Chambers laugh, which was often, the toes of those white Nikes with blue swooshes jittered left and right. His other assistants and trainer Steve Jacobucci sat behind Chambers.

In the back of the bus, Scott Dysinger always sat in the last seat on the right side. Bryce and Bryan Harper usually settled into seats back there on the left side. Opposite Dysinger was the cubbyhole of a bathroom that everyone—even black, sixty-nine-year-old volunteer coach Robert Cox, known to all as Mr. C—reached via a gauntlet of a hike. With hands on the right and left rails way up by the storage bins, those with business to tend to vaulted from row to row, treading their way with their feet, avoiding all the bodies and ankles and wrists and noggins in the aisle, on the narrow shoulders of the head rests, crouching so their heads didn't bump the ceiling. Number two was strictly prohibited. Someone had recalled assistant coach Steve Chatham stinking up the bus on one sorry trip in 2009. "He had *diarrhea*," appealed Dysinger. "He was *sick*."

At the first stop along the side of the road, in the swirling snow, Chambers yelled back that there was a problem. Another bus would have to be called. Could be a two-hour wait. After a dramatic pause that brought the groans and moans that Chambers had expected, he smiled and said, Relax, just a bathroom break for Kenny, who stepped outside. I followed, not wanting to execute the Olympian task of hurdling so many appendages and bodies for relief.

Twenty miles later, Kenny actually needed to call for another bus because of a near-total loss of power due to a computer-chip malfunction. He slowed the bus to a crawl. It sputtered. It stopped. We were out in what appeared to be a no-man's-land, somewhere between Lund and Ely. This was turkey-vulture territory. Chambers knew exactly where we were.

Just minutes away was his wife Kim's family's White River Ranch, a spread of more than three thousand acres along the foot of the Egan Range in the White River Valley. Ridgelines on both sides were covered in bristlecone pine trees. Juniper, piñon, and lush riparian vegetation dotted the rolling hills. Golden eagles, hawks, great horned owls, prairie falcons, mule deer, and elk soared through or roamed the terrain. To the west, rugged limestone had formed the massive, crenellated cliffs and mountain spines of the White Pine Range.

The immense ranch included a school and work program that annually housed as many as thirty wayward boys, a herd of nearly eight hundred cattle—including some prized bulls—and two dozen horses. The left wing of the boomerang-shaped main home, bowed toward visitors as they approached it, had been constructed thanks to the removal of tons of limestone from a sloping bed. This would be our oasis.

Kim Chambers's maternal grandfather, the late Floyd Lamb, had served as a Democratic member of the Nevada Senate from 1956 through 1983. A major boulevard and state park in Las Vegas had been named after him. Kim had grown up on her Turley family's Buckhorn Ranch, in the rich Mormon farming community of Alamo, which we had passed a couple of hours earlier.

Tim Chambers stood up, straightened his back, and puffed out his chest when he recalled Floyd Lamb. Stoic, Chambers said. "Dominated a room with his presence. You entered a room and said hello to him, never the other way around." Lamb played a key role in founding the College of Southern Nevada, then called Clark County Community College, in 1971.

In 1983, Floyd Lamb and four other politicos were caught in an FBI sting dubbed Operation Yobo, which the *Las Vegas Review-Journal* had ranked fourth in a 2008 feature on the top ten scandals in the history of the "Gritty City." Lamb had demanded a 1 percent finder's fee for his influence in helping an undercover FBI agent secure a $15 million Public Employees Retirement System loan. Lamb served nine months of a three-year sentence. He died in 2002 at the age of eighty-seven. Kim Chambers said Lamb tried rebuilding his life. "But, politically, that was it."

The powerful family included Floyd's brother Ralph, the longest-tenured Clark County sheriff, who served from 1961 to 1978. He once grabbed Chicago mobster Johnny Roselli, who had been chatting with Desert Inn owner Moe Dalitz and Nicholas "Peanuts" Danolfo in a diner booth on Dalitz's property, dragged Roselli across the table by his necktie, slapped him around, and threw him in jail for disrespecting a deputy's request to visit headquarters. Darwin, another Lamb brother, served a stint as Clark County commissioner.

Kim remembered two statements by her grandfather. When the topic was mob figures, Floyd Lamb had told her, "You would never know how many bodies there are out in that desert." About the presidency of the United States, he said he had been in government for twenty years and he still "had no idea who ran the country . . . it's not the Senate, or the Congress, or the president . . . you have no idea." Kim Chambers widened her eyes. "I was pretty young when he said that. Even so, I knew that was shocking."

Charlie Brown, Kim Chambers's stepfather, picked us up in a rickety 1960s-era white school bus at the end of a long, hilly, and winding driveway on Route 93. Before most of his players had boarded, Coach Chambers told them to mind their language—the devout Mormon family frowned upon certain four-letter words—and where they chewed and spit their tobacco. "Best behavior," Chambers said. "No cussing." Some kid, long ago, had etched ZIPPY IS A MONKEY on the metal frame of the seat in front of Bryce Harper. Two players who hadn't heard those commands said some choice words on the two-mile trek, but Brown didn't flinch or turn his head.

Brown's office was a testosterone shrine. Thirty-three animal heads, skulls, or stuffed birds surrounded the thirty-foot-by-thirty-foot space that was heated by a rustic wood-burning Defiant cast-iron stove fronted with a glass plate. Charlie Brown warmed up his audience with a tale of nailing a twelve-point buck at close range with a crossbow. He nodded five feet above him at his victim's head and antlers. He slipped a disc into a narrow, black DVD player and narrated, second by second, the hunt on a television screen; Brown hunched behind a tree as the animal almost brushed against him. The vertically paneled walls gave way to horizontal ash strips, rising like a pyramid to a point on the ceiling.

The thick, fudge-brown, furry head of a buffalo, from Eastern Washington, adorned the wall above Brown's desk. The ugly and perpetually snarling head of a former 750-pound wild boar kept the buffalo company to its right. Pitcher Tyler Hanks pointed to an unusual sight: "An owl?" Teammates howled. It was the rear end of a deer, with strategically placed false eyes. A rabbit's head had antlers, producing more quizzical looks; but it had been a Charlie Brown creation, something to confound and confuse his visitors.

His amusing ways knew few boundaries. A vintage Winchester rifle had been encased in glass on the wall. TAMPER WITH THIS GLASS, read the scribbling on an index card inside the case, AND THESE STICKS OF DYNAMITE WILL EXPLODE. Three red sticks could be seen. Everyone took a few steps back after reading those words, and they usually did so just as Charlie Brown unleashed his hearty chuckle. The dynamite, like the elusive eight-point mountain rabbit, had been props in Brown's perpetual comedy play.

On one hunting excursion, he hadn't even given Tim Chambers proper instructions on how to operate the power archery bow in his hands. The tension was so tight, after Chambers had taken a shot at whatever had been in his crosshairs, he was left with a baseball-size blood blister on his right arm. He said, "Charlie! What the . . ." Brown, twenty feet away, had doubled over, unable to control his amusement. "Laughing his ass off," Chambers said.

Charlie Brown looked like some combination of Charlton Heston and Clint Eastwood. Laurelie Brown, Kim Chambers's mother, saw rocker and wild woodsman Ted Nugent in her husband. Lean and rugged, Charlie had bushy, gray eyebrows and a cagey smile.

The Coyotes settled into the many comforts of the White River Ranch. Trent Cook sat in a recliner and toiled on a paper on his laptop computer in the family room. Six other players, lying or sitting on the off-white carpet around Cook, watched the New York Mets and St. Louis Cardinals play a goofball 17–11 spring training opener from Port St. Lucie, Florida, on a flat-screen television. The game echoed throughout the home, even on the right panel of the large, white refrigerator in the kitchen.

Bryce Harper and several teammates sat on high stools around the center island in the kitchen and munched on pub snacks, from a tall plastic tube, and drank lemonade. Outside a nook window, to the northeast, the valley spread out below. A water tank stood in the distance. Cattle roamed. Heavy snowfall ringed the 10,899-foot Ward Mountain peak like icing on a cake.

Enough canned goods and other nonperishable food items were in the large walk-in pantry to last a decade. Coach Chambers pointed it out and made me look again. This place was prepared for anything. Other players had scattered in rooms throughout the one-story palace, doing homework, fooling around on their computers, or talking into their cell phones. Laurelie Brown tossed fusilli, chopped sirloin, diced tomatoes, and sprinkled bay leaves and other spices into two huge metal chili pots for the crew of visitors that had dropped into her home without warning.

Not a problem, Charlie Brown said. His petite wife is a dynamo. Designed this entire house that they had been living in for a year and a half, he said. She always made Thanksgiving dinner for sixty or seventy family members and friends. A baseball team popping in without notice? No sweat, he said. Charlie eased into a story about an elk hunt.

Bryce Harper flipped through a coffee-table book in the immaculate living room that featured a rustic piano, and white couches on white carpet. Two or three times, he circled in front of that room, just inside the front door, and paid more than glancing attention at the color eight-by-ten of McKenzie Chambers, her blond locks flowing like angel hair inside the wide silver frame, on prominent display on a sofa table. The coach's daughter had caught Harper's eyes long ago. He wrote *P4MC*—Play for McKenzie Chambers—on the inside of his white CSN cap.

Harper had been making his way through *Willie Mays: The Life, the Legend,* the definitive 628-page tome that James S. Hirsch penned about one of the game's luminaries, but Harper had not lugged the book inside the ranch house. He said he had plenty of time to kill, so we wound our way into the quiet bedroom that Chambers and his wife had always occupied when they visited.

Bryce sat on a white comforter on the edge of a queen-size bed. He spoke quietly and confidently, keeping eye contact but with no hint of his between-the-lines intensity. He confirmed that the commitment of his older brother, Bryan, the lanky lefty who had played at Cal State Northridge the previous season, to CSN was a big reason why he'd made his move to junior college. They called each other Harp around the diamond and on campus. Many outsiders had still mistakenly believed that Bryan, whom the Washington Nationals had picked in the thirty-first round of the 2008 draft, followed Bryce to CSN.

A major theme of the CSN program, Bryce Harper acknowledged, had been every Coyote's desire to play for Chambers. If Chambers had not been running the CSN program, Harper admitted, he wouldn't be playing for the Coyotes. "He's *the* reason," Harper said.

Harper played inside linebacker and fullback as a freshman at Las Vegas High, and he beamed when talking about making a big hit on the football field or having his number called when a few yards were needed on a critical fourth-down play. As a kid, he had always dreamed of playing football and baseball at Alabama, Clemson, or Louisiana State; the uniforms, helmet colors, stadiums, and rabid fans of those teams looked so enticing and vivid on television.

One of his role models had been Tim Tebow, the former Florida quarterback who was as busy off the field, with all of his charitable endeavors, as he was on it keeping the Gators in the national-championship spotlight.

"There's nothing better than Tim Tebow. He has an incredible drive and he's a great leader. He's so good . . . and godly. He played every play like a bulldog. He'll run it down your throat, and he does everything through God and Christ. He's an inspiration to a lot of kids in the country with what he's done. What's not to like about him? They say, 'He's like God.' But you can't say anything bad about him."

I asked Harper about Luke 1:37, the scripture inscribed on his black Marucci bats where his name belonged and which he often added below his autograph. " 'For with God, nothing shall be impossible.' It's pretty much self-explanatory. If you do everything through Christ, it will be done. It's so profound. You've got to have someone by your side to get through hard times."

Harper's responsibilities were so demanding in junior college that he hadn't been able to attend church nearly as often as he desired. Still, he made time at the end of every day, before sleeping, to read scripture and say his prayers. "I want to be a leader and I want everyone to know 'he's a good Mormon boy,' not just a baseball player. I'm strong about God in my life. Definitely, few people know I'm Mormon and I talk about God."

The chewing tobacco, cussing, and sometimes crude banter about girls that are so much a part of baseball seem to run counter to someone of such strict faith, but so it goes. The Coyotes, like any team, often talked about the opposite sex like sailors on shore leave. Harper often joined in without pause.

"On a baseball field, you don't think about that. You shouldn't do it, but it makes you feel better [by being one of the boys] . . . like anything else."

Harper's hero was indeed his father, Ron, the longtime ironworker who could easily have been mistaken for an older brother or cousin. The touch of gray in his goatee barely gave away that Ron is old enough to be the father of Bryan and Bryce Harper.

"He taught me to try to be perfect," Bryce said. "There won't be anyone who works harder. I won't take a day off." Ron Harper's backaches inspired his boys to push and always do better. "It's brutal,"

Bryce said. "I tell him I love him all the time. He has worked so hard to make life good for my whole family. We've had so much fun, traveling around and singing in his truck, since I was ten."

Since he started playing the game with a serious edge, at seven, Bryce had been competing with and against kids two and three and four years older than him. That's why this extraordinary season, to him, had been something like business as usual. When he started, a stage of the ten-and-under USSSA Elite World Series had been held in Las Vegas. As a spectator, Bryce had marveled that more than a hundred teams from all over the country had traveled to his backyard, at the Arroyo Grande Sports Complex in Henderson, for such an event.

Bryce remembered his first home run. At Arroyo Grande, he belted a pitch over the two-hundred-foot fence and a group of oak trees. "I was jumping up and down, all around the bases." He tried to get to second base by the time a home run cleared a wall. "Oh my gosh, like Scott Rolen. My dad taught me that. I sprint around the bases. No pimp walk."

However, some foes and even a few of his own teammates would accuse Harper of taking his sweet time to reach first, or pimp walkin' around the bases after driving a ball out of the yard, throughout the 2010 season.

Harper immersed himself with the statistics and mannerisms of legends Mickey Mantle, Pete Rose, and George Brett. He wanted to be like them, hustle like them, and go far in the game. Those guys could *rake,* as Harper liked to emphasize about anyone who was especially talented with a bat in his hands. That was Harper's highest praise for another player. He *rakes.* Just thinking about the game made Harper wistful.

"Being in the dugout, smelling the leather, throwing dirt, the dew on the ground . . . there's nothing you can't love about baseball."

Harper figured matriculating at CSN would have its challenges, but he knew he couldn't return to high school. And what, he said, walk fifty times? He agreed with Coach Chambers that he might have hurt someone with an aluminum bat. Still, when he returned from Venezuela and struck out those four times at Foothill High, he harbored some serious doubts. He didn't get too deep about it, but he admitted wondering if CSN had been the right move, if he had made a mistake.

Everyone had an opinion about his not living up to the immense hype. The *yip-yapping,* Harper's generic term for those who criticized him, did affect him. For someone who professed to never read headlines or stories about himself, he was always cognizant of them. As much as he would try to deflect or ignore criticism, it soaked into his system. Then he rang up that golden sombrero. Harper said Chambers's closed-door meeting with him was the best balm for his tough self-analysis.

Harper laughed at his own superstitions. He slipped on his game socks, often the dark dress ones with green-diamond patterns, at the same time: right *and* left, not right then left. Same with his shoes. He never stepped on the foul-line chalk. Before he settled into the batter's box, he touched the tip of his bat along the outside of the plate and dragged it, from left to right, then tapped the toe of his right cleat and took four practice swings, before he cocked his left elbow and prepared for the pitch. That second week, in a Thursday game, Harper had tossed his bat into the box, bent over to grab dirt, and spit in his hands for the first time as a collegian. The next night, he had applied the menacing-looking eye black on each cheek. With the return of his full routine, Harper sailed that titanic homer over the center-field fence at Morse Stadium against Yavapai.

"I'm a humble guy, but I felt like I was on top of the world and no one could beat me," Harper said with a slight smile. He straightened his back on the edge of the bed. He had played catcher, third base, and center field. In Idaho in two days, he would add right field to his collegiate résumé in a move that would have a horrifying consequence.

With all of those friends in Oklahoma, he explained, he was in his element. He started going there when he was twelve, missing school days but making up for them by hitting the books hard when he returned and making the honor roll. He called Oklahoma his second home.

"Everything disappears there. Those are my real friends. They're like a bunch of Pete Roses and Ty Cobbs. They don't take anything from anyone. They're cleats-up on slides. It's where I want to live one day."

Cleats-up and not taking anything from anyone, that's how thirty-five-year-old Sean Brooks, who coached the Westmoore High Jaguars during the season and in a summer league, learned to play the game from a former coach. It's how most everyone in the area had been taught. Old-school, Brooks called it. It wasn't even talked about. That's the way Bryce played and why he fit in so well with the rest of the Jaguars, Brooks said.

After he had appeared on the *Sports Illustrated* cover, Harper went to Oklahoma for a couple of weeks of games. In one, Brooks noticed over the first few innings that the opposing catcher always dropped to his knees and "lollipopped" the ball back to his pitcher. Brooks detected laziness and kept it in the back of his mind. In a middle inning Harper arrived at third base, where Brooks had been coaching. Brooks started to explain the catcher's habit, but Harper finished the sentence. He had been watching, too. A few pitches later, Harper dashed for home the moment the catcher had released the ball to his pitcher. However, the pitcher had walked up a few paces past the mound, so he was in point-blank position to fire it back to his catcher and barely nail Harper at the plate for the third out of the inning.

"We laughed. 'Golly, I thought I had it,' Bryce told me," Brooks said. "I never would have thought they'd do *that* in a million years. I've always tried to teach the little things that maybe others didn't notice. But I knew Bryce's brain worked in a different manner than most kids'. What sticks out about Bryce is, he was like a normal sixteen-year-old kid. They'd go fishing one night, hang out at a mall. Nothing was ever below him. Other kids didn't have near the talent he had, but you'd never know that. If you didn't see him play baseball, you'd have no idea he could play at that level."

I asked Harper about Clint Hurdle and Jon Peters, promising baseball prospects who had appeared on *Sports Illustrated* covers at young ages but who did not have star-spangled careers. Their reputations had been inflated to gigantic proportions. Harper flat out said he didn't care, that—God willing—he'll play in "the bigs" and thrive.

He hoped to someday study kinesiology and become a physical therapist, as a fallback option. As he matured, emotionally, Harper hoped his six-foot-three, 208-pound frame would bloom, with help from Mama's cookin' and weights, into a commanding six-four or six-five, and 230 pounds.

The June 2010 draft, he said, wasn't such a priority for him. Plenty of excellent players would be available. Another year of college ball and classes would not be detrimental. Without blinking, he even talked about playing at Clemson or LSU as a junior.

"I left high school to further my education, get an [associate in arts degree], and try to get better at baseball," Harper said with the smell of the chili peppers, tomato sauce, basil, and oregano drifting around the hallways and sneaking into every crevice of the White River Ranch like cartoon fingers. "And I want to win the Junior College World Series."

What about those flashbulbs on opening night at CSN?

"I love it," Harper said. "It never gets old."

Chambers ducked his head in the bedroom and said, Hustle, the chili is being served and Laurelie wouldn't like it if anyone missed the prayer—which Chambers would deliver, surprising Trent Cook and Casey Sato, who usually covered team blessings—before the meal.

I asked Harper about his signed Team USA playing card going for $1,200, jerseys for $400, and autographed *Sports Illustrated* covers for $200 on eBay.

"Crazy. Nuts. I'd get a Josh Hamilton card. I wouldn't waste money on me. Not where I am now. Or I'd get something by Derek Jeter or Joe Mauer, or a Mickey Mantle Hall of Fame card. I haven't done anything yet."

The chili was the ideal comfort food for a junior college base-ball team hardly stranded out on the Great Basin of Nevada in what sometimes looked like a driving blizzard outside. Charlie Brown watched the Mets and the Cardinals among a half dozen players and offered pointers about the game as if he had logged a decade or so in pro ball.

Hugs and thanks were exchanged after word reached Chambers that Kenny and his new Grand Canyon Skywalk would be cruis-ing back up to the meeting point along Route 93. Charlie Brown walked outside, into a brisk wind and scattered flurries, to warm up the old school bus for the two-mile trek back to civilization. Chambers hugged his mother-in-law. The eighteen to twenty-two-year-old play-ers, more than four hours after entering the cozy ranch headquarters, doled out thanks and smiles as they filed out. The seventeen-year-old with baseball stardom at his fingertips slinked out as just another face in the procession.

The last one had walked out of Charlie Brown's office door when, oh, wait, Laurelie had almost forgotten. She turned to Chambers and whispered, "Who's the famous one?"

7

IN WHAT FELT LIKE an episode from the popular cable television show *Ice Road Truckers,* Kenny steered us back on the road to Twin Falls with snow blowing all around, drifts piling up on the side of Route 93, and visibility fading every few minutes.

The Grand Canyon Skywalk special powered on through the middle of the winter wonderland. Near dusk, the sun tried slipping through the clouds to the west, but the Ruby Mountain Range ensured that Kenny's coach absorbed no sunshine.

Jamie Foxx attempted to keep Philadelphia from panicking about a deranged killer, making all of his moves from inside jail, in *Law Abiding Citizen* on the half dozen small video screens as assistant Steve Chatham explained why Chambers did not want to switch this series, with the threat of inclement weather in Idaho, to Southern Nevada. Every other conference team always had weather issues, especially at the start of the season, but if too many early-season CSN away series were switched to Southern Nevada, the Coyotes would wind up on the road for the final three or four weeks, or more. That would not be a smart recipe for postseason success.

The weather changed every ten minutes, from whiteout conditions, to no precipitation and no sticking snow on the side of 93, to a few hazy rays of sunshine, to sleet, more snow, and then total darkness.

Fourteen hours after departing CSN, including the unscheduled stop at the ranch oasis, we reached the Twin Falls Holiday Inn Express. An easy jog to the east, along the Snake River, stood a granite-monument tribute to Evel Knievel's 1974 canyon jump attempt, which had failed when the parachute deployed prematurely in his rocket-powered Skycycle X-2 vehicle.

Inside the hotel corridor, the local *Times-News* had trumpeted, on the top strip of its front page, about the College of Southern Idaho playing SOUTHERN NEVADA AND PHENOM BRYCE HARPER. Seen by nobody, blended into the flowery wallpaper background like a chameleon, a brunette Russian woman with Bryce Harper on her mind sat on a bland couch near the entryway.

Chambers gathered his players outside the bus, handed out room keys to all of his players and coaches, and to me and Mr. C, and called for an eleven o'clock curfew.

"You know why we're here," Chambers said. "Baseball."

Diana Cox had no doubt that her husband, Robert Cox, would not be here today if not for Chambers and the CSN program. Mr. C had suffered a stroke in 1998, and Mrs. C believed the Coyotes had been responsible for bringing him back to a near total recovery.

"For sure, he would not be where he is today, and he might not be *here*," she said. "I'll tell you what it's meant to him. It brought him back from a severe stroke, that baseball program."

Mr. C, who had made significant strides particularly since 2008, walked at a leisurely pace, with a slight hitch on his right side. When the Michigan native bent over to pick up a baseball, he did so gingerly. On his way up, it helped to have something nearby to grab for leverage.

He talked, around the players, like a felon. A slew of F-bombs were hurled back and forth. That was his term of endearment, and they loved it. If he cared about you and you were male, he would smother you in four-letter words and a strategically flipped finger. Flip him back and he'd say, "That your age?" His cell phone was kept busy by former Coyotes who rang to tell him about their latest accomplishments, check how he was doing, and poach him for advice.

With women, he was as sly as he had been during his bachelor days in Kalamazoo. For them, he was always quick with a mint, from a constant stash in his right pocket. When he encountered kids and dogs, Mr. C turned into a doting grandfather. When he and Diana dined or shopped in the District, the outdoor mall across the street from their home in Green Valley area of Henderson, he could not pass a mutt—the plaza catered to them with walking areas and pit stops with plastic bags—or a child without patting a head or smiling with a hello. He introduced himself the same way to everybody he met:

"I'm Mr. C, a baseball coach at CSN."

The game meant everything to him. He had played all sports in Michigan as they changed with the seasons, but there was something about baseball. He coached Little League in Las Vegas and watched his son Robert Jr. play some pro ball in the New York Mets' minor league system.

Mr. C had been a fixture since he'd attended that first CSN tryout, at Basic High School, in 1999. Mrs. C had worked in CSN's human resources department, heard about the tryout, and forced her husband to attend. At Basic High, Mr. C could not walk or talk well. He had trouble rising from his fold-up chair. However, Chambers recognized the unmistakable glint of passion for the game in Mr. C's eyes. Chambers insisted he returned the next day, and the next, and the next.

Jonathan Slack, the outfielder who had played on Chambers's first two CSN teams, often chauffeured Mr. C to and from practice in his beat-up, green Ford Taurus. The rear bumper had been split in an accident, but Slack just said his car had wings. It did not have air-conditioning, so it tortured its occupants in Sin City summers.

Who are you? Some players initially questioned Mr. C's status as an assistant coach. They couldn't understand him. He had difficulty just moving around, so trying to explain and show a slight adjustment in a batting stance or throwing motion challenged Mr. C. Some Coyotes wondered why he was even there. Chambers told them to lighten up, that Mr. C had had a stroke and he was going to get better. They were too young and immature to comprehend that *they* would play incredible roles in helping Mr. C find the path out of his woods of despair.

A few years ago, Mr. C talked about retirement. At a dinner function Chambers presented him with a plaque, which gathered dust on Mr. C's garage wall, next to the photo of him and his wife on their wedding day. Both wore big Afros, and Mr. C is smiling from puffy sideburn to puffy sideburn. But he kept returning to CSN after having accepted that trophy. He traveled to road games, enduring the grueling bus rides just to lurk in the dugout or bullpen to support the Coyotes. He said little on the bus.

Mr. C and I were roommates for the season. I smiled the moment my olfactory glands first detected Aramis, the citrusy medicinal cologne—my dad's brand—that Mr. C dabbed on his wrist, neck, and chest before we went out to dine on butterfly shrimp or to grab a margarita. We shared personal tales and countless laughs, over his snoring that sounded as if he were sawing down sequoias and my occasional flatulence that could clear out a ballroom. Yes, Mr. C, there *is* a duck in the room. He got in the habit of asking me to put the jazz on my computer, on the Pandora application, soon after we had checked into another hotel. He'd lightly tap some fingers on a table and close his eyes as Bird and Miles and Monk soothed our souls.

At one hotel Mr. C sauntered out to the pool, where a couple of Coyotes were talking with a couple of girls. He stuck out an index finger. Not a big deal, he said, but it's 9:59. (Curfew was ten.) One minute, Mr. C said. The players said their good-byes and scampered away.

Here again and *that's my opinion* were two of his favorite sayings. Mr. C said plenty in foreign ballparks, where he constantly moved. He chided CSN pitcher Donnie Roach, slated to start the second game of a doubleheader, when Roach spent too much time during the first game walking around the dugout, wasting energy, and yapping at the other team. Mr. C casually coaxed a hitter to alter his batting stance a few inches. Traveling, and seeing new sites and meeting new people, thrilled him, as did providing guidance to young people.

"Baseball is a family, more than any other sport. It's important to me to help these young guys strive to get better. Not just in sports, but in life. Sports and education go hand in hand. If not for sports, some of these guys might get into trouble. It's the best thing that could have happened to me, I'll say that. I would tell myself I can't [do something, soon after the stroke], but that's not right. I learned to try. I learned that a long time ago. Try. People have told me that's how I came back the way I did."

As the Coyotes practiced on a sunny afternoon, Mr. C picked up a black bat and slowly mimicked a right-handed golf swing. That's how, with a three-wood or three-iron, he had started most days in his front yard. One December morning in 1998, he couldn't get the club perpendicular to the ground on his backswing. Something was impeding his right arm.

The blood supply to his brain had been disturbed, which affected the right side of his body, especially his right arm. Smoking cigarettes, high blood pressure, shaky cholesterol, diabetes, and genetics—his older brother, Theodore, never spoke after suffering a massive stroke and died from its complications—contributed to his affliction. It had altered Mr. C's visual field and speech pattern. At St. Rose Dominican Hospital he wore an oxygen mask as he was fed an IV and treated with other medication to stave off the stroke's effect. He communicated with God. However this turned out, Mr. C told Him, he wouldn't be mad.

But that hadn't been entirely accurate. Mr. C admitted that he had been a "sad sack," that his rehabilitation regimen had initially been too formidable, both mentally and physically. He battled poststroke depression. He contemplated suicide. When pressed, Mr. C explained that he didn't carry that thought to another step—planning how or when to take his own life. But he was close. He believed he was a hindrance to his wife and family. He had been accustomed to taking care of himself. He ate properly and exercised. That was gone. He was angry and upset.

"It just eats at you. You ask certain questions. I always say God put us on this earth for a purpose. What that purpose is, I don't know. But I shouldn't take my life. I'm happy I didn't take my life because of what happened. That would have been a mistake."

Out of convenience, Mr. and Mrs. C slept in a downstairs bedroom after his stroke. The stairs were difficult to climb. But the downstairs room was smaller than the master bedroom upstairs, and so was the bed. Mr. C was determined to escape those ground-floor quarters. Diana watched her husband constantly work at getting himself up those thirteen stairs. It became part of his therapy. He'd drag that right leg up there, step with his left, and drag his right. "That determination, I call it a hard head," she said. Diana Cox unleashed the rich laugh of someone who enjoyed life. "You know what? If a hard head is what makes you survive, then go with the hard head."

Then Diana Cox saw the note publicizing CSN's first baseball workouts. "The baseball just took over from there," she said. "That's all he needed."

Mr. C had worked at Bekins Moving & Storage with Diana's brother, Maurice, in Los Angeles. Robert and Diana had met at barbecues and card games, but Robert stopped cold in his tracks outside Norm's Restaurant, in Santa Monica at Colorado and Lincoln, one day in 1973. He saw Diana's red Pinto outside. He saw her inside. "She was kind of cute," he said. "She gave me a smile and we connected." Mrs. C noted the spark and thought, *He might not be bad to date.* She also noted that he needed a haircut.

They were married on March 30, 1974. Mr. C had five children (three from a previous marriage) and ten grandchildren. Junior is known as Rob Cox in a minor league data bank. The Mets had picked him in the ninth round of the 1994 draft, but by the end of 1998 he was out of the game. He worked a graveyard maintenance shift in a Henderson office building.

Mr. C was practical. Sure, he admitted he had been proud watching Junior play pro ball, but Mr. C also knew that his son had been "just another player." Mr. C could divorce his emotions from the reality of any situation, especially baseball.

"A lot of kids don't really understand what goes into pro baseball," Mr. C said. "You have to put your time into it, and you better get your education. If you don't, you'll get lost. Most young men want to look at their [batting] average, but I don't really think it's average that will get you noticed in pro ball as much as work habits and knowledge of the game of baseball."

Mrs. C is grateful to Chambers and the Coyotes. She knew most stroke victims were left paralyzed, in some form. A lack of motivation zaps their desire to rehabilitate. Baseball gave Mr. C life. "Once he got involved and once he was able to get back on his feet . . . he did a lot of therapy, and both of our children and I would work half days so we could be here with him. But once he got back to where he could function, as far as walking and talking and moving around, baseball brought him all the way back."

He wore blue Russell sweatpants and a blue jacket with two yellow stripes down each side, and a white CSN baseball cap with the blue *C* on the front, at a Morse Stadium practice when he traced some of his past. Mr. C had worked at Bekins for twenty-seven years. He had been earning $120,000 a year. He moved Cher and other celebrities. One guy tipped him five $100 dollar bills. After the stroke he couldn't keep working. Watching the Coyotes gave his brain a workout and made him attempt those mechanics, bit by bit every day.

"I couldn't *do* it. Probably never could do it as well as they could. But you forget about your illnesses when you get out here and see kids doing some things you did. I had excellent coaches in Michigan."

In Idaho, Mr. C called a home run by Bryce Harper two pitches before the phenom parked it over the right-field fence. Yes, Mrs. C said, her husband had a gift. Veteran pro scouts and collegiate re-cruiters chatted with Mr. C when they visited CSN. Players might have toyed with him frequently and exchanged rapid-fire F-bombs with him, but they listened to him, too.

"If a player is very good, physically, but has a bad attitude, Rob-ert tells them," Diana said. "He'll say, 'Your attitude on the field will take you away from baseball sooner than it will put you in baseball.' There aren't a lot of people who can say that."

After years of struggles and therapy, Mr. C turned a major corner at the end of 2008 and the beginning of 2009. Diana could have told him what to do, she said, or his children could have or his grandchil-dren could have, but he's the one who did all the grueling work, by himself, to regain his independence. In no small way, CSN's baseball team helped.

"It's been a long struggle," Mr. C said. "But, to me, it's been re-warding."

The week of the road trip to Idaho had included a supposedly random NJCAA audit that Chambers learned about in a Tuesday lunchtime e-mail he received on his iPhone. He had been prepared. In 2006 an audit cost him fifteen victories because of a vague transcript rule, which made two players ineligible, that got quashed from the confer-ence bylaws by the next season.

Perhaps this latest audit had been random, but Chambers knew it was coming. Adding someone as talented as Bryce Harper drew attention from all angles, so Chambers ensured that his players' tran-scripts had been updated through the first several weeks of 2010. They were prepared and ready to be shipped when needed.

More than 250 pages of that evidence were sent, overnight, to NJCAA headquarters in Colorado on Wednesday. Late Thursday night, in Room 219 of the Holiday Inn Express in Twin Falls, Chambers checked his e-mails on his iPhone and saw the one sent to him at 1:32 that officially declared his players' schoolwork accurate, in order, and a moot issue. Chambers high-fived assistant coaches Jay Guest and Steve Chatham, and me. We celebrated with a Bud Light or two.

The Scenic West Athletic Conference, as Western Nevada coach D. J. Whittemore had pointed out, was funky for the distance between its six programs. No other school was closer than seven hours, by bus, from CSN. They were in Idaho, Northern Nevada, Salt Lake City, eastern Utah, and western Colorado. Conference games were played in doubleheaders on consecutive days, seven and nine innings on Friday, seven and seven on Saturday. Nobody knew how that odd nine-inning game got thrown in there.

It was chilly, windy, and overcast when the 13-3 Coyotes arrived for the Friday, March 5 doubleheader at Skip Walker Field, a simple but unusual diamond that faced west. The low sun would cause some havoc for hitters late in the day.

Bryce Harper had saved my dugout hide with his outstanding hitting against Central Arizona in the first game of a doubleheader on February 13, but he had a seven-game hitting streak snapped when he went oh for three, with a walk and a strikeout, in the nightcap. He had hit in the second, third, and fifth holes until that day, when Chambers turned Harper into CSN's cleanup hitter. He had collected at least one hit in each of his next four games, but he went oh for three, with two walks, against Chipola before leaving for Idaho.

In the first doubleheader against the College of Southern Idaho, Harper scored three of CSN's seven total runs in two victories. Five CSI players had worn eye black, mocking Harper, and taunts were aimed at CSN from the moment batting practice started. Afterward, a pocket of fans waited outside the visitors' dugout to ask Harper to sign baseballs, bats, or *Sports Illustrated* covers. Some wanted a photograph with the star. He complied with every request. Kenny's coach had been full, save for the seventeen-year-old star, for fifteen minutes when Harper finally walked toward it. "Here he comes," CSN players said. "Here comes the kid."

Harper boarded and sat in the seat across from me. He hadn't been able to decompress for more than twenty seconds when assistant coach Jay Guest embarked and sheepishly approached Harper holding a sock full of seven baseballs and a clipboard holding three of Harper's famous magazine covers. For the three umpires, Guest said with an awkward smile. "You don't have to if you don't want to." How unprofessional, barked some of Harper's irate teammates. However, he knew he was in a bind. Guest did, too. There were games to play tomorrow.

"I have to!" an exasperated Harper quickly concluded as he stared at the lined ceiling of the bus.

Second baseman Scott Dysinger complained the loudest. He has no choice, Dysinger thought. If he had been the coach, Dysinger doubted that he would allow a star player to pander to such a request, in between doubleheaders, from the umpires. Then again, do you turn the officials down, possibly make Harper look bad, and maybe jeopardize your team with the umps the next day? Dysinger thought of every possibility. "He's just young and they're attacking him, trying to get his autograph. I don't get it."

Harper signed the three copies of the magazine cover. He paused, looking at the sock. He said he would sign three balls.

"Would you sign my balls?" said Mr. C, like a little kid with wide eyes, a seat in front of Harper and leaning toward the phenom. Harper didn't hesitate. "Yeah, motherfucker. Give me a silver Sharpie!" About a dozen teammates, within earshot and disgusted over the compromising position the umpires had put Harper in, erupted in laughter. Harper had diffused the situation with aplomb.

Trent Cook figured the most professional and sensible way to ask Harper for something would have been after the weekend series, but Cook had never been in such a situation so it was difficult for him to judge. "He did the right thing," Cook said. "Still, even though umpires put him in that situation, they shouldn't have. . . . I don't think it was by any means the right way to go about it." Even when adults around Harper don't act professionally, Casey Sato thought, he still tries to do the right thing. That's admirable and respectable. "Adults see one thing," Sato said. "But when you spend an entire fall and spring with him, you get a glimpse of what he goes through on a daily basis."

Bryan Harper did not learn about the umpires' wanting his younger brother's autograph in between those doubleheaders until the regular season had ended. Bryan pondered the situation as he stared at the ground and said, Oh my God. Then he laughed. "Amazing. Uh, yeah, sure . . . I'd sign them to open up the strike zone. Yeah, it's unprofessional. But there would be nothing I could do about it. If they want their baseballs, they want their baseballs. I'd sign them."

At the end of the next Thursday kangaroo court inside the CSN dugout, I presented Bryce with a silver Sharpie, so he'd be ready the next time Mr. C asked him to sign a couple of key pieces of his anatomy. Harper wailed and doubled over from his perch on the back of the bench. Teammates closest to Harper understood the joke. Later, Harper told me whatever I did with this project about him, this season, and this team, that I had better include his line to Mr. C about the silver Sharpie. It was too rich, Bryce said. And too funny; he laughed about it for weeks.

Chambers had had his own issues with the umpiring crew in Idaho, but he showed discretion when he confronted one. Chambers had wanted to argue a call, so he pulled his lineup card from his back pocket as a divergence. He calmly pointed to the card so fans would think he was talking about a potential switch or lineup issue. Actually, Chambers had been ticked about the inconsistency he had seen behind the plate. "I know I have been shit," the ump told Chambers. "But what a fun game!"

Just before 1:00 a.m. Saturday, Chambers had received notice of a curious smell down the third-floor hallway. Upon reaching it, there was no doubt about the earthy, pungent aroma of marijuana. Chambers's blood pressure raced. He awoke all of his players and checked their rooms. He found no evidence of extracurricular activity. When we had first rolled into the Holiday Inn Express, three shady characters were huddled outside the hotel; they were the culprits who were having some sort of party in a room at the end of the hall.

Chambers had reason to be concerned. During the 2008/9 academic year, pot had been an issue with a few of his players. However, the 2010 season was different. Many Coyotes had made a pact to party only on Saturday nights, when the week's games had concluded. Beer was their main indulgence, with an occasional appearance of rum and tequila. They'd gather at various teammates' apartments. Bryce never attended those gatherings.

Earlier that Saturday night, the brunette Russian woman had parlayed a panicky visit to Bryce's room seeking help into obtaining his cell-phone number. When she sauntered to the second floor, she found Harper and Marvin Campbell, Harper's roommate for the trip, just outside their door. Yelping about a car emergency, she said she needed to use a phone. Campbell hesitated. His phone was recharging on a table inside the room. Bryce let her use his cell phone.

CSN sophomore Gabe Weidenaar walked toward his room directly across the hall from Harper's and initially thought the woman was Harper's sister, Brittany. When Weidenaar discovered her identity the following day, he told Bryce, "If you have a stalker and she's too old for you, pass her off to me. I'm good to go." Weidenaar laughed.

On Harper's phone, the woman had called her mobile phone, giving her Harper's number. Later, in a text message she thanked him for being so kind. Then she inundated Harper with texts, telling him how hot he was and how she wanted to be with him. Harper pointed to his phone and told Campbell, "You believe this?"

In the morning, as Scott Dysinger and Ryan Scott ate scrambled eggs and pancakes in the hotel's small café, Dysinger spotted her eating breakfast. Three times Dysinger played a gag on her in which he raised his voice and said, "Hi, Bryce" or "Morning, Bryce." Each time, Dysinger and Scott saw her nearly get whiplash as she turned to look for Bryce Harper . . . only to find nobody there.

About that time, Ron Harper called Bryce from the Gold's Gym across the street to ask him if he wanted to come over for a protein shake. "Yup, Pop, be right there." He left. She followed in a gold sedan. Chambers was right on her tail after quickly learning about the details of the unfolding drama. At the gym, informed of the situation by Chambers, Ron Harper became infuriated. Chambers calmed him down, telling him to let the authorities handle it. They didn't see the girl again.

"His first stalker!" said a stunned Chambers before boarding the bus for the second doubleheader.

From that moment on it became CSN team policy for at least one player or coach to always accompany Bryce wherever he went. Between that day's doubleheader, Ron Harper was still concerned. He had changed his son's cell number for the fourth time. That was a new scenario, he said. Others talked about former tennis star Monica Seles getting stabbed in her back by a deranged fan at a tournament in Hamburg, Germany, in 1993. Extra precautions would have to be heeded.

"That was a little weird," Bryce Harper said. "Kind of scary, actually, really scary. That freaked me out. She needed to use my phone. Yeah, okay. No problem. I get a text from her later. Uh, what the hell?" She wanted to get together. *No shot,* he wrote her. "I just kept getting texts. Then Chambers said, the next morning, someone is following me. Kind of freaky."

Was he starting to feel like a veteran of the game, on and off the field?

"No. I'm still growing up, still a kid in that mind-set. Trying to grow up in the game of baseball."

Before that first Saturday doubleheader, sixty-six-year-old Skip Walker—who had coached the Eagles for thirty-one seasons, had guided them to an NJCAA World Series championship in 1984, and had been assisting his son, Boomer, for the past five years—and the rest of CSI's coaches were still raving about a play by Harper the previous day.

Harper had tried to throw out an Eagle, who had singled up the middle, from center field. Harper had casually picked up the ball as the hitter rounded first, then fired a bazooka shot, which never rose higher than seven feet off the ground, to Ryan Thomas at first base. It appeared that Harper got his man, but a moment later the ball trickled to the ground. The CSI player had run into Thomas's glove, jarring the ball loose.

"I jammed my wrist on the kid," Thomas said. "He threw it at the kid and the kid wasn't paying attention. As I caught it, he hit my wrist, and it came out. It was really, really close. I never would have thought he had a play. I'm going, 'No, no, no.' An incredible throw."

Skip Walker had spent more than fifty years in the game. Born in Minneapolis, he had played in the Philadelphia Phillies' organization way back when baseball had a Class C minor league. He chain-smoked in the dugout when he ran the Eagles. After one horrible road trip, he told his players to keep their spikes on for the long haul home. When they arrived, they went straight to the park for a midnight practice. Walker, who had helped coach several US national youth squads, had a paunch that hung over his belt, skinny legs, and a high-pitched voice. And he had never seen such a brazen attempt from an outfielder such as the one Harper tried in throwing to first base from center field.

"That was unique," said an excited Walker. "To have the presence to do that shows he has a lot of confidence. I said, 'Oh!' I tip my cap to him. He has a lot of God's gifts. He has the body and the foot speed, but you have to have the makeup to go with it. We have a five-tool player in our program, but he can't show anybody he can play.

"It's not easy for Tim [Chambers], I'd think. This can't be a dog and pony show. The rest could feel slighted and it wouldn't work, either. Tim has to balance all that. I've seen a lot of good players with potential, but what [Harper] is doing is beyond what I could think of, with all those expectations. It's just very, very unusual. It's crazy. Actually, it isn't, because he's succeeding. You have to keep your humility and perspective. That's the big thing. We've seen too many athletes lose that. They think they're invincible and they forget the little guy.

If he does that, I will lose all respect for him. He'll be just a guy . . . talk, talk, talk. You've got to give back."

During the second doubleheader, only one Golden Eagle mockingly wore eye black. Few sarcastic or smart-ass words were tossed at Harper or his teammates. In reserved silence, CSI players leaned on their dugout rail and watched and heard the ball explode off Harper's black Marucci bat during batting practice.

In between games that second day, Ron Harper informed me of writers who had been trying to secure his services for a book about his life story and raising Bryce. The elder Harper had a way of locking eyes, like a pilot locking his jet's missiles onto an enemy plane, with whomever he was talking. I understood—even though Ron Harper had said he had been impressed by the time and effort I was devoting to his son and this team, attending every practice and in the dugout for games—that Ron had his own agenda. A dinner invitation went unanswered, as did mail and cell-phone inquiries. We would exchange hellos, maybe even a handshake, but rarely anything more than a brief greeting. He allowed me to have only two conversations, one for less than four minutes and another that didn't last thirteen minutes, with him.

Two hours later, Skip Walker Field became as silent as a morgue.

Bryce Harper had been enjoying his best stretch as a Coyote. He flew out to center in his first trip to the plate that Saturday, then smashed the ball around the park. He pounded a home run to right at the end of the first game and belted another one to start the second game. In seven consecutive at bats, he had accounted for sixteen total bases. He had scored five times.

In the bottom of the fifth inning in the second game, at 5:06 on March 6, Harper, playing right field for the first time in college, sprinted after a deep fly ball that was slicing right of the right-field foul line when he slipped on a sliver of concrete. One of the quirky aspects of Skip Walker Field was that foul territory, which had an elevated area for the home team pitchers' bull pen that was surrounded by concrete and a brick toolshed.

Harper had lost his footing and fallen in a tangle of arms and legs that, from the visitors' dugout, looked as if an octopus had been tossed from the window of a moving vehicle. The home team's bullpen mound obscured most of Harper's body, but every few seconds he rolled around, in agony. Fans could see him holding a knee. Thirteen hundred eyeballs were glued to the area as CSN players, assistant coaches, and trainer Steve Jacobucci bolted after Harper.

Chambers sat on the far right side of the dugout bench. He didn't want to move. He felt—no, prayed—that Harper would jump to his feet any second, and the game, and the once-in-forever season, would resume. Showtime walked by me and said, "There goes the book."

Bryan Harper broke a heavy cloud of concern with some keen levity, although few were around to hear him. "Is there a doctor in the house?" he said to himself in the dugout. He answered his own inquiry, "No, but I did stay at a Holiday Inn Express last night!" Bryan laughed. That, he said, was his father's clever wit and quick sense of humor. Bryan also knew his brother's history with injuries and how much pain he could tolerate.

"He and I always played rough," Bryan said. "It's not like he'd come hang out with older kids, get hurt, and run home to Mom. He'd get hurt or something and keep playing. He never wanted to be the little kid that couldn't hack it with the older kids. I think that's the instinct he had sliding in there. Even if it hurt, I knew he'd be fine."

Others weren't so sure. Casey Sato, at third base, thought the silence was eerie after Bryce had run so hard after a ball he had no business thinking he could catch. "Your heart stops," Sato said. "You don't want to see the hopes and dreams of this great kid disintegrate in a split second. You never know what could happen running into a wall like that. Maybe bust an ACL? Definitely, there was a lot of suspense in the air."

Shortstop Danny Higa had never seen someone go so all out for a foul ball, especially into a brick shed. Josh Demello shot out of the dugout. Harper was in pain when Demello reached him. Demello thought Harper's season would be over, smashing his knee like that, and Demello began warming up, thinking he'd be replacing someone in the outfield. You've got to know your limits, thought Trevor Kirk, who watched from center field. But Harper was a big kid and it would take a lot to hurt him.

Idiot, Scott Dysinger thought to himself at second base. "I thought, 'You stupid motherfucker,'" Dysinger said. "There were a few people who were yelling, 'Fence! Fence! Fence!' He just knows better. He plays the game one way, that's hard as fuck the whole time."

It's definitely one thing to be aggressive, thought first baseman Trent Cook, it's another thing to be aggressively stupid. Maybe that was one of the times, but that showed he would always go full speed. The play reminded Cook of Pete Rose.

"That's just the way Bryce plays. He put on a show for the sold-out crowd. They hadn't seen a sellout in years, their first-base coach told me. They definitely showed a lot of respect for him. I had a feeling that, no matter what, he'd play through it, even if he were hurt. No doubt in my mind. The mentality he has and the person he is, he'd still be able to play."

As soon as Jacobucci, the trainer whom everyone called Bucci, and others reached Bryce out there by the equipment shed, Bryce asked them all not to laugh; as Bucci rolled up Bryce's left pants leg, a dark dress sock, with green-diamond patterns, had been exposed. Even though he was in pain, Harper did not want them to make fun of his wearing the socks he often wore to church. They were comfortable, and they reminded him of his priorities.

Finally, Chambers ran out to his fallen right fielder when the injury appeared to be serious. Chambers looked down at Bryce and said, "Rook, if there is any way at all that you can get up, do it. Stand up. Your mother is in the stands." In a few seconds Harper rose to his feet. There was nothing to be concerned about when, a little gimpy,

Harper told Chambers he could stay in the game. Chambers even had him catch for the final two innings of an eventual extra-inning defeat, via a walk-off homer yielded by relief ace Aaron Kurcz.

"It was pretty bad, sliding in, and getting crushed," Bryce Harper said. "I just went down. Holy crap, did that just happen? I rolled into it hard. I didn't think anything was that wrong. I've had problems with my knees before, but to slide into something like that always scares you."

Assistant coach Jay Guest had told Harper before that double-header that he needed to make at least one foul-ball play over in that area. "I was like, 'All right,'" Harper said. "Why not try to slide into it? I got crushed."

Told of his older brother's quick quip, that Bryan knew he would eventually rise from that horrible fall and walk it off, Bryce smiled. Ron and Sheri Harper weren't making jokes to each other, though, in the back row of the stands along the third-base side of the stadium.

"I was scared when I first saw that," said Sheri Harper. "He plays the game 110 percent. He'll go for it, no matter what, if he can help his team out. But he's tough. He's a catcher. He loves that contact. I knew if he was hurt, he'd play it off like he wasn't, so I was all right with it. . . . He was a little sore, but he was fine."

Ron Harper caught his breath when Bryce didn't get up. He knew his boys were warriors. They laid it all out on the line every time they stepped on a diamond. They played with reckless abandon. When all that happened, so could injuries. Came with the territory.

"I figured he'd get up and battle through it, but my heart did sink," Ron said. "You could hear everyone in the stands . . . the ooooohs and aaaaaahs. When he got up, it was a big relief."

Jim Brooks heard the crash and Joan Brooks closed her eyes when their grandson crumpled on the concrete. Plenty of times they had seen him come home black-and-blue from taking a physical beating behind the plate.

"But that was a tough one," Jim Brooks said. "Ronnie called it at the beginning of the series. He said, 'That's gonna be a bad spot. Someone will get hurt.' Who, of course, does it happen to? Bryce. His grandma is quite a religious young lady and she was a-prayin', and he got up. It was scary when he was down ten minutes. But I always see him coming back.

"Ronnie was concerned with him sliding into second base, just not right, a couple of times, maybe tearing up an ankle. But it's just the hard work they put in. They condition the body to those situations. Working with iron, Ronnie says the same thing. You condition your body to those situations. I had a broken leg, a back operation, the bad knee and shoulder . . . but you condition your body to take that kind of abuse. I really believe it. The man upstairs helps a bunch, too."

The reaction of the CSI team and its crowd, and their applause when Bryce rose and walked and jogged it off, pleased Sheri Harper most. CSI players bolted out to right field and were just as concerned about Bryce Harper as the Coyotes.

"There had been a lot of 'talking' in that game, they were being competitive. But when it came down to it, a fellow ballplayer, a brother, was down. The other team felt that. I was very impressed with that," Sheri Harper said.

"The camaraderie comes through," said Ron Harper. "You play hard, but you don't want to see anyone get hurt. CSI was a class act. That's a great thing."

Ron and Sheri did laugh, however, when told of Bryan's Holiday Inn Express line. "Bryan knows that's Bryce," Ron Harper said. "Bryce will run through a brick wall."

Jacobucci wrapped Harper's left knee in ice after the game. Thanks to Kirk "What a Team" Gibson, Bucci had a World Series ring from his late-1980s stretch working for the Los Angeles Dodgers. Bucci had tended to much worse injuries, including a player who had his left eye explode when he was hit by a fastball at the plate.

The forty-seven-year-old trainer resembled actor Tony Shalhoub, the star of the cable TV series *Monk,* but Bucci's curly black hair was a tad more unruly. Bryce once mimicked Bucci's guttural, drone monotone to a tee: "Get him an IV. . . . C'mon, guys, get a hit. . . . Whaddya mean where was I? Takin' a dump!" Bryce's teammates screamed in laughter. Bucci remained devilishly quiet, with a wry grin under the cap he had pulled down over his eyes, when the most rancid farts expanded and drifted through the bus.

When we returned to the bus, Bucci applied three electrical-stimulant patches, attached to a battery, around Harper's bruised kneecap to promote healing. Harper would miss no games. For an hour, sitting in the seat across from me, Harper made some calls on his new cell number. He chewed some Copenhagen, wintergreen, long-cut tobacco. Eventually, he eased to the back of the bus.

Five hours later, in Jackpot, Nevada, Kenny pulled over and most of the players zipped across Route 93 to a convenience store to load up on snacks. Harper, hopping as if he had a peg leg, was among them. They laughed like Little Leaguers and looked as if they had just won a trophy.

Back on the bus, catcher Ryan Scott slipped *Major League: Back to the Minors* into the DVD player to fuel more dreams. Kenny hauled ass, pulling into Morse Stadium at two in the morning. He turned on the speakers, flicked on all of the lights, and picked up the microphone with his left hand.

"Pick up the back, bitches!" he said, instructing the players to clean his coach, to yawning laughs. "Meow! You won three and lost one, but I still love you."

8

TIM CHAMBERS SET THE stage for a home weekend series against archrival Western Nevada as soon as his players had boarded Kenny's coach in Twin Falls for the long haul back home. Chambers told the Coyotes they had accomplished what they had set out to do against CSI, namely taking the series by winning three of the four games. Now, he said, let's concentrate on the Western Nevada Wildcats.

"Our favorite people," Chambers said drily.

CSN won the NJCAA World Series in 2003, but it hadn't been back to junior college baseball's grandest stage, in Grand Junction, Colorado, since then. In its first four seasons, Western Nevada went to Grand Junction in 2007 and 2009.

Wildcats coach D. J. Whittemore and Chambers often recruited against each other. Whittemore had signed more players from the Las Vegas area than Chambers had from Northern Nevada, although Southern Nevada had more high schools and better talent. Whittemore often staged early-season games in Las Vegas, for the better weather and so his players from the area could play in front of family and friends. But one that got away from Whittemore was Trevor Kirk, the slick outfielder for the Coyotes. After he had committed to Chambers, Kirk received angry text messages from Whittemore.

Whittemore's father was one of the more powerful legal figures in the Reno area. Whether that influence had bolstered D.J.'s ability to start his program or not, his foes used it against him. But taking his team to the World Series twice in his first four years confirmed Whittemore's abilities as a baseball manager.

Whittemore had also believed Bryce Harper's playing in the Scenic West Athletic Conference after his sophomore year of high school was ludicrous. Those words had trickled back to Chambers through his many baseball channels in the state, and they made him bristle. A series between the two programs always had tension, with swarms of animus in the stands. With Bryce Harper, it escalated to Jets vs. Sharks territory, a *West Side Story* that always seemed a choice word away from a rumble.

During one tight and prickly conference tournament championship game a few seasons earlier, both sides constantly badgered each other at Morse Stadium. When CSN pushed across the winning run in its last at bat, Coach Chambers, in the third-base coach's box, turned to the visitors' dugout and yelled, "Fuck you! What now?" The stunned Wildcats sat silently. Chambers glared at his foes as he continued walking toward his guys. After a round of high fives, Chambers kept walking, out the dugout and into his clubhouse, out the other door and into his black F-150, and home to Red Rock Country Club.

Chambers informed flame-throwing reliever Tyler Hanks, the proud farm boy from Spanish Fork, Utah, that he would be the team's fourth starter, in place of Kenny McDowall. As Hanks performed arm exercises and stretched during a practice that second week of March, his eyes glistened about starting.

Hanks grew up on his family's ranch and disregarded city slickers. His grandfather Ted, who never swore or drank alcohol, ran a five-thousand-acre spread. Hanks had baled seven thousand blocks of hay, at about 150 pounds a pop, in the summer of 2009 on his father Jason's ranch. Hanks attributed his power to the many strenuous chores he had performed on the ranch.

He knew people who had only eight or nine digits on their hands;

thumbs are common casualties for ranch hands and cowboys. His family had box seats to all of the prestigious National Finals Rodeo and Professional Bull Riders events. Hanks's girlfriend's father rode with rodeo legend Trevor Brazile, and Hanks talked about that roughneck sport with fervor.

"Bodacious was the Bryce Harper of rodeo," Hanks said, during a lopsided CSN victory, of the most fearsome bull in rodeo history. "Look what he did to Tuff Hedeman." In 1995, Bodacious, the firebreathing Charbray bull ridden for eight seconds by only 7 of the 135 cowboys who had dared to crawl on his back, broke every major bone in Hedeman's face when they knocked heads. Hedeman required more than six hours of reconstructive surgery and six titanium plates.

Hanks was detailing the farm life he loved so much just as Bryce Harper smacked a long two-run homer in some runaway victory by the Coyotes. Hanks shook his head. "He's on cloud nine," Hanks said, "and everyone else is on cloud one." Hanks had been astounded when Harper told him he would not get a luxurious new vehicle with his first paycheck. Harper told him the dependable black Toyota Tacoma with six figures in mileage worked just fine.

Redshirt pitcher Gentry Croft walked by. "Gentry," Hanks said, "you got a dip, you big-nosed bastard?" Croft stopped, he and Hanks turned their back to the field, and I looked out for any umpires' peering eyes as Hanks pinched some Copenhagen from Croft's tin and stuck it in his front lip.

In the first game of a Friday doubleheader against Western Nevada on March 12, Trevor Kirk singled to start the bottom of the first, and Scott Dysinger doubled down the left-field line. Bryce Harper walked to the plate, tossed his bat, and grabbed a few handfuls of dirt. Chambers had moved him to third in the batting lineup, to ensure that Harper would get to hit in the first inning, and that's where he would stay for the rest of the season.

In the visitors' dugout, the Wildcats stared. One of them mimed LeBron James, the basketball player who poured a handful of talcum powder into his hands and tossed it high into the air in a grand gesture before every game. Other Wildcats laughed at their teammate's gesture that followed Harper's grabbing the dirt around home plate. Harper shut them up with a four-pitch walk, and Kirk, Dysinger, and Harper all eventually scored to give CSN a 3–0 advantage. The bickering escalated by the inning.

In the third, Harper flew out to center to move Dysinger from second to third, but the kid with the eyes of the baseball world constantly on him wasn't pleased. When he returned to the dugout, he yanked off his batting helmet and didn't high-five any of his teammates who had wanted to congratulate him for moving a runner along, a fundamental baseball play that coaches demand and professional scouts seek. Bryan Harper tugged at his younger brother's left arm. In a jolt, Bryce was eye to eye with Bryan.

"Hey!" Bryan said. "Way to play the game, boy!" Bryce had a thousand-yard stare; he hadn't tattooed one out of the yard, so he hadn't been comfortable with plaudits.

The Wildcats scraped together three runs, two that scored on wild CSN pitches, which led to the Coyotes winning the opener in the bottom of the seventh on a single up the middle by Danny Higa that scored Matt Medina—running for catcher Ryan Scott, who had doubled off the center-field wall. The nightcap featured a one-hitter by CSN ace pitcher Donnie Roach, and home runs by Ryan Thomas and Bryce Harper, for a 3–0 victory to pump the Coyotes' record to 18-4.

The Harper homer, however, triggered much more as it appeared to land five hundred feet from home plate, closer to the CSN Student Union than the right-field fence. Harper didn't get rid of his bat until he was halfway to first, and he exchanged words with Western pitcher Jeremy Gendlek.

"I like having Bryce on our team!" yelled Roach, by far the most vocal Coyote in the dugout. In the first, Harper had laid down a bunt to third base that drifted foul. On the next pitch, he did it again. This time, it stayed fair. Western third baseman Andrew Garcia didn't even attempt a throw. "What *can't* he do?!" Roach barked. Harper sailed past first base. When he returned, he called time. He took six steps into foul territory and bent over, holding his left knee. The Twin Falls tumble flashed back into his teammates' minds, but Harper returned to the base seconds later and stole second.

After Harper's deep solo shot in the eighth, Gendlek hit Trent Cook, prompting an umpire's warning to both coaches that the next batter to get hit would result in the pitcher's being tossed and the guilty skipper getting booted from the yard, too.

Before the first pitch Saturday, the CSN dugout had been on edge. After Showtime, and assistant coaches Jay Guest and Cooper Fouts, had almost finished preparing the infield for the game, laying the foul lines and the batter's boxes, dragging the infield dirt, and placing the shiny bases in their slots, Fouts had marched into the dugout to find several pitchers sitting and chatting.

"You're fucking spoiled brats!" Fouts yelled. "We don't play in the field, you do! Why can't you help us?"

The caustic atmosphere only mushroomed during the doubleheader, played under mostly sunny skies but with an increasingly chilly gust blowing out to right field. When Ellen Whittemore, D. J. Whittemore's aunt who is a lawyer in Las Vegas, won fifty-five bucks in the fifty-fifty raffle during the first game, CSN players shook their heads. She had other reasons to smile when the Wildcats scored three times in the top of the first in an eventual 8–2 victory.

When Bryce Harper reached the plate to hit in the bottom of the first, Western catcher Pat McMeel warned him about posing and showing up the Wildcats if he hit another home run. Harper dropped his arms, stuck out his chest, and leaned toward McMeel. "Fuck you!" Harper said. "I hit that ball five hundred feet. I can do what I want!" The umpire stood between the two catchers, calmed them down, and Harper drew a walk, but he was left stranded on third.

"When the catcher says, 'Get your ass in the batter's box or next time we'll put one in your ear,' Ronnie or me or any other ironworker in this town would have knocked him flat on his . . . Bryce says the same thing," Jim Brooks said of his grandson. "That's why the ump got between them. Bryce said, 'Did you hear what he said to me?' The ump said he didn't hear anything. But it was being filmed and you could hear it on the tape."

In the top of the second, CSN was dealt what looked like a big blow when Trevor Kirk sped after a long fly ball in right-center field. It bounced wickedly off the fence, causing Kirk to adjust his route and twist his right foot. He fell in a heap. He writhed around as trainer Steve Jacobucci ran after him. Kirk needed help from two teammates to leave the field. Bryce, who had been catching his brother, Bryan, was shifted out to right field, and Ryan Scott entered the game to catch.

Trailing 7–1, with two outs in the bottom of the fifth, Harper tried to make something happen. He turned a bloop hit into shallow center field into a double, stole third, and scored on Trent Cook's single. Near the end of the game, Chambers paced the dugout and appeared flummoxed about his team's lack of preparation, as he was two days earlier when he had watched sloppy and lazy play after sloppy and lazy play in an intrasquad scrimmage—which prompted a twenty-minute chewing-out session about not respecting the game. Chambers had badly wanted to sweep the four games from Western on his own turf. That wouldn't happen.

"We didn't show up today," said Chambers, walking back and forth in the dugout. "Fucking embarrassing. Bullshit."

The dramatics escalated in the second game, when Harper slammed another home run to right in the bottom of the first. As he rounded third, he saluted the Western dugout. The Wildcats roared with indignation. When he stepped into his dugout, Harper angrily threw his two batting gloves at the bench and yelled, "Let's go!"

Before Trent Cook, the next batter, belted a triple to deep center field, Western catcher Chris Sinclair told Cook, "How does someone hit the ball like that?" The smack of the ball off Harper's bat had been that vicious.

It wasn't long before the game became volatile. In the top of the second, Western designated hitter Kyle Conwell slapped a single into right, and Harper, as he had in Idaho from center field the previous week, fired the ball back to first to try to catch Conwell napping as he rounded the base.

The Western dugout responded to the throw with claps, cheers, and jeers, mocking Harper for the daring play and trying to show up one of their own. Harper responded by bowing. Umpire John DeLuca darted out from the home plate area and ejected Harper for unsportsmanlike conduct. Their dugout was only cheering the hit, DeLuca claimed of the Wildcats, but Harper had taunted them with his silent bow. But clearly, the Western players had responded to Harper's throw, not Conwell's hit.

Chambers was shocked. He shouldn't have been. His poor history with DeLuca went back twenty years to an argument at Durango High School, when Chambers coached Bishop Gorman. Chambers claimed DeLuca had poked him in his chest. Chambers responded by spitting his tobacco chaw and juice in DeLuca's face, causing the ump to run from the grounds as Chambers challenged him to fight. Chambers admitted that that wasn't one of his finer moments. DeLuca declined to comment.

Bryce Harper raised both arms. Huh? "Gotta be kidding?!" he yelled as he galloped into shallow right field. Bryan Harper ran out to corral his brother, to steer him off the field and into the clubhouse. It wasn't an easy task, but it was made to order for the phenom's bigger and older brother. Many teammates and CSN coaches considered Bryan Harper to be the most levelheaded and rational Harper male.

"It's kind of rough, having people come at you all the time," said Bryan Harper. "I know if I was in his shoes, I'd be doing the exact same thing, if not more. As a junior in high school, I did not want people talking to me or saying stuff to me. I would say something to them. He's the exact same way. A competitor wants to be the best. If someone says he's not the best, he'll prove them wrong. In that situation, with him bowing . . . I knew me being the older brother, I had to get him back in or he could have been suspended for more games. We didn't need that. A one-game suspension was enough. Our team was fine. We have plenty of guys. But we didn't need him missing the Salt Lake or CSI series, or a good-team series. He'll always be under a microscope because of all the hype."

As Bryan directed Bryce off the field, Ron Harper, wearing jeans and a gray-hooded sweatshirt, screamed at the umps from just beyond the fence along the right-field foul line. The first-base umpire yelled for school police to escort Ron, who did not go quietly, from the premises. Then the second-base ump pointed to the CSN dugout and ejected "the guy on the crutches"—Trevor Kirk—for his baiting. Earlier in the dugout, Kirk had boasted to teammates how he had ventured into the stands, wearing a gray sweatshirt with a hood almost completely covering his head, to badger DeLuca.

"D.J., act like you're innocent!" Chambers yelled as he walked by Whittemore, coaching first base, to enter the Coyotes' dugout. Whittemore, staring straight ahead, never turned his head toward Chambers or said a peep. An ejection came with a one-game suspension, which Chambers had earned for his outburst against Cypress a few weeks earlier. A second toss would result in a two-game suspension, so Chambers wasn't about to tangle with DeLuca in that situation. Chambers and Harper would have to be careful for the rest of the season.

Amid the tense situation, sophomore reserve infielder Casey Sato stood on the other side of the dugout rail and called his teammates together. Some looked his way but stood still. He demanded they gather in front of him. A few more turned to him. His face turned red as he raised his voice. "Get over here. Now!" Sato howled. "Fuck them! Let's forget them! Let's send them back to Carson City with a ten-spot! Let's focus on us!"

The explosive atmosphere overshadowed a strong six innings by Tyler Hanks in his debut as a starter, and Aaron Kurcz bounced back from a couple of rough appearances by shutting down the Wildcats in the seventh and final inning of the 3–0 victory.

After the game, the third time CSN had beaten its rival in four tries over two days, Whittemore and his coaches led their players in a line to shake the hands of the Coyotes' coaches and players, but Chambers wasn't part of those proceedings. After the final pitch, he had angrily left his dugout for his clubhouse. Chambers wasn't about to shake the hand of anyone in a light blue jersey or in a black umpire uniform. At least in this series, none of them had asked for the seventeen-year-old's autograph.

Upon reflecting about playing Southern Nevada, Western coach D. J. Whittemore praised Bryce Harper. He would need to mature, Whittemore said. What seventeen-year-old doesn't? After seeing Harper in person, Whittemore looked forward to playing him and the Coyotes again in Carson City. The intensity with which Chambers had yelled at Whittemore during the dustup of Bryce Harper's getting ejected—"D.J., act like you're innocent"—hadn't been lost on Whittemore, either.

"The thing that sticks out with [Chambers] is he always puts so much pressure on himself and his guys because he wants to win so badly. They bring out the best in us. We hold their program in such high regard. Our coaches, our players . . . we feel it's a special opportunity to play against them and try to prove ourselves. It's just a lot of fun for us."

When the two teams met at Western Nevada, the series between the two bitter rivals would be much more fun for D. J. Whittemore. The most colorful exchanges and dramatic action in Carson City, however, would take place between Tim Chambers and Bryce Harper.

9

THE WEEK BEFORE CSN played host to Colorado Northwestern, the MLB Network dropped into Morse Stadium for a rare interview with Bryce Harper, and he would miss a game for the first time from suspension.

Late the morning of Thursday, March 18, Jonathan Mayo of the MLB Network appeared in the Coyotes' tight, blue-and-yellow locker room, made even more claustrophobic by a cluster of cameras, lights, microphones, sound equipment, and crew. When I walked in and sat on a metal bench out of harm's way, next to the sound engineer, Mayo glanced at me. He looked again, and again, but said nothing. Coach Chambers and Ron Harper stood in the recesses of the entryway out of sight.

On a four-legged stool, Bryce sat opposite the bald and pleasant Mayo and fidgeted with his feet, uncomfortable but accommodating. He wore a dark blue Coyotes cap. He looked down and to the left, a position he would occupy for most of the thirty minutes and twenty-one seconds of the interview. The rattle of the air-conditioning unit disappeared when Chambers turned off the system.

The sound guys synced, or time-coded, with the video guys by having Bryce count to ten. Camera One? Mayo said. You okay? Have to get in tighter. We have to move so that pole is outta the way. We will center up for this shot, then switch to an offset. Denny? Brad? Any issues? We're pretty good. How does the reverse look? Yeah, the reverse is good. I can get a little over the shoulder, too. Want me to mix that up? Yeah, feel free. Center it for the open then go to the offset.

Bryce looked bored. He would rather have been home playing with Harley, his yellow Lab. We just need a little black wrap over here, on this camera, someone said. The help crunched a black piece of foamlike material. Sorry about this, guys, he said. Good, Randy. I'm happy. Ready to roll the tape? All cell phones off, please. Camera Two, be careful moving in and out of the frame. Yes, copy that. Okay. Speed. One, two . . . time code . . . eleven oh seven . . . eleven nineteen, twenty, twenty-one, twenty-two . . . John, when you're ready.

Cameras rolled.

"His story has been well documented," Mayo said. "He left high school early to . . . t-t-t . . . we'll do it again."

"Tilt your head up just a little Bryce," said a voice in the shadows. He tilted his head up just a little. "Thank you."

Bryce Harper was ready for his close-up.

"His story has been well documented," Mayo repeated. "He left high school early to have the challenge of going to junior college and moving his draft day up a year. Right now, Bryce Harper probably wants to be known as just another baseball player trying to win a national championship for CSN. Start out there, with your transition from high school to junior college."

"It's been a fun transition from high school to junior college," Harper said. "I've known Tim Chambers for some time, and having all the guys around that I've grown up with, like Scott Dysinger, Trevor Kirk, Marvin Campbell, and my brother . . . being around all those guys, it's been real easy having them around and stuff. . . ."

Harper continued in a manner that would have pleased Jerry Seinfeld; cool, professional, and vague. He has always "played up," from when he was seven playing with ten-year-olds, to being the youngest player on the US U16 and U18 teams, to now, when he arrived at CSN playing fall ball at sixteen, he said. He has teammates who are twenty, twenty-one, and twenty-two. That's a lot of support, Mayo told Harper, all around you.

"Having that core of guys growing up, playing with them, and being around them all the time, always playing up and stuff like that . . . it was hard at the beginning, but it got easier as I was around them more. . . . Those guys made it so much easier for me. Like I said, Coach Chambers and his staff were huge assets to that."

The comforts of home that Harper cherished included his mother's cooking, sleeping in his own bed, piling up the dirty laundry in the hamper that he knew his mother would tend to, and being able to tap Harley on his head when he came home "and just say, 'What up, boy?' " said Harper, smiling.

As he figured he would, Harper told Mayo he had big adjustments to make from the start, facing tough pitchers such as fellow Las Vegan Donnie Roach—who hit ninety-five and ninety-six miles an hour on the radar gun—and Joe Robinson (who topped out at ninety-four) and older brother Bryan (whose movement was devilish). It wasn't a surprise that he did not mention Taylor Jones's wicked curveball. Neither Mayo nor anyone else outside the CSN family knew how close that particular pitch and that specific October practice game almost sent Harper scampering back to high school.

Bryce Harper came back from Team USA's successful trip to Venezuela tapped of energy and weighing only 185, but he regretted none of it. He talked glowingly about representing his country and continuing to do so in future world tournaments.

Mayo reiterated the misconception that Bryan had left Cal State Northridge to follow Bryce to CSN, which Bryce corrected. Bryce explained his decision to leave high school after his sophomore season. To keep testing himself, he said, in the classroom and on the diamond. Had nothing to do with the draft, he tried to convince Mayo. "Could care less" about the draft, Harper said. Like so many sports figures who used that phrase, Harper meant *couldn't* care less.

The high school curriculum, even his honors classes, had been way too easy. He had wanted to expand his mind, he told Mayo, get a jump on college courses, and mature quicker, on and off the field, around older peers.

"If I could come back and play here next year, I will come back here. God willing, I'll play pro baseball. It's not all about the draft. It's about furthering my education and trying to see what else I can do in life other than baseball."

In talking about the talent all around him, and that he didn't have to carry the burden in every game of the team's scoring, Harper said he was relieved to not have to be the "Cinderella man anymore, if that makes sense." He didn't have to go four for four every day. He could go hitless and CSN could still win. In theory, on paper, that sounded believable, but Harper's mettle and moxie were always severely tested when he did not get four hits in four trips to the plate.

"That's all that matters to me. As long as we get the W and by the end of the year we have that ring on our fingers. That's all that matters. . . . I don't have to be The Guy anymore. I want to be, but I don't have to be."

He said he would play anywhere, from catching to outfield to third, and he dreamed of some day making his first appearance as a relief pitcher in junior college—that's always in the back pocket, Harper said—but he preferred to catch, to be involved in every pitch of every game.

"I want to get run over. Not really run over, but I want someone to try."

He deflected the hoopla of all the interest in him.

"I'd rather track Joe Mauer or Josh Hamilton, see how they're doing. They're everyday guys and will be Hall of Famers one day . . . but, yeah, it's surprised me a little bit. But there have always been scouts around, people watching. I like that. You're in the middle of it."

Mayo asked Harper how much attention he had paid a year earlier to ace hurler Stephen Strasburg, who was drafted first by the

Washington Nationals. Harper said he never even took a glancing interest in Strasburg's situation or negotiations that led to his signing for $15.1 million.

Harper wished he could have faced Nolan Ryan or played with Mickey Mantle, Roger Maris, Pete Rose, and George Brett, recurring names when he reminisced about his favorite legends. Harper talked about sitting in the dugout next to CSN assistant coach Kevin Higgins during an intrasquad scrimmage when Higgins turned to him and called him a test-tube baby.

"What do you mean?" Harper said.

"You have everyone in you," Higgins said. "Jackie Robinson. Mickey Mantle. You have Joe Mauer in you. You have everybody. Your parents just haven't told you yet . . . nah, just messing around."

"Do I think I have all those guys in me?" he told Mayo. "I guess. But I don't. I'm Bryce Harper."

He ended the interview by saying he hoped the team finished its season in Grand Junction, Colorado, dog-piling after the last game of the NJCAA World Series. Telling everyone "we did it," and playing for Team USA in the summer "against all those guys from Cuba, Venezuela, and Korea."

"Don't mess with the USA. If the draft happens, God willing, I'll go in the draft and play pro baseball. All I'm worried about now is trying to win the national championship and then the world championship, playing hard, and getting those rings."

That had not been accurate, either. Plenty worried Harper, he just didn't let on how much he was concerned about producing, and convincing the Washington brass that it should take him first in the draft.

Moments after the interview, Harper slid into the clubhouse and joked with teammates, telling some he had mentioned them in the session with Mayo but telling others, uh, sorry. Laughs, including big smiles from Ron Harper and Tim Chambers, filled the spacious room.

The following day, after the first inning of the series-opening game against Colorado Northwestern, Harper sat alone on a blue-cloth-covered couch in the quiet clubhouse, watching the opening games of the NCAA basketball tournament. Enter the clubhouse through the blue metal door on the field side of the building, and immediately to the right, the couch and a smaller one formed an upside-down *L,* with a small pine coffee table between it and a sixty-inch television screen. Thirty feet to the left, against a wall, a line of desks had five computers on top. A few circular, white tables dotted the area.

Straight ahead, atop a large cinder-block wall, hung the framed Philadelphia Phillies and Chicago White Sox jerseys of, respectively, Matt Smith, who had played for Chambers at Bishop Gorman, and Aaron Rowand, the San Francisco outfielder. Behind that wall a narrow room contained the assistants' desks. Off to the right were the showers and the bathroom, a heavy-duty washer and dryer, and the small locker area. Coyotes blue-and-yellow trim was everywhere.

This was the game that Bryce Harper served the suspension, for the farce that had taken place the previous weekend against Western Nevada. Clemson played Missouri in hoops on television. No doubt Harper wondered how sharp the Clemson baseball uniforms looked. I sat next to him and asked if big interviews, such as the one he did the previous day with the MLB Network, were exciting.

"It just gets old. I don't want to do it, but it's really a lot of fun. If someone said, yeah, being on the cover of *Sports Illustrated* wasn't fun, they'd be lying to you. That was insane. Everyone dreams of that since they're five years old. You want to be like *him* [the guy on the cover]. *He's* my hero. To do all that stuff. It's a lot of fun, but it gets crazy sometimes."

Harper was agitated about not being available to help his teammates against Colorado Northwestern out on the diamond. He sent text messages to buddies at Las Vegas High. He paced around the clubhouse. He peeked through the window blinds in Chambers's office to check up on the action. Being restricted from a game, as his teammates competed without him, was a spooky harbinger for Harper.

As he tried not losing his mind, watching Clemson take a 28–19 lead on Missouri, outside that blue metal door pitcher Donnie Roach finished as well as he started in throwing a seven-inning no-hitter against Colorado Northwestern. Roach improved to 5-1 by walking three and striking out nine. He celebrated the first no-no of his life by dining out with his girlfriend's family on her father's fortieth birthday.

Of all the Coyotes, Donnie Roach possessed the deepest and richest roots in Las Vegas, in maternal great-grandfather Ed Von Tobel. In May 1905, he had left Los Angeles on the San Pedro, Las Vegas & Salt Lake rail line, disembarked on a triple-digit afternoon in Las Vegas, and participated in a historic land auction. Von Tobel began his business empire by acquiring a $100 plot for three bucks; the auctioneer spurred the bidding by crediting the winner's train fare against a 25 percent down payment, and Von Tobel had paid $22 for the ride from Los Angeles.

When the city became incorporated in 1911, Von Tobel was appointed to one of the five positions on the first City Commission, the precursor to City Councils, with an annual salary of $12. He had started a lumberyard and would endure some rough years, but the post–World War II building boom gave Von Tobel Lumber a firm financial foundation. In 1965, the family expanded the company into an eighty-thousand-square-foot indoor building on Maryland Parkway that became a blueprint for Home Depot and Lowe's. In the 1980s the family sold the business and enhanced its real estate holdings. A middle school on North Pecos Road is named after the patriarch of the Von Tobel family.

Von Tobel's son George, the father of Donnie Roach's mother, Julie, helped build runways on Pacific islands in World War II. He raced a red Jaguar XK150S around California in the late 1950s and early 1960s. He served four terms in the Nevada Assembly from Clark County, and as part of the Nevada Gaming Commission he once blocked Howard Hughes from buying the Stardust and monopolizing the city's hotel and casino industry. George's brother Jake was part of an initial group of investors, which included Nate Mack and E. Parry Thomas, that Cliff Jones had assembled to start the Bank of Las Vegas in 1954, which was reorganized as Valley Bank ten years later and became part of Bank of America in the 1990s.

With so many familiar faces such as Donnie Roach's around him, Bryce Harper couldn't have felt more comfortable in making his big leap to junior college baseball.

You didn't get a hit off me, Roach told slugger Marvin Campbell as he walked by Roach in practice. Their one face-off, pitcher to hitter, had occurred long before they became Coyotes. Roach got the better of Campbell. "I was fourteen!" said Campbell in stride. No matter, said Roach. Bryce Harper then walked by. This guy, Roach said as he pointed at Bryce, got a hit off me. "A double," Bryce said. "I was thirteen," said Roach, who quickly added that he picked Bryce off second a minute later.

A year after he thought about quitting the game, when he won only one of five decisions and had a 7.84 earned run average at Arizona, Roach eased into a comfort zone at CSN. He became serious about his workout regimen and pitch patterns. Coyotes pitching coach Glen Evans helped a great deal, too, by returning Roach to the three-quarter arm slot he'd favored at Bishop Gorman.

"I'm a thousand times better," Roach said. "I was horseshit last year with everything, including work ethic. Arizona tried to change me a little bit. It was just a bad situation all around. Not the place for me. . . . I threw a shitload of off-speed splitters. They called a lot of splitters. It was wrecking my arm. It hurt. I had forearm tendinitis. It wasn't good. Last year, I fucking hated it."

Roach had a prodigious beak and a shrewdness throwing a five-ounce mass of cork and rubber and wool and yarn, all wrapped in cowhide. His repertoire and tenacity made him the standout hurler of what the well-regarded PGCrossChecker.com scouting guide arguably called the most talented pitching staff "at any level of college baseball."

CrossChecker named the six-foot-one, 200-pound Roach among

its biggest early-spring surprises in the college ranks as Roach showed vast improvement in his ability to confuse batters and get ahead on counts. Chambers most often started him in the second game of league games because of Roach's stamina; he had the best chance to complete all nine innings and keep the CSN bullpen fresh.

Roach also led the team in dry wit. Let's not talk about the past, a teammate said during a game. Why not? Roach shot back. "I love the past." One is longer than the other one! He barked it again, emphasizing the first *one* and *other.* Teammates, perplexed for a few seconds, said, "Huh?" "My pants!" Roach blared at the opposing pitcher, whose right pant leg was indeed longer than his left. That was before Chambers ended the needling his players—led by Roach—engaged in with opponents. "Toxic," Chambers said before he heard it go overboard and become a distraction.

Roach had a tic—a jaw twitch to the right that sent his left ear down, as if he were cracking his neck—after delivering a barb to an opponent or a quip to a teammate. He also whistled the national anthem, alongside his teammates on the first- or third-base line, or on the mound before a start. Julie Roach did not know that about her son, but she knew why. In his youth, Donnie had been a promising trumpet player until baseball trumped the brass for his attention.

He was deliberate on the mound. As Roach delivered the ball, he ever so slightly slid his right foot, his anchor leg, a few inches forward, away from the rubber to which it was parallel. The closer a pitcher is to a batter, obviously, the better. No umpire, though, called him on it all season. He knew the pulse of his team, too. Roach also had some vaudeville somewhere in his lineage.

He marveled over the nearly six hundred Bryce Harper items on eBay, many signed by Harper. Those included cards, bats, jerseys, and helmets. Their prices ranged from $189.99 to $350, $500, $1,499.95, and $3,500. A card whose asking price was $850 came with this note about Harper—*He is really good!* Roach even saw the framed, three-card set going for $25,000. No doubt, Roach said, that could inflate a young star's ego.

"It could, but he's used to it. He's not going out there and showing anyone [his eBay listings]. He's something special. He's going to be real good. He's a great kid and I love him to death."

Bryce Harper seethed and steamed inside the clubhouse. It was pointed out to him that that's why he made the leap to CSN, to grow and get some of that brashness, those reactions that got him tossed from that Western Nevada game, out of his system. "It is a learning experience, for sure," he said. "I'd never done anything like that before, so it's a great learning experience."

The series of events that led to his getting ejected—the throw to first from right field and the subsequent bow to the Western Nevada bench when the Wildcats were so obviously mocking that bold maneuver, and not cheering their player's hit, which the umpire thought—were stunning. After all, home-plate umpire John DeLuca hadn't been in Idaho the previous weekend, when Harper, from center field, would have picked off the CSI hitter who had rounded first had first baseman Ryan Thomas hung on to the ball.

"I've been doing that all my life," Harper said of trying to catch runners leaning toward second base after they had rounded first on a hit. "If [an umpire] wants to throw me out, he wants to throw me out. It's his choice. I'm not going to bad-mouth him about that."

I told Harper how uncanny it is watching him play. In the field or in the batter's box, he demanded attention because it's never known what he might do next.

"It's been like that since I was ten. Everyone watches. Umps, other teams, are out for you. It happens in life, I guess. To come over here and play against older guys, I didn't think that would happen, that they'd worry about me so much. If I'm getting in their heads, so be it."

He admitted that this season was a great litmus test, a perfect transition for weaning certain tendencies out of his system. In the minors, in pro ball, Harper didn't expect that sophomoric yip-yapping from the other bench.

"You need to close your ears off. A-Rod and Josh Hamilton go through it every single day. They go out and show it with their bats. Jackie Robinson is the main guy who went through it all. Look where he panned out."

When Chipola College players had arrived at Morse from Florida and whooped it up in left field before their first game against CSN, the Coyotes were caught dumbfounded in their dugout when Bryce cracked up everyone within earshot with that line about remembering his first beer. Reminded of that scene, he laughed. That was a good one, he said. "Pretty funny. I remember that." But hilarity wasn't my point, I said. I asked him if he had ever had a beer, or even tasted the stuff. He laughed even harder and his eyes widened.

"No, I haven't. Never had a drink in my life. Ever. But it's a great line . . . I'll use it. But I never drank."

Once in a while, he licked his lips and told a teammate or two that Jack Daniel's was his favorite drink. But while older brother Bryan enjoyed an occasional beer or a Coke with a splash of Captain Morgan spiced rum, it was pure folly when Bryce talked about alcohol. Again, he was just trying to fit in, being one of the boys. Nobody had ever seen him sip any type of booze. As the season wore on, Bryce joked about maybe celebrating a Junior College World Series title with a can of nonalcoholic beer. Even that drew yeah-right looks.

Harper didn't plan to consume alcohol, and smoking and drugs were out of the question. There is no ambiguity in the Mormon faith's chaste principles, including forbidding premarital sex, avoiding alcohol, and tithing. LDS elders would cringe if they heard certain language, too. Those close to Bryce, once again, said, Hey, he's seventeen, using salty language or talking about girls is the way of the game. Would he mature into a model LDS sports figure, in the mold of former Atlanta Braves slugger Dale Murphy? That remained to be seen, but many believed Harper would embrace his growing images as a role model and a Mormon as he aged.

Harper had no problem with Western Nevada catcher Pat Mc-Meel, who had some words for Harper the next time he went to the plate after showboating a home run. Harper said he would have done the same exact thing.

"What he did wasn't part of baseball. What I did wasn't part of baseball, either, but when you have a team over there talking crap, yip-yapping, and your whole team is looking out for you . . . and you hit a bomb to go ahead . . . there's no feeling like that. The heat of the moment. It's how I've always played. I take that into every at bat, every play."

Did he feel like a pioneer, a trailblazing kid on the fast track to baseball superstardom? Harper quickly demurred. Jackie Robinson blazed a trail, Harper insisted, when he broke baseball's color barrier in 1947. What Robinson and others, such as Don Newcombe, Sam Jethroe, Willie Mays, Hank Aaron, and Larry Doby, had endured when racial tensions were taut in this country qualified them as heroes and trailblazers. Harper's sense of their rightful place in history was profound. He said he was just doing what he had always done: playing up against older competition. Nothing had really changed, he said. But junior college ball had thrown him a bit of a curve.

"It's just that attitudes of people are totally different up here. It's a totally different game from high school. You hit a bomb [here] to shut someone up and they'll look at you. In high school, it was different; someone hit a bomb and the next guy up won't get hit. *You* would get hit next time up. *You* are gonna get hit. And it's over. In the big leagues, you get hit, and it's over. If they were to hit me [in junior college], no problem; it's over. But they didn't hit me. They kept yip-yapping, doing everything. It's pretty crazy, being seventeen and playing college ball. But I love it. It's so much fun. There's nothing greater."

He would have relished playing with or against Mickey Mantle, Roger Maris, Joe DiMaggio, and Jackie Robinson, not just because of that golden age of the game but because of that era in general, and driving a slick, 1950s-era Bel Air with big fins. A big, yellow real one, although he adored the small die-cast one his grandfather had given him.

He was much more colorful and relaxed than he had been for the MLB Network cameras a day earlier. A few college-basketball brackets he had filled out had already turned to rubbish just a few games into the NCAA tournament. His teammates were outside, playing, and he couldn't wait to join them for the second game of the doubleheader. Harper did not regret one bit of his life in such a pressure cooker.

"I thrive on it. I love it."

10

IN A PRESEASON CHAT with Bryce Harper, Coach Chambers had told the budding superstar not to get too carried away with thoughts of obliterating every pitcher he'd face in 2010. The quicker you realize how difficult it will be to hit .600, much less .500, Chambers told Harper, the better off you will be. You'll be steady, instead of swinging with every dramatic high and low of the game, like a pendulum. You'll be prepared for life as a pro.

But by the time of that talk, Harper had rebounded mightily from his golden sombrero episode. "I *should* be able to hit .500!" Harper responded. "Don't tell me I can't. I should!"

The most exciting prodigy since LeBron James, according to *Sports Illustrated,* entered April as, well, the most exciting player in amateur baseball. He returned to the lineup against Colorado Northwestern and drove in four runs on two singles, and he hit a couple of doubles in the next day's doubleheader as CSN swept the four games by a total score of 29–2. Two days later, Joe Mauer signed an eight-year, $184 million contract extension with the Minnesota Twins.

Mauer was the player to whom Harper drew regular comparisons. He won American League batting titles in 2006, 2008, and 2009. Both the six-foot-four, 215-pound Mauer and Harper hit from the left side. Many experts considered Harper to be more advanced at seventeen than Mauer was at that age. That Harper had been excelling with a wooden bat, against older competition and the best pitchers he had ever seen in big yards, had impressed scouts.

Mauer's rich contract was the talk of the CSN practice Tuesday, March 23. Maybe within ten years that figure would be the ballpark for Harper's bounty. As the Coyotes stretched, that was the theme. When they broke up and Harper was far enough away, one Coyote, capitalizing on the popular movie theme of that time, turned to another and said, "Can you imagine what Bryce's avatar looks like?" For all of their effort, sweat, and toiling, most of them would never know what it's like to warm up on a major league field, much less ink a deal worth eight or nine figures. That was the chasm that separated Harper from so many of his teammates.

Just getting to the big leagues is a battle for most players, as Dick Scott, father of CSN catcher Ryan Scott, and Coyotes assistant coach Kevin Higgins could attest.

Privately, at least a few of his teammates continued to speculate if Bryce Harper was as driven as they were to reach the play-offs and go far, reaching the Junior College World Series and, hopefully, winning it. Because for all they knew this would be the last baseball of their lives. They had no offers to play anywhere in the fall of 2010. Nothing was guaranteed beyond the next several months. The only one with guarantees, it seemed to them, was number thirty-four, who was swinging his way to fame, riches, and glory regardless of how the Coyotes fared in late May.

At that Tuesday practice Harper thumbed around in the dugout for his Hawken, wintergreen chewing tobacco, the green tin with the orange, circular stripes, and the logo of the trigger portion of a Winchester rifle. Chambers laughed. That stuff is like candy, he said. "I could chew it and swallow it." In that day's intrasquad scrimmage, Harper tried stealing home. The ump, with a bad angle, called him out. It looked as if Harper had slid under the tag. Even in practice, he always went full bore to test himself and those around him.

NJCAA World Series officials, in telephone chats with Chambers, salivated about the prospect of a CSN team with Harper playing in Grand Junction, Colorado, in June. Harper's domination wowed Al Williams, the regional director for men's sports in the Scenic West Athletic Conference, who had dropped into Henderson to visit Chambers and watch the Coyotes practice. Williams, whose sturdy frame gave him the appearance of someone who had played fullback in college, leaned onto the yellow-padded rail of the CSN dugout and marveled at Harper's batting-practice power drives.

"Can you imagine if this were happening in basketball? It would be a national *holy funk* if a kid did this in basketball. I like it, because it doesn't seem like he's been exploited. He's grounded, academically, and he's handled it all very well. His confidence is growing, and it seems like he's just a good person. Those kinds of kids don't come along very often."

Someone told Williams about the homer Harper hit to dead center field, a shot of about 450 feet.

"That's a poke, and with a wood bat? You don't see many young guys like that out there at this level. Everyone else seems to be overwhelmed by him, but he just wants to play ball."

During the last weekend of March, CSN belted fifteen home runs and outscored the College of Eastern Utah by a combined score of 47–16 in a four-game sweep in Price, Utah. Harper had hit four out, including two in the same inning—another CSN first. Harper had pulled off that feat once in high school and at an all-star game in Cooperstown, New York. That gave him twelve on the season, tying him for the school record, which had been set when CSN hit with aluminum bats.

Marvin Campbell, benefiting from hitting behind Harper and with renewed confidence after undergoing eye exercises for a couple of weeks with Dr. Craig Hamilton, an optometrist, to strengthen his lazy right eye, belted five over the fences in Utah.

As Kenny's coach sailed down the east side of Las Vegas toward home in the wee hours of Sunday, March 28, a documentary of basketball player LeBron James and his prep team, *More Than a Game*, came to an end. It had showed James and his teammates playing video games and carousing in a hotel until the early morning before a big game. They weren't even concerned about their opponents. Hubris, and the other guys, defeated James and his crew. Bryce Harper had watched every second. He poked a text message to Coach Chambers in which the prodigy thanked his mentor for keeping close tabs on him and limiting his exposure to certain elements. You are welcome, Chambers wrote back as Kenny steered his beast left on College Drive.

After nineteen conference games, Bryce Harper was hitting .500, tops in the league. He was slugging at a goofy 1.036 clip. Nobody else in the league was over .700. His ninety-five total bases were easily atop the SWAC. His next closest competitor was teammate Trent Cook, who had sixty. Harper's thirteen doubles also were far and away the most in the conference. His twenty-two walks were among the top.

Harper was nonchalant about what he had been doing and his statistics. Still, many others marveled at the raw numbers. In his online PGCrossChecker, Allan Simpson, who had started the popular *Baseball America* magazine, raved about the possibility that Washington would select Harper with the number one pick in the draft. Even though that meant dealing again with superagent Scott Boras, Simpson believed Harper might own the most advanced raw tools, at his age, of any American who had played the game in the past half century.

"Harper has had to deal with the immense pressure that has been thrust on him by his unique situation . . . [sidestepping] the traditional draft process, all in the hope of reaping millions this summer," Simpson wrote. "Some observers believed that a young and inexperienced Harper was put in a position to fail with his bold move . . . [but] he has thrived on the field in the sheltered environment."

Salt Lake Community College coach D. G. Nelson noted the attention Harper was drawing to junior college baseball in general and the Scenic West Athletic Conference in particular, and how Harper was making his team and its foes better.

"I don't think you can put words to it. He's making other pitchers better, the ones who don't pitch around him. Junior college baseball has never seen anything like it. He's aggressive and smart. I think he's done nothing but improve his stock. It must be frustrating when they try to pitch around him, when they don't challenge him."

Two people close to Harper knew how his challenges would increase as he rose in the game.

Dick Scott had lost track of his oldest son, Ryan, at the old Yankee Stadium. When he was a minor league coordinator for the Toronto Blue Jays, the elder Scott had business to tend to in Boston and New York, so he brought Ryan and younger son Zach with him on the road trip to see the Yankees at home and the Red Sox at Fenway Park.

At Old-Timers' Day at Yankee Stadium, in the Blue Jays' clubhouse, Ryan fit right in. He raided the well-stocked fridge of its chocolate milk and feasted on the ample candy supply. He sat on a couch next to the big leaguers and watched a movie with them. He bolted to an elevator when he saw Reggie Jackson had just entered it. Ryan had heard that Mr. October did not like signing autographs, but he dove in anyway. Jackson kept the doors from shutting and complied when Ryan asked him for his signature.

After meetings with Toronto brass, Dick searched all over for Ryan. He finally meandered toward a dugout. As he scanned down the bench, he noticed eleven-year-old Ryan in deep discussion with the great Al Downing. Uh-oh, Dick thought. Downing had yielded Hank Aaron's record-breaking 715th home run in April 1974, in Atlanta. In 1967, against Cleveland, Downing became the thirteenth pitcher to strike out all three batters in an inning on nine pitches.

When Dick Scott reached them, Ryan piped up, "Dad, have you met Mr. Downing?"

"No, I haven't. Nice to meet you. If there are any problems, send him back."

Dick Scott, a minor league field coordinator for the Houston

Astros in 2010 who moved on to a similar position with New York Mets in 2011, still chuckled about that scene at Yankee Stadium. "He was having a great conversation. It was humorous, my son introducing me to Al Downing. He just dismissed me to the clubhouse. Everything was under control."

Ryan Scott smiled at the memory of talking with Downing, who had more questions for the young catcher than Ryan had for him. Downing was truly interested in what Ryan thought of baseball and his future in the game, but he also inquired about school.

At SkyDome, the Blue Jays' home field that was renamed Rogers Centre in 2005, Ryan once caught pitcher Ted Lilly's bull-pen session. On one throw, the young catcher missed the veteran pitcher's wave-off signal, and some wicked heat was unleashed at Ryan when he thought something far slower was on its way. Crossed up by a major leaguer. "That's the scariest thing for a catcher," Ryan said. "I was shaking. I hadn't seen that yet."

The first fastball he tried catching from minor league hurler Jayson Rodriguez knocked the mitt off Ryan's left hand. He was working out by himself one day in the Toronto weight room when Roy Halladay, one of the game's premier pitchers, joined him. Already drenched from running, Halladay hit the weights hard, then he pedaled on a stationary bike as if he were in the Tour de France. Ryan Scott thought, *That guy is good. I have to work like him.*

Ryan was in an odd position the first week of June 2009, after vacationing with family in Maine. Scott had snatched the *Sports Illustrated* from his grandmother's house. At the airport in Bangor, Scott began reading the six-page feature with the five photographs of Harper. "I saw that he was going to a JC, so as soon as I read that, I was like, Vegas, junior college . . . we're the only one. I knew Chambers had his ways."

A moment later, Scott received a text message from teammate and roommate Wes Hunt, a freshman utility player out of Shadow Ridge

High School in Las Vegas. *Hey,* Hunt wrote, *You hear Harper's coming to our school?* Scott wrote back, *No way.* In 2009, Scott had started twenty-seven of thirty-two CSN games at catcher, the versatile Harper's most-desired position. Scott hit .277, slugged two homers, and drove in nineteen runs. He wanted to work hard in the off-season to break out in 2010. *What, Chambers told Ryan, you scared of a sixteen-year-old?*

"It's definitely a funny experience and pretty cool. We knew it would bring a bunch of people to the games. I've heard a lot of stories about guys getting exposure from other people. On opening night, we had two thousand people here. That was a first. I don't think Bryce will be the only one on this team that will be a big name, either."

Perhaps more than any other Coyote, Ryan understood what awaited many of those who would get drafted and pursued careers in professional baseball, the long bus rides along empty state routes, and midnight stops at gas stations for water and junk food.

The Yankees had drafted Dick Scott, a shortstop from Ellsworth, Maine, in the seventeenth round in 1981, but he did not play a major league game for the Bronx Bombers, toiling in their minor league system for eight years. In 1989, the Oakland Athletics signed him as a free agent and he filled in, briefly, for Walt Weiss on the parent club. Scott played a total of 2⅓ innings in three major league games. He had no hits in two official at bats. It made headlines in the Northeast that Scott was the first position player from Maine to reach the majors in more than forty years.

He played eight hundred games in the minors, including seventy-nine at Triple-A Tacoma in the Athletics' system in 1989 and twenty-one in 1990 that served as the final chapter of his playing career. When Ryan was a year old, in 1991, Dick Scott started his managerial career. In the first seven years of his life, Ryan lived in Huntsville, Alabama; Modesto, California; South Bend, Indiana; Medford, Oregon; and Madison, Wisconsin; and he enjoyed the journey. "Pretty much a different team every year. It was fun. Dad got different jobs and I loved being around it. I know how it all works. A lot of these guys are definitely heading that way. You can tell."

At five, Ryan started spending some time with his father on buses traveling the minor league circuit. When someone put an R-rated movie into the VCR, Dick Scott made sure his son listened to music on his earphones, attached to a radio. When his father wasn't looking, Ryan turned the volume down so he could listen to movies like *The Rock*. When Dick managed a team in Medford, it was traveling to Bend, Oregon, for a series when *Harlem Nights* was the featured attraction. Dick glanced at Ryan and saw him twisting the volume down on his music. "I thought he'd figure this out sooner or later, just not at five. What are you going to do? He got some great language right out of the chute."

In South Bend, Ryan always snuck Tootsie Rolls from a canister atop the bat rack. He learned another valuable early lesson when one of his father's players always screamed and threw his helmet after making an out at the plate. Ryan never forgot those images. It didn't look good then, and he aimed to never mimic those counterproductive actions.

At Chaparral High School in Mesa, Arizona, Scott had his first physical challenge when the medial epicondyle tendon on the inside of his right elbow detached from the humerus bone. The forearm muscles, responsible for finger and wrist movements, connect at the epicondyle. A doctor for a major league team declined to perform the necessary operation because he wasn't sure if screwing the tendon back into the humerus would shatter the bone.

The Scotts thanked him for his candor and turned to Steve Mirabello, a Blue Jays team physician who had performed two such successful surgeries. Dick Scott flew with Ryan to Florida, where Mirabello performed the surgery. Ryan's right arm was in a brace for six weeks. He missed his entire junior season and part of his senior year. He had a frozen elbow from his arm's being immobilized for so long.

In a classy move, the Blue Jays picked Ryan in the thirty-second round of the draft after his senior year. Nobody knows our pitchers better, a Toronto executive told him, you've been catching them for so long. But that guy knew Dick Scott had wanted his oldest son to get his education. When you're ready to turn pro, call us, the executive told Ryan. His friends had been excited about Ryan's getting drafted; Ryan wasn't unhappy, but he wanted to be recognized for his own abilities.

Kristin Scott held her right forefinger an inch from her thumb; that represented the stack of letters her son had received from colleges that were interested in recruiting him before his injury. After Ryan had healed, he weighed his future: should he go to a four-year school and maybe get sent to a junior college anyway, or go the JC route from the start to ensure he'd get playing time?

At a tournament in Las Vegas, Ryan caught the eye of CSN assistant coach Jay Guest. The next day, Cooper Fouts, the Coyotes' catchers coach, checked out Scott and saw a durable and steady player who would need to add a few pounds. Dick and Kristin were there, but Dick was leery when Ryan told him that someone from the College of Southern Nevada wanted to offer him a scholarship. "I don't think it works like that," Dick hesitatingly responded. Actually, it did work like that. The Scotts met with Coach Chambers the following day and liked what they saw and heard, and they were all comfortable with the coach and his program.

"Nobody—not me, my wife, or Ryan—knew what all this meant for Ryan," Dick said. "For any parent, you want your son to do something he loves, and to be around people who will take care of him and look after him, and do what's best for him. We felt that was all possible there."

Dick Scott had watched teammates of Ryan's go to USC and UCLA, where they languished on the bench. Dick had told Ryan and his friends that it's most important to stay active, getting at bats and innings. Wherever that can happen, so be it. Playing is more important than going to a prestigious institution to please the parents and rusting away on the bench.

Dick Scott remembered his first telephone conversation with Ryan after it was clear that Bryce Harper would play at CSN. *Babe fucking Ruth?* Dick told Ryan it's not a big deal, that "you two are on different career paths." He wanted Ryan to help Bryce because that's how it goes in baseball, veterans taking time for the younger guys. "That's how you're supposed to do it in sports," Dick said. "Ryan's been around the game long enough to know that's how it's supposed to be done."

Dick Scott said the word on Harper, in major league circles, was wait and see. When you see Albert Pujols, Ryan Howard, Derek Jeter, and Roy Oswalt perform at such a high level day after day, and season after season, it's difficult to be impressed by someone who has never played a game at the elite level of the sport. Until then . . .

"And it's not a knock on Bryce," Dick Scott said. "The *SI* story got his name into a lot of clubhouses. People at the major league level, their reaction is . . . whatever. They see great players every day. To be impressed with a high school kid that is being compared to the next LeBron James . . . okay. As soon as he gets here and starts proving it, great. Until then, it's not a story. Pujols was not a common name until he was drafted. Now he has the best ten years of stats in the history of baseball. That's the beauty of it. Guys are not spending a lot of time talking about [Harper]. Sure, with scouting directors, like the Washington Nationals', there's a lot of discussion.

"But with Bryce, the difficult part is yet to come. Getting his GED and passing on two years of high school, that's his call and his parents' call. They seem to be very grounded. I can't fault them. But it's going to be difficult. Signing to play pro ball isn't everything it's cracked up to be for younger people. Bryce is a talented guy. He has a lot of confidence, which will assist him greatly. Hopefully, he continues to mature at the rate he has. That's the downfall of a lot of players who get into baseball: handling adversity. When he finally signs, the clock starts. Hopefully, he ends up in an organization that is extremely patient and understands that he will only be eighteen his first year. He won't be a big leaguer in his first year. He'll have ups and downs that he'll have to manage."

All that Bryce Harper had to manage, as soon as he showed up at CSN, bowled over his teammates. Ryan Scott couldn't comprehend how Harper could handle all of the attention, demands, and expectations that had been heaped upon him at such a young age. Ryan was three years older than Bryce, and Ryan had no idea how he could have survived with the constant pressure that must have felt like an ever-tightening noose.

"But he comes out every day and does his deal, and it doesn't really faze him. People here haven't experienced that. But he's been on that level before. He knows what he's doing. He's pretty experienced in that field, handling it. He's pretty humble for a kid in his situation."

Ryan eventually talked with sports psychologist Ray Karesky, a protégé of Harvey Dorfman, who wrote *The Mental Game of Baseball* with Karl Kuehl. Ryan's father gave him a copy long ago. Infielder Alex Rodriguez and pitcher Roy Halladay have credited Dorfman, a former teacher and writer who started seeing Oakland Athletics players in the 1980s, for saving their careers. Ryan also read Dorfman's *Mental Keys to Hitting: A Handbook of Strategies for Performance Enhancement* on road trips during the season. Donnie Roach dog-eared Dorfman's *Mental ABC's of Pitching: A Handbook for Performance Enhancement.*

Based in Scottsdale, Arizona, Karesky ran employee assistance programs for the A's, Toronto Blue Jays, and San Diego Padres, and he conducted counseling sessions for the Arizona Diamondbacks, Tampa Bay Rays, Washington Nationals, and the Major League Baseball umpires. He has advised corporate executives, firefighters, and Vietnam War veterans. In an ESPN.com article about Justin Duchscherer's issues, Karesky expanded on the pressures that athletes faced that could be applicable to Bryce Harper or anyone else making a good living by playing the game.

"Just because somebody gives you money and fame doesn't mean it gives you wisdom, common sense, or maturity," Karesky said. "The reality is, ballplayers are in an extremely demanding environment that produces stress they're not trained to deal with. It's a pressure cooker, and over time that stress can build up and take a real toll." Karesky told *Sports Illustrated*, "God wanted to give males something to do to keep them occupied and make them crazy, other than war, [and] he came up with baseball. So much time to think is likely to produce problems, especially if you're a perfectionist."

Unlike the many players who spoke with Karesky and called him Doc Ray, Ryan Scott just called him Ray. Dick Scott had befriended Karesky years earlier, and Ryan remembered making small talk with Karesky on many diamonds. Karesky has had meals in the Scott home, and he was always a text message away from Ryan. Karesky declined to discuss his chats with Ryan Scott with me. Ryan called his conversations with Karesky informal and helpful. Karesky told Scott that he couldn't be Bryce Harper. Scott couldn't hit like him or play like him. Nobody could. "You have to be yourself. You must have your own approach," Karesky said. For the first time, Scott seriously addressed developing the mental aspects of his game. He zapped every negative or selfish thought, minute as some were, turning every practice into healthy competition to make himself, and Harper, better. Anything else would have been counterproductive.

Still, the challenges seemed constant. During Ryan's recruiting trips to the University of San Diego and Cal State Fullerton, coaches and players spent the first fifteen or twenty minutes asking Scott about Harper. Is he *that* good? Is he a jerk? Many outsiders seemed to see only the war paint or an interview, in which Harper's confidence came across as arrogant or cocky, and made rash conclusions on the kid based on scant evidence. He's a seventeen-year-old kid and he's a good kid, Scott told them. As Chambers said, if you don't want the answer, don't ask the question.

Dick Scott told Ryan and some of his CSN teammates how the 2010 season could be special, that they had a chance to do something that a lot of kids only dreamed about. "A lot of times, kids are looking at the next 'best thing,' where they'll go to school their junior years, where they'll be drafted, can mom and dad afford 'this'? But those guys have to look at what's happening *now*. You don't always get that opportunity to be in a good place and possibly play in a [junior] college World Series."

Of all the personnel that Coach Chambers had assembled for support, Kevin Higgins dealt with the most striking dilemma. The five-foot-eleven former infielder rose through Los Angeles Harbor College, a junior college, to earn Division I All-America honors at Arizona State, helping the Sun Devils play for a national championship against Stanford. And he was the lone Coyotes assistant coach who had scraped his way to the big leagues, for the San Diego Padres. He should have talked. Others should have listened.

However, Higgins—Higgy to every Coyote—often kept his mouth shut because, even with all that experience and knowledge, he wasn't on the CSN payroll. Running a sign company was one of several family priorities that kept him from showing up at the diamond every day. It wasn't uncommon for a week to pass without seeing the forty-three-year-old Higgins at Morse Stadium. He'd show up with full facial hair. The next week, he'd be clean-shaven. The next week, he'd be wearing a salt-and-pepper goatee looking like U2 guitarist The Edge, *Joshua Tree* era. Higgins missed road trips. When he attended practice, he'd see other assistants giving improper instructions or direction, or a player holding his glove the wrong way, but he didn't feel it was proper to act like a full-timer.

That didn't mean he didn't have influence or always wore a muzzle. When the Coyotes believed they had been hoodwinked by umpires at Western Nevada, Higgins would take center stage in an Oscar-worthy performance. But his irregular appearances made it difficult to get to know him. Only after a clinic for his son and his Little League teammates did the other parents discover Higgins's history with the game when they stumbled into his trophy room during a team pizza party. They saw his thirteen baseball cards and the dugout lineup placard from his major league debut. We had no idea, they told him.

Finally, over a beer one night long after a game, Higgins talked about his past. He had RIP and GONE FISHIN' tattoos on his right shoulder in tribute to his late father. While attending Los Angeles Harbor College, he had committed to Nebraska, but only with a nonbinding verbal commitment. Arizona State coach Jim Brock, whose Sun Devils were in Southern California to play UCLA, dropped by Higgins's Redondo Beach apartment to sign him at two minutes past midnight on signing day.

"It can happen just like that," Higgins said. "I never thought I was good enough to get a scholarship to a place like that."

He quickly realized that the league's reigning player of the year, a second baseman, was returning to Arizona State the following season. "I thought, 'Oh, shit, what did I just do?' " said Higgins, who played second. "My 'Bryce Moment.' Oh, shit! You question yourself and your ability." He beat out the player to start at second base and was named captain in fall practice. "I always tell my kids, you have to be willing to learn and play the game the right way. If possible, with a little luck and being in the right place at the right time, a little bit of talent can take you far."

His determination to reach the majors, and his stories, inspired and entertained every Coyote. San Diego had picked him in the twelfth round of the 1989 draft and signed him for $2,500. At Triple-A Las Vegas, Higgins once played all nine positions in a game. He made his major league debut on May 29, 1993, and collected 40 hits in 181 at bats during his only season in the majors. "But I hit well in Montreal and Candlestick Park [in San Francisco]," he said. He had one triple, "in

Philadelphia." Higgins went to the plate eight times against Las Vegas legend and occasional golf-foursome mate Greg Maddux and hit two singles, with a walk and a pair of strikeouts.

One of his Padres teammates had been shortstop Kurt Stillwell, who hit .215 that season and went on to work for agent Scott Boras, who had wisely assigned Stillwell to advise Ron and Sheri Harper.

One night in Reno, playing for the Triple-A Las Vegas Stars, Higgins and Doug Brocail took young teammate Joey Hamilton out to a Western-themed bar that featured a mechanical bull. When Hamilton climbed aboard, Higgins slyly handed the patron a few twenties to twist the dial to ten. The bull's first move was a swift jolt up from the front, kind of what Bodacious did to Tuff Hedeman. Hamilton needed twenty-seven stitches to patch his chin, which just . . . kept . . . bleeding. Manager Russ Nixon implored Higgy and Brocail to leave the young guys alone.

When Higgins was with the Padres, slugger Fred McGriff invited him to the back of the plane for a poker game. Higgins had $1,300. He went on a winning streak and stepped off the plane with nearly $7,500. In Atlanta, Gary Sheffield escorted Higgins on a shopping spree that included a stop at the famous Friedman's shoe and clothing store. Gonna play in the big leagues, Sheffield said, gotta look like a big leaguer. The suits, dress shirts, slacks, and shoes cost more than $6,000. Sheffield paid the tab.

Several CSN players told Higgins they had seen him on the MLB Network, when it ran a feature about a July 2, 1993, doubleheader in Philadelphia that took twelve hours and five minutes to complete. San Diego won the first, 5–2, and lost the second, 6–5, in ten innings. It's the longest elapsed time for a doubleheader, involving an extra-inning game, in major league history.

"Seven rain delays!" Higgins said. "That was an ugly night."

At spring training in Yuma, Arizona, Higgins and Brocail, roommates who always had high jinks on their minds, snuck into first baseman Dave Staton's hotel room and dropped a rancid elk steak into the breast pocket of one of Staton's sport coats in the closet. Staton and his roommate complained of the horrible smell in their room for days. They tore it apart and finally discovered the steak and the pranksters.

Later that week, Higgins, Brocail (nicknamed Broke), and other teammates celebrated St. Patrick's Day with a few green beers. They returned to the hotel to sleep, but Higgins couldn't get comfortable and noted, "Broke, it feels like something's moving under my bed." Higgins turned on a light, and a rat the size of a loaf of bread scampered out from beneath his box spring. When one bolted out from under Brocail's bed, the players, wearing only boxers, quickly slipped on their cowboy boots. They grabbed golf clubs and stood on their mattresses. Higgins wiped one out against the wall with a seven-iron. In the hall, Staton and teammates cried with laughter. They had put the rats under the beds, in the wooden support structure, with big blocks of cheese.

"We called a truce right then," said Higgins.

Higgins played for Las Vegas from 1990 through 1992. In 1994 he hit .309 for the Stars in his final professional campaign. A rash of injuries had taken their toll. By the time he quit the game, he and his wife, Debbie, called Las Vegas home. She managed payroll at the Mirage, which had begun the megaresort phase on the Strip when Steve Wynn opened it in 1989.

Kevin had a lucrative job selling automobiles. He had also been influential in starting—and maintaining, as its chairman—the Southern Nevada Sports Hall of Fame in 1997. That Hall inducted Greg Maddux in 2002. Higgins had worked as a radio analyst for the Las Vegas 51s, the Triple-A franchise for the Toronto Blue Jays, during the 2009 season.

Higgins had six of his nine knee surgeries done on his left knee; when he bent it, those next to him could hear the bone-on-bone crunch. He spent much of his six years in pro baseball traveling the minor league circuits, which will be the lifestyle some of the Coyotes—the lucky ones—will experience in the coming years.

"Seventy-two games in seventy-four days. Twelve-hour bus rides. And you don't get in the day before a series, like here. You get into a town, after playing, at two in the afternoon. You have batting practice at four. You play the game and then do it all over again. You're looking over your shoulder to see what other guys are doing. In Double-A, you're seeing what guys are doing below you [in Single-A] and above you [in Triple-A]. Bryce won't have to deal with all *that,* but a lot of the others will."

Higgins met Chambers during off-season workouts, in 1992 and 1993, at Bishop Gorman. They stayed in touch. Chambers didn't have an opening on his 2010 staff, but he invited Higgins to help out as a volunteer when his schedule allowed. "A good year to get back into the game," said Higgins, pausing for effect. Indeed, coaching a team with Bryce Harper on it had been a wise move. There could be traps, too, which Ryan Scott, the full-time CSN catcher in 2009, and Tomo Delp, who thought he would start at third on opening night, had discovered.

"Veterans have to adapt to a seventeen-year-old. If you're not that good, you'll be on the bench, because of the situation, and if there are jealousies . . . those are some of the negative aspects that can come with it. But I've been a part of a lot of teams, and from the first guy to the twenty-sixth, or twenty-seventh, I've never seen a team so close, so extremely close, as this one."

Anywhere, at any time, Coyotes broke out in hugs. Maybe that's a baseball thing, as assistant coach Cooper Fouts tried to convince me. I disagreed. CSN had an inordinate tightness. Higgins, in all of his travels and all that he had seen and heard in the game, confirmed the bond of these Coyotes.

"There are no cliques. Bryce has always just been one of the guys. He'll never change who he is or what he's about. That's a credit to his upbringing and his parents. He's been under the spotlight for seven years now, and to handle it the way he does, graciously, is special. His support system and these teammates have taught him the right way to go about it."

Higgins watched Harper sign autograph after autograph, for clutches of kids and fans eager to get a glimpse of him, and was reminded of Cal Ripken and Tony Gwynn, accommodating and even-keeled superstars. Higgins expected Harper to fit into that mold. "Bryce gets who he is and he understands the responsibility to the game and the people, who will eventually be paying [his] salary."

Higgins tried to give Harper's season some perspective. Of all the players he had ever seen and competed with and against, Harper easily made Higgins's list of top three players.

"And that's at seventeen. I've never seen anyone at twenty that approaches his talent. He's a five-tool player that can play four positions. He has to stay healthy. That's a huge part of it. Time will tell whether he'll be an all-star, or whatnot, but I think he'll be making an acceptance speech [in Cooperstown, New York] five years after he retires."

Bryce Harper hitting at Morse Stadium with his dugout behind him.

(Rob Miech)

Bryce Harper swings a pink bat, a common Mother's Day practice by major leaguers, in Salt Lake City.

(Rob Miech)

Morse Stadium at dusk. The Strip is just starting to glisten at the far right.   *(Rob Miech)*

Morse Stadium in the late afternoon, looking southeast, during a 2010 game. *(Rob Miech)*

The entrance to Morse Stadium, home of the 2003 National Junior College baseball champions. *(Rob Miech)*

Harper with MLB Network's Jonathan Mayo after a locker-room interview.

(Rob Miech)

Harper and second baseman Scott Dysinger after a victory in the conference tournament. Harper is wearing the jersey that Dysinger would don for CSN's final game in the Junior College World Series in Grand Junction, Colorado.

(Rob Miech)

Harper applies his infamous eye black, in his reflection off assistant coach Cooper Fouts's sunglasses, before the final Western District doubleheader in Lamar, Colorado. He would go six-for-six, with four homers, to drive in ten runs in the second game to vault the Coyotes to the Junior College World Series in Grand Junction, Colorado.

(Rob Miech)

Bryce Harper applies his Franklin eye black, in big blocks, under Marvin Campbell's eyes at the Junior College World Series.

(Rob Miech)

Harper chats with ace pitcher Donnie Roach *(left)* in between games in Lamar, Colorado.

(Rob Miech)

Bryce Harper gets mobbed for his autograph at the Junior College World Series in Grand Junction, Colorado.

(Rob Miech)

CSN coach Tim Chambers during an MLB Network interview.

(Rob Miech)

(Left to right): Bryce Harper, Gabe Weidenaar, and Bryan Harper keep their eyes on the volleyball during an off-day barbecue at the Junior College World Series.

(Rob Miech)

Bryan (number 33) and Bryce Harper are flanked by their grandparents, Jim and Joan Brooks. Between the Harpers, Marvin Campbell holds the Western District championship trophy. *(Rob Miech)*

The lieutenants to Coach Chambers *(left to right):* Mr. C (Robert Cox), Glen Evans, Kevin Higgins, Marc Morse, Cooper Fouts, trainer Steve Jacobucci, Steve Chatham, and Jay Guest, at the pre-Junior College World Series banquet in Grand Junction, Colorado. *(Rob Miech)*

Reliever Aaron Kurcz goofs in the dugout during a lull. Behind Kurcz, to his left, sits Sean "Showtime" Larimer.

(Rob Miech)

Infielder Casey Sato *(left)* and first baseman Trent Cook, both of who were enriched by taking Mormon missions, after practice.
(Rob Miech)

Marvin Campbell gets slapped with a shaving-cream pie after CSN wins its conference tournament.
(Rob Miech)

Outfielder Trevor Kirk with his grandfather, Harold Shrader, who always played sports like he "had a pair." The Coyotes had just defeated Western Nevada in their conference tournament to advance to the Western District championship in Lamar, Colorado.
(Rob Miech)

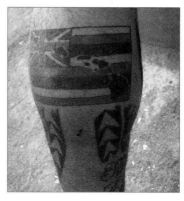

Shortstop and Honolulu native Danny Higa wears his heart on his left calf, where he features a tattoo of the Hawaiian flag.
(Rob Miech)

Robert Cox, the volunteer assistant coach known by all as Mr. C, outside Morse Stadium. *(Rob Miech)*

The author gingerly makes his way back from the lavatory on the CSN coach. *(Rob Miech)*

11

COACH CHAMBERS EXPLODED AT the end of the practice. A Washington Nationals scout had attended the session, but Chambers didn't cool his words with company inside his stadium. This is hardly the time to be complacent and lazy, he yelled. "The field was not ready when we started today!" Chambers yelled. Assistant coaches did extra work to prep the grass and the infield.

"Get it together!" Chambers said. "This is no time to start slacking off! We can still finish forty-eight and eight, which would be our best regular season ever. We're off to a good start. Don't start taking it easy! Now get to the line!"

Sprints were coming, probably more than a few, from the right-field foul line to center field. Some Coyotes grumbled as they slogged out to the line. Assistant coaches Jay Guest and Cooper Fouts, who remained behind on the dugout rail, smiled and whispered, "Watch this." Chambers implored his players to pick up their pace. They were dragging from the three-hour practice, and now they would have to run sixty-yard dash after sixty-yard dash. Chambers told them all to get the tips of their cleats to the line. He told them to pay more attention to detail in the coming days and weeks. Chambers raised his voice and . . .

"Okay, let's *all* . . . go home!"

April Fools'. Yup, it was April 1. The players clapped, hollered, or fell to the ground, happy that the day was done. Bryce Harper just sighed a little, smiled, turned around, gathered his equipment, and ducked inside the clubhouse. After winning fourteen of their first sixteen conference games, the Coyotes were in fine shape. Overall, they were 27-5 and rolling after hammering the ball in Utah the previous weekend. Chambers saw no need for extra exertion. Rest was in order.

Trevor Kirk, wearing a black boot on his right foot after aggravating his ankle injury in Utah, hobbled around and caught the groin of a teammate or two with the back of his right palm.

Marvin Campbell looked forward to a checkup call with Dr. Hamilton. Campbell beamed about his newfound vision. Basically, he focused on something—the top of a flagpole, even a tree—in the distance in the seconds before a pitcher threw the ball. That helped him concentrate on a tight, boxed area in which the ball would be delivered. Away from the field, someone would hold a finger near a picture frame and slowly walk toward Campbell, who focused on the fingertip, to improve his focusing abilities.

Campbell said Dr. Hamilton could tell, from a series of tests, that his right eye had become stronger in just two weeks. As Campbell left the office, he noticed a framed picture of CSN's 2003 national championship team on a wall. "You know," Hamilton said, "I have room for another one." Campbell smiled as he left.

The first weekend of April, though, turned out to be forgettable for Bryce Harper. He walked into the dugout before the first game of a series-opening doubleheader against Salt Lake Community College holding a coin. "Hey, just found a nickel," he said. "Is that good luck?" Not if it's tails down it isn't, said Tyler Hanks. "Throw that shit away." Harper turned around and tossed it away with contempt, as if the thing had scalded his fingers. Judging by his next twenty-four hours or so, Harper should not have picked up the coin.

Freshman reserve shortstop Wes Hunt, who had a blond patch under his lower lip, had been popped in the throat and upper lip by bad-bounce grounders at shortstop in practice a day earlier. He shook his head at how the rest of his day went. One gag had led to another with roommate Ryan Scott, the Evil Genius. Hunt couldn't get into his computer or two iPods—Scott had altered the entry passwords on both. When Tomo Delp and Hunt left to get some Copenhagen at a nearby convenience store, in ten minutes Scott, his girlfriend, and pitchers Chasen Shreve and Bryan Harper had switched everything from Hunt's room to Canadian pitcher Burke Seifrit's, and vice versa. Hunt just lowered his head and closed his eyes. "He's so evil," said Hunt.

Seifrit took what Scott and Bryan Harper did to his Nissan Altima with a laugh; Scott and Harper had wrapped a few miles of Saran wrap, a CostCo superpack, around Seifrit's rig. The keys were visible in the wrap on the driver's door. All of Seifrit's possessions were inside his Altima. Seifrit smiled as he tore through the layers of clingy plastic with a knife.

When Trace Evans, the stout, ten-year-old son of stout pitching coach Glen Evans, cruised through the dugout and didn't see his dad, he wondered aloud, "Hey, where's my dad?" A moment later, Scott said, "I don't know, but he left us a note. 'Take care of Trace.'"

The edge came when anyone messed with Scott, a computer expert. Scott got even with pitcher Matt Gardner by sending him a photograph of an old, naked lady in a tub, with a picture of Scott's face superimposed over hers, at the end of the 2009 season. Gardner had been pestering Scott all season, tripping him in the dugout, turning a hose on him, and calling him Skeletor because of Scott's 165-pound frame. Scott sought revenge. He set up Gardner for weeks, posing as a supposed online babe who lived nearby and promising a blind-date meeting, and fun. Voilà! The Wicked Witch of the West, nude and bearing Scott's smiling mug, finally showed up on Gardner's computer screen as teammates looked on. Embarrassed, he bolted out of the CSN clubhouse.

Kirk, nursing his sore right ankle, moved around slowly in shorts and a gray Coyotes T-shirt. He pointed out a color newspaper photograph that had made its way onto a clubhouse bulletin board—a blond-haired, pudgy Bryce Harper accepting an award at a tournament in Cooperstown, New York, at the age of twelve. Above it on the board were color photos of Barry Bonds and Carlos Delgado in full swing. "Even at twelve he could mash it," said Kirk, pointing at Harper. "He could hit it out of here" at spacious Morse Stadium.

Maybe they didn't show it often, if at all, but every Coyote had been a fan of their famous teammate's.

"We ain't scored *yet*?" Donnie Roach said seconds after the national anthem as he walked into the dugout. As the lineups were announced over the speakers, assistant coach Kevin Higgins paused when J. R. Rowland was announced for Salt Lake. "Didn't he write the *Harry Potter* stuff?" Higgins said. "That's *J. K. Rowling*, Higgy! A *she*!" Dysinger shot back. When Rowland stepped into the batter's box in the first inning, Dysinger yelled, "C'mon, Harry!"

Bryan Harper and a few teammates, after some disagreement, walked up to Marvin Campbell and asked him which singer is "more black," Justin Timberlake or Eminem? For one second, they waited for the decisive word to settle this latest major debate. Justin Timberlake, Campbell concluded. "Easy. He has more soul."

For all the banter going on around him, Bryce Harper often wasn't in the middle of shenanigans, laughs, or jokes. In the dugout, he usually sat at the far left side in one of three white plastic chairs just outside the dugout, where the batters in the hole awaited, and Chambers and other coaches discussed strategy. When Harper wasn't due up, and if he was catching, he sat just inside that end of the dugout on the bench. He was always close by when any of them had a tip for him or he had a question.

Against Salt Lake, when Harper fouled his second pitch straight back into the netting, nearly every teammate let loose a low "Ooooooooh!" in unison. He had just missed belting it into Utah. Harper wound up striking out. That was usually grounds for him to smack his helmet against the bench or the dugout floor, but this time he was more reserved and just slipped it into a wall slot.

Harper walked and eventually scored the first run of a nine-run fourth inning, and he came across home for the ninth run after singling, taking second on a wild pitch, and scoring on a Trent Cook single. In the sixth, Harper smacked a ball to deep center field, just right of dead straight, that was caught at the base of the wall—about four hundred feet from home plate. The wind blew from right to left, likely holding up the ball. The shot had weighed on Harper.

It's a wonder his helmet didn't shatter into a hundred pieces after he threw it to the dugout floor with such ferocity. Three batters later, he sat on the dugout bench and said, "That was thirteen!" as he stared straight ahead. That was it. He had wanted the CSN record. After the 10–2 victory, Harper still dwelled on the one that got away. He exchanged vector theories, with infielder Danny Higa and assistant coach Steve Chatham, on how that thing had stayed inside the park. The trajectory angle, they agreed, had been too high. It got caught up in the wind, maybe. In either gap, in right center or left center, they concluded, it would have been gone.

"I hit that so hard," Harper said. "*So hard.*"

Several Coyotes talked about signing their first autographs. Kids congregated in a walkway between the dugout and the clubhouse to get Harper's autograph, and they stuck around to get anyone else's signature. Ryan Thomas sheepishly returned to the dugout. "A kid just asked me, 'Are you Bryce Harper?' I said, 'Yeah,' and I signed," said Thomas, smiling. "I'm sure I'll get popped by the FBI for identity fraud."

In the second game, Harper grounded out to second and struck out in the third inning. He was so incensed at the whiff he slammed his black bat on home plate, shattering it in half. He had flashed his anger in an incredibly public way. He had flared his temper in full view for the world. The shocked umpire and the opposing catcher didn't move or say a peep.

It brought to mind the massive self-expectations, and destruction, of another highly rated player. In 1980, the New York Mets took outfielder Billy Beane with the twenty-third overall pick in the first round of the draft. Beane's implosion had been monumental. Scouts didn't seem to care how this exceptional five-tool player behaved as he threw helmets and hit whatever he could in the dugout with his bat when he didn't perform at the plate, when the inevitable frustrations of the game vexed Beane.

It's all in *Moneyball,* Michael Lewis's outstanding book on how Beane transformed the player evaluation process as general manager of the Oakland A's. The cautionary tale lies in Beane's longevity in the front office rather than on the professional diamond, because of his tantrums. Relief pitchers sped down to the dugout to see what Beane would do next after a poor at bat. Teammates lost count of how many bats he busted on those walls. He once wrecked a toilet. Another time he went after a fan. The batter's box had been described as Beane's personal hell. One or two poor plate appearances would ensure he'd be useless in the third and fourth at bats.

In a six-run fifth that decided the second game, Bryce Harper singled, stole second, and scored on Marvin Campbell's bloop single. An inning later, Harper's hustle again paid dividends when he walked and stole second and third on consecutive pitches. Stealing third always is ideal, Chambers preached, immediately after swiping second. The pitcher, he said, just gives second a cursory glance. Chambers, in the third-base coach's box, gave Harper the steal sign by pointing his left index finger into his left hip. Harper scored on a double-play grounder.

In the Saturday doubleheader, Harper singled, stole second, and scored in the third inning of a 4–1 victory over Salt Lake. In the nightcap, he grounded out to second in the second inning. "Get your ass down the line!" Scott Dysinger yelled as Harper jogged to first base. When Harper reached the dugout, he again slammed his helmet into the ground and it caromed around.

Harper kept walking, outside the dugout and into a clubhouse that he thought was empty. He slammed everything in his way. When he reached his cubicle, he hit the sides with his hands and made a commotion that drew Don Cooper from the laundry room, where the seventy-three-year-old former pilot had been bleaching all of the Coyotes' pin-striped uniforms. Cooper held one as he peered around the corner to check out the tornado that had just touched down.

Harper flinched when he noticed he wasn't the only one in the small locker room. Fit with trim gray hair, Cooper hailed from Bartlesville, Oklahoma, which endeared him to Chambers. Cooper had flown private jets for Las Vegas hotel magnate Steve Wynn. He also flew commercial aircraft, and on December 11, 1988, he served as a reserve pilot on Pan Am Flight 103 from London to New York. Had Cooper assumed that post ten days later, he would have been on the Flight 103 that blew up over Lockerbie, Scotland. A terrorist's bomb killed 259 people on the plane, and 11 on the ground. Cooper kept his cockpit pass, a bit smaller than a business envelope, from that 1988 voyage in a sealed clear bag as a tribute to those who perished in the tragedy.

He placed a hand on Harper's arm and said, "Bryce, you've got a long way to go buddy. You've got to cool it." Harper didn't respond. Cooper thought Harper appreciated the heartfelt words. Later, Cooper reflected on Harper, the incredibly high standards he had set for himself, and that explosive temper. "That's in all the good ones. I'd be fifteen times worse."

In the fifth inning of that second game, Harper had singled and made his way to third base when the opposing pitcher threw to first base to try to pick off Marvin Campbell. Harper dashed for home. The ball appeared to beat him to the plate, but Harper jarred it from the catcher's mitt as he slid home with CSN's second run. CSN didn't score again and lost, 3–2.

CSN was 30-6 overall and 17-3 in the Scenic West Athletic Conference. As speculation heated up about Coach Chambers replacing Buddy Gouldsmith at UNLV, Chambers had some stern words for

Harper in their weekly meeting the Monday after the Salt Lake series. There will be no more throwing the batting helmet in the dugout, Chambers insisted. No more smashing a bat on home plate. "Yes, sir," Harper said.

That afternoon, Harper finished his work in the CSN batting cages and sat on a concrete embankment at the back of the pitchers' bull-pen mound. He watched a high school team from Utah warm up for a game that night at Morse Stadium. He was alone in the half-light. He gazed out at the giggling kids, some who were older than him. Soon enough, in a stressful stretch, he would inform Chambers of his most personal thoughts about not wanting to be a superstar, about how he just wanted to be a kid again, to enjoy playing the game as he did in high school. However, as he watched the Utah players throw the ball around, joke, and goof off, he didn't look weary and wore no pained expressions.

Bryce Harper yawned.

WITH THE SHARPEST SENSE of timing, pitcher Donnie Roach bounced out of the CSN clubhouse in the sixth inning of the second game of the second doubleheader against the College of Southern Idaho at Morse Stadium the second weekend of April. Bryce Harper had dropped two fly balls hit directly at him in right field; the sun had played havoc with his vision. A year would pass before someone finally forced Harper to have his eyes examined. At the moment, Coach Chambers showed his irritation with his young star player.

"Guess the eye black isn't working?" Chambers deadpanned in the dugout. Or the sunglasses. "I'll have to replace you with someone who can catch," Chambers chirped out to Harper, warming up with a team-mate in shallow right field before an inning. The coach and the prodigy were beginning to wear on each other. The rubber band of their relationship, their friendship, was stretching, tightening by the day.

No matter, for Donnie Roach knew how the team's, and Harper's, heart beat. He knew how personal Harper took any minute error, failure, or miscue. So Roach entered, dugout right, with his own Harper-like eye black blazing. The war paint looked like the state of Florida, but thicker, under Roach's left eye. His right was a mirror image. Just like Harper, batting gloves stuck out of Roach's rear pockets. He swung a bat like Babe Ruth from a newsreel.

Harper smiled and laughed, dropping his shoulder and closing his eyes as his head tilted toward the ground, making him forget about how he had twice looked like a Little Leaguer. "We were a little tight," Roach said. "I was just trying to mess around, trying to get everyone loose. Joking around. Nothing too big."

It had not been an ordinary week for Harper. Then again, there had been nothing ordinary about the season he was writing, so it might have been business as usual when he stepped to home plate for batting practice on Thursday, April 8, and smashed—absolutely bruised—the ball. The sound of the ball jumping off his bat sounded like a .44 Magnum. Explosions came every four or five seconds like wrecking balls echoing off the outfield walls.

Asked about that performance, between games of the second doubleheader against CSI, Harper acknowledged it was not a usual batting practice. Something had gotten under his skin, ticked him off and driven him. What was it?

"Everything."

He might have just missed another home run or two in recent games, but Harper had also had that talk with Chambers about his helmet-bashing and bat-smashing antics. Something was building, or bubbling, like molten lava just below Harper's surface.

In the first game of the CSI doubleheader, Harper wore gloves while hitting. He did not drop his bat or grab handfuls of dirt and spit into his hands. He lined out to third base his first time up. He returned to the dugout, handed his black bat to a teammate, and softly placed his helmet in its slot in the dugout wall—the kinder, gentler Bryce that Chambers had demanded in their Monday meeting. It didn't last long.

In the fourth, he bounced out to first base. Entering the far right side of the dugout, Harper yelled, "Fuck!" and furiously tossed his helmet, then his gloves, into the ground. When he put his catcher's gear on, he sat on the bench with his head in his hands, staring at the ground. He clasped his hands in front of him without moving his head.

Chambers admitted that he had been employing a double standard. Harper was getting away with plenty with the heated throwing of his equipment. But the rest of the Coyotes, who wouldn't have been able to get away with such juvenile tantrums, knew what was going on. They knew it from that practice game against Fullerton in Cashman Field, when Bryce drew that line in the dirt with his bat and had not been penalized, in any way, for the gross indiscretion. This situation, this kid, and this season were different from anything any of them would ever experience.

Some of them, like those former teammates of Billy Beane's who couldn't resist witnessing his next act of self-destruction, looked to see what was coming next. Some glanced after an object had been flung or rifled somewhere. It became part of the program. But because Chambers had so many veterans on the squad, Chambers knew nobody would make a big deal of Bryce Harper's petulance.

Roach paced the dugout with a small red-brown mark on the seat of his pants. Someone asked him if he had "shat" himself, and Roach, nonchalantly in between strides, just said he had sat on a piece of gum. He was in a zone, so it would take plenty to distract him from an eventual 2–1 victory. A little stain on the rear of his pants didn't even register on his radar, nor did Harper's continued battering of his batting helmet on anything in the dugout.

In the top of the seventh, Roach threw a seventy-seven-mile-an-hour breaking pitch to a foe on a three-two count for the first out of the inning. Gentry Croft, the sophomore, right-handed pitcher redshirting with shoulder tightness, explained that that's why Roach was so superior. "He has a fast tempo, he's composed, and he never falls behind," Croft said after offering me the first bite of a Snickers bar. I declined. "Plus, he throws ninety-four. But he's not afraid to throw that breaking stuff on a three-two count. Filthy."

In his final at bat in the sixth, just before Marvin Campbell doubled in Scott Dysinger with the go-ahead and eventual winning run, Harper returned to some normalcy by shedding his batting gloves, tossing his bat in the dirt upon reaching home plate, and grabbing three scoops of dirt before settling in. "C'mon, Bryce-a-roni!" Gabe Weidenaar yelled. After Harper flied out to right field, he lobbed his helmet at the ground, where it caromed below my right foot, as he entered the dugout.

He started the second game with a single to right-center field as the setting sun turned the River Mountains beyond right a golden hue. But after flying out to right in the third, Harper sat on the bench, tormented once again, with his head in his hands, once again, and stared at the ground. The pressure he put on himself, every time he grabbed a bat, was indescribable. Forget the words of any critic, scout, recruiter, or opponent; if Harper did not do something thrilling almost every time he stepped to the plate, in his mind something was terribly wrong. He was inconsolable.

He was like a matador. It was him against the world.

In the fifth, clouds of blue-gray smoke from hamburgers and hot dogs on Bo's concessions barbecue drifted by the end of the dugout and engulfed the home-plate area. With no gloves and three scoops of the dirt, and one final swipe at the ground with his right hand before settling into his wide stance before the first pitch, Harper belted the first delivery from Tyler Vavra over the left-center fence for a school-record thirteenth home run of the season.

Harper exchanged wide smiles and big hugs for everyone in the dugout, including Wes Hunt and Burke Siefrit, reliever Aaron Kurcz, and pitching coach Glen Evans.

Saturday, in the first of two, Bryce was hit in the right thigh by CSI pitcher Casey Lish. Payback for last night's homer, Harper's teammates said. Harper wanted it that way. Don't hit a teammate for something he did. And he belted number fourteen in the third inning.

When the doubleheader started at noon, it had been about eighty degrees and sunny, but an ill southerly wind started howling from right field to left. It created a power alley of which the Coyotes took extreme advantage, but it terrorized the senses. Gusts of crushed red clay, dust, dirt, several varieties of pollen, and whatever else could be lifted from the desert floor kicked up in and around the CSN dugout to make breathing difficult. Matt Medina, charting pitches on white paper bound to a white folder by three rings, constantly wiped the pages clean of the grime.

The miserable mixture seeped in ear holes, nostrils, and eyeballs. Players breathed into their caps for some measure of comfort. Trainer Steve Jacobucci poured saline drops into the eyes of players and coaches in the far-right corner of the dugout, the only area out of harm's way. Rubbing eyes wasn't a remedy because that could scratch a cornea. Dirt could be tasted in the swig of a Pepsi can. Even after showering, it felt as if another were necessary to rid every pore of dirt. It was a preview of the play-off hell into which the Coyotes would descend in a few weeks.

In the fifth, Harper faced the first Ted Williams Shift of his collegiate career. CSI coach Boomer Walker placed shortstop Tanner Craswell just behind and to the right of second base, and second baseman Ryan Cooperstone played out in medium right field, between first and second. Cooperstone grabbed Harper's bouncer way out there and threw to first to get him out. CSN scored six times in the fifth, which led to a 16–5 victory.

CSN assistant coach Marc Morse, whose last name sat high over the stadium's press box, thought of Harper when he watched Ryan Howard, on an MLB Network show, describe how Barry Bonds once helped him deal with exaggerated Ted Williams Shifts. They're playing the Shift, Howard said Bonds told him, you smash the ball to the second baseman, and he throws to first. Why are you mad? You did what you're supposed to do, that's hit the ball hard. You put it where it would normally be a hit. You can't control what they're doing. A guy is throwing ninety or ninety-two, and "it's a round ball hitting a round bat," Bonds said, "and you're going to put that thing in a box, not trying to hit it hard and hope it lands somewhere they aren't playing?"

"Howard said that helped him when he struggled with the Shift," Morse said. "You're oh for four, then you blink, and it's oh for thirty because you let that Shift get in your head. Bryce will have to realize that, because they'll shift on him. But the great thing is that every time they shift on him, he'll drop a drag bunt down on somebody."

Harper could go two for three in a game, with home runs in his first two trips to the plate, but he would fume about failing in that third at bat. Those sky-high expectations of himself, Morse explained, separated and would continue to separate Harper from his peers. Morse saw someone who aimed to have an advantage, hitting better than .500, against pitchers.

"Wait until he's nineteen or twenty, when he has two or three more years under his belt. You might see the next .400 hitter. Then he'll be thinking, once he does hit .400, about .500. Why not? He'll think, 'Why can't I?' That's what's scary about the kid. He's honestly trying to break the mold, the thought process of history in this game that says .300 is good. He says, 'Bullshit, .400 is good. And you know what? I'll do .500.' Watch. Boy, you can't ask for a better mentality."

Morse, who played for Chambers at Bishop Gorman, arranged for the stadium tribute, to his late grandfather William R. Morse, with Chambers and the CSN hierarchy.

In the late 1930s, Bill Morse starred at quarterback at Las Vegas High. He had planned to join his father, Harold, in the legal profession when he heard the reports of the Japanese attack on Pearl Harbor, on December 7, 1941, with two fraternity brothers at the University of Nevada in Reno. Bill Morse became a naval aviator, flying 145 combat missions in the North Atlantic and Pacific Oceans in a TBM Avenger torpedo bomber. When an oil leak covered his canopy in boiling fifty weight, he became the first pilot to safely land his plane on an aircraft carrier at night with no visual aid. The flight-deck officer guided Morse over "the groove," the optimal landing path on the ship. Morse cut the throttle on command. The Avenger's arrestor hook snagged one of

the carrier's three deck cables, halting the plane in an instant and triggering a wild celebration.

Bill Morse started his law practice, which he interrupted for a
year to serve as a district court judge, after the war. After his death in
2004, Marc Morse and Chambers coordinated the dedication of the
stadium to William R. Morse. At Mother's Day dinner with his family, John Morse, William's son who had adopted Marc as an infant,
told Marc how much enjoyment he got from reading about Coyotes
games in the newspaper and always seeing the references to Morse
Stadium.

"It means a lot, more than anybody knows," said thirty-one-year-
old Marc Morse. "William Morse was a great member of this community. He set a lot of legal precedents in this state. The college afforded
us the opportunity to do that and I couldn't be more grateful. That's a
lot of pride for me."

Some in the Las Vegas baseball community were skeptical of
Marc Morse's coaching credentials, he knew, with his last name on
that stadium. But the memories of his grandfather overshadowed what
anyone might think of his own track record as a baseball coach. As for
being adopted and his affluence, Marc Morse said his background is
incredible. "But that's for another story," he said.

Christina Hixson, the executor of the Lied Foundation—whose
vast generosities have benefited many organizations, with hundreds of
millions of dollars in aid, in several states—had been another of the
CSN baseball program's key benefactors. However, Chambers doubted
that the Coyotes would have been able to survive and thrive, with such
a winning tradition, without Marc Morse's financial influence.

In 2003, Morse was studying architecture in Colorado when he
drove to Grand Junction to watch the Coyotes win the Junior College
World Series. Chambers outfitted Morse with a uniform and had him
sit in the dugout, alongside Mr. C, for the ride to the championship.
Afterward, Chambers and his other coaches didn't let Morse say *they*

or *you* in reference to the team. It was *we*. This doesn't happen, they told Morse, without you.

"I did it because I believe in Tim Chambers. He bettered my life as a coach. I had a dad at home, but it was also [Chambers] not letting me get away with shit, holding me accountable for my actions. That's a huge part of growing up." Morse detailed drinking exploits that, in high school and college, were his claims to fame more than any athletic endeavor. Morse said Chambers helped when, in the fall of 2008, Morse sought help to kick his drinking habit.

Chambers had to press Morse, who wanted his donations to the CSN baseball program to remain anonymous, to allow Chambers to publicly recognize him for his assistance. Finally, Morse relented. At a press conference at the stadium, after the Coyotes had won the national title, Chambers leaned over to Morse and said, "You *gotta* let me tell them. No way you don't deserve credit for what you've done to make this possible." Five hundred times, Morse figured, Chambers had asked him to let him divulge his chief benefactor. No, Morse said. Finally, with the national championship, Morse relented.

"My parents were on board with that. It was about developing a program that could stay here to help kids get to the next level, a stepping-stone to UNLV or wherever. It was an opportunity for guys to learn from the guy I learned from."

Soon after that press conference, Morse told Chambers how disenchanted he had been studying architecture. Chambers invited him to come around the stadium. When Morse showed up every day that summer, to work with players in the batting cages with their hitting or in the field with their gloves, Chambers invited Morse onto the staff.

Which led to the highly anticipated 2010 season, coaching a kid that everyone knew would be playing in the big time sooner rather than later, someone earmarked for stardom. Morse detailed the usual adjustment period for eighteen- and nineteen-year-olds to adapt from swinging aluminum to hitting with a wooden bat.

"But what Bryce Harper is doing right now is stupid. These kids struggle for a little bit, at least. You hope they struggle in the fall, then get it going in the spring. Sometimes, it takes a full year. What Bryce is doing is just not normal."

In between games, Harper beamed. This wasn't about just having won a baseball game, either. Something else was up, to where I had to ask him about his happy mood. Goin' to the fair tonight, Harper told me. The Clark County Fair & Rodeo was taking place about an hour to the north in Logandale, Nevada. Jake Owen, the popular country singer, had performed the previous night, and Harper was excited to see Owen that Saturday evening. (Somehow, it wasn't relayed to Harper that Owen had taken off that day for Reno.) Harper couldn't wait to get out of the yard, change into one of his many favorite flannel shirts, and hit the fair.

Harper was in such good spirits en route to the batting cages for some pregame swings he took a teammate's cue when he passed a blond-haired man, maybe in his late thirties or early forties, wearing a blue golf shirt and dark slacks, and standing in front of the club-house.

"Excuse me, but do you know who you look like?" Harper said.

"No, Bryce," the man said. "Who?"

"That guy from the Joe Mauer commercial!"

In a popular video-game commercial, Mauer, the catcher for the Minnesota Twins, told a blond-haired executive, sitting on his desk and on a split screen, that they had fished together in Mexico. I'm not even allowed in Mexico, the guy responded. When Mauer showed the framed eight-by-ten color photo of the two in a boat off the Mexican coast, the blond man said, "Well played, Mauer."

When Harper reached the cages, his father, Ron, asked him if he knew that guy. Nope, Bryce Harper said. Neal Huntington, Ron Harper said, the general manager of the Pittsburgh Pirates, who had the second pick in the Major League Baseball draft behind the Washington Nationals in June.

"We were all stretching and Ryan Scott says, 'That guy looks like the dude from the Joe Mauer commercial,'" Bryce said. "Wow. He really does. That's good. We were all cracking up. So I finally had to ask him if he knew who he looked like. . . . He said, 'That's pretty funny. That's pretty good, but I'm not him.' I told him, 'I know that, I'm just sayin' you look exactly like him.' My dad told me who he was and I thought, 'Ohhhh, are you kidding me? That's even better!'"

Well played, Harper.

In the second game, with Trent Cook on first, Harper singled to right, and Campbell followed with a bouncer to CSI second baseman Blake Lively, who ran at Harper. Never backing away from physical confrontation, Harper barreled into Lively, who hung on to the ball, but the double-play possibility had been foiled. Harper slowly rose, rubbing his left knee—the one that had been tweaked in Idaho. He limped noticeably en route to the dugout.

"[Cook] didn't score on that?" Harper said on the bench, as trainer Steve Jacobucci checked on the knee, to his right. During the confusion on Harper's run to second base, Cook did not try to leave third for home. "Are you kidding? He didn't score on that? Seriously, he didn't score on that?" It was a rare circumstance in which the aggressive Harper, who again dented and discolored his protective helmet on the dugout floor, walls, and bench, showed he could be as demanding on others as he was of himself. His having aimed his anger at Cook, the most unassuming Coyote, added to the impertinence of the emotional display.

The next inning, with Cook on first and Scott Dysinger on second, Harper—who mocked himself by saying, "That's odd," when he finally found his banged-up batting helmet a few feet from my left leg under the bench—strolled to the plate and CSI coach Boomer Walker replaced pitcher Chris Kerns with Tyler Vavra, whose motion and stuff Harper knew well. Harper belted a ball to deep left-center that caught the wind tunnel and might have come close to hitting the roof of a house.

Before the pitch, CSI shortstop Ryan Cooperstone had asked Dysinger, at second, "What do you think he'll do?"

"If he gets a strike, he'll probably park it."

"Really?"

"Yeah, he's pissed he dropped that ball in right field."

"Really, he gets down on himself?"

"He's seventeen!"

Harper reserved the biggest hug in the dugout for Donnie Roach, whose sense of timing proved to be invaluable thirty minutes later.

After Harper dropped a second ball in right field in the top of the fifth inning, which allowed CSI to score a run, he kicked one of four dugout poles so hard it's amazing the bunker didn't collapse or Harper didn't break his left foot.

Roach went to work. He left the dugout, grabbed Harper's Franklin eye black in the clubhouse, and zipped to the mirror in the bathroom. He wrapped his left wrist in tape. He stuck batting gloves in both of his back pockets. He grabbed a bat. He donned a helmet. He bolted out to the dugout, with one out in the top of the sixth, and drew laughs and *Oh my God*s the moment teammates saw him.

"Gonna be a hitter," Roach said. "Gonna be Bryce. I'm Bryce."

When Chambers changed pitchers, Roach ran out to the right-field foul line to keep Harper warm by playing catch with him. Harper doubled over when he saw his mirror image.

"Everyone was a little heavy, pissed off at each other and blaming each other . . . ," Roach said. "I like being the guy that gets things in motion. I've always felt a need to be that guy. I like to show people that there are ways to win. You have to do whatever it takes. It's a game you have to play lighthearted because shit's going to happen."

Skip Walker, the former CSI boss who was assisting his son, said he gained even more respect for Harper seeing him the second time around. Harper had a game plan, Walker said, to go to the opposite field. In all four games, Harper never wavered from that tack.

"That shows pretty good maturity. He stuck with it. I tip my cap to him. He not only hurt us but he adjusted to what he needed to do. That's pretty big at this age. Kids don't always adjust. If they don't have success, they'll go back. He stayed with it for four ball games and did a very, very good job. I think he believes he can probably do about anything."

In the sixth inning, the Eagles gave Harper an intentional pass to first base. Skip Walker told pitcher Casey Lish not to even think about getting one of those wide pitches anywhere close to the plate. "He'll reach out and hit it, I bet," Walker told Lish.

Told that Harper did just that on opening night, smacking a pitch that was intended to be an intentional ball to deep center field for a sacrifice fly, stunning everyone in Morse Stadium, Walker laughed.

"He's gifted. But he uses his gifts the right way. Here's a kid that's seventeen, and he's got good instincts for this game, really, really good instincts. Going the other way was the biggest thing. That's huge. And when I watch him behind the plate, he's really aware of the runners. He's not afraid to throw it. You can see he's always ready to make a play. That's pretty good."

The second time around, much less chatter came from the CSI dugout when Harper, eye black blazing, dirt grabbing, and hand spitting, stepped into the batter's box. But some stared and incredulously shook their heads. Walker called that jealousy. Harper could do a backflip into the batter's box and it wouldn't surprise Walker, he said. Harper's routine was just part of his makeup that the CSI players didn't understand. Walker predicted that Harper would lose the "war paint," and maybe a few other habits, at the next level.

"They have a way . . . especially in the minor leagues . . . of saying, 'Eh, it's *our* way or Trailways.' They're a little stricter in the minor leagues with their prospects. He'll make mistakes, but he'll learn from them. He'll look at role models in spring training and say, 'This is how I'm supposed to act.'"

Harper was the best prospect Walker had ever seen. He said Harper was better than 90 percent of the players in the big leagues right now. The Real Deal, Walker called Harper. "Good for him. With all this pressure, he just keeps within himself. There wasn't any show in it. He just went up there and did his job, and did it quite well." Walker chuckled. "I just hope we don't see him next year."

After CSN's 9–6 victory, after exchanging high fives with his teammates in the usual postseries line on the field and then doing the same with the CSI Eagles, Harper waltzed into his dugout. He didn't favor his left knee to any degree. He hustled to the yellow Gatorade cooler on its perch about five feet off the ground and drained the last drops of liquid into his mouth. He was looking forward to the evening.

A seventeen-year-old kid stoked to be going to the fair.

13

KENNY STEERED HIS Grand Canyon Skywalk charter out of the Morse Stadium parking lot at 6:18 in the morning. All but one of the players had been on the bus twenty minutes earlier. Shortstop Danny Higa's alarm clock forgot to buzz, or something, and at 6:17 he had performed the walk of shame from the parking lot above the stadium down the little S-curved road to the coach. A wave of applause greeted Higa, who showed no emotion as he strolled down the aisle.

Bryce Harper had enjoyed the county fair. At one booth he had thrown a baseball that hit ninety-four miles an hour on a radar gun. For that effort, he admitted with a slight blush, he had won a big, yellow blowup bat. This trip to Carson City, to play archrival Western Nevada, would be no weekend at the fair for Harper.

The journey past the desolate desert terrain of sagebrush and weeds finally became interesting when Kenny rolled by Walker Lake, about fifty miles outside of Carson City along the east side of US Highway 95.

Assistant coach Steve Chatham, in front of me, said he had read that the navy once had a Thresher-class submarine in there that could launch its nuclear missiles in a flash, but it had sunk to the bottom under mysterious circumstances. As he gazed at the still, salty lake, Chatham sounded as sure as an admiral or Cold War expert. The Naval Undersea Warfare Center and a US army depot, full of munitions bunkers, were nearby. Stories had circulated about UFOs on that land and underground aquifers that stretched from the Pacific Coast to Walker Lake and beyond, to St. Louis, maybe even to the Eastern seaboard.

When we arrived at John L. Harvey Field, many Coyotes scoffed at the unusual all-artificial-turf diamond. Lines divided the field, in long and narrow pie strips, from home plate to the outfield fence, in alternating shades of light and dark green. Every grounder kicked up tiny rubber pellets, causing a rooster tail behind every bounce; the pellets kept the fake blades standing and created a playing field akin to real grass.

The polyurethane turf meant sunflower seeds were prohibited because their shells became impossible to extract. The previous season, the Coyotes had chewed seeds. Rules and Western Nevada be damned. A sign on the fence showed 314 feet to the right-field foul pole; Chambers knew it was actually 300. Harper made a mockery of the place in batting practice. The usual wind blowing in over the mountains beyond the right-field pole wasn't there, and Harper jacked six or eight way over the fence as Tom Petty howled "Don't Do Me Like That" over the loudspeakers. A few kids stood back on a ridge to try to catch the balls before they landed in a steep, deep ravine. "This is going to be like playing in a cartoon," said pitcher Donnie Roach.

CHEMISTRY. HARD WORK. RESPECT. SWAGGER. Those black words hung on a square, white sign in the Western Nevada dugout. By the end of the series, CSN could drum up a few more words for that board of inspiration.

Mr. C and I checked into our room at the Holiday Inn Express and found one bed. But a couch to the left, as we walked in, contained a rollout cot. Not even a peep, I told Mr. C. That's my bunk. You dab on your Aramis and let's get out of here. He had his beloved butterfly shrimp. I had something from the local river. We both had margaritas.

"Who would have thought junior college baseball would be *this* much fun?" Mr. C said before dozing off and attacking the Brazilian rain forest.

The *Reno Gazette-Journal,* as most papers did when Bryce Harper visited, glowed about the *Sports Illustrated* cover boy. His skills are "almost nonhuman," the paper wrote. "He bashes home runs that soar over freeways like flying saucers disappearing in the distance. . . . He does things you would laugh at and ridicule as implausible if you saw them in a movie . . . but Harper isn't a video-game creation or the result of some computer nerd scheming the system to make an unstoppable, almost unfair, player. He is a living, breathing baseball-playing phenom whose talents rarely align themselves in one person."

Laughs bounced around their dugout when Harper's teammates read those words before their first doubleheader against Western Nevada. Here's another, they said. Bryan Harper screamed at the flying saucers line. In an hour, the sports page had become faded and tattered from all the paws that had been on it. Seconds after the national anthem, Donnie Roach yelled, "We ain't scored yet?" "That's enough Donnie," said Chambers.

Harper continued his capricious ways at Western Nevada, triggering a series of events that turned a lost weekend in Carson City into one of the most important periods of his growth and development.

The previous few weekends, Harper had reacted swiftly when something had gone awry. He shattered a bat on home plate after whiffing. Other times he slammed his batting helmet on the ground so hard it resembled a racquetball. His four-letter expletives rang off the outfield walls. On one trip to the plate in Carson City, after the first pitch the umpire looked at Harper's cracked helmet and made him return to the dugout to don one that would adequately protect him. Western Nevada coach D. J. Whittemore became so spooked at the damage Harper might inflict on his visitors' dugout he gawked in there more than once to check on its status.

Mike Brown, a Reno-area architect dating Stephanie Turley, the sister of Chambers's wife, Kim, sat in the dugout and jumped considerably when Harper returned and drop-kicked an orange Gatorade cooler, like Bruce Lee, three feet from Brown. The orange liquid erupted out of the container.

After bashing his bat against a wooden trash receptacle, Bryce Harper dropped the weapon, grabbed his glove, and strode through the visitors' dugout, exiting on the right side, about twenty yards ahead of Chambers. When Harper reached shallow right field, his coach yelled, "Stop throwing your shit! I'll yank you!" Harper turned to face Chambers and feigned deafness. "I'll yank you!" Chambers repeated.

Harper straightened his eyes toward the right-field wall and said, "Then do it!" Fortunately for Harper, an already dumbfounded and exasperated Chambers did not hear that response.

When Harper returned to the dugout and leaned on the left side of the rail after that inning, Chambers stood next to him. "I can't believe you'd turn your back on me," Chambers said. "I can't believe that just happened. After all I've done for you, you treat me like that? You stabbed me in the heart." Chambers walked away before Harper could respond.

After two tight and tense defeats, and the drama between Chambers and Harper, the Coyotes were becoming corrosive. Catcher Ryan Scott had been offended at the way the Wildcats celebrated, whooping, hollering, and dog-piling on their field after getting a walk-off hit to win the second game. "You fucking kidding me?" said a frustrated and red-hot Scott, normally one of the more mild-mannered Coyotes. Casey Sato told Scott to shut his mouth. They confronted each other in front of the dugout. "That's what you do, how you celebrate, when you win," Sato said. Within twenty seconds, Scott had apologized and they hugged. When you have a day like that, said third baseman Gabe Weidenaar, nerves can fray and friends go at each other.

On the way back to the hotel, Steve Chatham, the assistant coach, talked with San Francisco Giants outfielder Aaron Rowand, his former

Cal State Fullerton teammate who had been hit in the head by a Vicente Padilla pitch that night at Dodger Stadium. The conversation was brief, but Rowand had broken bones and would be out for a while. "Take it easy," Chatham said. "Chat with you soon."

At the Holiday Inn Express, concerned assistant coaches asked several players to gauge the tenor of the team. "How you guys doin'? You okay?" Some of the Coyotes knew what had been transpiring. "All the coaches were trippin' a little," said Gabe Weidenaar. "It was like there was a big thing going on with Bryce."

An hour later, Bryce Harper, shortstop Danny Higa, and Ryan Scott bounded onto the white coach. Kenny didn't want to chauffer any players the two and a half miles down North Carson Street to Red's Old 395 Grill, the town's best barbecue joint, where many Coyotes had unanimously predicted a sweep of Western Nevada the previous evening. Kenny didn't think they deserved any rides anywhere after their poor showing against the Wildcats. Yet, the three Coyotes and Mr. C and I were en route to Red's. Harper spoke to his father, Ron, on his cell phone.

"He said he'd yank me . . . then do it," Bryce said. ". . . such a prima donna."

A boiling Ron Harper then called Chambers, who did not get in many words. Ron Harper, without being in the dugout to witness exactly how Bryce had been reacting to whiffing or bouncing out to the other pitcher, said Bryce wasn't acting that bad. He's just competitive, Ron said. He wants to win. Ron downplayed the transgressions. He had no idea what had been taking place.

When Chambers could squeeze in a word, he told Ron that Ron didn't know the true measure of the situation. Chambers finally hung up. He plugged his phone into its charger and left it in his hotel room. He and Mike Brown went to get takeout at Red's.

At the restaurant, Chambers and Brown ran into Pat Mahoney, a seventy-two-year-old retired New York firefighter. After hearing about Mahoney's background, his love of the game, and how he had once met Joe DiMaggio, Chambers directed him to the young man sitting outside. Mahoney had known all about Bryce Harper. Chambers and Brown left with their ribs, beans, and slaw.

When Chambers returned to his room, he picked up his phone and saw that Ron Harper had called twenty-four times. Sheri Harper reached Chambers and begged him to call her husband. Chambers did, and Ron Harper apologized. It had been a mercurial few hours, but it could have been much, much worse; had Chambers heard Bryce Harper's response—"Then do it!"—out there in right field, Chambers would immediately have yanked the prodigy from the game and sat him on the bench, maybe for the rest of the weekend. Repercussions would have been immediate and severe and might have bled into other confrontations. That, Chambers confirmed, would have ignited a powder-keg exchange between him and Ron Harper that might permanently have dented their friendship.

Trainer Steve Jacobucci and CSN sports information director Dan Barrera had joined Bryce Harper's dining party at Red's, where Mahoney walked up to Harper amid a gaggle of wild, chirping ten- and eleven-year-old girls celebrating a soccer tournament. In the dusky chill everyone at the table wore multiple layers except Harper, who didn't shiver in his white T-shirt. Mahoney pointed at Harper and asked, "Is this the one?" Harper's dining mates either smiled or nodded.

"Just wanted to shake your hand, son," Mahoney said slowly, as if he were introducing himself to royalty. "I shook the hand of Joe DiMaggio and it would be an honor to shake yours."

In 1951, when he was thirteen, Mahoney and a buddy had leaped out of the right-field stands at Yankee Stadium to dash by Mickey Mantle in right field to get to DiMaggio in center. Mahoney's pal got pinched. Mahoney made it to Joltin' Joe. "What are you doing?" DiMaggio asked Mahoney, who said he just wanted to meet Joe and shake his hand. "You shouldn't do that," DiMaggio said. They shook hands. As Mahoney turned to run, DiMaggio tapped him on his rear with his glove and said, "Now go on."

Security personnel banned Mahoney for life; he kept going to the fabled stadium but always kept his head on a swivel, feeling as if the police would toss him in the can for life if they had spotted him. Initially, Bryce Harper had been relieved that someone had wanted nothing more than to say hello and shake his hand. Later, told of Mahoney's brush with DiMaggio, Harper flashed a big smile and said, "That's so cool."

Harper ordered ribs and chicken, and he asked a waitress if he could get macaroni and cheese instead of beans. She said, Uh, that's on the kids' menu, but she'd try. Two or three at the table laughed at the unintentional joke at the expense of Harper, the baby superstar of baseball. He got his macaroni and cheese, but it was watery and bland, nothing like his mother's. He barely stabbed at it with a fork.

Harper was jovial during the meal. He extended a fist for a bump after making a joke or arched an eyebrow as he caught the form of a cute girl. He looked forward to playing for the U18 national team in a big summer tournament in Canada. Underneath, though, he had been bothered. That came to a head a few hours later when he watched Chambers run three teammates, who had broken curfew, in the Holiday Inn Express parking lot.

Hunched over with his hands on his knees, Harper stared out the window of Room 210 at a quarter to one as teammates Josh Demello, Tyler Hanks, and Ryan Thomas ran sprint after sprint, with Chambers fuming at them, in the hotel parking lot. Chambers had nabbed the trio, thirty minutes after their ten o'clock curfew, playing blackjack at the Carson Nugget. They had screwed up royally.

In his mind, Harper had royally messed up, too, at the diamond, only he wasn't running for his indiscretions. "I should be out there running with them," Harper told roommate Ryan Scott. "Come look at this." Scott rolled out of bed, watched the three Coyotes run in the parking lot, and told Harper to stay put. "This is not a good time," Scott said. "Leave them alone." At 12:56, Harper reached for his iPhone.

Sitting on his bed, Harper punched out a text message to Chambers to apologize for his antics in the doubleheader hours earlier, specifically, and for the pettiness he had generally displayed in recent weeks.

I won't be a little baby bitch anymore! he told Chambers. *You deserve a lot more respect* than he had given him. He said he would keep his mouth shut and focus on playing the game.

I'm just trying to teach you some things, Chambers wrote back to Harper when he returned to his room. *I love you very much.*

I love you too, coach, came the reply and Harper thanked the coach for everything he had done.

The messages capped a taxing stretch for Chambers. He had blown a fuse right there in the Carson Nugget the moment he saw his three players at the blackjack table. He yelled at them in no uncertain terms. A security official closed in, but assistant coach Kevin Higgins told the man that this is a baseball coach, those are his players, they had just dropped two close games to Western Nevada, and these guys had broken curfew. Smiling, the security man nodded and turned away, letting Chambers run his show. Rather than immediately bolting for the exit, though, Demello, Hanks, and Thomas walked to the cashier's cage to exchange their chips for cash, raising Chambers's ire even more.

"They said it was only a little," Demello said of the ground he, Hanks, and Thomas had covered. "I thought it was a lot." He shook his head in the dugout before the Saturday doubleheader. Moments later, Demello exchanged a long hug with Chambers and the two shared a few personal words. Chambers tapped Demello's cap as he walked away. Thomas played and Hanks pitched, as scheduled, which started with Pat Mahoney handing Chambers a large manila envelope—containing black-and-white, eight-by-ten photos of Mantle and DiMaggio, and one with those Yankees legends on either side of Boston Red Sox star Ted Williams—at the edge of the dugout. Those would wind up, framed, in the CSN clubhouse.

When Chambers had returned to his room after running Hanks,

Demello, and Thomas, he saw Bryce Harper's text messages and thanked him. Chambers sent a copy to Ron Harper, who also thanked Chambers. You can only control so much, Ron Harper wrote to Chambers. "The rest is in God's hands."

Bryan Harper had seen his younger brother make strides with his emotions. He never wants to make an out, Bryan said. He wants to hit one hundred home runs. His high competitive spirit can set him up for a hard fall at times. Bryan did the same thing . . . when he was a junior in high school.

Gabe Weidenaar, the versatile six-foot-four weapon and possibly the most athletic Coyote, was one of the few teammates that Bryce Harper literally looked up to. Known as Gabby, the Montana native had curly brown hair, a laid-back demeanor, and an easy smile. Unlike fellow country boy Tyler Hanks, however, Weidenaar hadn't been reared on a farm. His father was an expert computer technician. Gabby once stunned his teammates with a powerful windmill dunk in a pickup basketball game.

Bryce Harper wasn't the only Coyote who had left high school early and obtained his GED, either. Gabby had earned his GED halfway through his junior prep year to concentrate solely on improving at baseball with older brothers Nate, who played minor league ball in the Atlanta Braves system, and Zach, who played football for a year at Wyoming before switching to baseball at an NAIA school in Oklahoma.

That year and a half had turned Gabby into a force on the diamond; he could pitch, he was adept in the outfield, and he could hit from either side of the plate. But the timing of a back injury at CSN in 2008 was even more fortuitous. Had he played one more game that season, Gabby would not have been eligible to play in 2010. But he received a medical redshirt in 2008. Therefore, he was able to play as a sophomore when Bryce Harper landed at CSN.

Gabby didn't hear about those early-morning text messages Harper had sent Chambers until a month later. A change had, Gabby recognized, happened that weekend. That wouldn't have taken place in high school, Gabby said, which could have set Harper up for an even bigger fall had such shenanigans occurred in his first professional season in the minor leagues.

"Those messages were big," Weidenaar said. "He's a *Sports Illustrated* cover boy and he apologized to Chambers? That's huge on his part. Anyone else in his shoes could be, like, 'Fuck off, I don't need you at all.' That says something."

Late in the first Saturday game, CSN players thought they had registered two outs but didn't get one. A Wildcat racing for third, on a hit by a teammate, appeared to slide into Weidenaar's glove at third base after he had caught a bazooka throw from the outfield. Weidenaar quickly tossed the ball to catcher Ryan Scott to get another Wildcat—delayed by a base-running gaffe—scrambling for home. That runner appeared to dart out of the baseline as Scott seemed to tag him on his head before he had reached the plate. However, neither runner had been called out. Chambers sprinted out of his dugout to argue with umpires. Chaos reigned.

"I've seen a lot of shit in Montana," a stunned Weidenaar said in the dugout, "but I've never seen shit like that!"

Harper had singled, stolen second, and scored in the first inning. After grounding out to second in the third, he calmly returned to the dugout and coolly placed the helmet in its slot and his bat in the rack. That surprised infielder Tomo Delp, who knew Harper had to have been frustrated. "I thought he'd come in and slam his bat, but he set it down. That was huge. Western Nevada fans were so chirpy and annoying, but Bryce doesn't need to throw stuff."

"It's a reality check," said second baseman Scott Dysinger. "The pros would be all over him. . . . He's young. Sorry, he's supposed to be a junior in high school. You can understand it a little bit. But, yeah, that would not fly next year in the minors. Not going to happen."

Pitcher Donnie Roach likened some of Harper's low points during the season to funks he'd experienced during his own miserable year, in 2009, at the University of Arizona. The quicker you pull your-self out of those spins, Roach said, the better player you'll become.

"He's learned that it's a little different here than high school, with the wood bat and better pitching. He'll mature more as his game pro-gresses. He's hard on himself. Many are, especially when you're sev-enteen and you're Bryce Harper."

After the stirring events of the previous day, and early-morning hours, Bryce Harper belted a solo home run off the top of the fence in right field in the fifth inning of Saturday's first game, which went ex-tra innings. He was a model of composure after popping out to the catcher in the top of the eighth. The five hundred or so fans were treated to Harper's lone pitching performance of the season, in the bottom of the eighth inning, at 1:57 in the afternoon.

He had yearned for that adrenaline rush. He had begged Coach Chambers to let him throw a Diamond baseball in a game. He had thrown well in intrasquad scrimmages, but he told teammates he didn't think Chambers would ever let him pitch with a game on the line. He had dreamed about inheriting the bases loaded and victory or defeat riding on his right arm. He needed that spotlight. He got it when Cham-bers, with his pitching staff getting stretched, nodded to him to take to the hill.

Harper held his glove up high, covering his war paint, as he peered in for Ryan Scott's signals. "We're ready to hit *this* guy!" yelled someone in the Western Nevada dugout. Harper induced a Wildcat to bounce out to him on the mound and got the next one on a called third strike. He was throwing ninety-three miles an hour, but Scott never knew where the pitches would wind up. One would be fired down the gut, the next would make Scott stretch. Six pitches later, a Wildcat grounded out to second base. "He can pitch, *too!*" roared Donnie Roach.

In the bottom of the ninth, a Wildcat rocketed a double off the left-center wall and a throwing error sent him to third. A few fans chanted, "Overrated!" at Harper. A single gave Western the victory and Harper the defeat. He showed no emotion as he walked off the mound. Harper signed bats and balls for a dozen kids outside the CSN dugout. Got a new favorite player? someone asked a kid wearing a San Francisco Giants cap. "Yeah!" he said as Harper signed his baseball. "Especially if the Giants get him!"

Infielder Casey Sato observed, with curiosity, Harper doling out his latest autographs. No doubt some parents of those kids had been calling Harper a spoiled brat and a showboat. Totally classless, Sato said, but there's Harper signing baseballs and caps. "The things he goes through on a day-to-day basis are completely unreal, but he responds in such a classy way. People need to get off his back and understand he's only seventeen. It's amazing. He's just a good person, a good kid, and he should be completely respected for what he does for other people."

Trent Cook shook his head about the offspring of some of those heckling parents asking Harper for his signature. Harper, though, lived to give kids his autograph. The hype and the pressure, all of Harper's teammates had learned, came with the fame. To be fair, though, CSN fans had goaded and verbally sparred with their Western Nevada counterparts that weekend. The state motto—Battle Born—was on grand display every time Southern Nevada and Western Nevada played baseball against each other.

To start the second game, CSN assistant coach Kevin Higgins, not Chambers, walked the Coyotes' lineup card to home plate for the usual pregame meeting with the opposing coach and umps. Higgins had wanted to give the umpire crew an earful for botching that potential double-play call in the first game. Chambers gave Higgins his consent. Higgins got tossed four seconds after shaking his first hand.

"You guys really fucked that one up!" Higgy had said with neck veins bulging. "I've been in the game more than thirty years, and I've never seen a game fucked up like that one!" Higgy didn't slow down. "You're really fucking terrible," he told one umpire. "You ever cuss to one of my players again and I'll fuck you up," he told another. "And *you*," he said to the plump first-base ump, "had better mix in a salad once in a while, you fat ass!"

Higgins grabbed a backpack and left the diamond as the Coyotes gave him a rousing ovation. Higgins had grabbed a twelve-pack of Bud Light and had stashed it, on ice, on Kenny's bus, and that's where he went after getting ejected.

In the second game, Harper struck out into a double play in the first, flew out to left in the third, and smacked a two-run homer to left in the sixth, a breath after a woman in the stands had yelled, "Go back to high school, Bryce!"

CSN, which had entered the weekend three and a half games in front of Western Nevada atop the Scenic West Athletic Conference, left Carson City in second place to the Wildcats. The weekend had been a disaster, but CSN was grateful to have Carson City in its rear-view mirrors. The Coyotes had not been too surprised by the many close calls that didn't go their way. They stopped for pizza, hamburgers, chicken sandwiches, and tins of chewing tobacco.

Harper had made some strides during the trip.

"Growing up, getting more mature, dealing with the outs I made, and dealing with all the adversity we had . . . that first day, I acted pretty much like a little bitch. The second day, I matured a little bit, took everything in stride, tried to help the team win and do what I could do. If I got into the big leagues, or minors, and went oh for my first thirty-five . . . hopefully I don't do that, but if it happens, I'll know how to deal with it, not go out there and go, 'Oh, crap! I need to change,' and do all this stuff. I'll walk into the dugout, put my stuff down, and say, 'Hey, let's go, guys!' Nothing I can do. I don't need to be throwing my stuff or kicking the water jug. That's not baseball and that's not me."

Western Nevada won the final game of the series, 3–2. It ended when Gabby Weidenaar hit into a bases-loaded double play. Bryce Harper had been standing on deck.

"I ain't perfect," Harper said. "I ain't Superman. That weekend wasn't that much pressure, they just had a good weekend, got some calls we didn't get. I could have had a good weekend. I helped us behind the dish, stole a couple of bases, hit some balls when we needed them. I hit those two home runs in really big situations, when we needed them. And if I had got up in the last situation, it would have been perfect."

14

AFTER HIS CARSON CITY epiphany, the new-and-improved Bryce Harper showed up at Morse Stadium on Tuesday, April 20, for practice in *GQ* form after getting his hair cut. He had dyed it black all season. He had preferred that look for a long time. Now, his natural brown mane tight and trim, Harper and the Coyotes started a stretch in which they played host to league bottom-feeders Colorado Northwestern and the College of Eastern Utah in consecutive weekends.

His first day in uniform with his hair au naturel, Harper belted a home run to left-center field that nearly smacked another house. The ball sailed in the fifty-mile-an-hour jet stream to left that had torn an enormous American flag from its thick steel pole beyond center field. Thunderhead clouds that looked like chocolate cotton candy had threatened the day, but Harper exchanged exuberant high fives with Marvin Campbell in the dugout and chest-bumped Ryan Scott as if the Coyotes had just defeated the Red Sox to earn a spot in the World Series. It was the usual Tuesday practice scrimmage, but it meant a little more to Bryce Harper.

That week, Harper turned in a progress report from an anthropology class to Chambers, who turned it over and chuckled. On the other side were about sixty scribbled Bryce Harper signatures. He had been practicing his autograph in class. In a Psychology 101 class in the spring, when the topic of people in their sixties having sex came up, Harper said, "Ooooooh," and he got up and left.

The 4.0 grade point average he had earned in the fall took a hit in the spring, when that Psych 101 professor gave him a C. He received another C in Basic Math 91, and a B-minus in US History 2, but he flunked Composition. He aced Baseball; every player who participated was rewarded with an A.

A snowy weather forecast in Rangely, Colorado, forced Northwestern to shift its series with CSN to Southern Nevada, and Chambers happily agreed to pay the Spartans' travel expenses. That meant no twelve-hour bus ride, the last hour or so winding through the steep edges of the Roan Cliffs, which had usually forced Chambers to his stomach in the aisle. He cannot hide his deathly fear of heights. Mice and snakes also rile him. When he was a kid, he had put a cage with six mice in a closet and forgot about it. A few weeks later, he went to grab something out of that closet and saw that a few mice had been eating dead ones; Chambers had been scarred for life. On a golf course in Utah, Chambers only needed to hear what he thought was the rattle of a snake to send him running and wailing to the middle of the fairway. Assistant coach Cooper Fouts relished the scene.

Certain writers always sent Chambers into a tizzy, too. The day before the start of the Northwestern series, Kevin Goldstein of the Internet-based Baseball Prospectus wrote a piece on Harper titled FUTURE SHOCK, detailing the questions that remained in Washington's decision whether to take Harper with the top pick in the draft. In the fourth section, "The Makeup," Goldstein quoted an anonymous scout about Harper's "top-of-the-scale arrogance, a disturbingly large sense of entitlement, and on-field behavior that includes taunting opponents."

"He's just a bad, bad guy," Goldstein quoted the scout. "He's basically the anti–Joe Mauer."

That ignited Chambers and Ron Harper. In the grand scheme, wrote *Las Vegas Review-Journal* columnist Ron Kantowski, "I doubt that a hatchet job by an obscure Internet Web site is going to influence

Major League Baseball general managers and/or impact Harper's potential to make an obscene amount of money by playing baseball." Kantowski had clouted that one out of the yard, by a country mile, but it didn't mitigate the animosity in the anonymous Goldstein quotes.

"That's why I don't read that junk," said Dick Scott, the father of CSN catcher Ryan Scott, who had played or worked in professional baseball all of his adult life.

Chambers had always blasted anyone's condemnation of Harper's bold move. Nobody has *ever* done this, Chambers always repeated. Harper has a lot to learn and there are going to be growing pains. He will learn plenty this season. So will I, Chambers admitted. But we'll both be better for it. In the end, Chambers believed Harper's performance would stifle each and every critic. And, oh, yeah, Chambers added, "He's only putting together the best amateur season *ever!*"

Bryce Harper acknowledged the Goldstein story. "I don't know . . . the guy doesn't know me very well. He doesn't know me on the field or off the field, with my family or with my coaches. I don't really have a comment on that. I couldn't care less."

When I asked him to elaborate, Harper didn't blink when he admitted, as he had previously told me, that he doesn't play the game to make friends between the lines. "Well, I'm an asshole on the field. I'm not going to lie. I'm an asshole. I'm a dick, in the aspect that . . . I don't talk shit or crap about anyone, but if you're a dick to me, I'll be a dick back. I'm going to try to ram it down your throat, hit a bomb, and say, 'Gotcha! There you go! Shut up!' But I won't ever taunt or anything. I haven't taunted anyone this season. I never [verbally] taunted anyone this year, not once. Twenty other guys on Western Nevada did. But if I were on their team, they'd be happy as hell. But I really couldn't care less. Whatever, dude. I've had a lot worse stuff than that written about me. It's okay. Gotta learn."

A second round of acupuncture, which had included a needle that he swore scraped his spine and would result in his missing two starts, stung Bryan Harper more that week than anything anyone might have said or written about a family member. Comes with the territory. Nothing we can do about it, he said.

"People will always have their opinion about everyone else . . . you see it all the time in the media with celebrities. Look at Tiger Woods and that sex scandal. Oooooooh. He's a bad person, the Antichrist. Really? Mistakes off the field when he's not playing? He doesn't have girls standing around at every hole, waiting for him to make the putt. Everyone has their own opinion, even if they truly don't know anyone."

The Harpers' teammates weren't so diplomatic. Donnie Roach, the starting pitcher, didn't temper his rage. "I'd be fucking cocky if I was [Harper]. On the cover of *Sports Illustrated* at sixteen? I'd be walking around with it pasted on my chest. He's not even that bad. He's somewhat cocky, but it's how you play the game. The best athletes in the world are cocky people. It's the ten-eighty-ten rule. The upper ten percent are cocky, and the lower ten percent want to complain about everyone else and not fix themselves. They don't know anything. They want to talk like they know, but they don't know what it's like to be him. Nobody does. So how can you say anything? It's a joke. It's a guy sitting in the stands wearing a forty-year-old T-shirt, eating a hot dog, and getting mustard all over, going on the Internet and typing."

Trent Cook and Casey Sato noted how Harper had grown during the season and that he was maturing. Cook figured the comparison was being made because fans never saw Joe Mauer toss his bat up in the air or smash it on home plate. Also, Harper's expectations of himself were extraordinary.

"He gets frustrated. That's human nature in all of us," Cook said. "He's a great kid and he has great moral standards. He comes from a great family. For someone to say that about him, I don't think it's right. We're all human and we all have our own issues. At some point, we all grow up and mature. At some point, we were all a seventeen-year-old kid and we needed to learn. Whether it's media or fans yelling in your ear, it'll get tougher. But he's proven he can overcome all that and deal with it."

Sato would much rather have a teammate who is aggressive, competitive, and passionate about stepping between the lines than someone who was nice, smiling, and not taking the game seriously. With a runner on second and two outs, there's nobody Sato would rather have at the plate than Harper. "He won't go down without competing or fighting. That's what you want. I don't understand where the negativity comes from. They look at some of the things he does, and, yeah, some of them aren't right. At the same time, you take that for the things he gives back in return. Besides, he's a great kid, somebody you want to be around, and somebody you want on your team."

Jim Brooks had a rational reaction to the second- and thirdhand ripping of his grandson in that Internet report. From talking with knowledgeable sources, Brooks figured that three Major League teams, maybe more, were behind such stories because they didn't want Washington to draft Bryce; they wanted him to slip to them in the draft.

"I think that's the whole thing," Jim Brooks said. "They'll beat him up and beat him down, just beat him down. The Nationals said Bryce is a good kid. He works hard and runs hard and slides into bases hard. When you've done that all your life, you have an aura around you, and you're going to keep doing things hard."

Likely the only opinion that would matter to Bryce Harper was that of Mike Rizzo, the Washington Nationals' general manager, whose responsibility it would be to pick Harper with the first selection of the June draft or pass on him. Kris Kline, Rizzo's assistant, enjoyed how Harper carried himself like a big leaguer, that he held himself to such a high standard, that he never felt that he should make an out. Kline told the *Washington Post* that Harper would have to make adjustments, of course, as he rose in the professional ranks—if the Nationals drafted him and if they could sign him—but that Harper was a class act. As far as the "bad, bad guy" line, Kline had other words for the Goldstein story.

"Absolutely the worst, most ridiculous, stupidest article I've ever read. That was horrible." He called the unnamed quoted scout "gutless" for not giving his name.

With his newly trimmed do and a batting helmet repaired with narrow blue tape—it looked like something from a crash-test dummy— Harper bounced down his dugout on Friday, April 23. As "T.N.T." blared over the loudspeakers, Harper mocked flamboyant AC/DC guitarist Angus Young's bent-down and skipping strumming style, acting as if his black Marucci were the Gibson Signature SG electric guitar that Young favored. "Yeah! Yeah! Yeah!" said a smiling Harper. All that was missing were Young's trademark black shorts.

Harper mock-kicked an orange Gatorade cooler and slightly laughed at himself as he looked at me. No doubt Mike Brown, the Reno-area architect who nearly got drenched in Gatorade when Harper booted that cooler at Western Nevada, would have approved of Harper's self-deprecation. Those immature, petulant "baby bitch" actions were gone forever.

Or were they?

The oddity of the series with Colorado Northwestern had been CSN playing at home but batting first because of the venue switch. The Spartans still had the benefit of hitting last, since the games were supposed to have been played in their park. The Morse Stadium scoreboard, however, had CSN permanently in the bottom-inning slot, with VISITORS in the top-inning slot. CSN's scores were kept in the bottom line and Northwestern's in the top line, with the bottom-rung figures going up first because the Coyotes hit first.

Try explaining *that* version of the game to a foreigner.

Then again, it didn't matter much. Scott Dysinger led off the first game with a single and Gabe Weidenaar drew a walk. Four pitches later, Harper belted the ball 450 feet over the right-field fence for his eighteenth home run of the season and a 3–0 CSN lead. Now add on, Dysinger said in the dugout. "Add on! Five fuckin' innings or that's a loss!" Player comments were much more directed at themselves after Chambers's early-week declaration that talking smack with opponents was now finished. Too much of a distraction, he said. Worry about us and let's move forward. Was Donnie Roach listening?

The league's mercy rule ended a game if a team went ahead by eight runs after five innings or ten after seven. Dysinger's message was about the Coyotes' continuing to test themselves, not letting up or coasting, to defeat someone you should beat by margin, and getting this thing over early.

The Northwestern team was in disarray after the winter break, when almost enough sophomores to fill out a starting lineup had left the squad. It was the first time that the tranquil Trent Cook had ever felt sorry for another team. They will have trouble catching routine fly balls, he said. He did not laugh when he spoke those words.

Harper bounced out to first in the third inning and laid his batting helmet on the grass, where first-base coach Jay Guest picked it up and took it to the dugout. Then Harper smacked a two-out grand slam in the fourth to give CSN a 10–0 advantage.

In the top of the fifth, it was announced that CSI had defeated Western Nevada. So CSN had picked up a game on its nemesis and would pick up another when that was the same outcome of both second games.

But in between games, the Coyotes mended, manicured, and patched their own field, which every home team does in junior college. At least the players who move on to the low minor leagues wouldn't have to tend to their own field. Everybody but Chambers pitched in to prep the field for the next game.

Jay Guest, the assistant coach who taught high school history, laid down the chalk for the first- and third-base foul lines with, uh, not exactly chalk. Rust-Oleum's inverted striping paint was also used to give the bases at first, second, and third, and the seventeen-inch-wide home plate, clean white sheens at the start of every game, and it's sprayed on the pitching rubber. It should not be used within a hundred feet of fire

because its vapor and liquid contents—toluene and xylene, namely—
are extremely flammable. In California, those chemicals had been
found to cause cancer. Or so read the Rust-Oleum label. It is a toxic
mixture that zapped the pons and medulla like a three-martini lunch.

Guest didn't even flinch when that stuff tickled his nostrils.

Bryce Harper signed bats and balls for a half dozen kids outside
the dugout. Asked if he might have signed about a million autographs
so far in his young life, he thought for a moment and nodded. "Maybe."
Then he said, "But I haven't done shit."

Harper bounced into a double play in the first inning of the second game, and upon returning to the dugout, he gently placed his gray
batting helmet, with the narrow, blue tape lines, into its wooden wall
slot and laid down his black bat.

In the next inning, Harper crushed his twentieth homer of the
season, a two-run shot off the scoreboard in left field. A Northwestern
outfielder badly misplayed a Trent Cook drive that landed Cook on
third—he had been prescient about those foes missing shots hit right
at them—and Tomo "Helicopter" Delp belted a two-run homer.

In the fourth, Harper hit an infield grounder, and as he sprinted
down the line, Northwestern first baseman Nathan Holt drifted into his
path to make a catch. In a flash, Harper lay, stunned, flat on his back on
the dirt. Holt lay crumpled and dazed to Harper's left. Steve Jacobucci,
the trainer, tended to Harper, who shook off the contact, stole second
and third, and scored on Ryan Thomas's bloop single to right.

Over the next two innings, Matt Medina contemplated lunging
over the dugout rail from a bench jump, using the black metal I beam
supported by the four flimsy posts as a swing-launch for his hands. It
looked doable, maybe even easier than it appeared, like jumping off a
roof into a pool. But the cost might be rough for his spine on the rail.
Trevor Kirk and Scott Dysinger weighed the chances and thought it
could be done. It would be sick if you could do that, said Kiel Harmon.
"You can do that?" said assistant coach Steve Chatham. "Yeah, I'll do
it," Medina said.

Reserve infielder Ray Daniels thought it could be done, but he was occupied with his left eye. He had fielded a bouncer just below that socket in an energetic practice the previous day, but Gabe Weidenaar came to the rescue. Actually, Weidenaar's seventy-year-old grandmother, Sharon Finch, who dabbled in holistic medicine and herbal remedies back home in Montana, came through when she gave instructions for Daniels to rub egg whites under the eye to prevent it from bruising.

"Your grandma and her witchcraft," a disbelieving Bucci told Gabby whenever he distributed another Grandma Finch remedy to a teammate. No black-and-blue marks surfaced, which disappointed Daniels. "He was upset because he wanted to look like a badass," said, Gabby, laughing.

After CSN's second mercy-rule victory in a row, the Coyotes grabbed lawn tools to clean the field and manicure its edges, put away the bases, and tidied up the dugouts. Medina eyeballed the rail for a minute and wisely shelved his vaulting plans.

CSN had taken Dysinger's five-inning challenges and capitalized on them. Saturday, Harper hit another homer, and he lined a single and a double to score three times and knock in three runs in a 9–3 victory. In the second game, he grounded into a fielder's choice and toppled the second baseman when he ventured into Harper's path. When Harper struck out in the fifth, he swung his bat at the bench in the dugout. Teammates to his right and left peeked over shoulders or under elbows to witness what Harper might just do with his bat.

It took a while, but Harper walked and scored in a three-run seventh inning that capped CSN's 4–0 victory.

On Wednesday, April 28, for the first time Bryce Harper was one of the six CSN players who faced the rest of their teammates, in lines opposite each of them—facing them—in their prepractice stretching routines. Jokes flew. They talked about girls. They zoned into baseball for the day. With back spasms sidelining Marvin Campbell, the seventeen-year-old superstar slugger became one of the de facto captains, if only for a day, of the Coyotes. Gabe Weidenaar was on the far right, with Bryce Harper to his left. Aaron Kurcz, Ryan Scott, Donnie Roach, and Scott Dysinger filled out that day's leaders.

It was so subtle, Chambers never noticed. Bold move, Chambers said months later, on Bryce's part. Had that been ill-advised, his teammates would have badgered Harper out of there and into the fold with the commoners in seconds. But he felt as if he belonged as an unofficial captain for the day, and so did his teammates.

For the second consecutive week, players noticed that Mr. C hadn't been coming around much. Strong winds had been the norm lately, so they figured that had been keeping him away. Fallout from ash, juniper, mulberry, and olive trees, with a buffet of various ragweed, created a special form of sinus torture when spring winds whipped through Las Vegas.

Ryan Thomas and Josh Demello asked Mr. C where he'd been when he finally appeared at practice, and a few Coyotes gave Mr. C a bear hug. "What are you, a warm-weather fan?" one of them said. Actually, Mr. C confided to me, that horrible weekend in Carson City had made him irritable and sullied his outlook on the season, so he had wanted to stay away for a little while. I'll be fine, he said, I just hope they come around. He even apologized to Trevor Kirk for a quick temper that had made him snap at Kirk.

Before the first game against Eastern Utah, Bryce asked me if I lived on Pecos Road, about ten miles west of Morse Stadium. Yup. I told him I had thought that black Toyota Tacoma pickup truck behind me the previous day had looked familiar. It had been Harper. He had been visiting a friend in the neighborhood, he said, and we talked about the many police officers—even the fat motorcycle cop who thought he could hide behind a few skinny baby pine trees—who always staked out strategic spots along that road, heading north from the freeway. Right there, the speed limit sliced from forty-five to thirty-five miles an hour, which was tailor-made for speed traps because of a subtle downhill slope. Soon enough, the limit bumped to forty-five.

Again, however, it sliced to thirty-five just before another descent. It was Shark Alley, just the remedy for a city's budget-strapped bottom line. With radar guns aimed at Pecos, police picked all kinds of nooks and entryways in which to hide. It wasn't uncommon to see multiple vehicles pulled over to the side as officers slowly wrote them up.

Some of those were near entertainer Wayne Newton's Casa de Shenandoah, a forty-two-acre gated and high-walled compound that contained peacocks, penguins, wallabies, sloths, and fifty-four horses at the corner of Pecos and Sunset Roads. His white mansion had a curved, four-pillared, two-story entry. The tail of his white, twin-engine Fokker F28 jet airplane could be seen sticking out of the northwest section of his property. Newton planned to turn it all into a kind of Graceland West, with a tour and a dinner theater that could seat three hundred. Oak, pine, cottonwood, and Mexican fan palm trees, and a few Italian cypresses, dotted Newton's land.

Harper and I nodded to each other about always being careful and vigilant on that stretch. Oh, yeah, I kidded with him. You were the one with Madonna blaring on your stereo? His smile turned into a frown as he said, "Uh, no."

On the diamond, Kenny McDowall became the first pitcher to register triple figures on the radar portion of the CSN scoreboard. He had hit ninety-four, ninety-five, and ninety-six. . . . When McDowall hit one hundred, with Bryce Harper catching him, the CSN dugout burst out with claps and cheers as if they were at a New Year's Eve party and the clock had struck midnight.

A few minutes later, an Eastern Utah batter zinged a sharp liner into the CSN dugout. In a blur, everyone scattered. But someone had banged into the sturdy, black metal overhang, above the back of the bench, that is used as a shelf for players to store their gloves, caps, tape, shoes, and chewing tobacco during games. That thing had absolutely no give. Thirty feet to my left, a body was crumpled in a fetal position. Chambers and his players slowly addressed it.

Assistant coach Steve Chatham finally rolled onto his right side, his face as pale as home plate. Instead of dodging that bullet left or right, his first reaction had been up. Blood trickled down Chatham's dazed and confused mug. Bucci and Showtime whisked Chatham to an emergency room.

Chambers picked up Chatham's cap ten minutes later and found a mess of blood, minute chunks of Chatham's scalp, and a few hairs, on the inside where his head had dinged the metal. When Chambers rang Showtime for an update, he said, "Not good, his head just rolled off his neck." The dugout roared. By the middle of the second game Chatham, with his head wrapped in tan gauze, had returned. Chambers gave him a helmet. That night Aaron Rowand, due to return to the San Francisco Giants' lineup the next day after suffering head injuries of his own when he had been beaned a few weeks earlier, was the one calling Chatham for a medical update.

CSN sophomore third baseman Tomo Delp hit safely in eleven of thirteen plate appearances against Eastern Utah, with a solo home run in the opener, to become the first Coyote to earn national junior college Player of the Week honors. Delp hit nine singles and a double, in addition to the solo shot, and he walked, stole a base, and one of his two outs had been a groundout to the right side that moved Ryan Thomas from second base to third; Thomas scored on a sacrifice fly by Danny Higa.

CSN swept the Eastern Utah series by scores of 5–3, 8–1, 5–0, and 7–1, but it hadn't been just another weekend. Mike Rizzo, the Washington Nationals' general manager, attended the only CSN games he'd watch all season. Rizzo had tried to avoid all reports and opinions of Harper, even from his own people, so his views wouldn't be tainted when he saw Harper with his own eyes. Showtime was correct: it wouldn't matter what any "clown boy" thought of Harper except a Major League team's general manager.

Rizzo saw Harper get six hits in twelve at bats, with three doubles. He tried stretching one, slapped into deep left-center field, into a triple but was thrown out. After another, he tried stealing third but was gunned down by the catcher. He knocked in five runs and scored five times. He struck out twice, once on a sixty-six-mile-an-hour floater, and stole a base. He caught a fifteen-strikeout performance by Donnie Roach and the 7–1 victory by Tyler Hanks and played right field twice. Rizzo saw Harper's aggressiveness and tenacity, and he especially liked the way two of Harper's hits went to left and two were blasted up the middle. Harper also beat out an infield hit for a single.

On their flight home from Las Vegas, Rizzo, his assistant Roy Clark, and Washington scouting director Kris Kline agreed that Harper would be the best player available in the draft. Kline, like Coach Chambers and many of Harper's own teammates, kept reminding himself that this wunderkind was only seventeen years old. Kline believed Harper was savvy beyond his years, that the young lefty slugger had a simple approach but advanced abilities.

Rizzo told MLB.com that he had no concern about Harper's makeup and that the Nationals were sold on him, his character, and his family. Rizzo confirmed that Bryce acted as if he was seventeen, at times, but Rizzo didn't want to reveal how he had acted when he was that age.

"He is mature beyond his years as far as performance on the field, tools development, and even his social skills. This guy has had more hype and more publicity than most twenty-five-year-olds have had already. He has handled it remarkably. Between the lines, he is going 110 [miles an hour] all the time. He is a baseball rat. I love the way he gets after it."

And with a wooden bat, no less. That played an important role in how Rizzo and his staff evaluated Harper, by giving them a long-term look at Harper's bat speed and how he made adjustments. "It kind of takes the guesswork out of a few of the particulars," Rizzo told *The New York Times.*

The frustrations that had zapped Harper at Carson City had been addressed and dealt with, but the next couple of weeks confirmed that the pressures of all that hype and publicity were latent, always simmering just below the surface, and could make Harper boil with a certain trigger. Soon, he would yearn for those days when it seemed as if life was so wonderful, when he wore that red-and-black Wildcats uniform for Las Vegas High, when his scintillating swing took up an entire *Sports Illustrated* cover.

OKAY, STEP AWAY FROM the door. I'm going to ramrod it open. Metal could fly all over so step back. Get away from the door! Coach Chambers stood on the outside of the closed dull-silver Otis elevator doors on the ground floor of the Holiday Inn Express in Salt Lake City and implored his fifteen players inside to watch out for shrapnel. He turned to a few people around him and muted a laugh. The elevator would be stuck for thirty-four minutes. Chambers had taken advantage of the situation. It was the best thirty-four minutes of his season, so far. No media pestering. No blind-mice umpires. No heckling from the stands or jeering from the other dugout. No curveball antics from the prodigy.

Just a coach having fun with some of his players.

CSN had traveled to Salt Lake City, courtesy of Kenny hauling the Grand Canyon Skywalk up I-15 in less than seven hours, with its sixth conference championship in nine years locked up. After playing host to CSN in Carson City, Western Nevada had fallen apart in the ensuing weeks.

As Bryce Harper boarded the coach just before six on the morning of Thursday, May 6, with a faint orange glow rising along the rim of the River Mountains, he held three new custom-made weapons, pink bats individually wrapped in protective cellophane. Marucci had produced the CU26 Pro Model bats—cut from Pennsylvania maple, handcrafted, and bone-rubbed in Baton Rouge, Louisiana, the choice sticks of the Philadelphia Phillies' second baseman—and applied the blushed hue just for Harper. To celebrate Mother's Day, he said. Again, where his name should have been displayed below HANDCRAFTED FOR, it read LUKE 1:37. On the handle hub, BH had been enscribed above (5/5/10).

During the trip, someone sent Chambers, on his iPhone, a photograph of a fan wearing a red NATIONALS T-shirt, with number thirty-four and HARPER on the back, from the game at Nationals Park the previous evening. Another first. Chambers showed it off to everyone. Someone had released a toxic bomb of intestinal gas that smelled like a decayed swamp-skunk corpse and awoke Mr. C in a panic.

"Ho-ly . . . ," said Mr. C as he rubbed tears away from his wide-open eyes. Trainer Steve Jacobucci, a seat in front of Mr. C, might have been grinning.

"One hundred and nine at-bats," Chambers said to assistants Jay Guest and Chatham behind him, "and one hundred and nine total bases." Bryce Harper was slugging a ridiculous 1.000 in Scenic West Athletic Conference games.

As Kenny pulled into a convenience store in Cedar City, Utah, assistant coach Marc Morse congratulated Tomo Delp on winning national NJCAA Player of the Week honors for his hitting prowess the previous weekend against Eastern Utah. The unassuming Delp didn't know he had been so honored.

Thirty minutes outside Cedar City, as Robert Downey, Jr., hunted for clues and battled bad guys in London in *Sherlock Holmes* on the tiny TV screens, I finished *The Boys of Summer,* Roger Kahn's epic account of Jackie Robinson's Brooklyn Dodgers and what those players, long after their glory years, had remembered of those watershed days. It is considered the Holy Grail of sports literature.

I thought of Harper during a passage in which Kahn met up with the great Duke Snider after Snider had retired. During Kahn's final road trip with those Dodgers, he had a drink with Snider in Milwaukee.

Snider had been hitting .335 but was sullen. Kahn asked what was wrong. "Everything."

At twenty-six, Snider had soured on the game. Fans threw marbles at him as he chased fly balls in center field. He disliked the endless travel. He didn't care for the press. In a World Series game with seventy thousand in the stands, he had made a fabulous catch. What was on his mind at that moment? Farming avocados in California.

"I dreamed of being a big leaguer once, but that's not it for me anymore," Snider told Kahn. ". . . If it wasn't for the money, I'd be just as happy if I never played a game of ball again." Kahn had Snider elaborate on those thoughts and turned Snider's statements into an infamous magazine article long before *Boys* came out.

I wondered what Harper would think about the game when he was twenty-six, or thirty-six. At CSN a month earlier, a serious-looking Harper had belted ball after ball with some extra-vicious swings in a Thursday batting practice. Something seemed to be up. I asked him what was wrong. "Everything," Harper responded.

In the back of the bus en route to Salt Lake City, Harper, who had zipped through a paperback copy of *Beyond Belief: Finding the Strength to Come Back,* about Texas Rangers slugger Josh Hamilton's drug-filled past and turnaround, had been digesting a hardback edition of *Willie Mays: The Life, the Legend.* Mays had just turned twenty when, on May 24, 1951, the New York Giants held a press conference to introduce their latest call-up from the minor leagues; Mays had been the youngest black player to reach the majors.

Harper read how Mays shunned alcohol. Mays had also been tagged with a golden sombrero; he struck out four times against nineteen-year-old rookie Gary Nolan in 1967. Mays wore eye black, was known for outwitting runners by throwing behind them, and often slid into home with his spikes up. In a 1959 game against the Dodgers in San Francisco, Mays went to the plate with runners on second and third, and one out, and the Dodgers tried to intentionally walk him. But on the fourth wide pitch, Mays leaned over the plate and took a poke at it; unlike

Harper on opening night, Mays didn't drive in a run as he popped out to the catcher.

CSN's four games with Salt Lake Community College were meaningless, with the regular-season conference crown locked up, but Chambers told his players in practice a few days earlier that he didn't want them taking it easy, as if they were in some adult rec league or softball beer league.

During batting practice at Salt Lake Community College, whose acronym induced the Coyotes to call the place Slick, later that chilly, cloudy afternoon, the Bruins looked on in some awe at Harper. He wore a dark Detroit Tigers cap with an orange, Old English *D* on the front, and he cranked a few balls out of the park with one of his three pink pieces of lumber. Kaz Smith and Scott Dysinger, at half speed, swung and admired Harper's other pink bats near the dugout.

At Trent Cook's home, a forty-minute bus ride north to Bountiful, Utah, early that evening, an endless feast of grilled pineapple, assorted salads and vegetables, shrimp, bacon-wrapped bratwursts, and a gourmet-burger bar had been prepared by Cook's parents for the Coyotes. There was even a fruit pizza. "You have to understand my dad," said a smiling Trent Cook. A two-man band played in the cozy twilit backyard of the Cooks' comfortable home just west of the majestic Wasatch Mountains.

Upon returning to the hotel, the fifteen Coyotes had crammed themselves into the elevator that could transport up to three thousand pounds of human freight. In the early stages of the lockdown, Ryan Scott had tallied weights and come up with 2,675 pounds. Did you jump? Outside, talking through a tiny peephole at the top of the elevator doors, Chambers communicated with his players. With this situation, he said, laughing, he was going to have some fun. "Did you jump?" he yelled again. "That's very important. If you did, it could take twelve hours to get you out!"

"I swear to God we didn't jump!" someone yelled back.

The Coyotes steamed inside the metal box. Eventually, all the players removed their shirts. Ryan Scott and Bryan Harper, being cagey veterans, alternated quietly dropping down on one knee—down by the vent that pumped in fresh air. Some took camera-phone snapshots of the situation.

"Get out of the way!" Chambers yelled. "I'm gonna ramrod the door!"

"Really, Coach?"

"Get out of the way! Bryce, make sure you're in the back, way out of the way!"

"It's not a safe," Ryan Scott said. "It's an elevator."

Chambers turned to fellow coaches, assorted players, and several hotel guests standing around him, and he laughed some more.

"You sure you didn't jump?" Chambers implored. "That will make a big difference if we're able to get you out before tomorrow. Or I'll have to play with the guys I have."

"Good luck with the team out there!" Bryce Harper shot back. He looked around him. "We've got Dice [Scott Dysinger], [Trent] Cook, and Marvin [Campbell] in here."

That line didn't register well with a few of the veterans and would be remembered. Harper panicked the most. The itching he had experienced on the bus and after batting practice—he had asked Jacobucci for some aloe lotion—disappeared. Chambers rolled up a small piece of paper and squeezed it through the peephole. Write your last wishes on this, he said. He cupped his mouth as he laughed. Pitcher Kiel Harmon poked another little sheet of paper through the tiny hole and asked Harper for his last autograph.

When fire department officials showed, they inquired if anyone had jumped—on Chambers's request. "If so," a fireman said, glancing at Chambers and smiling, "this could take up to twelve hours."

"No!" came the response, in unison.

"It freaked me out," Bryce Harper said later. "Ohhh, man, I'm really claustrophobic. I hate being in tight places with other people. Hate it. It was really scary actually, because we were all sitting there saying, 'Oh, shit . . . no way did this just happen.' Thank God we were on the first floor, because if we would have jumped . . . it would have been really, really bad."

His panic meter soared when Chambers said it might be half a day before the fire department could get them out. "That *really* freaked me out," Harper said. "I didn't like that at all. I got really scared, really quick. Donnie and I were yelling, 'We've got the draft! What are you doing? Get us out of here!'"

The draft was a month away.

Scott Dysinger thought the first five minutes were funny. Ha ha ha, he said. "After that, okay, this is fucking stupid," he said later. "It was hot. We were cramped. It seemed like hours. It felt like I was in there the whole night."

He recalled that they all got in the elevator, entered floor numbers, and then someone said, Okay, on three, everyone jump. One, two . . . but nobody jumped. The elevator didn't budge. They pressed more buttons and ground lights went off. The lights on the buttons all shut off. Only the thin ceiling lights stayed on. Marvin Campbell had a half-full plastic water bottle that they rationed. The autograph request for Harper had not made its way into the elevator.

Firefighters finally opened it, the players walked out in single file. Ray Daniels was the last one out. They were all dripping in sweat. Chambers howled about the incident all night. Actually, all weekend.

"The fire department said that's going to cost ten thousand dollars," said Chambers, turning to Harper. "And *you* are going to pay it!" Chambers walked away laughing.

Harper was the lone collegiate player who wielded a pink bat, which became an annual tradition in the major leagues in 2006 to celebrate Mother's Day weekend and to bring awareness to breast cancer research. It was as if he had already arrived.

"Awesome, I liked that he did that," Scott Dysinger said.

"He's really a big leaguer," said infielder Tomo Delp. "He knows it. We all know it."

Many Coyotes used the stairs to reach the ground floor of the hotel the next morning. Before the first doubleheader, Harper remembered a drill Mr. C had taught him ten years earlier, in the far right of the three batting cages at Morse Stadium. Standing on a four-foot-long two-by-four, with Mr. C watching, Harper had learned about keeping his feet parallel and balanced when hitting. Harper remembered something else Mr. C had told him that day. "You ain't worth shit," Mr. C told seven-year-old Bryce. "Prove me wrong."

Before the first doubleheader against Salt Lake, both Mr. C and Harper laughed at those memories. CSN lost both games. It seemed as if the players would have had the same blasé and unaffected reactions had they won the first two games, but that first day included a harbinger when reliever Aaron Kurcz lost the first game 4–3. That marked a stretch of thirty-four games in which the Coyotes had only lost eight times. In those eight setbacks, Kurcz had either yielded a game-deciding home run, thrown poorly, or got slapped with the defeat five times. In Iowa, coaches at another junior college had been charting Kurcz's failures and tendencies.

Kurcz had not enjoyed the Air Force Academy. The hazing wasn't so bad, but he felt the upperclassmen were taking far too many liberties in barking at him and giving him additional orders when he had missed some duties due to road trips with the Falcons baseball team, while representing the institution. That's when he knew his stint at the academy would be short. He wouldn't miss staring at the little blue eagles—and nothing else, like all good plebes—on the shiny white plates during breakfast.

In twenty-one games for the Air Force, the six-foot, 175-pound Kurcz had won three games, lost four, and collected seven saves. He got drilled. In thirty-three innings, he yielded forty-five hits, including ten home runs. He struck out thirty-six batters, but he walked twenty foes and had an 8.10 earned run average. The product of Durango High was thrilled to return home and grab a spot on the incredibly talented CSN roster.

Donnie Roach lost the second game to end a remarkable stretch. After he had been pounded by Cypress in that metal-bat game at CSN on February 19 and before that game at Salt Lake City, Roach had tossed eight gems in nine outings; the one anomaly coming in the Coyotes' horrible weekend in Carson City. In those eight sterling starts, all victories, Roach had recorded a 0.92 ERA. And four of the six total earned runs he had allowed came in one game, a blowout victory at Eastern Utah on March 26. In those fifty-nine innings of work, Roach had yielded only twenty-six hits, and he had struck out eighty-one while walking only twelve.

That night, after the first doubleheader in Salt Lake City, Matt Medina and Marvin Campbell walked by the semicircular, red-padded booth that Mr. C, Kenny, and I occupied at the nearby diner to say hello after they had eaten dinner. Medina, standing to the right next to Kenny, who was sitting at that edge, started walking away when Kenny grabbed his arm. Aren't you forgetting something? Kenny asked. Medina stood perplexed as Kenny handed him his wallet; it had been in his front left pocket.

Using the silky touch he had developed in his youth to survive on the mean streets of the Bronx, where he had watched the games at Yankee Stadium from the roof of his tenement, Kenny could pickpocket a walnut from a squirrel. He could also spew the finest string of Spanish invectives this side of Puerto Rico. Kenny explained to several Coyotes that, indeed, he's black, but a Hispanic family had adopted him when he was an infant. In Twin Falls and Salt Lake City, he spent stretches on the CSN dugout rail blasting opponents in high-pitched, ornery Spanish, to the delight of every Coyote. At the start of every road trip, as he guided the bus out of the Morse Stadium grounds in the early morning, Kenny always told Scott Dysinger and Trevor Kirk that their cars would be stolen from the CSN parking lot while they were away.

That weekend, Chambers kept his hurlers on a rare tight pitch count to avoid any arm or depth issues for the pending postseason. Still, the games counted and getting swept was never easy for him to digest. "Let's have some fucking fun, boys," said Gabby Weidenaar after CSN dropped the first game Saturday. "Let's have some fun!"

The Coyotes put up a fight in the fourth game. Bryce Harper smashed a two-run homer to right field in a four-run fifth inning. The color of the bat didn't matter. The distinctive sound of Harper's home runs, and many of his hits, got a rise out of his teammates.

"That bomb he hit . . . oh, it's Bryce," Tomo Delp said with a shrug. "You kind of get used to it. Still, it's amazing. The sound of the ball off his bat is a gunshot, compared to everyone else."

David Segui had logged fifteen seasons in the majors and believed that the sound of the ball off Harper's bat was as uncommon as its trajectory. The forty-four-year-old Segui likened the arc of many Harper home runs to left field to what he saw fly off the bat of Ken Griffey, Jr.; instead of the usual slice from a lefty's bat, those two sluggers could crush homers to left that appeared to soar out of stadiums on straight lines, with scant slice, and rise a second time, like a well-struck golf ball, due to the incredible underspin. Segui just shook his head.

In the dugout, Josh Demello had been unusually quiet. He hadn't been humming any reggae or singing lines from a popular Oahu band. He told me that he felt that he "could have" played at the next level, as if his future had already been determined and that chance had dwindled away due to his erratic playing time. We exchanged small talk and I tried boosting his spirits.

In the sixth, Chambers tapped Demello to hit for Marvin Campbell, and Demello responded with a bunt down the third-base line that eked by the charging third baseman, hit the bag, and dribbled into shallow left field. "That was the best bunt ever," said Gabby. Demello sped into second base and scored on Trevor Kirk's single.

Marvin Campbell leaned on the rail next to Mr. C and admired the watch Chambers had given him to commemorate the Coyotes' 2003 World Series championship. "Mr. C, that's a dope-ass watch!" Campbell said. "I want to get one like that. Miech, you seen this?" I had. Yup, I told Campbell, "It is dope-ass."

Harper led off the seventh by flying out to center field. He returned to the dugout and smashed his batting helmet on the ground. He sat on the bench and stared down with his head in his hands.

Taylor Jones threw a complete-game four-hitter in CSN's 7–0 victory. Late in the game, when the Coyotes were hitting, Jones threw his left arm—the valuable one that was responsible for that three-two curve that had so confounded Harper seven months earlier at Foothill High—around my shoulders, as players are wont to do on the dugout rail. At first, it was surprising. Then again, they'd gotten used to me. I'd gotten used to them. After the final out, Demello flashed a knowing smile my way. It was wild, he said, how that worked out—Chambers calling for him, and his bunt for a double—after our conversation.

That night, Harper stayed in Salt Lake City. Coyotes pitcher Taylor Larsen had seventh-row center tickets to the Utah Jazz–Los Angeles Lakers NBA play-off game at EnergySolutions Arena. Jazz coach Jerry Sloan, it had been rumored, wanted to meet Harper.

"It was a good game, too. A great game," Harper later said of the Lakers' 111–110 victory that give them a three-games-to-none edge in the series. A few weeks later, they would successfully defend their NBA title. "I couldn't have gone to a better game than that. Kobe [Bryant] was lighting it up. [Derek] Fisher lit it up. [Ron] Artest had a great game. [Pau] Gasol had a good second half. Taylor's dad got the tickets, and he's friends with Jerry Sloan. Taylor said [Sloan would] like to meet me when we're over there, so I met him."

Nobody bothered Harper, for his autograph or a quick photograph, at the basketball game. He was at a rare sporting event with thousands of fans and nobody recognized him. Afterward, he hung out with Larsen and infielder Casey Sato, and some of their Utah friends, in Murray, south of Salt Lake City. At twelve thirty in the morning, Ryan Thomas, who had also stayed in Utah to spend time with family, was shopping at a Wal-Mart for Mother's Day cards for his mother and grandmother when he looked at his cell phone. It was Harper.

"Hey, man, let's go hang out. What the heck is going down tonight?"

"It's not a poppin' night," Thomas chuckled.

"You told me it's poppin' every night in Salt Lake City."

"It would be if I wasn't buying Mother's Day cards."

Thomas would marvel about Harper having reached out to him in Utah and his attending a Jazz play-off game for months. "Seventh-row center, and it's not even his home state. That's impressive."

Kenny steered the coach into the Morse Stadium parking lot at 1:00 a.m., and Trevor Kirk's white, two-door Acura and Scott Dysinger's black, four-door Ford Expedition were right where the players had left them, as usual.

A few days later, J. C. Paquin, one of coach Boomer Walker's players at the College of Southern Idaho, examined Harper's statistics. Harper had collected 123 total bases in 121 at bats. Forty-two of his seventy-five hits had been for extra bases. Twenty-three had sailed beyond the fences. A six-foot-two native of Montreal, Paquin shook his head and told a small group of coaches and teammates, "If it looks like a chicken, smells like a chicken, and tastes like a chicken, and Bryce Harper says it's beef, it's beef."

WITH THE REGULAR SEASON completed and the Scenic West Athletic Conference, or Region 18, tournament, next up for the College of Southern Nevada, writers for the *Washington Post* and *Pittsburgh Post-Gazette* parachuted into Morse Stadium for practice on Tuesday, May 11.

Chambers had made an exception and allowed Dave Sheinin of the *Post* and Chuck Finder of the *Post-Gazette* a few minutes with Bryce Harper after the hitting and fielding sessions. During batting practice, Harper dazzled the newcomers with a show to which the Morse regulars had long become accustomed. But his first full-bore swing, after laying down bunts along the third- and first-base lines, was a bullet at first base. Somehow, it missed first basemen Ryan Thomas and Chris Sambol, who had not been looking toward home, and catcher Kaz Smith, who had just hit and was rounding first. The few people who had watched the ball rifle so close to three skulls, take your pick, just stared in quiet amazement that nobody got nailed.

A few pitches later, Harper bet anyone within earshot that he would belt a homer over the Brando's Pizza ad on the fence in right-center field. Nobody took his challenge. He might have actually pointed at the pepperoni pie, too.

"He delivered," Finder wrote in his piece that ran on Sunday,

May 30, of the ball that sailed high over the fence. Finder called him THE WONDER KID, but Harper revealed little, with Coyotes assistant coach Cooper Fouts sitting within earshot to quickly object to any inappropriate question from Finder or Sheinin. As he did when MLB Network plopped in and hung all those lights, cameras, and microphones in CSN's tight locker room, Harper belied his age when he mostly gave brief and generic answers to every inquiry.

"I love it. I've had a lot of fun," Harper had told Finder. "It crosses my mind where you miss [high school] and stuff, but I wouldn't take anything back."

But at the very moment Harper was talking with the two reporters, he had been missing high school far more than he let on. He had been attending play-off games in the area with Showtime, which laced Harper with guilt because he couldn't help Las Vegas High. Harper felt as if he had deserted the Wildcats. He said nothing to the outsiders.

Sheinin, a bit more timely with a piece that ran five days after he had been in Henderson, focused on the eye black, the tossing of his bat at the plate, scooping up dirt, spitting in his hands, exasperation with umpires, and the slamming of his helmet at the dugout floor. Sheinin wrote of a scout shaking his head at those antics and mentioned the "bad, bad guy" line from the notorious Baseball Prospectus piece. "People can talk, do whatever they want," Harper told Sheinin. "I don't really care." Ron Harper told Sheinin, "I always tell my boys, be John Wayne out there. Be a gunslinger."

Assistant coach Cooper Fouts had finally reached Dallas Braden, the Oakland Athletics pitcher who had tossed a perfect game against Tampa Bay on Mother's Day and whom Fouts caught at Texas Tech, to say hello and exchange small talk. Fouts recalled Braden scaling an outfield fence to reach a teammate who had been tardy to a game and teach him a tough punctuality lesson with his fists.

Landon Powell had caught Braden's gem. Powell was the one-time hot prospect from North Carolina who, upon the advice of agent Scott Boras, got his GED after his junior prep season in 2000 and became a free agent, only to have no major league team interested in signing him. So he went back to high school and attended the University of South Carolina. Oakland picked Powell—who had signed with the SFX agency by then—in the first round of the 2004 draft, and he made his major league debut in April 2009.

The SWAC tournament started on Wednesday, May 12, but because CSN had won the regular season title, it got a bye and did not play that day. The Coyotes had batting practice at Foothill High, across Heather Drive, which was haphazard at best as only a few coaches ran it and some players were missing. Since they were hosting the tournament, several Coyotes had to stay behind to prep the Morse Stadium diamond, to rake the mixture of dirt and sand and clay back into the base paths and home-plate area and water the infield dirt, before every game.

At Foothill, a pack of Coyotes stretched and taped hands and bats, in front of the third-base dugout, and conversation, as usual, revolved around female conquests. Bryce Harper casually mentioned how he had screwed one girl that morning and received a blow job from another at lunchtime. Not one teammate within earshot called Harper on his claims or even glanced at him with a nod of acknowledgment or approval, as if they knew he had just been talking. To fit in. Folly.

After a round of foul tips into the cage and infield pops, Harper walked away from home plate and said, "I fuckin' hate this sport. Not kidding. I just want to play football." He smirked as he swung his black Marucci into the air and squinted into the sun at the site of his inglorious golden sombrero.

At dusk, before the final game of the day, league officials gave out season awards. Chambers won Coach of the Year, Bryce Harper Player of the Year, and Donnie Roach shared Pitcher of the Year honors with six-foot-five Kramer Champlin of Western Nevada. In two regular-season games against Champlin, Bryce Harper had gone oh for four, with a pair of walks and runs, and a strikeout. While a swarm of players prepped the field for the final game that day, Harper sat in a black barber's chair, a choice perch near the entry of the CSN clubhouse. The Rook was oblivious to his teammates sweating and toiling. He was in his own world, which consisted of text messages on his cell phone.

Trevor Kirk admonished him for not helping on the diamond. Harper responded, "I do my work during the games." That incensed Kirk even more. "You don't think you're part of this team?" Kirk snapped. "You don't think you should do your part?" Harper stayed put as that anger drifted inside the clubhouse among several other Coyotes. The draft isn't for a couple more weeks, one said. He's already coasting? said another.

The morning of CSN's first conference tournament game, on May 13, did not start well for Roach, whom fellow pitcher Tyler Hanks couldn't believe was even walking around the premises a few hours before game time. "I hit him right in the head with a Semtex bomb!" Hanks gleefully proclaimed. "Blew up his head!" Hanks looked at Roach as if he were an alien. Roach acted as if Hanks weren't there. They had played the video game *Call of Duty* that morning, and Hanks's soldier had lobbed a Semtex device, or sticky bomb, perfectly so Roach's figure ran right into it, uh, headfirst.

Gabe Weidenaar had complained the previous day about not having a good bat. All of his had cracked. For the hell of it, I brought him a store-bought Manny Ramirez model of a Louisville Slugger I had toyed with while hitting baseballs at local parks with friends. I gave it to Gabby, as a lark, and he marveled at its lightness—probably not even thirty ounces, he said—in the cages. It hadn't even cost me thirty bucks. Gabby took a few swings, and I walked away. I never saw that bat again. Hopefully, Claim Jumper got it and did something useful with it, like turn it into toothpicks.

It had been the rare occasion that I'd ventured around the three batting cages before a game. That was the players' domain to hit and prepare, to concentrate. But scouts, kids, some looky-loo fans, even a television cameraman who shot footage of Bryce Harper as he hit in the far-right cage, mingled around. The Coyotes, and one in particular, felt as if they were zoo animals. No security was around to police the area. The blue gate between the dugout and clubhouse that was usually locked or guarded was wide-open. Bryce walked around the far-right cage and glared at anyone who dared to look at him.

Combine his guilt over not being there for Las Vegas High, Trevor Kirk's chastising him for not helping with the field work, the grumbling over hitting at Foothill, where he had been fitted for one of the few sombreros of his life, and the discomfort in his own batting cage before a play-off game, and Bryce Harper smoldered.

Bryan Harper, wearing a blue Dwight Howard Orlando Magic jersey, tended to the mound. Nine bases lay off to the right of the home dugout, with three cans of the white Rust-Oleum inverted spray inches away. Nobody was around, so I gave the dirty bases fresh white coats. Ron Harper walked by and laughed. "Finally putting you to work?" he said. About time, eh? White specks stayed on the tips of the fingers on my right hand all day.

An hour before the game, Bryce appeared to have settled himself. He strolled through the dugout and perfectly belted out the first few lines of "Thunder Road"—*The screen door slams, Mary's dress waves . . . like a vision she dances*—blaring on the Morse Stadium speakers. Bryce Springsteen? Harper jogged in beat to the song out to right field, where he warmed up by tossing a baseball with Wes Hunt.

Trevor Kirk talked about wanting to win this tournament to keep playing, to get to the next one, the districts in Lamar, Colorado, where the prize would be a spot in the Junior College World Series. A Texas-Arlington scout had informed Kirk and Scott Dysinger that the Mavericks weren't going to continue recruiting them, so Kirk was more uncertain than ever about playing the game in 2011.

The tournament did not begin well for Harper. His random thoughts had so distracted him that he forgot and left his pin-striped number thirty-four uniform at home on Cantelope Court. He had worn it the previous night to the league's awards ceremony. Events were beginning to stack up and affect him, and that had been a mindless error.

For the Coyotes' first game, Harper wore number twenty-two. That had been pitcher Kiel Harmon's jersey, but the Sierra Vista High School graduate had been left off the play-off roster. Harmon effectively ended his CSN career when he chose to stay home instead of coming to the stadium to support his teammates, even if he wasn't on the roster.

With the foreign twenty-two jersey, and the pregame batting-cage crowd that got under his skin, and all the other foibles on which Harper had been dwelling, he struck out twice, grounded and popped out, and drew an intentional walk. In the bottom of the third, after flying out to left field, he angrily slammed his helmet to the dugout ground.

Donnie Roach went the distance to pace CSN to a 9–2 victory over the College of Southern Idaho. "I'm going to get you another ring!" Roach told Chambers. Harper was trying to deal with his crises. His high school team's playing poorly in the play-offs seemed to cement his torment.

An hour after the game, at 4:28, a serious-looking Ron Harper bolted from the clubhouse to the right-field chain-link fence, which he opened. At 4:33, Chambers escorted Bryce Harper, wearing his gray number twenty-four Team USA hitting jersey, out of the stadium through that gate so he wouldn't have to wade through about thirty autograph seekers at the stadium entrance. By Bryce Harper's body language, it would have been a stretch to believe that CSN had just won a game.

Harper was feeling overwhelmed, which he admitted to Chambers in a dramatic exchange of text messages that night between 8:59 and 9:32. Chambers had started the exchange.

How you doin'? It's a new day tomorrow. The sun will come up, I promise. Get your mind right. I will keep the vultures away. You just play and have fun.

Harper immediately answered. He texted back that he was feeling okay. His head just wasn't in the game today and he wasn't having fun. *I love this game but today I didn't.*

Chambers wrote that he had not known that all that commotion had taken place in the cages hours before the game. He had been in his office, filling out his lineup card, and talking strategy with his assistants. It would have been different had Chambers known those outside influences had infiltrated his team's private workouts.

I know why u didn't love it today because you are tired. Everybody wants a piece of Bryce and the blue gate will be locked tomorrow. It is about you and I will keep them away from you.

The next morning, Ron Harper policed the area around the CSN dugout and clubhouse as if he were with the KGB. That blue gate, between the end of the dugout and the clubhouse, had been shut and would be monitored by two security officers. Nobody who didn't belong in the Coyotes' private areas roamed around that territory.

Harper continued his Thursday-night text messages to Chambers:

He expressed his love for the game, but complained about the toll being in the spotlight was taking on him. *I can handle it, but I just wanna have fun again like high school.* He said he missed just playing the game.

Chambers responded that that's all he wanted, too.

Everything will be OK. You be Bryce and fuck em all. I promise they will not get near you and I will take all the heat for it because I don't give a shit what they think of me. And if you were in hs you would still be getting all the attention. So have fun and lets go get a ring together.

Harper replied yes.

By the way fuck off. Ha. Love you so much and I will always be here for you. Let's finish what we started. Don't look into the future. Let's live in the now (win). That's important now.

Love you too coach! Harper texted back thanking Chambers for everything.

Sleep, please. You my boy (blue.)

Harper said he'd try.

That last line by Chambers had been a reference to Will Ferrell's movie *Old School,* in which Ferrell's character, crying, says, "You're my boy, blue!" at the funeral of an elderly man. Chambers and Harper had exchanged that line before. Chambers had wanted to leave Harper laughing. He didn't.

Harper's first junior college play-off game wasn't another golden sombrero, but it might as well have been. All of his thoughts had derailed him. In his mind, everything was on the line. His team won, and by margin. Hadn't he said all he cared about was the W? His melancholy mood showed that might not have been such a sincere statement. It was the postseason and he had not performed. How would scouts view that? What would the Nationals think? Are number one picks determined by producing when it mattered most? Harper did not shy away from explaining the events of that day.

"I like to get work done with nobody around. Nobody should be back here when we're getting loose. When we get done, they can all be back here. We play the game, and then they can be back here . . . and only a few, not a million with cameras and crap like that, and scouts. We got work to do. And there are cameras. Shit like that gets annoying."

About bolting that evening with Chambers through the right-field gate, where his father awaited, Harper sighed.

"It was a tough day. Just had a breakdown. Came back the next day, nobody was back there, and went four for four. I was missing high school a lot, for my team. It had a good shot to make it to state. I kind of left them. If I came back, I think we would have won state. No one would have beaten us. That happens. It sucks. I felt like I was letting down coach [Sam] Thomas a lot, but I talked to him and everything was good. It was all fine."

The Las Vegas Wildcats had gone 1-2 in the area play-offs, bowing out in the quarterfinals. Sam Thomas confirmed that Bryce Harper had told him he had felt guilty about not being there for the Wildcats, but Thomas told Harper that that was nonsense. Sure, Harper could have helped, Thomas said. He would help any team. But there are no guarantees.

"There are a lot of what-ifs, but I'd rather think of what he did and what he's going to be able to do. I told him, 'Move on.' It was a thought of his. I won't lie. He could have helped anyone win a state title. But we had some seniors that didn't step up. I won't dwell on the fact that he wasn't there—I'm more excited about what Bryce is going to do than what he could have done."

Thomas wore a short, salt-and-pepper goatee and hadn't missed many meals; he resembled a well-fed Ben Kingsley. Thomas was born and raised in Las Vegas. As a senior, remember, he caught junior pitcher Greg Maddux at Valley High. Thomas's father, Charlie, still worked at Titanium Metals Corp., in Henderson. Anyone who played golf or flew in an airplane or had a knee or hip replacement, Charlie Thomas or a colleague probably had had his hands on some part of the device used.

Sam Thomas was fortunate to have had Bryce Harper play for him for two years. Bishop Gorman had been an option for Harper when he started high school, but the annual tuition of more than $10,000 had been prohibitive. Bryce had participated in Thomas's summer camps, and then he enrolled at Las Vegas High, less than a half mile from his front door, when he could have played at any high school in the city. Bishop Gorman would have required a daily round-trip of more than thirty miles.

"He could have gone anywhere," Thomas said, "as illegal as it is, with the exception of [the private] Bishop Gorman. Every high school was trying to get him. What he did this year didn't surprise me. The people that don't know him are jealous or have an opinion that doesn't seem very positive. They look at him as being cocky or overrated. Yet, if you have the opportunity to be around him, he'll make you a fan of him. That's one of the special gifts he has. It's not his game so much, but *him*. Once you become a fan of Bryce, the kid, the person, then you sit back, and you can't help but root for him."

New York Times reporter Alan Schwarz might not be such a fan. He had the misfortune of getting a few minutes with Harper, via Chambers, scheduled for after that Friday game. But after Thursday's events, Harper was in Operation Shutdown, by Chambers's decree. Schwarz fumed at Chambers, who did not budge. Schwarz stormed out of the CSN clubhouse without talking to Harper.

Harper's four for four effort against Salt Lake that Friday helped CSN win, 6–5. He had slammed a two-out, one-hop double off the left-field wall in the first and scored the first run of the game. He singled to right in the third inning and got picked off trying to steal second base.

Heading into the top of the fifth, Alice Cooper's "School's Out for Summer" blared on the stadium speakers. Harper had grabbed his glove and was bolting out of the dugout when he stopped right in front of me and altered the last line of Cooper's ditty to "School's out for-*fuckin'-ever*!" Harper laughed to himself as he ran out to right field.

He singled to right in the fifth inning but made the last half of an inning-ending double play. In the eighth, Harper doubled down the right-field line, and Gabe Weidenaar and Harper tallied the tying and go-ahead runs, respectively, on Trevor Kirk's single to left.

Kirk had produced the play of the game when he ended it, in the top of the ninth with two outs, by diving in front of him and to his right, to catch a liner with a man on third. Bryce Harper had been shifted to catcher two innings earlier, and Kirk had moved from center to right.

The morning of the final, Dysinger and Kirk showed up at eight thirty, nearly five hours before first pitch. A couple of hours before the game, Chambers laid 120 older CSN jerseys on a table by the stadium entrance, to layer the crowd in pinstripes. I grabbed number twenty-seven. Joe Robinson wore that number and smiled when he passed me. Tomo Delp entered the dugout holding his white cap and admired a ladybug on the bill. "Yeah," he said of the good-luck symbol.

Chambers leaned on the far right side of the dugout rail and shook his head. His sixteen-year-old daughter, McKenzie, had wrecked his wife's silver Lexus that morning entering a freeway on-ramp. Neither Mac nor the other driver had been injured, but the front of the Lexus had been rolled up. Yup, Mac told her dad, she had been looking at a text message on her cell phone when it happened. She had had her license for three and a half weeks.

Bryce Harper heard what happened, and when that chatter had drifted out of the dugout, he told me how he had been in a similar accident exactly a year earlier, the morning of the *Sports Illustrated* photo shoot. He had been driving his buddy's Ford F-150 truck when he checked his text messages at Warm Springs and Green Valley. Harper nailed an Acura with an older couple inside. Nobody was injured.

Harper had no driver's license and no permit. He called his dad. "What the . . . ," said Ron Harper, who soon fishtailed from the other side of the street as he pulled a U-turn to get to the scene. Police were startled and asked Bryce, who's that? My dad, he said. "Uh-oh," said the officers. As part of his penance for driving without a license, Harper nearly gagged when he had been forced to view corpses in the morgue at the Clark County Coroner's Office.

Harper flashed a ghastly look in the dugout. Have fun today, I told him. "Oh, yeah! Especially after *that* story." He was cool and relaxed, a million mental miles from that guy who had just wanted to be a kid again and have fun playing the game.

CSN was just as cool and relaxed in the championship game a few hours later, when it all but locked up its 8–2 victory over Western Nevada for a spot in the Western District tournament in the first inning with five runs.

Bryce Harper had singled to right and scored the third run, but he flew out on a deep fly to center and struck out three times in his other at bats. The first one he was caught looking, but he wasn't even in the box; the umpire hadn't called time when Harper stepped out so quickly, so the ump continued with his punch-out call after the pitcher had followed through with his pitch and thrown a strike. In the sixth,

Harper whiffed on a one-two pitch and busted his bat on the dugout floor.

Wildcats coach D. J. Whittemore had been impressed, not about this game by Harper but by the stunning impact he had made on the game with a wooden bat in the challenging league. Recall that Whittemore, in the fall, thought it was the most foolish situation—a high school *junior* thinking he could swing a wooden bat in *this* junior college conference—he had ever heard of. He thought twice about that statement long after the season had been put to bed.

"He proved me wrong. I'll admit it was certainly fun playing in front of large crowds at our park and theirs. I think, a lot of times, the quality of the other players on that team got overlooked. The depth and quality of their pitching was incredible."

Whittemore came around to admire Bryce Harper's competitive drive and fortitude, his willingness to bear so much of the publicity burden. That allowed so many of his teammates to operate under the radar, Whittemore said. None of them felt that white-hot spotlight. It was all focused on Harper.

"I had no idea the pressure he must have been under. It must have been immense. Certainly the hype was immense, and I thought he absolutely lived up to the hype. I asked our pitchers to make sure he didn't beat us, to pitch around him. They didn't listen. They kept pitching to him."

Although CSN had defeated Western Nevada in the one game that mattered, in the conference tournament final to advance to the Western District tournament, Whittemore took some measure of pride in his Wildcats' winning five of nine games against the Coyotes and in beating Bryce Harper, in Carson City, in his lone pitching appearance of the season. Critiques of certain umpires weren't mentioned.

"But he's a great talent," Whittemore said. "He was good for junior college baseball and good for the state of Nevada, and I'm happy for all the success he had. It was enjoyable to be a part of that."

While Marvin Campbell conducted an interview for a local television station, Bryan Harper smacked him with a shaving-cream pie. Coyotes hugged and high-fived each other, but they were controlled. They had bigger plans. Western Nevada respectfully hung around to watch all the festivities, and Whittemore said the Wildcats lost to likely the best junior college team ever assembled.

Trevor Kirk earned the tournament's MVP honors by going six for eleven at the plate, with a pair of doubles, and scoring four runs. He had mostly lived with his grandparents after his parents divorced long ago. For the past year, after his maternal grandmother, Mary, lost her battle with cancer, Kirk had been keeping his grandfather company.

Out in center field Kirk always stood facing the wall, with his cap over his heart and his head bowed, and said a prayer to Mary before the other team hit in the first inning of every game. In the preseason of 2009, CSN had returned from a tournament in Florida as Mary slipped away. "People said she hung on just to give me one more hug and say good-bye," Trevor said. "She would do anything for me."

Harold Shrader, Kirk's seventy-one-year-old grandfather, was a mess after the game. He wore an untucked pin-striped Coyotes' number sixteen jersey—Kirk's number. Before the championship game against Western Nevada, Shrader had grabbed Chambers on the edge of the dugout and, already with glassy eyes, told him that nobody could have molded Trevor, and matured him, the way Chambers had.

"I had a coach like that in the 1950s," Shrader told Chambers. "He wouldn't holler. He just knew what to do." Trevor reminded Shrader of himself, when he played six sports every year in high school twenty-five miles south of Fort Worth in Alvarado, Texas. Shrader had wheels, hit well, and his right arm was a bazooka.

Before every CSN game, Shrader always gave his grandson the same advice: "Play like you have a pair." Shrader wasn't referring to eyes or legs. His bear hug of Trevor after the game confirmed that his grandson had listened.

17

BRYCE HARPER LICKED HIS lips and paused for a few seconds, giving my question serious consideration. Should it be illegal for him to hit with an aluminum stick? He laughed and finally deferred to reason. "I don't know. I'm just looking forward to this tournament."

The Western District championship, a double-elimination affair to be played in Lamar, Colorado, would determine which of four teams, including CSN, would advance to the Junior College World Series in Grand Junction, Colorado. In this tournament and in Grand Junction, if the Coyotes advanced to the grand stage of junior college baseball, aluminum bats would be employed.

The tin had made its way into the college game in 1974, as a cost-saving measure. Aluminum bats cost about $300, three times that of wood, but could be used all season. Sometimes, Bryce Harper broke two wooden bats a day. Coach Chambers and his assistants said the expense difference wasn't even close. Harper had been quite fortunate that a collegiate program that participated in a wooden-bat conference existed just down the freeway from his home.

The Coyotes flew to Denver on several flights, on two different airlines, on May 19. Those flying Southwest, where bags flew for free, were given the brunt of the equipment. I got to McCarran International Airport in Las Vegas at 7:00 a.m., just in time to walk through security with Coach Chambers, and a few assistants and players. On the plane, Trent Cook sat next to Bryce Harper, who stepped aside to let another passenger by. "Thanks, Bruce," said the man, who had misheard the first name of the most famous amateur baseball player in the country. Minutes later, another teammate wanted Harper's attention. Cook said, "Hey, Bruce." Harper didn't respond. Cook nudged Harper. "Hey, *Bruce,* he wants you." Harper finally giggled.

In Denver, we had a wait of nearly four hours as the players gathered from their scattered flights. In a huge concourse we made camp, piling dozens of black CSN equipment bags and satchels and backpacks in a mound. Bryce Harper took out a metal bat, glanced up at the fabricated, undulating canopy that looked like a half-closed accordion, and asked nearby teammates if they were up for a game of pepper—a batter knocks grounders and liners to three or four teammates fifteen feet away, hitting the ball again as a player lobbed it back to him. There were no NO PEPPER signs—common in ballparks—anywhere. He wound up playing catch, with a baseball and gloves, with Wes Hunt thirty feet away.

When all had finally gathered, Kelly pulled her Coach America, with the dark-tinted windows and red and blue stripes on the white sides, to the boarding curb outside the airport and we headed east toward Lamar. We were on a two-lane road passing abandoned shacks and dilapidated buildings. An HBO show called *Eastbound & Down*—yup, baseball was its theme and a washed-up good-ol'-boy relief pitcher was its main character—on the video screens failed to grab my attention.

Rolling through a town called Fowler along US Highway 50, the coach drew a few stares. "First bus they've ever seen," said someone from the back. Kelly made a pit stop at the Tank N Tummy, where pretzels, candy, soda, and water were hoarded. Josh Demello was brave enough to try a slice of pepperoni pizza that looked as if it had been baking under a heat lamp for a month. Might pass out, he said. Might have the Nike logo on the other side, I said.

Dark-tipped clouds looked like a lurching, growling ten-thousand-foot tsunami unfolding to the north. A blanket of hail stormed down upon the last half of the players, who had to run the fifty feet between the store and the bus. "What the hell is that?" said Danny Higa, who had never seen hail in Honolulu. "There should be a wet T-shirt contest," said Ryan Thomas. It pelted pitcher Chasen Shreve, the best-dressed Coyote, wearing dark slacks and a blue dress shirt. Always like to look good, he said. Shreve's older brother, Colby, threw for Chambers at CSN and spent 2010 pitching for Philadelphia's Single-A squad, so Chasen knew the drill about feeling good if you look good, and throwing good if you feel good.

The nimbus fangs hovered as the bus passed a dairy farm in Rocky Ford, curved right along long, tall, and deep rows of hay bails, and dipped in a cluster of oak trees. We lost? said Trent Cook. Marvin Campbell thought we were in someone's driveway. Where are we going, said Gabby Weidenaar, "the Field of fucking Dreams?" Kelly had been following her GPS device. Assistant coach Marc Morse, from the front left seat, tried to find where we were on a county map.

The bus stopped in what looked like that desolate crossroads in Texas where Tom Hanks, at the end of his hit movie *Cast Away,* attempted to deliver the package that had washed up to him on that island somewhere in the Pacific. We stopped. Morse, pointing at his map, talked with Kelly. Finally, with hesitation, we continued. Fifteen minutes later, we rounded a left curve and stumbled onto Highway 50 east, back on track.

Tyler Hanks, the country boy from Utah with Polynesian ancestry, pointed out the alfalfa off to the right of the bus. We passed thousands of cows, in pen after pen, the immensity of which surprised even Hanks. "Thistle," he said two minutes later, as if he had just found termites under the carpet, when he peered down out of the window with his nose to the glass. Hanks shook his head. "That's bad. You don't want thistle."

We pulled into the Super 8, next to the long, narrow, and abandoned redbrick BMS Truss Plant, sitting high on a concrete foundation. Two minutes inside Room 209 and it was apparent we were not staying at the Waldorf. The toilet didn't flush, so I opened the back and lifted the flange. Take me back fifty years, said Mr. C, wincing.

Fifteen minutes later we were back on the bus to take batting practice at Merchants Park. Kelly had been diverted to the right, past homes of varying degrees of decay and stature. Cops had shut down Main Street. "Someone spit on the sidewalk," said a Coyote. "That's funny," said another player as half of the bus howled.

Lamar, with a population of almost eight thousand and a median household income of almost $24,000 less than the Colorado average of $56,993, had been in a slump since the 2006 collapse of bus manufacturer Neoplan. Pitcher Doug Brocail, who went to Lamar High School, had played with CSN assistant coach Kevin Higgins on the San Diego Padres in 1993. Higgins said Brocail and his family enjoyed Lamar and the great outdoors. "He'd show up at spring training with nine guns. The redneck loves hunting," said Higgins, laughing.

Wind energy was becoming a hot industry, and a sixty-foot propeller lay as a kind of badge at Lamar's train depot. CSN and Bryce Harper would come to understand why locals had to be proud of their anemology.

Merchants Park was a quirky yard full of dips and bowls and funky dimensions—the outfield fence was deeper in the alleys than to dead center field. Its dugouts didn't have rails. It would finish second to any diamond in Las Vegas. And this is where a spot in the Junior College World Series would be determined?

The Coyotes hit three at a time in the cages off the left-field line as the waves of dark clouds moved east at us. When the sun barely squeaked through the mash, raindrops fell. Ahh, the Midwest, I told Mr. C. Nothing like rain when it's sunny to give you a headache. Or when it's raining on the other side of the street, Mr. C said, but not this side. "Like Kalamazoo." Outside the cages, Mr. C showed a six-year-old boy how to hit by slowing down his hand speed. Harper looked up and said he'd seen six tornadoes in all his time playing in Oklahoma. A group of kids anxiously waited to acquire his autograph, but by the time the session ended, only one had had the patience to wait. After Harper signed a piece of paper, the seven-year-old Hispanic boy told Mr. C how poor his family was and how he was going to sell the autograph.

Upon returning to the Super 8, I entered Coach Chambers's room and grabbed a Bud Light as he fielded a text message from Bryce Harper. Chambers had sent Harper a note saying that he'd stay at CSN and not contemplate a move to UNLV, a rumor that had been building by the day for weeks, if Harper did not like his draft outcome or contract negotiations and wanted to play his sophomore season for the Coyotes.

No, go to UNLV. You have to go to Division I, do what's right for you and your family and win a national championship. I'll be fine, if I stay at CSN, with whomever.

From the two plastic, white chairs that each sat two people comfortably on the Super 8 porch, Mike the proprietor watched the world pass by on North Main Street, which doubled as the north-south link to the east-west Highway 50. To the right, a spiffy Holiday Inn Express had opened six weeks earlier. Mike shook his head over the business he had been losing.

A few minutes past eleven that first morning, Scott Dysinger and Trevor Kirk hung out on the porch as benign cumulus clouds drifted west. They couldn't take it anymore. They itched for the three o'clock game to start and wanted to get away from Room 118, which must have been known as the Pall Mall Room to locals for the way its decades of cigarette ash, residue, and smoke had seeped into the walls and the carpet, inducing every visitor to gag a half step inside the door. Good thing I brought extra Claritin, so Dysinger had something to soothe his violated sinus canals.

When Dustin Colbrin, the former Colorado Northwestern baseball coach who was tight with Chambers, arrived at the Super 8 to pick up assistant coach Marc Morse, Dysinger and Kirk took advantage of the ride to the park an hour and a half before Kelly was due to take the team to the yard. Dysinger was eager to gauge the competition and try to steal signs from the Central Arizona–Lamar opening game.

Kirk had been a bit too eager to leave the motel. After I arrived at the park, settled in to its nuances, and watched hometown Lamar pull away from Central, Kirk walked up to me and clasped his silver chain and cross around my neck. Good luck and safekeeping, he said. That okay? I nodded. I told him I am Catholic. I didn't tell him I didn't have good memories of the cold, gray church—weren't those gargoyles screaming down from the pillars?—from my youth. He placed his orange, wraparound sunglasses, upside down, flush against the *C* logo of my white cap.

Then he panicked. Kirk had left his peach Skoal in a pocket of his backpack somewhere back in the Pall Mall Room. I tapped Dustin Colbrin and we cruised back to the Super 8 in his little, blue, four-door Toyota. I finally found the orange tin and . . . wait, what's this? A pizza box? I opened it and a slice of sausage and pepperoni stared at me. I took a big bite and laughed. I took another and bolted. No doubt Kirk and Dysinger would think the maid got hungry.

Colbrin and I edged around the left-field foul pole. Kirk smiled when he saw me drop into the home-side dugout along the third-base line with the orange tin, which I only revealed by holding it between me and the red cinder-block back wall of the dugout, out of the umpires' views.

From that dugout, it wasn't possible to see Kirk's feet when he had trudged out to right field because of the crest of one of the goofiest fields in the country. Merchants Park was 375 feet to each power alley. Those points were connected by a straight wall, which marked dead center at 365. And the right-field foul pole was 310 feet from home plate. Bryce Harper salivated when he tossed his bat in the box. The quirk was that crest, and dips, bowls, and contours that made the infield, especially where the third-base area bled out to left field, look like a cross-country mogul ski run for rats. From the home dugout, Kirk looked as if he were amputated at the knees.

"There should be rules," Kirk said. "This is supposed to be like a superregional in junior college?" He had played on a field or two in high school that had potholes, but nothing as bad as the undulating joke of Merchants Park.

Trouble greeted CSN starting pitcher Donnie Roach the moment he saw the first Western Nebraska hitter, who reached first on a dribbler. Roach hit the third batter, but got out of the trouble. Bryce Harper gave Roach and the Coyotes a two-run advantage in the bottom of the inning by belting Tim Beard's first delivery over the left-field fence, but Roach didn't have an easy inning until the fifth. Roach hit another batter, walked one, and yielded two hits, and the game was tied. Two innings later, the dam broke on Roach when he gave up two doubles, a pair of singles, and a walk. Errors by third baseman Tomo Delp and shortstop Danny Higa helped Western take a 7–2 lead.

"Take some corn-hole looseners, boys," said assistant coach Steve Chatham before CSN hit in the bottom of the fourth. Chambers said to nobody in particular, "We tight? Huh?" He tripped over his own tongue with six regulation innings remaining. "We're fine! We got seven innings!"

CSN cobbled together pairs of runs in the fourth and fifth to get to within 7–6, but Harper was disgruntled at leaving the bases loaded with two out in the fourth. Tripping on the way to first, on the thick berm where the grass met the dirt, landed Harper on his mug halfway down the line as second baseman Josh Parker easily threw to first to end the threat.

Roach retired six of seven batters he faced in the fifth and sixth, but was given a spot on the bench by Chambers when he allowed a single to start the seventh. Bryan Harper came on in relief, fielded an easy grounder to throw out one Cougar, and watched Dysinger snag a liner and jump at second base for a nifty double play. That had come during a seven-week stretch in which Bryan Harper, with sore back muscles, had started only one time. He tried finding a groove by throwing out of the bullpen in four games.

In the bottom of the inning, designated hitter Ryan Thomas's two-run homer barely cleared the left-center wall and center fielder Jared Baros's glove. "One pitch at a time," CSN pitching coach Glen Evans softly said to Bryan Harper, sitting next to me in the dugout, moments after Thomas's big hit, "until you get six outs." Harper didn't even register another dozen throws.

In the top of the eighth, Western Nebraska chased him when he hit a batter, and a single and double made it 8–8. When Chambers lifted Harper for Aaron Kurcz, the Western bench chirped at Bryce Harper, who didn't back down behind the plate. Chatham had to pull the younger Harper away to diffuse the situation, and the umpire quelled the bickering. Kurcz walked a batter, but that set up a convenient double-play opportunity to start at any bag. Then he recorded a strikeout and got a batter to fly out to Gabe Weidenaar in center.

In the bottom of the ninth, Marvin Campbell got smacked in the shoulder with a one-out, two-strike pitch from Julio Davila. Chambers ran Matt Medina, the fastest Coyote, who covered sixty yards in six and two-fifths seconds, for Campbell. After Ryan Thomas flew out, pinch hitter Casey Sato and Danny Higa drew walks to load the bases for Scott Dysinger, who had so eagerly gone to the park seven hours earlier. Armani Gonzalez came on in relief for Western, and Dysinger slapped the first delivery through the infield, off shortstop Nelson Quintero's glove, for the victory.

Behind the CSN dugout, Marvin Campbell's father shook his head. The roller-coaster nature of baseball continued to confound the retired Las Vegas firefighter. "Here again, it's 'Harper,' 'Harper,' 'Harper,'" Mr. C said when he took his seat on Kelly's coach. "Well, our *team's* pretty good."

Did trailing 7–2 in such an important game qualify as the very jaws of hell? "Close," said Casey Sato, who had given the scripture that contained that line to Bryce Harper, ". . . especially with four errors!" Before Kelly pulled her big, white rig away from the park, Chambers leaned on the fifth-row aisle seats and spoke to his players. Proud of you guys for fighting. Can't believe we won that as crappy as we played. We've got to play better tomorrow against the home team. "And wherever you ate last night," said the king of all phobias and superstitions, "eat somewhere different tonight." In the back of the bus, Demello broke into a chorus of James Taylor's "You've Got a Friend."

Kelly turned a slow right into the Super 8 just as Western Nebraska's bus stopped in front of us to the right. The Cougars were about to disembark from a hauler that looked in worse shape than the one in which Charlie Brown tooled around the White River Ranch out there in the Great Basin of Nevada.

"Ahhhhhhh," said Donnie Roach, bent forward so he could peer out the right-side windows, as he made his way down the aisle of Kelly's coach, "we just beat you!"

That night I learned the depth of Chambers's eccentricities. With him and Dustin Colbrin, we plowed through a few pizzas and side sticks with marinara sauce and some Bud Lights. Soon enough I penguin-walked into the bathroom. Moments later, I heard Chambers yowl. Did his Dodgers just lose on a walk-off grand slam? Did he drop something on a toe?

Nope. Someone—me—actually had the audacity to use his toilet. I had finished my business and walked out when Chambers froze me. "Seriously?" he said. He was dumbfounded. Colbrin tried to suppress his laughter. He knew. I didn't. Nobody *ever* used Chambers's bathroom, especially for number two. He usually did his business elsewhere, in fact. He didn't even use the bathroom in his master bedroom at home. Chambers was busy making a mental list of all the cleaning supplies he would have to run out and get when I told him to relax, I'd take care of it. I'll wipe down and polish every square centimeter of that little room if you want me to, and I went at it. Twenty minutes later, he was somewhat calmer as I tried convincing him that that was the most sterile space in the western hemisphere. Months later, he could still not believe I had been so audacious.

The following morning, carrying a Big Mac and other goodies in a bag from McDonald's, Bryce Harper crossed Main Street back to the Super 8 wearing a white I'M THAT DUDE T-shirt. He had seen the Nike shirt in a Dick's Sporting Goods store two weeks earlier and quickly grabbed it. One of Donnie Roach's favorite sayings was "Be a dude!"

Harper lived up to that motto by hitting for the cycle, getting the triple in a ten-run eighth, in CSN's mercy-ruled 22–8 victory over Lamar a few hours later.

The first sound of championship Saturday, other than Mr. C's cutting down the redwoods of the world in his sleep, had been the sirocco outside. It never let up, staying at between forty and fifty miles an hour, and howled straight out to left and center field at Merchants Park. Birds couldn't fly against it. It blew caps off. Hitchcock would have loved it. Somehow, the American flag on the pole beyond center did not end up in tatters, with its strips landing in Wyoming.

A photographer shot Harper that long, dry, and ugly day for the June 7 issue of *Sports Illustrated*. In the upper-right corner of the cover, under BASEBALL'S NEXT SUPERSTARS, *Bryce Harper* appeared over *Stephen Strasburg*.

Central Arizona had to defeat the Coyotes twice to advance to the World Series. The conditions, and Central Arizona, teased and tested the Coyotes. By the time CSN starter Chasen Shreve was chased in the third inning, he had given up four homers and two doubles, and he had hit a batter. By the time reliever Taylor Jones was yanked in the sixth, he had yielded five home runs and two doubles, and he had hit two batters. CSN trailed, 21–4, heading into the bottom of the fourth.

Aluminum bats and a fierce wind are as combustible as a match and a tank of gasoline. Only Rommel and Montgomery would have enjoyed the perfect sandstorm. Dirt and dust funnels twisted into the CSN dugout for ten consecutive hours.

Fifth-year Central Arizona coach Jon Wente (pronounced *WEN-tee*) remembered a doubleheader being canceled once in Kansas when, at home plate, he and the other coach saw the light towers moving. Maybe we shouldn't be here, both coaches said at home plate. They didn't play; an official windout. Wente admitted that the conditions in Lamar were the worst in which a team of his had played a game.

Like CSN, Central had hit with wood all season, too. "The way it's supposed to be played," Wente said. With metal, you don't want to give away outs, he said. You need to scramble for every possible run, every extra base. That strategy would come into play in a big way.

CSN tried mounting a comeback in the first game, scoring ten runs to cut the final deficit to 21–14. A football score, Bryan Harper had correctly predicted early on. Bryce Harper had doubled in two and scored in the four-run fourth, and he led off the five-run eighth with a single and eventually crossed home plate. Scott Dysinger had started a triple play at second base, catching a ball and stepping on second for the first two outs, for the Coyotes.

But Tyler Iodence, a six-foot-two Vegas native, had turned in the grittiest performance of the CSN season. "Eye-oh" to his teammates, he was tan and moved as smooth as a spy. He didn't think he'd pitch again after undergoing disk surgery. Rehab was so difficult, bending over just a few degrees pained him. Still, he rebounded to throw fifteen innings for Chambers in 2010. And he finished this disaster by allowing no runs over the final three innings. He walked one, allowed three hits, and struck out four. Chambers could save another arm or two for the second game. When CSN scored five in the eighth, the fear of an unbelievable comeback circulated in the Central Arizona dugout.

In the CSN dugout, Donnie Roach became incensed when Central, ahead by double figures, used a late-game ploy to sneak a runner from second to third base. The Coyotes' pitcher hadn't been looking.

Tomo Delp, at third base, wasn't looking, either. The Arizona runner easily took third.

From his dugout perch, Roach laser-eyed Vaqueros third-base coach Anthony Gilich. "You're a clown!" Roach screamed. "Here we go! I'm gonna get in the second game and carve you up. You're a piece of shit! Your program has no class! I *know* you can hear me!" Gilich didn't look at Roach until the inning had ended. Gilich strolled toward his dugout, and only when he nearly reached the mound did he sneak a peek into CSN's dugout as he acted as if he were marking something on a small sheet of paper.

Wente looked for such guile in players he recruited, and he coached his guys to always be alert, to swipe an easy bag when the situation presented itself. Always. Especially with metal bats . . . you just never know. It wasn't unheard of to make up a deficit—or lose a lead—of ten runs.

"If it's wide-open, take it," said Wente, who had been the Central pitching coach when it had won the Junior College World Series in 2002. "Was it borderline? I don't think so. We're trying to go to Grand Junction and do something you'd never forget in your life."

When Gilich stepped into the Central dugout, he told Wente, "I don't know who that is over there, but they're wearing me out." Don't make it a bigger deal, Wente said. Just do your thing. Donnie Roach had that effect on opponents.

After the game, McKenzie Chambers bawled like a baby as she talked to her dad from their home in Red Rock Country Club. "We aren't going to Grand Junction!" she said between weeps. Coach Chambers responded, What are you talking about? There's another whole game left! We'll be fine.

Chambers ran his team out to left field and told them to refuse to lose. "We deserve it more! They have no class! Jump on them early! The biggest prize is on the line right now!" Deep down, the searing wind and heat, and the absolute pasting his team had just taken, had affected Chambers, who wondered how he would rally his players.

Chambers mutated into Jack Torrance, Jack Nicholson's bug-eyed character in *The Shining*. He became more psychotic than he had ever before been on a diamond. He had started a chant late in the first game. During the lull before the second one, he continued it. "It's hot! Only gonna get hotter! We're not goin' anywhere! We're right here! *It's hooooooooot!*"

Wente and Gilich and everyone else on the Central squad stopped in their tracks and gawked over at the zaniness unfolding, and the increasing decibels, in the other dugout. Wente had been filling in his lineup card and figuring out his available pitchers for the second game when Chambers caught him cold.

"I was thinking we got 'em," Wente said. "We were one game away. We got momentum on our side. But something changed that made [the Coyotes] believe. Like, throw game one out the window. That took our attention over there, to their dugout. It was hot. Tempers were short. As a coach, part of your job is not just the X's and O's, it's the mental side. I'm sure Coach Chambers felt momentum was in the Central dugout and thought, 'What could I do to change that?' Sometimes you do things that are crazy and off-the-wall, to change momentum, so game two isn't like game one."

Central center fielder Bryan Karraker led off the second game with a single but pulled into first base with a cramping right hamstring. It looked painful and would affect him the rest of the game, but he stayed in, hobbling in the outfield to make catches and hunt down doubles and triples. His extraordinary effort would result in the Coyotes' giving him a standing ovation.

Chambers did not relent. "They're crampin'!" he yelled. "And we're comin'! We're right here! *It's hooooooooot!*"

Bryce Harper helped dial up the heat. He transformed the field into his own personal pinball machine and made CSN's line score look like pi. When his team needed him most, with a World Series berth on the line, Harper became a one-man highlight reel.

He walked and scored in the first inning, and he hit four home runs over the next six innings. A moment before Harper's first homer, a three-run bazooka blast that sailed over the fence about ten feet from the right-field foul pole, Marvin Campbell said, "He's due." Campbell knew that when Harper was due, he most always delivered in a big way. In Harper's other trip to the plate over that stretch, he tripled down the right-field line to score a run. He sliced a solo shot down the left-field line in the fourth and pummeled a two-run rainbow to left-center in the fifth. Before his fourth homer, in the seventh inning, he walked up to me and glanced at my scorecard.

What do I need? Harper asked me. He wanted to connect for the cycle for a second consecutive day. I didn't exactly know how the official scorer had ruled what I considered a double to center in the first inning, so I told him "single." He thought they might have figured that was a single, so he was thinking he needed a double. We both scratched our heads. I finally said, "Just keeping knocking the snot out of the ball, I guess." Ron Harper, at the front of the chain-link fence to the right of the CSN dugout, asked Chambers what Bryce needed, too, for the cycle. Chambers didn't give a damn. "I'll take another home run," Chambers said.

Bryce Harper creamed Josh Dahl's two-two pitch, with Gabby Weidenaar on second, deep over the center-field fence. Harper finished with ten RBIs in the 25–11 romp. Trent Cook had homered twice, and Dysinger and Danny Higa had also pounded pitches over the fence. In two innings of relief, Donnie Roach did carve up the Vaqueros; nineteen of his twenty-three pitches were red-eyed strikes. Closer Aaron Kurcz continued to struggle when he allowed Central to score four times in the ninth. He hit a batter and walked another.

From four strikeouts in his first swings wearing a CSN uniform in that fall scrimmage at Foothill High School to four home runs in Lamar to propel the Coyotes into the Junior College World Series, Bryce Harper had been building up to the golden performance.

"It felt really good swinging the aluminum again. Getting that in my hand, just getting used to it that first game . . . all of us were trying to get used to it again throughout the whole tournament. You put the bat on the ball, and it's gone. That's all it is. Put it on the sweet spot and let your hands do the work. I miss the wood. Yup, for sure. I love swinging the wood, but to get that aluminum back in your hands . . . it is like an arcade game, so it's a lot of fun. I wasn't really mad between those two games. It's just, Central Arizona's a good-hitting team. I knew we'd come out on fire and play like we did. I knew we'd come out and swing it."

He smirked when asked again if it's fair for him to swing the tin.

"I don't know. Maybe, maybe not. But I knew I needed to be the leader and get it for everybody, pick my game up, hit some balls hard. In pressure situations like that, I usually go over the top and do some things I don't think I could ever do. I wanted to do what I could do to help the team win. I'll step up every time I need to. I have Trent [Cook] behind me, Marvin [Campbell] and TK [Trevor Kirk] behind me. . . . I just had a pretty good day."

Months later, many friends and colleagues had consistently asked Wente why he did not just intentionally walk Harper every time he went to the plate. Well, Wente said, the guys behind him hit almost as well as Harper did, soooo . . . "What hurt us was the weather," Wente said.

I reminded Harper of the Doctrine and Covenants passage that Casey Sato had shown him during the season, the one describing the *fierce winds* and *heavens gather blackness* and *elements combine* and *the very jaws of hell gape open the mouth wide after thee,* how all of that *shall give thee experience* and *be for thy good.* Harper nodded. Yup, he said, Lamar had represented the very jaws of hell, with the winds, dirt funnels, and adversity, and the Coyotes had kept their composure. Harper, especially, with those four home runs.

"I didn't think that wind would be that bad. It's a huge thing, for both teams, having that wind. You can't let down. You can't shut down. You can score twelve or thirteen, and the other team can score twelve or thirteen, and it'll be tied. The wind is an equalizer. I've played in bad rain in Oklahoma, and I've played in some snow. But that wind was bad. In Oklahoma, tornado sirens have gone off during games. I'd lay in bed sometimes and tornado warnings would go off, and everybody would go crazy."

IT'S HOT screamed from the back of Junior College World Series T-shirts that Chambers would contract high school pal Clark Hill to print for his coaches and players, and all of the Coyotes fans who would travel to Grand Junction, Colorado.

Daylight quickly faded as Kelly guided the coach into the Super 8 parking lot. Chambers announced that they would depart for the long drive to Denver in one hour. There were a few, albeit quiet, dissenters. By the time most every player had walked into his room, the yell rang out through the hall that there was a team meeting, right now, downstairs. Chambers thought everyone had been in agreement to get to Denver tonight. Not so. Donnie Roach was the most vocal opponent, saying that plan didn't make sense. I nodded to him as we opened hotel doors directly across from each other. These rooms were paid for, Roach reasoned, so at the least, why waste more than $2,000? And after the long day at the yard, in such horrible conditions, Roach and others just wanted to clean up, relax, get something to eat, and take it easy, rather than endure another four or five hours on the cramped bus in this hellish wind, just to end up in another hotel by the airport.

The lobby became flooded, so Chambers moved the impromptu meeting out in the parking lot, where Bryce Harper, Gabby Weidenaar, and Ryan Scott stood in their underwear. One of the biggest team arguments of the season ignited at seven minutes past eight, but it was a measure of the players' bond that it had been such an unusual occurrence and it ended quickly. "I understand some of you want to stay and celebrate, but a district tournament?" Chambers said. "We've got bigger goals." Roach stated why it would be smart to stay, others agreed, those who wanted to head to Denver didn't have much ammo, and Chambers said the coach would depart Sunday morning at six.

That night, I dropped off Quarter Pounders and Big Macs for Chambers and Jay Guest. Nearly spitting out cheese, onions, pickles, and chunks of beef, they argued about losing a coach's spot in the dugout for the World Series. "I'll sit out," Guest finally exclaimed. "You will?" Chambers said. "Okay then, done. Thanks." Well, Guest mumbled, if someone has to . . . if there's an issue . . . it was still unresolved when I left the room.

Coughing, sneezing, and wheezing dominated the five-hour morning drive to Denver, where the Coyotes hopped on several flights back home to Las Vegas. Saturday's terrible conditions had clogged my sinuses to where I'd need to see my doctor for antibiotics first thing Monday. I hacked up Lamar dirt and dust, and blood, for a day and a half. No, I told a few curious players, I'm not chewing snuff, as I spit into an empty water container, and left it at that.

At Denver International, as a pack of Coyotes ate lunch, a shapely woman turned heads. From the neck down, I thought, outstanding. "All 'uni,' no hat," Coach Chambers said as he chewed his barbecued ribs.

Wandering around the terminal, a woman mistook me for a coach just beyond Gate C45. Your players are so well behaved, she said, and they're *soooo* funny. Good luck, Coach. I didn't have time to explain that I was just a fly on the wall, so I smiled and nodded. Bryan Harper tapped into a video feed of the Boston-Philadelphia baseball game on his computer. Others stood around Chambers as he regaled them with stories. Some players left for a flight. Others at the next gate tossed a baseball around as they sat in chairs. The two-thirty flight was announced. The A group lined up, then the B's. The area emptied, but as I stood to go for another stroll around the terminal, I heard what faintly sounded like my name.

Meek. I dashed to the counter. You mean *Miech,* like *Michigan,* right? I spelled my name. The attendant nodded. I hustled back to C45, touching my right wrist with my left hand way high. Look who just got called up, I told the Harper boys and several other Coyotes as I picked up my luggage and computer bag. I heard laughing behind me, not sure if it was with me or at me, as I entered the tunnel to the plane. The only seat available was in the middle, near the back on the left side, and the man in the aisle seat had to have pressed his scale to at least 350. I had to slip down the armrest. But I was ecstatic to be on the plane.

Chambers, in the back next to Scott Dysinger, was sweating, shaking, and bobbing his head, rolling his eyes and forming a big *O* with his mouth before the thing even became airborne. Dysinger laughed. Trevor Kirk, in front of Dysinger, smiled. By the time the bird lifted off, Chambers's head was squarely into the back of the seat in front of him.

Acrophobia, suriphobia, and ophidiophobia, I thought. Some combination of bacteriophobia and verminophobia, at least, with some obsessive something-or-other, had plotted to create a serious toilet phobia for the tortured Chambers, too. Toss plane travel somewhere into that menagerie.

Trent Cook sat behind me, Marvin Campbell was a row in front but on the other side, and Tyler Hanks, a row in front of me but in the aisle, tried to comprehend the game of cricket from an Indian man next to him. When Hanks explained the salaries of some American pro athletes, what surely awaited his famous teammate, his seatmate's eyes bugged out. Across the aisle, Campbell kept the man's kids laughing.

After a while, Hanks almost had glassy eyes when describing this team. "Best team I'll ever play on," he said. "Great guys . . . the camaraderie." Campbell was listening and chimed in, "I might be on a team with more talent, but not better guys."

Bryce Harper was eager to play before another crowd of thirty thousand, a figure that had become wildly inflated for a few weeks as the Coyotes dreamed about the Junior College World Series in Grand Junction. It would hardly be the largest audience to watch Bryce Harper play a game of baseball, but his spotlight had never been more intense.

"Everyone will come at us. Everyone will be gunning for us. I can't wait. It's going to be a great experience and we're going to win it."

The sweetest ending for a storybook season?

"Yup. For sure. I don't want to go out a loser. I want to go out a winner. I don't want to be pissed off sitting there on June seventh and watching the draft."

18

THE COYOTES SHOVED THEIR long, black equipment bags into the belly of Gabriel's Ryans Express coach, with the swooshes of aqua along each side of the white bottom half, a few minutes before seven on the morning of Thursday, May 27. It was the first time all year Coach Chambers had tapped that company for a ride, but it was the same one he had used to transport his team to the Junior College World Series in 2003. Could Chambers go two for two with Ryans Express, or would Kenny, who had befriended every Coyote, and his sassy Spanish be missed?

The issue was moot because Kenny and his Skywalk had switched to a Las Vegas–Grand Canyon round-trip tourist route, where the tips would be sweeter. Only making an extra hundred bucks per trip with the Coyotes had not been enough for his bottom line. Kenny did not want to embarrass Chambers, who had a tight budget, so he never made it an issue with the coach.

Before Scott Dysinger boarded, I caught him fidgeting with something in the left pocket of his jeans. His American Legion national championship ring glistened like a mini-disco-ball in the early-morning rays. He had won two state championships at Bishop Gorman, and his Legion title team had won seventy-five of eighty-two games. Dysinger did not have a *Sports Illustrated* cover, but he had every Coyote's respect for how he played and what he had achieved. He didn't show the ring to anyone but he brought it along for good luck. A faint smile reflected Dysinger's pride. He wanted more jewelry.

During the first stretch of our trip east to Grand Junction, a few hours northeast on I-15 and then a straight shot east for several more hours across the lower section of Utah on I-70 to just past the Colorado border, no players were awake. Pitcher Joe Robinson, on the other side and a row behind me, broke any existing record on sleeping in as many positions as possible within two hours.

I sat five rows back on the right side, facing the windshield. Coach Chambers drove his black F-150 so he could conveniently fulfill any personal obligations, separate from team functions, that could arise in Grand Junction. Plus, he took his golf clubs. Assistant coach Cooper Fouts assumed Chambers's spot at the front of the bus on the right side, shoes dangling over the rail. Kingfish Cooper.

When Gabriel stopped in Cedar City, Utah, he yanked off his sunglasses and did a double take, as if shocked that anyone would consider him much less chat with him, when I asked him if he wanted anything. The bald man with the thick, dark goatee and dark brown eyes shook his head. Turned out he didn't understand English well. Players had already started missing the gregarious Kenny.

Ryan Thomas boarded the bus wearing a curled-up frown after tasting his chocolate milk. "Tastes like a doctor's office," he said. Go get another one, a teammate replied. When Thomas boarded a minute later, he was asked, "What does that one taste like . . . a veterinarian's office?"

Trent Cook told a teammate how he beat redshirting player Andy Weissberg the previous night in a baseball video game. Weissberg was incredulous. Tied going into the bottom of the ninth, Cook coerced one of his players to slam a long shot to the warning track that had caromed off an outfielder's head, à la Jose Canseco in 1993, and bounced into the stands for a walk-off belt. Cook couldn't hide a Beaver Cleaver smile.

Kevin Higgins stood up as Gabriel gunned us back onto I-15. Higgy handed out $100 bills, the per diem, to everyone. Mistakenly, he shoved a bill toward me; I told him, uh, nope, I don't get that since I'm not a part of the official traveling crew. Chambers usually took care of doling out the meal money.

"Thirty-eight hundred dollars," said Casey Sato, shaking his head. "Man, that's a lotta money." Joe Robinson laughed and said, "Let's go to the strip club."

Ryan Scott, the Evil Genius, stood front and center when teammates yelled for a movie. Can't go wrong with *Bull Durham,* Cooper Fouts said, three feet from Scott. *Bull Durham* could run on an endless loop on every television screen Fouts ever came in contact with for the rest of his life, and it would be a happy life.

"This is business . . . it isn't personal" and "Life is a road" quotes kept blasting from the speakers because of glitches in the DVD player or scratches on the two DVDs, whatever they were. After fifteen minutes, Scott was resigned to putting *Bull Durham* into the thin, horizontal slot. "Like it," said Fouts.

Gabriel zipped through the red hoodoos, sandy spires, and sharp cliffs of the fringes of the Capitol Reef National Park and magnificent Southern Utah.

Bull Durham cut to the interior of the mythical team's bus.

"You've been in the Show, man?" someone asked Kevin Costner's character, Crash Davis.

"Yeah, I was in the Show for twenty-one days. The greatest twenty-one days of my life."

Gabriel could hear a pin drop. He sliced through canyons, past sand chollas and brittlebush, Joshua trees and creosote, Mormon-tea and mesquite bushes. This was John Wayne territory, and we would come close to the Monument Valley area that the Duke had made famous on the silver screen.

A wedding had been taking place on the video screens when GRAND JUNCTION—198 MILES appeared on a green, rectangular sign.

A Coyote pointed out, five seconds before it happened, when the right nipple of actress Susan Sarandon's Annie Savoy would appear on the screen during a brief lovemaking session with Davis, er, Costner. "Right . . . about . . . there," the player said with precise timing.

Sarandon ended the movie by quoting Walt Whitman on baseball, saying, "It will repair our losses and be a blessing to us."

Ryan Scott put in another DVD. When it blurted, "This is business . . . ," he yanked it out and slipped in *The Sandlot,* one of Bryce Harper's favorite movies. "Yes," said Fouts, who no doubt believed the ten best movies ever made, perhaps even the top hundred, were all about baseball. "Hell, yes."

Gabriel bent the bus around a long left curve and dipped it through what looked like a mini–Grand Canyon. Hoodoos stood out like funky stalagmites on an ocean floor. Layers of red shale angled out of the earth. A stunning peak soaked up the windshield in the distance. "This is some of the coolest fuckin' terrain," a player said.

With fifty miles to Grand Junction, Bryce Harper moved to the front of the bus to sit next to Fouts. Harper wondered who would do his laundry during what the Coyotes believed would surely be a long stay at the World Series. "Just pick out a girl in the stands," said Gabby Weidenaar, drawing scattered laughs.

We passed a John Deere plant and the Canyon View Park baseball diamond, where the Coyotes would take a few batting practices. It looked as if Harper might just be able to reach the freeway beyond the left-field fence with one of his oppo boppo specials. Exit 3 came into view. Harper smacked Fouts on his shoulder, and Fouts smacked Harper back, making Harper giggle.

The Book Cliffs—a miles-long mesa looking like a shelf of books—to the north marked Grand Junction as we left the interstate for the Clarion Inn. I remembered them from the 2003 trip with the Coyotes. Compared to Lamar, this was San Francisco, a bustling metropolis with character and culture, and some well-regarded vineyard patches not far away.

* * *

After a short rest, we bolted to Bergman Field at Mesa State College for a round of batting practice. As Harper would do throughout the week, he hit with wood for a couple of rounds, sometimes even into his third set of pitches. On one of his first smacks with aluminum, he belted a ball so far in deep right field it landed on the other side of the school's softball field fence and rolled to a rest at the pitcher's mound.

The following day Chambers debuted a ten-minute video, produced by his daughter McKenzie, that highlighted the team's run to the World Series and was backed by the music of Whiskey Falls, Fabolous with Jeremiah, Eminem, and Murphy Lee, King Jacob, Prentiss Church, and Fala Beats. Scott Dysinger and Trevor Kirk soundly approved a preview. The whole team raved when they watched it in the clubhouse at Mesa State.

That night, former major league pitcher Dave Dravecky would speak at a pretournament banquet for all ten teams. Chambers insisted that all of his players wear collared shirts and slacks, no jeans. Donnie Roach looked spiffy with silver links on the white French cuffs of his tailored, dark blue dress shirt. Dysinger wore all black, including a sharp vest, with a pink tie. I turned a hall corner in the hotel and nearly ran into Bryce Harper, who wore a thin, dark tie on his crisp, white dress shirt.

That a clip-on?

"C'mon, bro," said Harper, disappointed that someone would think he couldn't tie his own tie. "I'm Mormon."

More than fifteen hundred people packed into a convention-center ballroom. Three coaches were inducted into the NJCAA Baseball Hall of Fame, and the visitors stabbed at chicken and steak medallions with mashed potatoes, gravy, and carrots. Dravecky stood out on the dais in his white, Hawaiian, short-sleeved silk shirt with green and red flowers. He'd put on a few pounds since he last donned a San Francisco Giants uniform. Anyone who didn't know him figured he'd have a story to tell, since his left shoulder and arm were missing. His shirt had been sewn in that area.

In 1989, Dravecky's left arm broke as he delivered a pitch. He dropped to the ground in agony. A cancerous tumor had been discovered in that arm a year earlier. After surgery, he battled to return to the majors, a journey that ended in amputation after his gruesome fall. Actually, Dravecky explained to his audience, that represented the start of an enlightening journey. He revealed how his setback transformed him into a more considerate and less selfish person, a better husband and father, and a dependable friend.

It had been a tightly crafted forty minutes, no doubt honed over the years. But Dravecky had tailored the ending to fit this event. He told the junior college players to be respectful, to not take this World Series for granted. This game will humble you, he said. Embrace it. Play to win, he said. But keep it all in perspective.

"It's a gift, a privilege you all have."

Harper had heard every word.

"I thought it was an awesome speech. It was cool the way he approached everything and how he talked about it. He was a pretty funny guy, too. It was great listening to what he did and how everything happens for a reason. You could tell he loved the game a lot. It's just that something unfortunate happened. He has a great faith. Dravecky knew He was first in his life. He loves his family and the game of baseball."

Dravecky's strong faith and spirit had resonated with Harper. During the tournament, a man, with his wife and son by his side, sidled up to Harper and asked him about the Luke 1:37 inscription on his black Marucci bat. Harper thought the guy didn't believe that he knew the meaning of the scripture, that it was on his bat for show. Through God nothing is impossible, Harper told the man, who said that impressed him more than anything the kid did on the field.

"It's awesome to know that people are looking at that, seeing what I write," Harper said. "I always put God in front of everything. Anytime

I can help people out . . . if a little kid reads that or asks what it means, or why do I do this or that, I talk of the gospel. That's just me."

As Harper hit during pregame batting practice the following day at Mesa State, a few blocks away from Suplizio Field, a gray-metal speaker high on a telephone pole behind home plate ran live audio from the action at the World Series. ". . . see Bryce Harper and the Coyotes against Pitt. . . . Everyone wants to get a look at Bryce Harper, and for good reason. . . ." Marvin Campbell blasted a ball that landed on the other side of the softball field fence, too, more than five hundred feet to right.

En route to the first game, Ryan Scott popped McKenzie Chambers's highlight video into the DVD player. As Gabriel pulled the bus to a stop at North Twelfth and North, at the southwest corner of the stadium, the video became more dramatic as it flashed images of every player and all the coaches from the season. The music rang off the tinny insides of the bus.

The ten-minute video featured "Load Up the Bases" by Whiskey Falls, "It's My Time" by Fabolous, and "Lose Yourself" by Eminem. When Murphy Lee, King Jacob, Prentiss Church, and Fala Beats finished it off with their pulsating, heart-pounding, lung-pumping "Stomp," the Coyotes were ready to storm Normandy.

They descended from the coach, yanked their equipment bags out of the bowels of the bus, eased by a throng of wide-eyed kids and smiling parents, and entered Suplizio Field via a blue-metal gate by the yellow right-field foul pole.

In the CSN dugout, as third-string catcher Kaz Smith changed out of his practice attire and into his uniform, a photographer snapped shot after shot of him, at close range and from various angles. Kaz was in his Skivvies and wondered what all this exposure was about. Kaz was all decked out in his number thirty-six uniform when "Y.M.C.A." started playing on the stadium speakers. He started boogying to the familiar tune.

Cool, the photographer thought, Bryce dances. Wait, Bryce dances?

Stumped, he asked around. Nope, Bryce didn't dance. The guy had been shooting the wrong catcher. It had only been for a short spell, but someone got to feel what it's like in Bryce Harper's shoes. And Kaz didn't like it.

The crowd of 10,339 surprised some of the Coyotes, especially outfielder Trevor Kirk. Unaccustomed to playing before so many people, Kirk was a mess in his first trip to the plate. On a two-two pitch, he hit a pop-up that didn't get out of the infield but still hit the dirt, and Kirk wound up on first. Four pitches later he scored on Marvin Campbell's four-hundred-foot home run over the left-center fence. His next time up, Kirk struck out on six pitches. He belted a two-run homer in the fifth inning that smacked the miles-per-hour readout board in right-center field.

Gabe Weidenaar committed two errors at third base, but he went four for five at the plate, with a double and solo homer, and scored four times in CSN's 13–5 mercy-ruled victory over Pitt Community College. Donnie Roach struck out eleven in pitching all eight innings in what would turn out to be his final game as an amateur.

After the game, Kirk admitted he had game-opening jitters. He had never experienced anything like that, with so many eyeballs on him. Other players talked about how odd it had been to be able to hear people chatting in the stands, to hone in on specific conversations between two fans.

Josh Demello had also been shocked, but not by the crowd. Playing football before tens of thousands of fans inside Aloha Stadium, the grand sporting stage on his home island of Oahu, had taught Demello how to handle himself in the spotlight. Chambers knew that and started his sterling defender in center field, even though Demello hadn't started in a game since May 7. He was solid, singling through the left side of the infield in the first inning and catching a fly ball in the fifth.

The Grand Junction Rotarians hosted a barbecue for CSN at a park the next day, a Sunday that the Coyotes had off. The Rotarians still

had horrible memories of playing host to Western Nevada a year earlier, when the Wildcats were the only squad in the ten-team field that
had failed to show for the annual Friday-night kickoff banquet. That
made the hosts look bad. However, the Rotarians were quite pleased
to be catering to the team in this tournament that had the famous Bryce
Harper.

Mingling among the large group of coaches and players, and
their relatives and friends, was the father of CSN infielder Casey Sato,
Michael Sato, who relished his memories of playing on Suplizio Field
for Southern Utah State College in the mid-1970s with catcher Bruce
Hardy.

Hardy and Bryce Harper both went from high school *Sports
Illustrated* cover boys to junior colleges. A three-sport prep star in
Murray, Utah, Hardy was proclaimed as BEST SCHOOLBOY ATHLETE by
the magazine in 1974. On a two-lane road to nowhere, with snow-
capped mountain peaks in the distant background, Hardy squinted
into the camera when he appeared on the cover on the blacktop wearing cleats, his white football pants, full pads, and light blue jersey with
the white number twelve, and cradling a football against his right hip.
Hardy went on to Arizona State and played in two Super Bowls with
the Miami Dolphins.

Michael Sato, an accounting and finance executive for a global
security firm, smiled when he said just *a few* more people were at the
stadium for this tournament than when he and Hardy played, in a series
against Mesa State. "This is really neat," the elder Sato said as he bit
into a cheeseburger. "These guys are so loose. What an atmosphere."

A few Coyotes were entertained by the multifaceted comedy
show I staged that starred Mr. C. An hour before we left for the park,
Mr. C had settled in for his afternoon nap. He looked adorable all
wrapped up in his white sheets and white, six-hundred-thread-count
comforter, with ultrasoft goose-down pillows in their luxurious white
cases cradling his head. He had drifted off into CandyLand. He snored
like a bushel of beavers gnawing down oaks. I could not resist. I

turned on my digital tape recorder and laid it on the night table next to his bed for two minutes. The combination of the photograph on my cell phone with the recording blaring his twin bugles made a few Coyotes double over in laughter at the picnic. Halfway through the barbecue, word had spread back to Mr. C. He confronted me.

"Mother . . . ," he said as his nostrils flared. But I detected a grin as he turned to walk back and gather more brisket.

On one of the sand volleyball courts, action broke out as CSN players picked sides. Bryce Harper rolled up his jean bottoms and the sleeves of his blue-checkered flannel shirt. He took off his shoes. He reveled in smacking a bigger white ball around. Ron Harper picked his youngest son's side and kept one point alive with a spectacular dive and elbow save. Bryan Harper took to the other side, with Marvin Campbell.

The game didn't last fifteen minutes before Chambers put a halt to it, with groans and grumpy reactions all around. Those guys couldn't just play for fun. Chambers knew it and wanted to avoid any unfortunate injuries on the eve of the Coyotes' most important week of their season.

Later that day, in Showtime's hotel room, Bryce Harper tried Copenhagen snuff—the serious stuff—for the first time. Showtime tossed him a dark-wrapper tin. Here, throw one in, he told Harper. No, I'll die. No, Showtime said. Just put one in. I can't, Harper said. "Aw, screw it," said Harper. Coaches do it and many players do it, he reasoned. I'll have to sometime, might as well be now. He pinched a bit out of the tin and stuck it in his lower front lip.

For twenty minutes, he was fine. This ain't bad, he thought. Then the tobacco zapped him like a donkey kick. The propellers quit and he spun toward earth. Mayday. Harper thought he was on a roller-coaster ride. "It was bad," he said. He didn't throw up, but he will not repeat the scene. "One and done, for sure."

A plan was hatched that day to get Kevin Higgins into the CSN dugout. NJCAA officials had tightened their bunker rules since the last time the Coyotes were in the World Series; this time around they had too many coaches. That became an issue for Chambers as his squad advanced in the postseason. He knew the numbers, and by experience and seniority alone that would have put twenty-eight-year-old Cooper Fouts in the stands with the fans. But Chambers also knew Fouts, as one of two full-time assistants, with Marc Morse, would complain, since he was always around the yard. He did, loudly and strenuously. I'll sit out, Jay Guest had said in Lamar.

It had been an issue for days, until it was decided that Higgins, the former major leaguer who had juggled several side jobs to support his family, would sit out. He did not object. Again, the only CSN link to the major leagues would be outside the action. For the first game, Higgins had sat in the stands with several redshirt players and CSN's fans.

At the barbecue, a Rotary official told Higgins, what if you quit? Huh? Higgins said. If you quit for the game, I can hire you to direct your batboys. It'll be your dugout pass. "I know how much it must have hurt not to be in the dugout for that first game." He handed Higgins a red Rotary shirt and a straw hat with a red sash around the bottom of its crown. "You're on the field." Higgins smiled. Afterward, Chambers "rehired" him. Before each game, Higgins would quit, only to be rehired afterward. Higgy could be with his guys.

The next morning, on Monday, May 31, several Coyotes, a couple of parents, and Mr. C ate breakfast at a long table at the Coco's restaurant that adjoined the Clarion. Rich Kirk sat across from his son, Trevor, and criticized some aspects of his game, such as his swing and pitch selection. Trevor did not say a word.

Mr. C sat with his back to a wall, with a view of the entire restaurant, and began taking mental notes of a pattern. He noticed umpire Don Gilmore eating his scrambled eggs, sausages, and crispy hash browns at a table by himself. This was not new. Mr. C had noted that the other umpires, all of whom were staying at the Clarion, ate meals in a group. Gilmore, a probation officer in Kentucky, always ate solo. That picture stayed with Mr. C for many months.

Before nearly ten thousand fans a few hours later, CSN thumped Faulkner State College, 18–1. Harper singled to right in his first trip to the plate. He wound up on third and electrified the crowd that had largely come to see him when pitcher Alex Layne tried to pick off Trent Cook at first. As soon as Layne went that way, Harper broke for home and beat first baseman Douglas Turo's throw to catcher Stephen Clarke for a 2–0 edge.

Harper walked and scored in the fourth and fifth innings, and he struck out when CSN sealed the game with eight runs in the sixth inning. Cook and Tomo "Helicopter" Delp homered in that inning, and Marvin Campbell hit a two-run blast over the right-field fence that smashed the front windshield of a tan SUV in the parking lot. Assistant coach Steve Chatham stole about a dozen signs, from a Faulkner coach to catcher Stephen Clarke. The result on half of them, for CSN hitters, had been positive, as in a hit or something to move a runner along. Of the other half dozen, most were balls. Kirk, who had three hits and was hit by a pitch, got a single and a double on fastballs that he knew were coming courtesy of Chatham.

Bryan Harper, billed as THE OTHER HARPER in a *Grand Junction Daily Sentinel* headline during the week, kept most of his sliders and two-seam fastballs at the knees of Faulkner batters to allow only one hit over five and a third innings. The gangly lefty with the goatee had struck out six and walked two.

After the game Bryce Harper was being interviewed by a young writer when, after a minute, Bryce abruptly walked away when the kid tried to ask him about his childhood. "Huh? No! You believe this clown?" Harper said with mocking laughter to some of his bewildered nearby teammates as he walked away, like John Wayne, from the cub reporter and sought the safe refuge of his dugout and coaches.

•   •   •

After a first-inning strikeout, Bryce Harper put on the show that 10,200 had come to witness on June 1 when he pounded Zach Willand's first delivery in the third inning over the right-field fence to tie Iowa Western, 3–3.

In the fifth, Harper's sky-high pop-up landed in shallow left field as no Reivers fielder could trace it in the dusky sky. That scored two, and Harper touched home on Cook's single to give the Coyotes a 6–5 advantage. In the sixth, Harper pummeled Jordan Kistler's two-oh pitch high over the lights in left-center, a three-run moon shot estimated to have traveled 440 feet, to cap a five-run inning. CSN left with a 12-7 victory.

Many kids mobbed Harper by the exit gate along the left-field line. He hated saying no to his legion of three- and four-foot fans. Veteran security personnel said Harper was the biggest celebrity they had ever seen at the World Series. He had been billed as the brightest star to ever land in Grand Junction, bigger than Kirby Puckett, with Triton College of River Grove, Illinois, in 1982. A week later, Minnesota selected Puckett with the third overall draft pick, and Puckett helped the Twins win two World Series championships. In 2006, at the age of forty-five, Puckett died a day after suffering a massive hemorrhagic stroke.

At an Applebee's restaurant, Harper was dining with his parents and Kurt Stillwell when two bikers, wearing leather and tattoos, paused and stood before Harper. The one with the scraggly goatee said, You *that* guy? Yup, Harper said. Mind if we take a photograph with you? Harper rose and stood between them for a most unlikely snapshot and gave each an autograph.

"That's cool," Harper said. "I don't mind doing that, as long as I'm done eating. I like going out with family and enjoying a meal, not talking baseball. We don't talk baseball off the field. It's awesome. People think I like to talk baseball all the time. I don't. I like eating with family, hanging out, and being with friends."

Some CSN teammates knew how often Bryce liked to talk about

baseball. It's all they ever heard from him, especially around girls. He would tell them about what he had done in the game and what he would do, and how much money he would make.

The following morning, I passed assistant coach Kevin Higgins in the laundry room and pinned him down, finally, for an interview about his time in the big leagues. I knocked on the door of Room 2024, which had been wedged open by a sliver with the swinging metal lock jimmied between the door and the frame. Fouts and Higgy said, Come on in. In a T-shirt and shorts, Fouts sat on the far bed with his legs crossed and the tournament bracket unfolded in front of him. He had filled it out with a ballpoint pen. He was pleased when he told me, Yup, this thing could end by Friday night. It wouldn't necessarily carry over until Saturday. Of course, he had CSN winning the rest of the way and claiming the championship Friday night.

I nodded but thought, Uh-oh. If there's a first rule of sports, especially baseball, doesn't it have something to do with not looking ahead or thinking certain games were certain victories? I just nodded. I would remember that scene at various times over the next thirty hours.

As I talked with Fouts and Higgy, Bryce Harper walked in to show them the big toe on his left foot. An ingrown nail had turned it red and puffy. Fouts directed Harper to trainer Steve Jacobucci's room for treatment.

That day, for the first time all season, I could not sit. Months of sitting on the back of dugout benches, tight bus rides, and foreign beds had taken their toll on a lower back I had first tweaked a year and a half earlier in an ill-advised outdoor basketball game on a fifty-degree night. Mr. C handed me a small silver board. Said it contained magnets and would constantly warm my back, but I resisted. Trainer Steve Jacobucci went into action at batting practice, pumping me with four ibuprofen tablets and applying an ointment and four pads on my lower back. Bucci handed me a small electrical-stimulation device wired to the pads, the same contraption Bryce Harper had worn on his left knee on the way home from Idaho after that terrible fall in right field.

The dials went from one to five. Turn it to whatever you can handle, Bucci said. I slowly turned them to three and felt dozens of tiny ticks zapping my back.

When Scott Dysinger walked by, I asked him if he had ever needed one of these and what number he could handle. Without saying a word, he turned a dial to five and laughed as it looked as if a lightning bolt had zapped me.

Harper eased into batting practice at Mesa State. The toe was a bother, so he sat on bench in a recessed, fenced-in dugout along the first-base line when his teammates took their positions, in the field and in the batting cage. A man, in his mid to late twenties, who appeared to have a developmental disability, walked up to the chain-link dugout fence. Harper sat on the other side. The visitor wore a blue Boise State Broncos shirt, plaid shorts, a tattered, light blue Denver Nuggets cap, and a glistening smile. He peered through the fence and wondered aloud where his hero, Bryce Harper, was; Harper was four feet from the man.

"He's out there," said CSN's Grand Junction host. He tried covering for Harper, to give him some solace at practice by saying he was somewhere out in the field. Not two seconds passed when Harper spoke up.

"I'm Bryce Harper. I'll sign that for you. Come on around the fence."

His newest fan couldn't believe he was shaking Bryce's hand. You are the best player ever, the guy said. "You were awesome last night. Are you catching tonight? I'll see you afterward. Is your brother around?" Harper put aside his left-big-toe woes and jogged out to left field, where Bryan Harper had been stretching. Bryan, Bryce said, you gotta sign this card for my new buddy. Bryce jogged back to the dugout and handed the autographed cards to the man.

"That kind of bothered me that [the host] did that," Bryce said. "That really bothered me. The guy was somewhat challenged, and he came up to the fence and was real happy. He knew a lot about baseball.

You could tell. He was rattling off our names. He knew our team. You can't turn someone down like that. I had to get up. . . . I can do that. I hate it when people say, 'Ohhh, he's out in the outfield,' and lie to them. It's not me. I got my brother's signature and it made [the fan's] day. You can't take things back like that. You just can't explain what that means to that kid. It was awesome."

Harper belted a few tape-measure bombs during the batting practice, and he had a noticeable gimp as he trudged to the dugout after hitting. At Suplizio, I stood by a gate down the left-field line, next to the Coyotes' bull-pen area, with my lower spine feeling as if it were being held together by loose chicken wire. Bending over about twenty degrees ignited a burning sensation and a free fall that was unstoppable. That was the gate that had been swarmed by hundreds of kids begging to get Harper's autograph, after CSN games. In less than two hours, it would be the gate through which Harper would depart junior college baseball.

Mr. C had had a bad feeling about the San Jacinto game when he'd learned that Don Gilmore would be umpiring home plate.

In the first inning, Harper glared at Gilmore when he called what Harper deemed a questionable strike. Gilmore did not take that stare lightly. Harper hit into a fielder's choice, which nearly turned into a rumble after he had run over the right calf of stretching San Jacinto first baseman Deric Hawkins in beating the throw from second. A pained Hawkins grabbed his right leg and griped, as did the first-base coach and many of the San Jacinto players in the dugout who saw up close what had happened at first base. Gilmore sped down the first-base line and warned Harper, "Cool your role." Harper later apologized to Hawkins, telling him it had been an accident.

According to CSN pitching coach Glen Evans, it wasn't. He also had a clear view of what had transpired. When he slid back into the Coyotes' dugout, he told Chambers that he didn't care what anyone else said or thought, Bryce had intended to spike that guy's leg. Evans had seen Bryce execute that malicious act when he played for a few of

Evans's Calvary Christian summer-league teams. Evans knew all about the aspects of Bryce's game that he called "dirty," and Evans hated that such a talented kid would resort to such tactics.

When order had been restored, Trent Cook smacked an opposite-field home run to left, and Danny Higa hammered a three-run homer to left in the second. However, Scott Dysinger's error to start the game had led to four runs for San Jacinto, and Higa's error to lead off the third allowed the Gators to score four more runs.

Harper walked on four pitches in the third but didn't score. With Gabe Weidenaar on first and no outs in the fifth inning, Harper stepped to the plate in what would be his final collegiate at bat. The partly cloudy, eighty-six-degree evening had turned dark a couple of innings earlier, so the lights illuminated the diamond like a stage. It took mere seconds for the curtain to come down on Bryce Harper's amateur career.

Harper took two strikes, then watched a Chris McKenzie pitch fly to the outside of the plate. Gilmore punched out Harper with an elaborate gesture. Strike three. "Fucking bullshit!" Chambers hollered at Gilmore. "Not even *close* to being a strike!" Harper stepped across the plate and etched, with the end of his black Marucci, a short line in the dirt from his right to left to trace his vision of the ball's flight path, before continuing straight to his dugout.

Gilmore quickly ejected Harper with a yell and an animated backward fling of his right fist.

In the CSN dugout, Marvin Campbell heard Gilmore's third-strike punch-out of Harper and, like many other Coyotes, bowed his head. They instantly heard an unusual buzz in the crowd. Campbell looked back up and said, "What just happened?" He saw San Jacinto catcher Ryan Hornback pump his fist as he walked toward McKenzie on the mound and say, "Yeah, we got him!"

Campbell repeated, "What just happened?"

Cooper Fouts said, "Bryce just got tossed. He just threw Bryce out!"

From his spot in the third-base coach's box, Chambers took a few steps toward Gilmore and said, "Are you serious?"

Gilmore made a gesture toward Chambers that told the CSN players in the dugout that Chambers had just been tossed, too, but that hadn't been the case. Gilmore was just trying to settle Chambers and quiet the Coyotes in the dugout.

A replay that quickly made its way onto YouTube showed the ball's path to be outside Harper's line in the dirt, more than six inches off the plate. Gilmore did not comment after the game, and tournament officials were not compelled to produce a statement from Gilmore. For a fifty-one-year-old national tournament whose organizers took pride in how well they ran it, the incident had given the World Series "a sort of Mayberry feel," wrote *Las Vegas Review-Journal* columnist Ed Graney.

Umpires reviewed controversial or close calls each night, and a rumor spread that Gilmore had supposedly responded to a replay of that particular pitch by bowing his head. As in, yup, missed that one. Not so, said Glenn Ballangao, who worked home plate on the night of the Coyotes' season opener at Morse Stadium and was the third-base umpire for the explosive San Jacinto game.

"We do review, but it's not so much watching tape," Ballangao said. "We talked about it. Don's reaction was, you can't just let something go like that, even though it's in a big situation like the World Series, because on any other given day you eject a player for doing something like that. If you let that go in a World Series, you're only going to open yourself up to worse things down the road. Don's reactions to it were, basically, if it were to happen again, he would do it again. He wasn't somber. He was not really sad. He was just more disappointed that he had to do it, that he had to eject the kid for what happened. But on the other hand he was doing his job."

About the wide pitch, Ballangao was in no position to definitively say whether it had been a ball or a strike. On the replay, viewers had the benefit of a camera directly over the plate. It's easy to decipher a ball from a strike. But if you were crouched behind the catcher, Ballangao stressed, your view would have been a bit distorted in real time.

"Right after the game, [Gilmore] felt it was on the corner," Ballangao said. "He didn't feel he had taken the bat away from Bryce. The following morning, [Gilmore] and I watched the video together . . . you know, everyone makes mistakes. At a crucial time like that, it's unfortunate. . . . You kind of just roll with the punches. [Gilmore's] thought was, 'Yes, it could have been outside. Did I take the bat out of his hands at the time?' He thinks he didn't. I didn't think the ball was *that* far outside."

The lone positive aspect of the situation for Chambers was that Harper just kept walking, silently, to the dugout after Gilmore tossed him from the game. Harper hadn't been so quiet when he was thrown out of that March 13 game in his own stadium against Western Nevada. Because of that ejection, the penalty for the World Series ouster would be two games, not one. CSN would have to win its next two games to be able to play one more, for the title on Saturday, June 5, with Bryce Harper. But that seemed like a long shot to even the most ardent Coyotes fan.

"Unfortunately, what he did . . . yeah, it was grounds for ejection," Ballangao said. "I told [Chambers] I would have done the same thing."

Plenty of Coyotes, including Chambers, unleashed some choice words at Gilmore. Ballangao had to restrain himself from tossing anyone from that dugout. Other umpires, Ballangao said, would probably not have been so tolerant, but Ballangao lives in Las Vegas and had a history with Harper and Chambers, having worked maybe eighteen Coyotes games during the season.

"My biased opinion is that if I wasn't at third base umpiring that game, there would have been more ejections out of that dugout. Some of the comments that came out of that dugout, I let 'em go. Then it stopped. With someone else [umpiring third base], I believe [ejections] would have kept on coming."

At midnight, long after the game, Bryce Harper told Chambers in Chambers's hotel room that he believed Gilmore had set the stage for acrimony before the game started, when Harper tried informing Gilmore of pitcher Chasen Shreve's arsenal, a common practice for catchers. According to Harper, Gilmore said he did not want to hear any of it and that he knew Harper could hit. "Now let's see how well you catch."

Chambers had no avenue to appeal the ejection. But he demanded a meeting the next morning with tournament organizers and junior college officials, and Chambers charged racism by Gilmore, who is black, not caring about any repercussions. There were none.

"The game officials control the action while the game is in play," NJCAA executive director Mary Ellen Leicht answered, in an e-mail, when pressed for her thoughts of the events of that evening. "The NJCAA has no additional comment."

Months after the game, Gilmore, from his home in Georgia, declined to talk about Harper and that game. Ballangao had, to no avail, contacted Gilmore several times about discussing those events. "He wasn't up to it," Ballangao said. "He said, 'I'd rather just not talk or say anything.'"

Ballangao said many catchers establish a rapport with umpires, and vice versa, before games regarding what a pitcher throws. Harper had dealt with plenty of umpires and opposing catchers who disliked his routine in the batter's box during the season, but Chambers said the prodigy had quickened the dropping of his bat and grabbing of dirt and tapping of the bat by the time of the World Series. Nevertheless, an umpire seeing that routine, even in truncated form, for the first time, might understandably have an issue with it. Bryce Harper's flashy and temperamental reputation preceded him everywhere he traveled. Ballangao denied that Gilmore might have held Harper's antics or celebrity against him, in any personal way, before or during that game.

"To have it out for someone? No. No. Not even close. It's something that happened. Donnie felt it was warranted and ejected him. I felt the same way. It was a blur. It happened so quickly. I got to see Bryce all season, so they would ask me how this kid is. Of course, I told them his tendencies of doing things and whatnot. Everything was positive. Watching him play, [umpires] were just as much fans as anyone else. To have a kid like that play the game, and you umpire his games, at such a high intensity level as they were . . . it was something really special."

That same night, almost at the same moment, major league umpire Jim Joyce entered the national spotlight when he made a bad call, waving his arms horizontally to signal "safe" to give Cleveland Indians hitter Jason Donald first base against Detroit Tigers pitcher Armando Galarraga, an out away from a perfect game, in Detroit. Replays showed Galarraga had touched first base, with the ball in his hand, before Donald. Joyce's decision had spoiled Galarraga's perfecto. Yet, Joyce was available for comment and said he regretted his mistake. The way Galarraga forgave Joyce became bigger headlines.

Harper gathered his equipment at the right side of the dugout. Ron Harper jumped to the field and escorted Bryce along the left-field foul line, through the gate I stood by and inches in front of me, and into his hulking red truck.

"It was pretty far outside," Bryce Harper said later. "I didn't agree with the call, but that's his call. If he wanted to bang me for it, he banged me for it. He got me, you know, and I learned from it."

Harper had played before bigger crowds in his life. In a game against Cuba, for a US junior national team, twenty-five thousand or thirty thousand fans must have been in the stands. The atmosphere at Suplizio Field, Harper admitted, had been electric, a fantastic stage. Now he was barred from the stadium.

"The first day being out there, walking on the field, it was just a lot of fun. You could see the atmosphere. We talked about it all year and finally getting there, it was so much fun. . . . I didn't say a word. I just swung my bat, and he got me. You know, I went out with a bang, literally."

Harper laughed but couldn't hide his disappointment or embarrassment. "It was unfortunate I didn't get to play in the last game and be out there with my teammates. It sucked. It wasn't a fun feeling."

Ryan Scott replaced Harper, and the onetime Toronto Blue Jays ninth-string practice catcher smacked a double to center field that was part of a three-run sixth inning. But Gabe Weidenaar struck out looking, with two on and two out, in the ninth inning of CSN's 10–8 defeat to San Jacinto.

As the Coyotes walked to a spot in shallow left field to hear Chambers's postgame words, Trevor Kirk spotted me as I slowly trudged, with my aching lower back, toward the dugout to hand Big Red to Trent Cook. Kirk fumed and pointed at me, as if to say the loss had been my fault. I had stood along a gate by the foul line, a new position. I had taunted the game's devilish superstitious gods, Kirk believed, with my move. It had upset the gravitational balance of the baseball universe.

Chambers saw that and jumped all over Kirk, telling him, "What did you do, get *one* hit?" Kirk apologized to me as soon as everyone had retreated to the dugout. It was just the heat of the moment, Kirk said. I'm too competitive, he said. No sweat, I said. I knew the feeling, which is why my basketball days were over.

"Keep your fuckin' heads up!" said assistant coach Steve Chatham on the bus after every Coyote had boarded and taken a seat. "We can still win this thing!"

"Hell, yes!" said Chambers.

When the bus pulled to a stop at the Clarion Inn at eleven twenty-five, Harper descended from his father's Ford Excursion—the huge, red, four-door monster with dark-tinted windows, and a big, wide, and shiny silver grille that seemed to snarl at lesser vehicles—wearing his white CSN cap, a white T-shirt, and dark shorts. Bryce Harper walked up to his teammates, hauling their equipment out of the coach, and slid into the building in line with them.

A local newscast led with "This was likely the last we've seen of the seventeen-year-old phenom." Minutes later, it showed the errant call Jim Joyce had made in Detroit. Bryan Harper, who would start the following day on short rest, was shaving in the bathroom of the room he shared with Marvin Campbell.

"You've got to be kidding me!" Campbell said as he sat on his bed watching the replay of Joyce's bad call.

"What happened?" said Bryan Harper, walking out of the bathroom.

"Umps are having trouble tonight."

"Who got tossed?"

"Nobody got tossed. Someone blew a perfect game with two outs."

"Noooooo," said Bryan Harper, who walked over to the television screen and watched another replay of Joyce's bad call with half a face of shaving cream.

Bryce Harper was next door in the room he shared with Scott Dysinger and Trevor Kirk. Bryan and Marvin heard a crashing noise, then the banging of walls. With the remote control, Bryan turned the volume of his television set all the way down. He and Marvin looked at each other. On the other side of Bryce Harper's room, Ryan Scott also heard the commotion. All heard the door of the room between them slam hard. Bryan drooped his head. Campbell walked outside.

The denouement of his landmark season had staggered Bryce Harper, who had just been informed by Chambers that he had indeed been suspended for two games.

Campbell saw a crying Bryce Harper leave the hotel. Burke Seifrit was one of many Coyotes who saw Harper balling, with snot running down a nostril. Harper punched a door. He bawled his eyes out in McKenzie Chambers's room. Bryce and the coach's daughter had been getting closer to each other as the season had progressed. "That was my last college game," he sulked. She didn't know what to say.

An irate fan in Las Vegas had seen the video of the wide pitch to Harper that had been called strike three and rang Mr. C to vent early the following morning, June 3. I feel bad for the kids, said the caller, whom Mr. C had put on speaker mode. "It was a foot and a half out-side. He was setting up Bryce. I woke up at three just thinking about it." Shit happens in life, Mr. C responded. "You have to relax. Calm down."

A few hours later in Bryce Harper's room, before the elimination game against Iowa Western, Scott Dysinger told Harper not to worry. "We got you," Dysinger said. Bryce Harper looked at Campbell, who said, "Don't worry, we'll get you another game." Bryce pleaded to Campbell, "Carry the weight for me. You've got to hit a bomb. You've got to get these guys going. You have to be the catalyst."

They exchanged a big hug. At Canyon View Park, where teams that lost always took batting practice the following day, a *USA Today* writer talked with Chambers and Dysinger. En route to Suplizio, Josh Demello sang Bob Marley's "Waiting in Vain." Ryan Scott put in McKenzie Chambers's season-highlight DVD, and Whiskey Falls and Eminem and Fabolous thumped inside Gabriel's coach. Campbell felt as if something special would happen, but it all seemed hollow and dis-tant. Concocted. Artificial. The songs from the DVD fell flat. Some-thing was amiss. Something was wrong. The thirty-four jersey was on the bus. The player who normally occupied those threads was no-where to be seen.

Before the Coyotes descended from the coach, Chambers told them that, traditionally, the team that lost a game like CSN had dropped the previous night came out the next day and folded in that game, too. "It doesn't recover," Chambers said. "But we'll still win the national championship! Let's come with everything. Let's win it for the kid. Let's get his bat back in the lineup Saturday."

Demello walked into the stadium and flashed a wide grin when he saw, along the fence at first base, his father, Monte, and best friend, Marcus, whom Demello called Sparky and who had played on the de-fensive line for Saint Louis in those state football title games at Aloha Stadium. They had flown in from Honolulu to surprise Demello. They would see Josh scramble desperately to save the CSN season.

At the field, when the players began to put on their uniforms to warm up, Campbell looked up and out of the dugout when he heard a big roar from the crowd. Dysinger, who normally wore number seventeen, had donned Bryce Harper's yellow, number thirty-four jersey. Tournament officials were not going to allow that maneuver, but Dysinger said he had misplaced his uniform. Chambers argued. The officials, who believed Dysinger and the Coyotes were showing them up, would not relent. Finally, Chambers just turned and walked away. Dysinger wore Bryce Harper's jersey for the entire game.

The team gathered for its usual pregame prayer, along the right-field foul line. The players talked about playing together now more than ever. "Show we're a family," Dysinger demanded. When they had returned to the dugout, Campbell pulled a stick of Franklin eye black out of his bag and smeared blocks under his eyes. One Coyote after another asked Campbell for the eye black. Fortunately, he had another stick of the stuff to pass around. Almost every Coyote wound up with big black swooshes under each eye, to honor their prodigy stuck back at the hotel. Campbell saw that Jim Brooks, Bryce Harper's grandfather, was in tears in the stands.

Fans and relatives of CSN players also smeared grease on their mugs, as they had threatened to do when Bryce Harper had first put it on four months earlier. They rejoiced when Dysinger was introduced as the CSN second baseman, "wearing number thirty-four."

Only 3,325 attended the game. Without Harper, two-thirds of the gate was lost. At the hotel, when he left for the stadium, umpire Glenn Ballangao passed by Harper, who exchanged text messages with friends and sat on a stairwell by a side entrance of the Clarion. Harper even stood silent as Don Gilmore, who had thrown him out of the previous night's game and, for that matter, the Junior College World Series, walked by him in the hotel parking lot. Gilmore didn't say a word, but he seemed to scoff at a red-eyed Harper as he passed.

Bryan Harper started on the mound for the Coyotes on only two days of rest. Donnie Roach had pitched two days before Bryan at the

World Series, but Coach Chambers had been concerned about the 126 pitches that Roach had tossed against Pitt in the opener. Against Faulkner, Bryan Harper had only thrown 73 pitches. It had been a taxing stretch for Roach, whose season-high tosses were the 133 he recorded when he went the distance to defeat Western Nevada at Morse Stadium on March 12. But that had been an anomaly. Roach hadn't logged triple figures in pitches in consecutive games until the playoffs, when he totaled 128 on May 13 against Eastern Utah, 121 on May 20 against Western Nebraska, and the 126 in the Coyotes' first World Series game.

Roach needed to rest his arm, and Coach Chambers could go to his ace on Friday if Bryan Harper and CSN could get by Iowa Western.

Bryan wore his brother's cap and scribbled a three and a four in the dirt behind the pitcher's mound. That started a battle between Bryan Harper and Iowa starter Taylor Eikenberry. Each time Eikenberry took to the mound, he erased the three and four with the bottom of his right cleat. When Bryan Harper went back out there, he scribbled the three and four. They went back and forth.

In the top of the third inning, with two outs, Chambers walked up to Campbell before he stepped into the batter's box. "I would sure like to see you run one to get this place going again, to change momentum," said Chambers, whose squad held a tenuous 2–1 advantage. "I want to see this place erupt like the first night when you hit one out."

For four years, Campbell had been getting occasional hitting advice from Bill Madlock, the four-time National League batting champion who had helped the Pittsburgh Pirates win a World Series championship in 1979 and had relocated to Las Vegas. Madlock usually had Campbell end every batting session with a home run. Madlock would say, "Let's go home." That would signal Campbell to get in the right frame of mind, to envision the perfect pitch and a powerful swing through the sweet zone. Maybe, Madlock told him, you'll get two such pitches in an at bat. Tops. Be selective. Chambers said, "Let's go home," to Campbell.

Campbell jumped on Taylor Eikenberry's first delivery to line it, like a two-iron shot, over the fence in center field. The heater was down, over the plate but in a little, and all Campbell had to do was get the head of the aluminum bat on it. It was his fifteenth dinger of the season. If not for the wunderkind who had leaped off the pages of *Sports Illustrated* onto the Morse Stadium diamond, Campbell would have been the program's new single-season home-run king.

"You have to deliver like that," Campbell said. "You get that pitch, you have to hammer it, just that quick." As soon as he touched home plate, Campbell raised three digits on his right hand and four on his left. Campbell could see Ron and Sheri Harper weeping in the stands along the first-base line. "Everybody was happy," Campbell said. "No way we could lose after that."

Bryce Harper, in a tangle of nerves, watched the play-by-play on his computer in his hotel room. Early on, McKenzie Chambers had sent him a picture via her cell phone of Dysinger wearing Harper's number thirty-four jersey and eye black. Harper couldn't believe it. "I got real emotional when I saw that," he said. "I love that kid. Sitting inside the hotel room and watching on the webcam, I was going crazy. It was not cool. I hated the feeling of being there and my team on the field. It's hard to explain. There's no tougher feeling. They're all my brothers."

Without Harper in the batting order, CSN struggled, scoring only three runs in the first seven innings. Campbell's euphoria wasn't so contagious, until late, long after Chambers had taken Bryan Harper from the game and put Tyler Iodence on the mound.

Danny Higa punched a two-out, two-run homer in the eighth to cut the Coyotes' deficit to 6–5. In the top of the ninth, with nobody out, Gabby Weidenaar—who chose to hit away after being given the option to bunt by Coach Chambers—smacked a home run off right-handed pitcher Scot Donner, with Tomo Delp and Dysinger on board for an 8–6 lead going into the bottom of the ninth inning.

Inexplicably, the home-plate umpire turned to CSN catcher Ryan

Scott and said, "See you at breakfast tomorrow morning." But after the first out was recorded on a grounder, the cloudy day with winds blowing in suddenly shifted. The skies parted. The wind blew out.

In left field, Marvin Campbell tried to shield his eyes from the sudden sunburst so he could nab a ball that Iowa catcher Anthony Bemboom had lined at Campbell's knees. It hit Campbell's glove. It dropped out. Bemboom wound up on second base. Tyler Iodence had given way to Joe Robinson, who had pitched well for three relief innings, but Robinson gave up a two-out double to Tanner Moore that scored Bemboom. "What a turn of events," Campbell said. "[We] had all the momentum. We were rolling. All of a sudden, someone hit the light switch. There it goes."

When Iowa Western third baseman Brent Seifert walked to the plate, Chambers turned to six-foot, 175-pound closer Aaron Kurcz, whose smooth face looked as if he had never needed to shave. In the World Series, Kurcz had only thrown in the previous game. He had looked strong in striking out three of the six San Jacinto batters he had faced. Before that, Kurcz had that horrible outing against Central Arizona—which had been masked by Bryce Harper's magnficent four-homer performance.

Iowa Western assistant coaches Rob Allison and Chad Ogden had done their homework. They had noticed Kurcz's glitches during the season. They had watched that San Jacinto game from behind home plate. They knew that Kurcz relied on a fastball that he could zing up to ninety-five miles an hour.

Seifert, one of five Reivers who had started in the JC World Series in 2009, had entered this national tournament with a .497 batting average. The six-foot, 195-pound infielder had displayed his versatility at Cameron High School in Missouri, where he also played defensive back and wide receiver on the football team and was the basketball team's point guard. His mother, Kristi, a second-grade teacher, had raised Brent and older brother Blake by herself in Cameron, about an hour's drive north of Kansas City with a population around ten thousand.

Brent had used a thirty-four-inch bat all season, but for this game he had switched to a thirty-three-inch Louisville Slugger TPX Exogrid model to shave a fraction of a second off his swing. The silver and black bat weighed thirty ounces, an ounce less than his usual weapon. He had singled and scored in the second inning, then Seifert struck out looking, walked, and popped out to Dysinger at second. Against Kurcz, Seifert knew what was coming.

Kurcz missed the plate with his first two pitches, then catcher Ryan Scott turned to his right to get the signal for the next pitch from Coach Glen Evans, who started touching parts of his face with his right index finger. As soon as he touched an ear, Scott knew the next move would be "live," for the pitch. After Evans went to his right ear, he tapped his nose; that meant fastball. Scott thought nothing of the call or the ensuing seconds. He had been in a robotic trance, gathering signals from Evans and flashing them to whoever was on the mound.

Kurcz delivered a ninety-three-mile-an-hour fastball down the middle of the plate, but just a whisker in and letter high, slipping into Seifert's wheelhouse. Scott instantly thought, Uh-oh, as the ball never hit his mitt. Seifert had drilled the heater. Kurcz, with a terrified expression, turned over his right shoulder. He shot a pleading look back at Scott, as if Scott could pull a string and bring the thing back. Kurcz bent to his knees and peered back out to center field. Josh Demello, whom Chambers had just put into the game for his defensive prowess, jumped high into the wall. Seifert thought, Uh-oh. He kept his head down as he sprinted to second base, only letting up when he heard that unmistakable reaction from the crowd that confirmed what every hitter lives for.

Home run.

Seifert heard his mother cheering the loudest from the stands.

He had crunched a two-run dinger, the first walk-off shot of his life, for a shock ending to the game and the Coyotes' season. Kurcz covered his head with his glove and right hand.

From his dugout, Iowa coach Marc Rardin had figured the strong hit would at least score one run, that the game would be tied. He knew the ball would sail over Demello's head. Rardin didn't think it would clear the fence, but the ball bounced into the parking lot after having soared over the top of that fence by twenty-four inches, tops.

Rardin had derisively called Kurcz "the little guy." When Kurcz missed with his first two pitches to Seifert, every Reiver knew a blazing speedball would be coming Seifert's way.

"A thousand percent," Rardin said. "Still, that doesn't mean Brent is going to do what he did. It just worked out that way. We knew [Kurcz] had electric stuff. We knew he'd empty his tank. We told Brent, 'Just get your front foot down and get the barrel of that aluminum bat on the ball.'"

Rardin felt as if he were watching it in slow motion as it all unfolded. "Front foot down. Hands through. Barrel through. Yeah, we knew what was coming."

Ryan Scott described an out-of-body experience as he saw the ball sail over the fence. "Unreal," he said. "I couldn't believe that was happening." Iowa Western defeated San Jacinto twice in the next two days to win the Junior College World Series.

Eight months later, Kurcz confirmed that he could have waved off the fastball request from Evans. With first base open, Kurcz remembered, he should have delivered a slider, something tricky that would have kept Seifert guessing. Walking him, Kurcz knew, wouldn't have mattered. "I don't know what I was thinking," Kurcz said. "But I knew I wanted to try to throw one by him. I couldn't believe what happened."

Brent Seifert had moved on to Missouri State, where he was studying psychology. As he rode a bus east on Interstate 44 for a weekend series in St. Louis against the Saint Louis Billikens, Seifert, on his cell phone, said he and his Iowa Western teammates felt like MLB World Series champions after they had defeated CSN.

"Because they were the team to beat. We knew [Kurcz] would come at me with a fastball. We knew he threw hard. I went down to that thirty-three-inch bat in that game because it was lighter and quicker. I guess it worked out."

Bryce Harper had watched it all unfold on his computer. "I was pissed I couldn't be out there with my team. I felt like I let my team down a little bit, because I wasn't out there for the final game. They battled as hard as they could. Unfortunately, what happened . . . it's just baseball. Not always the best team wins. I still think we're the number one team in the country."

At 5:44, cotton-ball-like clouds drifted eastward on the warm, late afternoon. Trace Evans, the bespectacled son of Coyotes pitching coach Glen Evans, hung on his father's thick right arm and cried a few steps from the visitors' dugout at Suplizio Field. "Dad, I want this team to be together forever."

Hugs were exchanged in front of the dugout as the finality of the season sunk in with every Coyote. I handed Cook's red bat back to him. A shell-shocked Aaron Kurcz didn't react to anyone who tried to console him. As CSN players walked out of the stadium down the right-field foul line, pockets of fans stood and clapped.

Scott Dysinger, with glassy eyes, boarded the bus first and went straight to the back. Wes Hunt, who had played fourteen games, stood outside and signed autographs. Trent Cook boarded, handed a black Sharpie to Casey Sato and said a kid outside wanted Sato to sign his cap. Chambers gave one of his many fans his yellow jersey and blue cap. He raced inside, told Cooper Fouts to take the jersey off his back, and bolted back outside to give it to another fan.

As Gabriel tried maneuvering his bus out of the parking lot, it came to a standstill. A bus in front of Gabriel had stopped, not allowing him to move. FOLLOW THE REIVERS read the rear of the bus. It was Iowa Western's ride. It had plucked its nickname from Middle Ages border plunderers between Scotland and England. They would be the ones with the fairy-tale ending. Little by little, CSN players talked as Gabriel finally pulled away from the heart of junior college baseball for the final time. Mostly, the short drive was punctuated by coughs, sighs, and sniffles. "At this point, I wouldn't mind getting drunk for the first time," said Sato, who made dinner plans with his family and Cook's. "Back to reality," said another Coyote.

"I love you boys," said pitcher Tyler Hanks as the bus pulled up to the Clarion, whose female front-desk workers were crying about the defeat. "I love every one of you."

Bryce Harper had been sitting on a curb in front of the hotel. He walked up to the door of the coach with a blank face as almost all of his teammates disembarked with the gaudy black marks under their eyes, more than two dozen mirror images of how Harper had looked all season. There were hugs all over the parking lot.

"I walked up there and just teared up, seeing all the guys and hugging them. I didn't get to be out there and it killed me seeing them walk off the bus. I just teared up. Everyone had the war paint on. It just killed me."

The longest hug took place between Bryce and Bryan Harper, six steps from the bus. Eight times, Bryan had started a game in 2010 throwing to his brother behind the plate. The Coyotes won six of those games.

"I was emotional," Bryce said. "It's just incredible playing with your brother and being around your brother. I loved playing with him my freshman year in high school, when he was a senior, and being able to work with him again, knowing him, and him knowing how I catch, and me knowing how he pitches and what to call . . . seeing him out there for the final game, I felt like I let him down as a catcher. Ryno [Ryan Scott] did a great job, it's just that feeling my bro and I have. It's unfortunate. It sucks. That hug, it's that brotherly love. Nothing is stronger than that."

Said Bryan, "That was knowing you probably won't play with him down the road, unless something happens. . . . That was just remembering all the times we had all year. It all set in that it might not happen again with us."

They held their clutch as a choked-up Chambers haltingly addressed his players. He told them they were champions regardless of the outcome of this tournament. The finality of the season weighed heavily on Bryce. "It just killed me. I started bawling. I couldn't be with my team."

The next morning, Gabriel edged out of Grand Junction a bit later than Chambers had planned. Many players wore weary expressions, courtesy of a beer or two, or twelve, from the previous hours. One had been a serial puker, having discharged in the sinks of at least two different teammates' rooms. Two pitchers talked about the crazy kid that one had nearly fought at a local house party in the wee hours. One player had drunkenly boasted to a teammate about having pinched the rear of another teammate's mother at a gathering. Another player had gotten forty-five minutes of sleep. Another never let go of a large bottle of Patrón Silver all evening. An assistant coach found his wedding ring, which he had misplaced early in the trip, behind the curtain in his hotel room.

Before the bus departed, Chambers called for Tomo Delp, Danny Higa, and Chasen Shreve to return to their rooms to clean them. "Is that girl still in there?" someone said. Mr. C had long ago taken off in his new, black Volkswagen CC, in which he hit 128 on his speedometer on the way home. The rig had been his early seventieth-birthday present to himself. In conducting a visual roll call, Chambers spotted me. "There's Big Bird."

On the way home, players handed out stacks of the team's baseball cards, which the NJCAA had produced for every team in the tournament to sell at the concessions stand, for everyone else to sign. Chambers passed a box of a dozen new Junior College World Series baseballs for all of his players to autograph. "For boosters," said Chambers, who raised his camera to take a photograph of his team. Every player, except Trent Cook, flipped off their coach and smiled for the picture. With a silver Sharpie, Chasen Shreve drew a perfect copy of the Copenhagen tobacco logo, with other designs, along the length of Canadian pitcher Burke Siefrit's left forearm. Then Shreve sketched a maple leaf on the left side of Siefrit's neck. *Zoolander* played on the DVD system as we knifed through the Utah plains and canyons and desert and broccoli-like shrubs.

I recalled what Ron Harper had told me after CSN won its conference tournament in its own stadium. That had springboarded the Coyotes into the postseason. In Oklahoma in the summer of 2009, the two Howard College coaches had visited Ron and Bryce Harper to inquire about Bryce and Bryan playing for the Hawks, in Big Spring, Texas, in 2010. They had just polished off a 54-0 regular season with a Junior College World Series championship in Grand Junction. But Ron Harper could not relocate. He had his job, continuing to build Las Vegas. He had a family to support.

"There's no other way it would have worked out," Ron Harper said. "I've told Tim [Chambers] that several times. Bryce being able to be home, to be around all these kids he's played with for years . . . he's known all these coaches since he was six. An amazing, amazing thing. There's just no other way it would have worked out. I believe that in my heart."

Midway through the trip home from Grand Junction, Bryce Harper took the seat next to me for what would be our final chat within the confines of the historic season he had just completed. His thirty-one home runs were the most for anyone at any level of college baseball that season. He went up against that artificial aluminum world with his black maple Maruccis, and three pink models, and pummeled the competition. He won his conference's Player of the Season award. The seventeen-year-old had proven himself mightily against players four and five years older than him, but the ending was bittersweet.

"I stayed up until three this morning, thinking, 'Holy crap! The season just flew by.' It feels like we were just in fall ball, at Cashman Field, playing that first [fall] game. I can't believe it's all over, all said and done. I couldn't have asked for a better season. There were some goods, some bads. I can't thank Coach Chambers, and Cooper Fouts and Jay Guest, and the rest of the coaches, enough. They made it a lot easier, so did the players. Having everyone around, I wouldn't take any of it back. Through all the experiences, at Western [Nevada] and [against the Wildcats] at our place, at CSI . . . it's real humbling, a great experience getting me ready for the next level."

Oklahoma and California were likely spots where he'd relax with friends, do some fishing, and maybe hit a batting cage or two, but foremost on Harper's list was a good friend of his for the past eight years.

"I want to see my dog," he said of Harley.

There was also the matter of the Major League Baseball draft in three days. On the topic of Bryce's ejection from the JUCO World Series, Washington general manager Mike Rizzo sounded as if he and his brain trust had not altered their assessments of Harper, as a person and as a player. If you took a snapshot of that incident, Rizzo told *USA Today,* and didn't know the kid "like we do, you might have a bad impression. But we know this kid. He's a high-strung, emotional seventeen-year-old. I like the fire he plays with. I like the fact he loves playing the game. He will learn to control his emotions."

Harper said, "Oh, yeah," when reminded of the draft, as if it were an afterthought, aboard the bus somewhere out in the hinterlands of southern Utah. "I'm not going to pump my chest and wonder how much money I'll make playing in the big leagues. I want to have fun playing baseball. It's supposed to be fun. It can be humbling. That's all you can say. You can walk on the field and think you're bigger than the game, and it'll bite you in the ass. I'm not going to go out and say I'm the best. I might think it. I've always thought that, that 'this guy' can't beat me. It's how I play the game. I don't think anyone is better. It's just a shock that it's already here. The season went by so fast. I should be a senior in high school. It's crazy. Buddies will be seniors, and here I'm a freshman in college going into the draft. It's what I've been doing since I was three years old, so I'll just have fun with it, enjoy it with family, and see what happens."

Marucci had been talking with Harper about keeping Luke 1:37 on the signature spot on his bats when he turns professional.

"But I'm still not where I want to be. If I get drafted Monday . . . I'll live in the moment. After Monday, Tuesday comes, and it's back to reality. In baseball, you better have fun. Baseball players have to stay young, in that mentality. You see the *Baseball Tonight* guys that are wired, they talk to Evan Longoria . . . those are some of the funniest guys in the dugout. You hear John Smoltz, he's forty and laughing like a kid. You have to keep baseball fun. You can't make it a pressured job. You can't get down, say, 'Screw baseball,' and get out or be in a bad mood for nine innings. It's a long game. I just had so much fun. Looking back, in the dugout and in the clubhouse, guys had so much fun. It was a blast, an absolute blast."

At the end of the journey, Chambers had asked Ryan Scott to slip in that highlight DVD one last time, as the bus descended the off-ramp to College Drive. It skipped horribly and was irritatingly loud. "Turn that fucking thing off," Chambers yelled. Scott ejected it. The bus quietly rolled into Morse Stadium.

"There's nothing I'd take back," Bryce said. "I love this team and I'll always be a CSN Coyote. We went out there and played every game like it was our last. Unfortunately, we didn't get a chance at the national championship. It was not the storybook ending I thought it would be. We tried our hardest. We tried to bring it back to Vegas and we got pretty far, but it didn't happen. The Yankees are the best team in baseball but they don't win it every year. That's the way baseball is."

After they had left the bus and before they made their getaways, Bryce and Bryan Harper were asked about the next time both might be on the same field. What if Bryce had to face Bryan? What if that took place in the majors?

"He knows better," said Bryan, flashing a smile. "He doesn't want to face me."

"It would be insane if that happens," said Bryce. "I hit him a couple times, and he got me out a couple of times in the past. He's absolutely filthy. It's weird. I don't know where Bryan will throw the ball, no idea, or where it'll move. It goes all over the place, this way and that way. That's how Bryan is. He's different every single time."

Pitching coach Glen Evans had coached Bryce when he was a chubby seven-year-old on a club baseball team. Bryce would show up for practice wearing football pads and pants, having just bolted over from football practice. The middle linebacker, Evans called him. For a few days, after returning from Grand Junction, Evans contemplated that last scene of the season, in the parking lot of the Clarion. As he poured drinks for customers on his graveyard bartender shift at the M Resort, Evans replayed Bryce, with nothing on his face, meeting the bus and almost every teammate wearing the war paint that had been the kid's signature for so long. Evans concluded that that's what was supposed to have happened. CSN winning the tournament would have been too nifty, too unreal. Too perfect.

"Instead, thirtysomething people showed how much they loved him," Evans said even softer than usual. "It was bigger than the game. He knows those are guys he can call, no matter what, anytime, for anything. I don't know if he'd have gotten that if we had won it. I believe he learned more because of that. I think this is the first time he felt loved, unconditionally, by his teammates. That'll be the biggest thing he carries with him."

EPILOGUE

BRYCE HARPER WAS SELECTED first by the Washington Nationals in the Major League Baseball draft on Monday, June 7, 2010. He was in Newport Beach, California, with his family at superagent Scott Boras's headquarters—a three-story, futuristic building whose three-thousand-pound, sheer-steel front door had no knob or handle—when he made history. Never before had a junior college player been picked at the top spot in the draft.

Harper had hit .443, with thirty-one home runs, knocked in ninety-eight runs, and scored ninety-eight times in sixty-six games for the College of Southern Nevada. With 225 total bases in his 228 trips to the plate, Harper had slugged an incredible .987. All but his batting average were school records; Jonathan Slack hit .446 in 2000, CSN's debut season.

A few hours later, Harper typed a passionate, seven-hundred-word e-mail to McKenzie Chambers, the CSN coach's sixteen-year-old daughter, in which he professed his adoration for her and promised that they would still be together despite travel issues that could beset a rising baseball star. He would frequently hang out with her at her house, where they watched movies and swam, for much of the next month. He wrote intimate entries in her diary and on its cover. *Wanna be a baseball wife?* She had a stack of notes from him.

In Big Spring, Texas, the Howard College baseball coaches had been keeping tabs on Harper, the one that had, sort of, gotten away from them. Hawks catchers coach J. Bob Thomas thought Bryce had been an admirable ambassador for junior college baseball.

"He brought the spotlight to junior college, no question. He's been a catalyst. It was very beneficial for junior college baseball. People need to understand how many good players there are in junior college. He brought some prestige to it, no question, being the number one pick."

Stephen Strasburg, the hard-throwing pitcher whom Washington had taken with the number one pick a year earlier, made his pitching debut for the Nationals the following day. That had been billed as a landmark twenty-four-hour window for the Nationals, a woeful franchise that now had two young cornerstones for what looked like a bright future.

Harper would play right field, the Washington hierarchy quickly announced, in a move to get him to the big leagues faster and to keep him around longer. The Nats might also have noticed Harper's throw-out ratio behind the plate: thirty-four of forty base stealers (85 percent) were successful against Harper at CSN. By contrast, twenty-four of thirty-four (71 percent) foes stole bases when Ryan Scott caught for the Coyotes. Coach Chambers's preseason prediction that nobody would run on CSN with Harper, and his outstanding glove-to-glove time of 1.84 seconds to second base, didn't exactly materialize.

However, after the draft, the Nationals still had to sign Harper to a contract. If that resembled how the team's negotiations went with Strasburg, it would not be settled until the end of the signing window in a couple of months.

On Friday, June 11, Tim Chambers officially became a Rebel when UNLV athletic director Jim Livengood presented Chambers as his new baseball boss at a formal press conference inside the Thomas & Mack Center. Chambers had been destined for the post since he had started Bishop Gorman on its roll to national recognition and then brought more glory, and widespread attention, to the tiny junior college outside Las Vegas. He had guided CSN to a record of 466-195-1 in eleven seasons. He had been so nervous, Chambers asked me to compose a few paragraphs to guide him in his first UNLV media session.

CSN players Ryan Scott, Trent Cook, Scott Dysinger, Trevor Kirk, Joe Robinson, Marvin Campbell, Casey Sato, Danny Higa, Gentry Croft, and Tyler Iodence accepted Chambers's offers to play for him at UNLV.

Five days later and bored beyond belief, Bryce Harper, wearing his white CSN cap, gray Coyotes shirt, and blue CSN shorts, and McKenzie Chambers spent five hours helping Chambers move into and arrange his new corner office on the second story of the Lied Athletic Complex on the UNLV campus. Out two rectangular windows behind his desk, Chambers could see Wilson Stadium, its right-field foul pole maybe eighty feet away.

The diamond lay directly under the landing patterns of two McCarran International Airport north-south runways—One Nine Right and One Nine Left—to the south of Wilson Stadium. It was Shea Stadium West. The former home of the New York Mets was notorious for the deafening noise from overhead planes landing at or taking off from nearby La Guardia Airport.

Just beyond his new stadium, Chambers gazed at the point of the Eiffel Tower of the Paris hotel and casino, the Venetian, Palazzo, Bally's, Caesars, and the bronzed Wynn and its sister property Encore. Out a side window, Chambers viewed the Stratosphere tower and the Hilton. At CSN, Chambers had been off-Broadway. Now he sat within walking distance of one of the world's most famous and brightest boulevards. He had a chance to make a name for himself at the high-school, junior-college, and four-year-university levels in the same town. "Not many can say that," Chambers said, beaming.

Chambers hired Jay Guest, Kevin Higgins, and Sean "Showtime" Larimer from his CSN staff to help him at UNLV. Steve Chatham also went to UNLV, as director of baseball operations, but he was uneasy being confined by a desk position and left after a few months for a volunteer assistant post at Loyola Marymount in Los Angeles. Cooper Fouts, who had coached the catchers at CSN, became a volunteer assistant on Steve Rodriguez's Pepperdine staff in Malibu, California. Glen Evans coached pitchers at a local high school and had been promoted to a manager at the M Resort.

When the Baltimore Orioles picked Joe Robinson in the thirty-second round of the draft, nine Coyotes—including seven pitchers—had been taken. Only two four-year universities, baseball powers Arizona State and Georgia Tech, with ten apiece, had had more than nine players selected to that point. Six of those Sun Devils had been pitchers, while four Yellow Jackets were hurlers. Indeed, CSN could have boasted, on draft positions alone, that it had the finest pitching staff in all of college baseball in 2010.

Ace starter Donnie Roach was a third-round supplemental pick by the Los Angeles Angels, who had selected him in the fortieth round out of high school in 2008. Roach accepted a signing bonus of approximately $250,000. He was hit hard in his first two appearances, but Roach settled. In the fall of 2010, an MRI on his right arm at the Arizona Fall League revealed no damage; throwing 165 innings of competitive ball that year had taxed his wing, so rest was prescribed. He had won seven of nine career pro decisions by the middle of May 2011, when he was throwing out of the bullpen for Single-A Cedar Rapids.

Through the same period Aaron Kurcz (tenth-round pick by the Chicago Cubs) had won four of five minor league decisions and had saved ten games. Chasen Shreve (Atlanta Braves, eleventh round) had lost his first two decisions of 2011 in Single-A Rome. Kenny McDowall (New York Mets, eighth round) underwent arm surgery and hadn't thrown in a pro game. Tyler Hanks (Washington Nationals, seventeenth round) had won eight of ten decisions and saved a pair of games.

Bryan Harper had been a twenty-sixth-round pick by the Chicago Cubs, but he honored a commitment to play for the University of South Carolina, which had won the 2010 College World Series championship.

Joe Robinson did not sign with the Orioles, and he claimed hardship to get out of his commitment to Georgia so he could throw for Chambers at UNLV. Gabe Weidenaar spurned Chambers's offer to visit UNLV and accepted a scholarship to Oklahoma State. Tomo "Helicopter" Delp went to the University of Maryland. Josh Demello, the speedy center fielder from Hawaii, matriculated to Mesa State, right where CSN took batting practice a few times at the World Series in Grand Junction, Colorado.

After the draft, Bryce Harper went to Oklahoma for a week to fish for trout and hang out with friends. He saw Sean Larimer coach an American Legion team in Southern California, and they watched Texas play the Los Angeles Angels in Anaheim. They were planted in Scott Boras's front-row seats by the Rangers' dugout. When slugger Josh Hamilton strolled to the on-deck circle, Harper marveled at Hamilton's broad shoulders and impressive physique on his six-foot-four, 240-pound frame.

Harper's family had been vacationing in Huntington Beach, California, and he left them to spend July Fourth with McKenzie Chambers and her family just down the coast in Oceanside. For a long time, she had resisted his advances and attempts to get close to her. She had grown up around ballplayers, so she knew how flighty they were, how selfish and shallow they could be. Yet, she had finally let him in that spring. She believed every word of the many messages—about how much he cared for her and wanted to be with her—he had written to her over the previous months.

But when Harper departed Oceanside the morning of July 5, McKenzie felt that something had changed between them. It had. They didn't have another meaningful conversation, and McKenzie never got an explanation. By the end of the summer, Harper had removed McKenzie from his exclusive list of Facebook friends. A *Washington Post* headline would eventually inform Nationals fans YOU'RE ABOUT TO FALL HEAD OVER HEELS FOR THE NATIONALS' NEWEST STAR. The story in the paper's Sunday magazine gushed, "Will he realize his galactic potential, or will fate, hubris or health stop him short? Will he fill our hearts with joy, or break them, or both? Or neither? Will we remember his name? Will we grow old together?"

McKenzie Chambers had her own answer.

On Tuesday, July 13, Harper won the Golden Spikes Award, given annually to the nation's top amateur player, in a ceremony at the All-Star festivities in Anaheim, California. Harper looked sharp in his dark suit with charcoal pinstripes, black dress shirt, pink tie, and pink kerchief in his left breast pocket.

Chambers sat behind Harper and marveled at the width of the slugger's shoulders. In the fall of 2009, Harper weighed 185 pounds, shocking Chambers when the prodigy showed up at CSN. In Anaheim, Harper had tipped the scales at 225. Unlike his four competitors for the Golden Spikes, who wandered and looked out of place, Harper glided around the Angel Stadium infield and casually spoke with major league players he knew, such as St. Louis slugger Albert Pujols. For the first time, Chambers met and exchanged a few words with Scott Boras.

Only one other junior college player, pitcher Alex Fernandez in 1990, had won the Golden Spikes. Fernandez had accomplished that at Miami-Dade Community College, a year after spending a season at the University of Miami.

The Nationals had until nine at night, Las Vegas time, on August 16 to sign Harper, and all signs pointed to both sides negotiating up to the deadline. The Nationals had signed Strasburg with seventy-seven ticks remaining. That long delay meant Harper could not play with the US eighteen-and-under team, which he had helped win the Pan American junior championship in October 2009 in Venezuela. It would not have been wise to risk injury, not with Harper so close to winning the baseball lottery. The Americans lost to Cuba, 3–2, in the first round of the play-offs in the junior world championship in Thunder Bay, Ontario, eliminating them from medal contention.

In the July 20 issue of *SportsBusiness Daily,* a team of corporate brand managers, marketing executives, agencies, and baseball media included Harper, even though he hadn't played a professional game yet, among its five most-marketable major league players under the age of twenty-five. "The hype makes him relevant to Madison Avenue," wrote staff writer Erik Swanson. In order, the magazine tabbed Stephen Strasburg, Evan Longoria of Tampa Bay, Jason Heyward of Atlanta, David Price of Tampa Bay, and Harper.

The downtime drove Bryce Harper so zany he wrote on his Facebook page on Tuesday, July 27, that it looked as if he would return to CSN for his sophomore season. He had also hated not playing for Team USA. He wrote:

Probably going back to CSN to try to win a National Championship!!! :) Wish I was playing USA more than anything!!! Summer has been crazy, and thinking about returning to CSN for another year!!! Very possible! Life without baseball = An early DEATH!!!!!

Three days later, mainstream media got ahold of his Facebook disclosures. The *Las Vegas Review-Journal* speculated that the page had been a fake, that someone was expertly impersonating Harper. Not true. It had been authentic. One of the five hundred "friends" that Harper kept in contact with via Facebook had to have outed him, said a friend familiar with that social network. Harper's page had been copied and was sent to someone, who sent it to someone . . . next thing Harper knew, it was public.

That site irritated Harper. Once he had to delete seven thousand friend requests, one by one. The page that went public showed Harper wearing board shorts, or long swimming trunks, and smiling without a shirt on. Ryan Scott responded to Harper's statements, about returning to CSN for his sophomore season, by writing, *Nice negotiating ploy,* to him. By Saturday morning, July 31, Harper had erased his photograph.

On Sunday, August 15, Harper told the *Las Vegas Review-Journal* that he would report to the first day of CSN's practice, on Monday, August 16, to work out and participate in practice. He kept saying it would be fine with him if he played his sophomore season for the Coyotes.

Chris Sheff, the former Bishop Gorman coach, had been named the new CSN head coach on July 9. Sheff removed all photos, plaques, and awards from the clubhouse walls. When he held his first practice on August 16, it was stunning to see the new caps. They were Western Nevada royal blue, with a white *C* in the style of the Cincinnati Reds' logo. The cursive, capital *C* that had so distinguished CSN for eleven seasons, and at two Junior College World Series appearances, was history.

Bryce Harper was nowhere to be found. Neither was Mr. C.

On that 111-degree Monday, an industrial-size, three-wheeled Toro lawn mower sat in shallow right field. It wouldn't start, and five assistant coaches couldn't push the thing or figure out what was wrong with it. Sheff finally added gasoline, but it had been filled with petrol and the overflow dumped onto the Bermuda grass. The stain on the diamond would soon cover the once-proud program.

Much later that day, with twenty seconds remaining—as Bryce Harper saw on his watch—in Washington's negotiations window, Nationals general manager Mike Rizzo and president Stan Kasten came to terms with Boras. Harper agreed to a five-year, $9.9-million deal. It included $1 million in roster incentives, for 2014 and 2015. It was the richest deal ever for a position player, surpassing the $9.5-million pact Mark Teixeira signed in 2001.

On the MLB Network, reporter Jonathan Mayo frantically exchanged text messages with Coach Chambers in the waning minutes before the deadline. Looks like a done deal, Mayo wrote to Chambers. Any idea of the terms? Ten million, Chambers wrote. For months, that was the oft-reported and repeated figure that would make Harper a Nationals player, just enough to surpass Teixeira's initial deal. Gotcha, Mayo wrote to Chambers as the cameras rolled live, but Mayo's eyes angled down, at his cell phone, under the slick metal-and-glass stage desk.

In the kitchen of his home on Cantelope Court, Bryce stood at an island, with Kurt Stillwell at his side, and poked at the screen of a laptop computer as the two sides concluded the deal. Ron said he had been completely behind Bryce's decision whether he chose to return to CSN or begin playing professional baseball.

What do you want to do? Ron asked his youngest son.

"I want to play pro ball. I want to go play ball. It's what I want to do in my heart. I've always wanted to do it. It's my dream."

"Okay, let's do it. It's done."

Months later, Ron Harper downplayed the scene. "You get the phone calls, you talk to people, discussing what they want and what we want, trying to make a good decision for your kid's career and the family, making sure it's the right thing. I want him happy, no matter what. All I've ever wanted in my life is for my kids to be happy: Brittany, Bryan, and Bryce. Sheri, too. That's mainly what it was about. It was never about money. It was never about anything but [Bryce] playing baseball and being happy."

Did Ron and Bryce, and others, keep a keen eye on the clock as the deadline approached?

"You kind of do," Ron Harper said. "You knew you had to make a decision in a certain amount of time. When you hear, 'Thirty seconds left . . . what do you think?' I sat there on the couch and told Bryce, 'I'm okay with whatever.' It wasn't a big deal. The most fun was going to Washington and being with [owner Ted Lerner and his family], and [team executives] Mike Rizzo and Stan Kasten, and Bryce getting to take BP on the field. That was the fun thing. Draft day was fun. [Signing] deadline day, it was what it was. But going there and seeing him put on that jersey and saying, 'I'm a Washington National,' that was awesome."

On Saturday, August 21, Stephen Strasburg winced in pain after throwing a pitch in the fifth inning at Philadelphia. He had torn an elbow ligament and underwent Tommy John surgery on Friday, September 3. Strasburg likely wouldn't throw a competitive pitch until the 2012 season. Whether he would return to form was anybody's guess, but Strasburg was buoyed by the recent success rates of those who'd returned from the delicate procedure.

John tore a ligament in his left, or throwing, elbow in September 1974. Dr. Frank Jobe performed the revolutionary surgery by replacing that ligament with one from John's right forearm. John pitched in the majors until 1989, going 164-124 after the operation.

In a flash, the face of the Washington franchise's future became the lefty slugger from Las Vegas. Early on Thursday, August 26, the morning of his introductory press conference, Harper ran up the steps of the US Capitol without a shirt, raised his hands, twirled, and howled like Rocky, even though he wasn't in Philadelphia. Passersby glared, laughed, or stepped aside.

At batting practice that afternoon in Nationals Park, Harper slammed a ball into the third deck in right field, a tough shot because of its distance and because only two sections jutted out a bit past the right-field foul pole. Only Adam Dunn had parked a ball in that lofty balcony. Tim Foli, a special assistant to Nationals general manager Mike Rizzo, pulled Harper aside and told him he was swinging too hard. Relax, Foli said. Harper then smacked half of his dozen homers of the day in his sixth and final hitting round.

Washington brass decided against having Harper report to its Gulf Coast League squad. It wanted to slowly introduce him to professional baseball. In the middle of September, Harper went to the club's instructional league squad in Viera, Florida. He had told me after the JUCO World Series that he had a clearer understanding of the game's intrinsic humbling qualities.

"I've just gotta learn that baseball is a game of failure. That's the way it is. . . . I have to learn, mentally, and get stronger and better. I will have to be mentally prepared for everything that comes my way."

Chambers had fielded a phone call from Jeff Johnson, who coached Chipola College in Marianna, Florida, up by the Alabama and Georgia state lines in the Sunshine State's panhandle. An outstanding sixteen-year-old pitcher had been considering leaving his Florida high school after his sophomore year to play for Johnson at Chipola in 2011.

Johnson was curious. He asked Chambers, exactly how did Bryce Harper do it? How did he leave high school so early? What was your first step in the process? How'd you go about it? How'd you handle him and the situation, and the rest of your team, and the jealousy and expectations and hype and . . . what am I leaving out?

"They want to get in position to play professional baseball at an earlier age, like they've done in the Dominican Republic and other countries for years," Johnson told me. "If you're a talented player, your body only lasts so long. You want to get in as many years as possible. It's a no-brainer, if they're mature enough and talented enough. They're all going to school to figure out a way to make a living, right? The earlier you make that living, the better. Playing baseball ain't that bad.

"What Bryce did was great for junior college baseball. For something to come out of it as good as Bryce Harper, it's a good deal for all of us. For him to open that door for others . . . it's a great thing junior college offers. To have him go number one in the draft? He's a heck-uva player. We'd pitch to him and I'd realize, 'He's supposed to be a junior in high school! Holy cow, is this guy good.' Not only was he young, but he did as well or better than anybody out there. Wow. No question, Bryce is a trailblazer."

Harper hadn't been hitting so well in Viera, near Cape Canaveral, so he begged his instructional league coaches to let him wear his eye black. They nodded. He reached for his black, Franklin, lipsticklike tube. He grabbed his black Marucci and bashed a 475-foot home run. He hit .319 against pitchers regarded at the low Single-A level in Florida. He also predicted that the Nationals would win multiple World Series trophies and the National League East would surpass the American League East in stature as the power division in the majors.

On the first Friday of October, I attended UNLV's first fall intrasquad scrimmage at Wilson Stadium. I caught a whiff of Aramis cologne. Mr. C, wearing a scarlet polo with UNLV stitched in black on the left breast and a white Rebels cap, traipsed around down there in the home dugout, steps from Chambers. Mr. C flipped off UNLV players and generally dispensed insight wherever he wanted. I'm not going to let him retire, Chambers said. I couldn't make out complete sentences, but I did hear Mr. C say *here again* and *just my opinion* a few times.

Bryce turned eighteen on Saturday, October 16. Bryan had returned from South Carolina to celebrate his brother's birthday with the family, and Bryan wound up in Donnie Roach's condominium for a reunion with Roach, Aaron Kurcz, Joe Robinson, Ryan Scott, and Casey Sato. The conversation turned to the Junior College World Series. Several said they couldn't believe they didn't win it. "I'm kind of getting over it," Scott told his close friends. But Bryan Harper became enraged. "I'm not. I'm still bitter. We should have won that thing." It turned fiery and Ryan Scott tried to diffuse the heat. But Scott was kidding himself that the ending of the 2010 season had stopped bothering him. "In the back of my mind, I knew they were right," Scott said. "Everyone chimed in. It brought back memories, not good memories."

After his birthday weekend, Bryce Harper drove to Phoenix with his father to report to the Scottsdale Scorpions, on October 18, in the elite Arizona Fall League. In the nearly twenty years of the league, for top prospects and major leaguers, 159 All-Stars and 18 Hall of Famers had participated in the AFL. Harper was the second-youngest person ever to don an AFL uniform. Only Fernando Martinez, who turned eighteen the day he had put on a New York Mets uniform in Arizona in 2006, was younger; by two days.

As a "taxi squad" player, Harper would play twice a week but practice full-time with the team. In an October 20 *Washington Post* story, which detailed his experience in Florida and previewed what he hoped to achieve in Arizona, Harper talked about having turned a high school crush with a girl named Kayla into his new relationship over his birthday weekend.

In early November, Marvin Campbell bashed a three-run homer over the right-field fence in Wilson Stadium as a UNLV team largely composed of players from the previous CSN season trounced a squad of returning Rebels, many of whom had been taking regular snipes at the former Coyotes, in an intrasquad game. Those veteran Rebels were either jealous of the attention their new teammates had received the previous season or said they would have done nothing without Bryce Harper on that squad, or both. This will shut them up, said Trevor Kirk. In both dugouts and on the diamond, Marvin Campbell was the lone black player.

That day, Jonathan Slack sat next to me along the first-base side of the stadium. He was scruffy in a T-shirt, whiskers, and jeans. His valet shift at the Rio had ended at three thirty in the morning, and, well, he just hadn't had the time to clean up before coming to the yard. Slack had been elated because he was about to get back into the game as a graduate assistant to the man who had taught him so much about baseball and life. "People are excited about the UNLV program," Slack said. "You can tell when people are feeling it. They are definitely feeling that Chambers will bring it back."

On Wednesday, November 3, less than four months after Chris Sheff had been hired to replace Chambers as baseball coach and athletic director at CSN, Sheff was relieved of his duties. A day earlier, the school had launched an independent investigation into the baseball program when administrators learned about potential rules violations and alleged mistreatment of players by Sheff. CSN president Michael Richards continued the investigation to ensure that the program was being run in compliance within National Junior College Athletic Association rules and regulations. Junior college baseball programs were allowed to dole out twenty-four annual letters of intent. But after it had found CSN guilty of three infractions in Sheff's brief tenure, the NJCAA penalized the program by docking ten letters of intent from its allotment in both the 2011/12 and 2012/13 academic years.

Nick Garritano, who had coached pitcher Joe Robinson at Green

Valley High, was hired to replace Sheff. Garritano vowed to run a well-structured, clean program. He told the *Las Vegas Review-Journal* that CSN's image had indeed been tarnished. Marc Morse accepted the post as CSN athletic director and promised to improve the program that played its games in the stadium that bore his grandfather's name.

Two days after Garritano had been hired at CSN, I trekked three hundred miles—through the Black, Hualapai, and Vulture Mountains, past Rattlesnake Wash, by vast stretches of Joshua trees, and the tiny desert towns of Wikieup and Wickenburg—into the heart of Phoenix, where eastbound I-10 bled into the 202 loop to East Van Buren Street.

The Scottsdale Scorpions and Bryce Harper had been scheduled to play the Phoenix Desert Dogs that Friday night in an Arizona Fall League game at Phoenix Municipal Stadium—where Willie Mays and other notables had played spring-training games during baseball's golden age. I arrived late in the afternoon and spotted Ron Harper's mammoth red truck, backed in to show off its gnarling silver grille to anyone who dared to glance at it, in the small parking lot, just in time to watch Bryce take batting practice and shag flies.

He wore the white jersey of the Nationals, with red letters on the front and a red thirty-four on the back. As a member of the team's forty-man major league roster, that's the uniform that would be waiting for Harper whenever the parent team called him up. A trainer stretched Harper's legs in a serious way along the left-field foul line. As Harper lay on his back, the trainer just about put all of his weight into bending Harper's straight left leg almost back to his left ear. Then they switched to the right leg.

As Harper jogged from right field to the third-base dugout with his teammates, maybe fifty fans had been lined against the stadium rail hoping to score Harper's signature. Harper had just passed second base when all of his teammates began chirping at him, like crickets all around him, mimicking the cries that always rained down upon Harper for his autograph. "Bryce. Bryce! *Bryce! Bryce! BRYCE!*" Fans were taken aback and none of them said a word to Harper, who smiled to his teammates as he slid down the dugout steps and up a tunnel to a clubhouse. His teammates continued yelling his first name at him, and those chirps echoed off the metal walls like a scene from a cheap horror movie, as all ran to the clubhouse.

A crowd of more than eight hundred had filled Phoenix Muni, as locals called the one-level stadium that had an accordion-like roof over its lone, small second tier of stands behind home plate. What's with all the fans? a kid said to his buddy as they entered the stadium. "Bryce is here," his buddy responded. It was a Chamber of Commerce sixty-seven-degree evening. At the concessions stand, a young woman peddled caps of all six AFL teams, including the Peoria Saguaros and Mesa Solar Sox, but by the third inning every Scorpions cap had been sold.

With a wide block of the black stuff under each eye, Bryce stood in the on-deck circle in the first inning when, with the bases loaded, a teammate hit into a double play. As if testing what he could get away with, the outside of each black swath had nubs dragging down, just a bit, onto his cheeks. Harper drew a walk in the second inning. He had severely curtailed his hitting routine, as expected. No dropping of the bat. No grabbing of dirt. Before jumping in the box, he took one mean practice swing. He stepped in, ran the tip of his bat on the other side of the plate, and smacked the tip of his right cleat with the bat. He drew a walk and was thrown out trying to steal second.

He singled to right field in his next at bat and was thrown out on the front part of a four-six-three double play. However, he had barreled into the right side of second base to make the shortstop's throw difficult. The shortstop had made a beautiful pirouette to avoid contact, but he barked at Harper as Harper jogged into his dugout and low-fived a teammate. The pitcher hit the next batter in the square of his back, and the umpire sternly warned both managers. If any foe had thought Bryce Harper would play the game anything but all out, they must have been from another country and not privy to the years of headlines about him.

Scorpions coach Randy Knorr, who would guide the Nationals' Triple-A Syracuse Chiefs in 2011, compared Harper to Ty Cobb. "He will put you on your . . . ," Knorr said.

As Bryce struck out, with strikes two and three coming against what appeared to be fastballs in the ninety-six-to-ninety-eight mile-an-hour range, Ron Harper heard some critiques from nearby seats. He didn't turn his head. These are some *good* pitchers, he told me. "Bryce will get the hang of this."

Ron had been impressed by his son's performance in Arizona, but he was not shocked. Look at these guys, Ron said. These are high-level players, topflight prospects. Ron told me Bryce would adjust and ascend.

"This game is about adjustments. Can you make adjustments, in-game adjustments? To try to do what these older guys are doing, at such a young age, I think he's doing it. He did it up there in college, in high school . . . he did it at every level he's been at. I don't expect anything different now. I think he'll try to outwork everyone and try to become the best player he possibly can, but he has a lot to learn. He just has to go out and work hard, and good things will happen. It's got to be the toughest thing in the world for him to sit around for three days, and play . . . sit three days, then play. He's never, ever done that in his life. But I think he's done really well. I'm proud of him. It's a privilege to play in this league, with such great players and great talent, and to be around the coaches and just be a part of it. It's amazing, so good for him."

Ron's presence was also good for Bryce, Ron believed. He seemed to have difficulty straddling the line of protecting his son or letting him out on his own, responsible for doing his own laundry and eating properly, and fending off any enticements that might lure him away from his goals and objectives. When I brought up Josh Hamilton as an example of someone who had given in to temptations, Ron widened his eyes and responded, "Exactly!"

Bryce ended the night hitting .348 in the AFL. Mike Rizzo, the

Washington general manager, parroted the organization's line that it was not going to rush Bryce through its minor league system. In the AFL title game, Bryce singled in the first Scottsdale run with a sharp single to left in a game the Scorpions would win, 3–2. On the MLB Network, former Los Angeles Dodgers manager Tommy Lasorda expounded about Harper's talents and predicted that he would be successful, "if he stays levelheaded, that's the big thing."

The education of Bryce Harper continued at Tim Soder Physical Therapy, an expansive workout facility in the southwest corner of Las Vegas. Members of the PGA Tour, MMA fighters, and many pro baseball players used the latest equipment to stay in shape and prepare for upcoming seasons.

At a winter session, San Francisco Giants outfielder Aaron Rowand, an All-Star and Gold Glove winner in 2007, tore into Bryce. An hour into it, Harper had apparently finished. Rowand blasted him, saying they were only halfway through the regimen. Rowand's steam had been building, as he had noticed for a stretch of days that Harper had been slacking off. "What the fuck?" Rowand yelled at Harper. "You think you're going to show up in the minors and skate? Everyone there works *hard*. You better learn that right now!" It had been a welcome-to-the-big-time moment for the kid who should have been preparing for his senior season of high school ball.

In between semesters, another call rang out. Some former Coyotes called others. Bryan Harper rang Ryan Scott. Someone called Donnie Roach, and it was on. Two dozen of the 2010 CSN Coyotes gathered on a Friday night at a Buffalo Wild Wings restaurant in early January 2011 for another reunion. One was missing: Bryce Harper had to spend some media-orientation time in the Washington, DC, area with top prospects from other teams, where major league officials guided them on handling certain interview questions or specific social situations.

"Like what do you do when a frantic woman is yelling for help and wants to use your cell phone for an emergency," Marvin Campbell chuckled, sitting next to me in a Wilson Stadium seat after a UNLV practice, about the Russian female who had stalked Bryce Harper in Twin Falls, Idaho.

The ex-Coyotes took up a thirty-foot table and talked for hours, occasionally skipping around and switching places with others to catch up and instantly resume jabbing each other with inside jokes and personal history. Ryan Scott didn't think he would ever be on such a tight-knit team again.

What would CSN have done in 2010 without Bryce Harper, without all of the distractions that came with having one of the most celebrated amateur players on the roster? At least a few Coyotes pondered that thought. One predicted they would have won the championship. Then again, in the end, CSN had had that chance. It could have won two games and, depending on the scenario, claimed the crown in Grand Junction without having Harper in the lineup. But with their star attraction serving his suspension in the hotel, the Coyotes couldn't win a game. Casey Sato laughed at the thought of whether the Coyotes would have fared worse or better without Bryce Harper for the 2010 season.

"What would be cooler, to tell my grandkids I won a junior college championship or to say I played with one of the best baseball players who ever played?" Sato said. "What would you rather do, win a championship or witness history?"

CSN opened its 2011 season on the evening of Friday, January 28, with a roster almost completely bereft of returnees. Only four were Coyotes the previous season. Pitcher Wes Johnson, the former marine who had made two tours of Iraq and so badly wanted to throw for Chambers at CSN in 2011, had not made the cut.

Before the opener, Bryce had his number thirty-four retired in a home-plate ceremony emceed by Marc Morse, who wore tan khaki pants, a blue dress shirt, and a yellow tie. Chambers's number six and Mike Dunn's number forty-four were also being retired, joining Sean Kazmar's number four on the wall in center field of Morse Stadium.

Morse gave Harper, Chambers, and Dunn their framed jerseys after making a few nervous comments about each former Coyote. Harper wore a gray, long-sleeve T-shirt, black jeans, and sneakers.

After the ceremony, Bryce was brief with former teammates. He, his father, and his girlfriend were on a tight schedule; they had to leave for Salt Lake City, where Bryce's sister, Brittany, was getting married that weekend. Outside the clubhouse, Harper signed stuff and took some pictures with fans. When he arrived where McKenzie Chambers and a few of her friends stood, he abruptly quit the autograph session and disappeared behind the dugout. Many visitors left before the first pitch. Maybe two hundred—far fewer fans than the record crowd that had packed into Morse Stadium for the 2010 opener—stayed for the game, which CSN lost to Arizona Western. The Coyotes barely had a winning season.

In February 2011, *Baseball America* listed Harper atop a chart of its top prospects. On Monday, February 28, 2011, at Port St. Lucie, Florida, in his first spring-training game, Bryce struck out in his two plate appearances against the Mets. Harper casually returned to his dugout after both whiffs. Michael Morse had homered twice in the Nationals' victory, but Harper's strikeouts were what made *SportsCenter* highlights on ESPN. On Tuesday, March 1, against the Mets at Space Coast Stadium in Viera, Florida, Harper drove a one-oh fastball from twenty-four-year-old pitcher Pedro Beato, a six-foot-four right-hander who had spent five seasons in the minors, into left field for his first spring-training hit. That, too, made the top of *SportsCenter*.

There's no blueprint for it, Washington general manager Mike Rizzo explained—sounding like Tim Chambers at any point during the 2010 season. "We're breaking new ground here," Rizzo said. "And every day is something different."

UNLV improved to 13-3 after crushing Valparaiso, 12–2, on Friday night, March 11. Trevor Kirk had crunched a three-run homer off Valpo pitcher Damon McCormick in the second inning, and a little kid traced the Rawlings baseball's path over the left-center fence at

Wilson Stadium, retrieved Kirk's first UNLV home run, and presented the ball to Kirk's father, Rich, who had been sitting in the ninth row behind first base. Some of Rich's friends from Rancho High, from thirty years earlier, had been sitting around him. In high school, Rich had dreamed of playing baseball at UNLV, but then-coach Fred Dallimore avoided signing players from Las Vegas. On the rail to the right of the home dugout, Rich's eyes were glassy as he high-fived and hugged Trevor after the game.

In the early spring, Bryce Harper bought new vehicles for his parents and helped out Bryan, on a partial scholarship to South Carolina; he had chipped in to financially assist Brittany with her wedding. For himself, Bryce splurged on a sleek, new pearl-colored Mercedes-Benz, with the license plate MY BABY. It was believed to be the only one of its kind in the state. Some of Harper's former CSN teammates were certain they had seen his girlfriend driving that spiffy rig around town.

In his first big league camp, Bryce Harper hit .389 and drove in five runs. He played in thirteen of fourteen games as a late replacement, mostly for new Nationals outfielder Jayson Werth. The Nats lost one game when Harper made an errant, late cutoff throw. On Saturday, March 12, the parent club optioned Harper to the Single-A Hagerstown Suns.

On his Twitter account a few days earlier, Harper had displayed a redesigned team logo that read HARPERSTOWN. The Suns planned to sell en masse T-shirts with that logo. In the middle of February, Bryce, with some coaxing from older brother Bryan, had signed up for Twitter. He had 271 followers on February 19. That had doubled three days later. He counted 1,750 on March 1; 2,398 on March 4; 3,409 on March 7; and 5,780 a week later.

He started the season sluggishly, hitting .250 after a few weeks, but during it he made rare contact with a former Coyote. For almost an hour, he exchanged text messages with Sean Larimer the night of Friday, April 8. "He's havin' fun," Showtime reported.

Harper wound up having his eyes examined. On April 19,

Washington Nationals team optometrist Keith Smithson told Harper, after he had struggled reading an eye chart, that he had one of the worst pair of eyes Smithson had ever seen. Harper had worn contact lenses only briefly at Las Vegas High because they had given him such headaches. Fitted with new and improved prescription contacts, Harper went on a hitting tear.

By mid-May Harper was closing in on .400. Through Friday, May 6, Harper had gone twenty-four for forty-seven (.511) at the plate with the new lenses. He had counted about 12,500 Twitter followers when he posted a photograph of the pink Under Armour cleats he would wear for the Mother's Day game on Sunday, May 8. By the time he hit his first professional grand slam, which was his eighth homer of the season, on May 11, Harper had disengaged his Twitter account. THIS USER DOES NOT EXIST read the official note when anyone tried tapping onto BHarp34. Opposing pitchers could only wish that were true. Harper couldn't turn off his notification e-mails, of new Twitter messages, so he zapped the page.

On Saturday, May 14, Bryce's solo shot to left was the only run in a game against Lakewood. He had also hit a single to raise his average to a South Atlantic League–best .393, and he had stretched his hitting streak to eighteen games. At the end of the month he appeared in consecutive *Sports Illustrated* issues, on the positive side of its WHO'S HOT/WHO'S NOT graphic, and then in the opening sentence of a short piece on talented minor leaguers on the rise.

So how did Bryce Harper record one of the most outstanding amateur seasons at CSN, which led to the Washington Nationals' signing him to a guaranteed deal worth almost $10 million and Under Armour inking him to another rich endorsement pact, with such poor vision? Harper downplayed the issue. Coach Chambers was dubious about the April 2011 reports of Harper's horrible eyesight.

"It's important to see the baseball to be able to hit it," said Chambers, after mulling the question between bites of a chicken-Parmesan sandwich. "I'm pretty sure he saw [the baseball]. I'm pretty sure he saw *something*."

On Monday, May 23, UNLV's baseball team piled into a coach and traveled to San Diego for the double-elimination Mountain West Conference tournament. The Rebels were 33-23. Late that night, I had a ninety-minute telephone conversation with Trevor Kirk. He confessed that his rebuke of me after the game in which Bryce had been ejected from the Junior College World Series still bothered him. It had taken place almost a year earlier. I cut him off before he could finish. I told Kirk that I had forgotten about it long ago. It had been a heated game with a disappointing conclusion. Forget about it. He laughed and said he'd sleep easy that evening.

The next night, against San Diego State, Kirk led off the game with a walk. Scott Dysinger, the next batter, also walked. Both eventually scored to give UNLV a 2–0 lead, which it didn't hold. The Rebels lost. Joe Robinson started on the mound the next day against BYU, and UNLV lost again to end its season at 33-25. It had been the Rebels' first winning campaign in six years.

Trevor Kirk and Ryan Scott had both hit above .300 in their first Division I seasons. Trent Cook, the only player to start in every UNLV game, hit a blistering .370, third best in the league. The Rebels had won sixteen of their first twenty games when they hit a rough patch. Casey Sato told me about the cliquish clubhouse. Every captain had been a returnee, but Sato said, "There are captains, and then there are leaders." Sato rang Coach Chambers and pleaded for him to start giving more time to some ex-Coyotes. Sato did not include himself. The main beneficiary was Scott Dysinger, at second base. Chambers had agreed with Sato.

Dysinger responded with solid defense in the field and hitting well. In what would be UNLV's final victory of the season, Dysinger knocked in the winning run with a shot down the left-field line in the bottom of the ninth inning at home against San Diego State on May

19. Chambers had appreciated Sato's boldness and feel for the team, and he asked Sato to be his graduate assistant after Sato's senior season of 2012. Sato told me he would likely accept the offer.

Bryan Harper threw sparingly out of the bullpen for South Carolina, but he boasted on Twitter about the total team effort that had been required when the Gamecocks won a second consecutive College World Series title by beating Florida in Omaha, Nebraska, in the last week of June. Just Average Joes, Bryan wrote.

In the South Atlantic League, Bryce Harper heard constant smack from the stands. A guy in West Virginia had been particularly crude, constantly yelling unpleasant remarks about Harper's mother and sister. Bryce had heard every syllable. But when asked about the nine-inning tirade, Harper didn't blink. He said that was just preparing him "for Philly."

The Rook had been prepped well. With the thick grease smears and the ultraconfident manner, he invited criticism. But he wasn't about to change his ways. He had his mother's compassion and sense, and his father's aggression and steel spine. He had a clever knack for turning a phrase, and a brash attitude on the diamond that could get him into trouble and embarrass him as easily as it could produce glory and single-handedly defeat an opponent.

That's what Washington brass wanted him to temper in the minor leagues. The Nationals were not going to rush him or expose him before he had been thoroughly seasoned. When former Washington Senators slugger Harmon Killebrew passed away on May 17, 2011, *Washington Post* columnist Thomas Boswell wrote of how invaluable Killebrew's 338 minor-league games had been in his development. He hit 573 home runs in his major-league career.

"As baseball celebrates Killebrew, let us underline what might be most unusual about him: For once, a wildly celebrated teenage athlete managed, both as a player and a person, to have a finish worthy of the start. Give Harper the same chance."

Washington picked Bryan Harper in the thirtieth round of the draft on June 7, 2011, the third time the elder Harper had been drafted and the second time he had been picked by the Nationals in three years. Chambers surmised that the Nats had wanted someone to temper Bryce, to cool and corral him when needed, such as when he blew a kiss at the Greensboro Grasshoppers pitcher off whom he had just parked his fourteenth home run. That happened twenty-four hours before Washington drafted Bryan. By then, Bryce had started a new Twitter page, dubbed BHarpersStache. Yes, he had been growing a mustache, which had widely been mocked as either a caterpillar from the garden or something from the porn industry. The page had ninety-six Twitter followers.

GRASSHOPPERS? MORE LIKE ASSHOPPERS! LOL! OMG! KISS MY STACHE!!!!!!! 11! SMOOCH! wrote Harper, or his mustache, the day the Nats drafted his brother. As usual, Thomas Boswell explained in a column a day later, Bryce had been reacting to a buildup of taunts, and a fastball that had tagged his left knee a day earlier. Boswell downplayed the kiss-blowing incident. Nothing to see here. Move along. Some welcomed the new blood into a game that had become somewhat stale. HARPER'S ARROGANCE JUST WHAT BASEBALL NEEDS headlined Yahoo! writer Jeff Passan's story about Harper.

By the end of June, Bryce Harper had been selected to participate in the Futures Game, featuring up-and-coming players, during All-Star Game festivities in Phoenix. And McKenzie Chambers had created a Twitter account. HarperMania, which posted regular updates of Bryce's progress in the minors, was among the first sites that she chose to follow. It supplied a link to Harper's first commercial, an endorsement for a SwingAway contraption that included a voice-over line from his father, Ron. After watching the ad McKenzie wrote, *I think I'm going to throw up. LOVE CONCEITED PEOPLE!*

On July 3, Bryce had been promoted to Double-A Harrisburg. He had hit .318, with fourteen homers and forty-six RBIs, in seventy-two games in Hagerstown. On Independence Day, he singled twice and scored a run in a Senators victory. Metro Bank Park had been filled with a record crowd of 8,092 fans. He played left field, and Washington general manager Mike Rizzo revealed that the parent club wanted Harper to play all three outfield positions in the minors to give him more versatility for his eventual call-up to the majors. Nationals manager Davey Johnson, who had replaced Jim Riggleman after his abrupt resignation two weeks earlier and had known Harper for three years, believed Harper had been ready to jump over Single-A Potomac to Harrisburg. "Bryce is never going to bite off more than he can chew," Johnson told *The Washington Post*.

Chris McKenzie had returned to the Nationals' Gulf Coast League team in Florida. The six-foot-three Massachusetts native had tossed the final junior college pitch to Bryce Harper and had been picked by Washington in the thirteenth round of the 2010 draft, 385 slots after the Nats had selected Harper at number one. McKenzie had started six games in Hagerstown before being demoted. An hour after winning a day game in Florida, McKenzie told me how he and Harper had become friends, that Harper was a model teammate, and it had been fascinating to watch all those fans flock to Hagerstown games just to see Harper play.

"He's legit," McKenzie said on his cell phone after ducking inside a locker room to escape the wind. "I believe he's gonna be one of the best to play the game."

I asked him how far outside that pitch had been in Grand Junction that ended up being called strike three by Don Gilmore, which made Harper etch that line in the dirt with his bat and caused Gilmore to eject him from the game? "It was a ball," McKenzie said after pausing for two seconds. "But I'm a pitcher. I'll take whatever I can get."

He had never seen a batter show up an umpire by drawing a line in the dirt, so the gesture alone had been quite dramatic to McKenzie. That it had been the last amateur pitch Harper saw punctuated the moment. But Harper, McKenzie, and Tyler Hanks, the other Coyote who had been drafted by the Nationals and spent minor league time with Harper and McKenzie, had all laughed about the episode.

"We joked with each other, saying, 'It was a ball!' 'No, it was a strike!' Just messin' around," McKenzie said. "It was exciting. But at the same time, I still had to focus on the game. Yeah, it was pretty cool to strike him out. I was just glad he was out. But he wasn't the focal point of my game; I really needed to throw well against their whole team."

Bryce had a cheery, unbridled way of laughing when he was with his teammates and his guard was down. His reaction to a question I had posed to him, on the coach somewhere in the lower part of Utah as we rolled home from Grand Junction, had left an impression. We daydreamed about his pro career and fast-forwarded to the end of it. Harper insisted it would only be at that point, when it was all said and done, that he would reflect about any of it, about doing something no-body before him had done and, quite likely, nobody after him would attempt—trampolining from his sophomore year of high school to professional baseball via a magnificently turbulent season swinging wood at the junior college down the highway from his home.

On the somewhat sullen busload rolling west, he had no interest in introspection or the past. He wouldn't turn eighteen for more than four months.

"The day I retire, that's when I'll be satisfied," Bryce said in a tone just above the rattle and hum of the bus's engine and wheels. "Hopefully, I'll be forty-five years old. That'll be when I'll be satis-fied. I'll look back on it with family and kids and have fun, relax, go fishing, and hang out."

And he'd let himself get fat, I suggested—having heard that line often from pro athletes over more than twenty years as a sports-writer—on his major league stats and spaghetti and mac and cheese, recipes handed down from his mother?

Harper erased his congenial look. "No. I don't want to do that. I want to stay in shape."

I'd seen that steely glare before in a Harper. In November 2010, Ron Harper had cringed when I informed him that Chipola coach Jeff

Johnson had a kid in Florida who had been giving serious thought to leaving his high school after his sophomore year to play for Johnson, to be eligible for the Major League Baseball draft a year before his high school class graduated in June 2011. Serious and blunt, as usual, Ron Harper slowly shook his head in the Phoenix Muni stands. As Bryce struck out against some high Arizona Fall League heat, Ron braced himself as a few fans yelled insults down at his son. He said nothing for five seconds, which became ten. Finally, he unclenched his teeth, locked eyes with me, and quietly spoke so nobody around us could hear him.

"I don't suggest it to anybody. It wasn't easy. Everyone sees that it worked out for him. They didn't see everything else."

2012 UPDATE

BRYCE HARPER SMOKED A soft lob from Kevin Higgins into the left-center gap at Wilson Stadium on the UNLV campus. The ball was sinking fast in the long late-afternoon shadows when, in a blur, Marvin Campbell snatched it an eyelash before it kissed the Bermuda turf. Harper gawked at Campbell from under the huge hitting cage.

"You make that play at the [Junior College] World Series, we win!" Harper barked at his lifelong buddy. Campbell rose to his feet and flipped the ball to a teammate who was collecting them in a white plastic pail at second base. "You *play*," he shot back at Harper, "and we win!" Both shrugged and laughed.

To prep for the Washington Nationals' spring training camp a few weeks away in Florida, Harper dropped by UNLV in February 2012 to work out with about a dozen of his former College of Southern Nevada teammates. Most of them were seniors. Harper was about to start his second full professional season. He wore a dark knitted skull-cap, down over his ears, on the chilly, breezy day. He hugged and exchanged small talk with Rebels coach Tim Chambers, and assistants Higgins and Jay Guest. He joked with Trevor Kirk, Scott Dysinger, and Sean "Showtime" Larimer. Harper blasted several Higgy pitches over the wall in center and right field.

It had been a hectic winter. Harper had MOM scrawled in ink on the inside of a wrist, POPS on the other. He spent some beach time with a *GQ* reporter and photographer. The latter captured Harper, bleach streaks in his brown mane, wearing a blue leisure shirt, with a baseball in his mouth, the setting sun and breaking waves behind him. The former captured Harper dropping three F-bombs in the first few paragraphs.

Harper had also dropped $762,000 for a luxurious home in the high-end Foothills at MacDonald Ranch for his family. He posted a note on Twitter about signing the bank documents. He had returned to that social network to banter with friends and answer inquiries from his many fans; quickly, he had more than twenty thousand followers. In another flash, Nats executives or Boras staffers, maybe both, convinced Harper to quit frittering with Twitter. Time to concentrate on baseball.

In Florida, Harper looked composed in the batter's box, quite different from that free-swinging kid with all those antics in junior college. He wanted to break camp with the parent club. He never wanted to play another game in the minors. He had a key ally in that quest in Manager Davey Johnson, who had been high on nineteen-year-old pitcher Dwight Gooden when both were with the New York Mets in 1984. The Mets front office had wanted Gooden to season for another summer in the minors. Johnson won the debate; Gooden was selected to the All-Star team and won seventeen games. Washington General Manager Mike Rizzo promised to keep an open mind. First baseman Adam LaRoche wondered how The Rook would deal with failure at the highest level of the game. "Can he handle the first funk he goes in? When you've got twenty media [members] standing in front of you, wondering why you're hitting [.120]? Do you let that go to your head and screw up the rest of the year? Or can you stop it and get after it?"

After nine spring games—in which he hit .286, with two doubles, two walks, and eleven strikeouts—Harper was designated for assignment, to the Nationals' Triple-A grounds; he broke camp with the Syracuse Chiefs. On a gloomy thirty-nine-degree afternoon the first

Thursday in April, he made his Syracuse debut wearing a dark blue hooded sweatshirt underneath his white uniform with the light blue CHIEFS logo, pant stripes, and sleeve piping. He singled and doubled. He stole a base. The Chiefs lost to Rochester before more than six thousand fans at Alliance Bank Stadium. A local columnist included Willie, Mickey, the Duke, and Roy Hobbs in a piece about Harper. He cracked his first Triple-A homer, at Alliance, on a three-one pitch from Buffalo's Jeurys Familia on April 22.

On Thursday, April 26, Harper singled in a game at Rochester. He was hitting only .243, in twenty-one games for the Chiefs. The next day, Syracuse's game was snowed out. Harper, however, was on a five-and-a-half-hour flight to Los Angeles, where the Nationals were beginning a series against the Dodgers. Chiefs Manager Tony Beasley had summoned Harper into his Alliance office and told him, "You're about to become the youngest player in the major leagues." On the parent club, Ryan Zimmerman and Michael Morse were injured. Johnson needed a left-handed hitter with some pop. Baseball's top prospect in 2011 and 2012, according to *Baseball America,* was available in Syracuse. Beasley saw a humble and grateful rookie who did not see the promotion coming. "None of us did," Beasley said. "I think he was kind of speechless. It's a big day for the whole organization."

Rizzo's master plan had been predicated on Harper getting three hundred at bats at the Triple-A level; Harper had had seventy-four. "This wasn't the coming-out party for Bryce that we had in mind," Rizzo confirmed. But because of Harper's makeup, attitude, and confidence, Rizzo didn't hesitate to send for him. Johnson knew Harper had earned an opportunity to play in the big leagues. "Enough said," Johnson said. When Bryce called his father with the news, Ron Harper told him, "It's the same game you've been playing your whole life." Rizzo had waited long enough to promote Harper to keep him in Washington through the 2018 season.

Seeing his mother crying at Los Angeles International Airport would be forever burnished in Bryce's noggin. He started on Saturday night, April 28, as did ace pitcher Stephen Strasburg. Harper strolled into the narrow, cramped Dodger Stadium visitors' clubhouse and navigated a quick left into Johnson's tiny cubicle of an office. Johnson told Harper to keep doing what he's been doing. "Keep playing the game you've been playing your whole life. Don't change." At 19 years and 195 days, Harper became the youngest player in the majors since 2005. It was everything Harper had ever wanted. "And it was just the beginning," he said. The *Las Vegas Review-Journal* devoted a daily strip at the bottom of its sports-section cover to update readers on his major-league statistics.

The debut did not disappoint the legion of Harper fans that had been awaiting his arrival since his *Sports Illustrated* cover anointment. On a three-two delivery from Dodgers starting pitcher Chad Billingsley, Harper scorched a double off the base of the center-field wall in the top of the seventh inning. He flipped the helmet off his head as he sprinted toward second for his first major-league hit. Harper would have picked off Jerry Hairston at the plate with a laser throw from left field had Nationals catcher Wilson Ramos hung onto the baseball. With one out in the ninth and runners at the corners, Harper tied the game on a lineout to left, off reliever Javy Guerra's first pitch, to score Rick Ankiel. Matt Kemp won it for the Dodgers with a home run in the tenth inning. Harper soaked up the energy from the crowd of 54,242. "Crazy atmosphere," Harper said. "Those fans love that team. It was a cool moment to see that and say, 'This is Major League Baseball. You're here. Hopefully you stay here and keep playing.'"

Showtime drained his bank account early Sunday morning to fuel his gray four-door 2008 Nissan Rogue for a trek to Dodger Stadium. Ron Harper left him a ticket at the will-call gate. High up behind home plate, he snapped photographs of the huge outfield video screen when Bryce appeared on it before hitting. Showtime marveled at watching Harper make a splendid catch as he crashed into the center-field wall. En route back to Las Vegas, Showtime tapped out a text message to Harper. *Congrats, Bryce. You'll never know how proud I am of you.*

Being able to watch you play is something very special. Best of luck. Before the Nationals' chartered plane left LAX, Harper responded. *Thanks for making it, Show! Love you, brother!*

Within his first week in the majors, foes had learned to pitch around Harper. Alfonso Soriano would be the lone major leaguer to see fewer first-pitch fastballs than Harper's 46.1 percent in 2012. Philadelphia starter Kyle Kendrick walked Harper three times in one game. "They know he can hit a fastball, his hands are so lightning fast," Showtime said. "They try to dice him up with breaking balls."

Phillies starter Cole Hamels welcomed the phenom to the big time by plunking him in his lower back with a ninety-three-mph heater in the first inning on May 6, a Sunday night game that ESPN aired to a national audience. Harper laid his bat down and trotted to first base, never looking at Hamels. Two batters later, Harper caught the twenty-eight-year-old lefty napping on a throw to first—where Jayson Werth preoccupied Hamels—and stole home. Werth, who once played in Philly, had discussed Hamels's typically slow move to first with Harper before the game. When Hamels went over there a second time, Harper took off. He became the first teenager to steal home plate in a major league game since the Angels' Ed Kirkpatrick pulled it off in Kansas City on May 5, 1964. Hamels admitted hitting Harper on purpose and was suspended for five games. Werth broke a bone in his right wrist, running in from right to catch a low liner, in that game. Harper would play every outfield position before his tenth major league game.

Thomas Boswell of *The Washington Post* had never seen a player relish his first ten games in the big leagues as much as Harper: "Just revel in them, rise to them, and gobble each day like he's waited for it since he was born. . . . This is a moment in baseball time that doesn't come often and won't last forever." Boswell witnessed Harper in batting practice, "which sounds like an evening thunderstorm." When Boswell asked Johnson if he had ever heard anybody swing so hard in BP while maintaining balance and mechanics, Johnson said, "Mantle." Irascible television personality Keith Olbermann called Harper

"The baby Jesus" after taking in The Rook's BP session at Citi Field in New York.

The Nationals witnessed some major-league volatility on May 11, when Harper smashed a bat against a concrete wall in the tunnel connecting the visitors' dugout and clubhouse at Great American Ball Park in Cincinnati. The splintered wood just missed Harper's left eye. The wound required ten stitches to mend. Blood ran down Harper's left cheek while he patrolled the outfield. Werth, fourteen years older than Harper and on the disabled list, watched the antics on television from his home and laughed. "He's entertaining, on and off the field. Just watching him being him, it's funny . . . he's nineteen, he's extremely talented, and he's just as messed up as anybody. He's just a normal guy."

Werth provided the kid with some much-needed direction three days later, as Harper stood in his dugout and 19,434 fans roared for him in Nationals Park. Werth patted him on the back. "Get up there, kid." Harper had just swatted his first major league home run, on a two-one, eighty-seven-mph slider from San Diego right-handed pitcher Tim Stauffer. Harper had poked it 429 feet from home plate, to dead center field. He became the youngest big leaguer to park one since Adrián Beltré in 1998. Harper had zipped around the bases and into his dugout; contrary to national-media exaggerations, showing up a pitcher was not in his DNA. After launching one in Atlanta on Saturday, May 26, Harper returned to home plate in 16.35 seconds, the fastest circuit in the majors since July 4, 2010. He dashed around the bases in 16.2 seconds after another homer, and those two times would be the fastest home-run scampers of the season. His teammates enjoyed Harper's enthusiasm. "What he's done for this team has been infectious for all of us," said veteran infielder Mark DeRosa. "Really, he's breathed a whole lot of fresh air into our team."

When he exhaled after his first five weeks in the majors, Harper was rewarded with the National League rookie of the month award for May by hitting .271, with four home runs, four triples, two stolen bases, and twenty-one runs. On the first Monday in June, a day off for the Nationals, Harper read to a class of grade-school kids. The following day, he became the first teenager to collect a walk-off hit since Gary Sheffield, in 1988, when he laced New York Mets hurler Elvin Ramirez's bases-loaded, oh-and-two, ninety-six-mph pitch into left field in the twelfth inning. The Nationals were alone atop the National League East Division.

Their young star was blossoming so early, some were compelled to make suitable comparisons outside the baseball fraternity. Grantland.com writer Rany Jazayerli highlighted Tiger Woods as another young phenom who had improbably exceeded unrealistic expectations. Jazayerli made a corollary between home runs by the age of twenty-two and greatness, in the form of career homers and Hall of Fame ceremonies. Of the top dozen on that list, topped by Mel Ott, Eddie Mathews, and Alex Rodriguez, ten were either already in the Hall or their plaques were being polished. Jazayerli wrote, "There is no stronger indicator of a Hall of Fame career than precocious power—the very skill Bryce Harper is most famous for."

That power led to the revelation of yet another skill, as an orator who could produce a phrase worthy of induction into the national sports lexicon. Harper drilled a moon shot, his seventh homer, four hundred and fifty feet off the glass façade of a Rogers Centre restaurant in Toronto on June 12. The blast helped power the Nationals to a 4–2 victory over the Blue Jays. Harper's batting average soared to .307.

A Toronto reporter tested Harper, inquiring if he would celebrate with a beer that night. The nineteen-year-old prodigy was of legal age to drink in Canada. But as a devout Mormon, he had never touched alcohol and vowed he never would. "That's a clown question, bro," Harper said. By sundown the following day, Kit M. Stetina—an attorney based in Aliso Viejo, California, not far from agent Scott Boras's lair in Newport Beach—filed THAT'S A CLOWN QUESTION, BRO with the United States Patent and Trademark Office, as serial number 85651210, on Harper's behalf. Red T-shirts bearing that phrase popped up all over Washington, Virginia, and Maryland. In an interview on 106.7 The Fan in Washington, Harper explained that he didn't carouse, that he felt the question had disrespected him. He called his body a temple. "I'm not going to put anything in it that will affect me or the way I play because I want to give everything I can for this team and this city every single day."

The Nationals swept the three-game series in Toronto to stretch a winning streak to six games. They were separating themselves from their NL East rivals. Harper had played a direct role in that success with ten hits in twenty-one at bats, including two doubles and two homers, and seven runs.

It was only the middle of June, but Washington was rolling—having won nine of its past eleven games—when it came upon one of the most compelling series of the regular season against the New York Yankees. When he signed his contract, Harper had predicted that the Nats would press the Yankees for East Coast, if not baseball, superiority; but the Bronx Bombers swept the three games. Worse, Harper struck out five times in the Saturday defeat. The platinum sombrero. Three of those came against six-foot-five veteran lefty Andy Pettitte. Bryan texted his brother, *It happens to the best of them*. Bryce responded, *Yeah, I know. It's fine*. Harper earned a not-so-small concession Sunday afternoon, when his frozen rope off the wall landed him a foot from Yankees legend Derek Jeter on second base. Months later, Harper would embed a photo of the meeting on his Twitter page.

As the Yanks were schooling the Nats, the Denver Beer Co. tapped its first keg of a limited edition Canadian lager named CLOWN QUESTION BRO. Harper learned about the killing of Officer Celena Hollis, a veteran Denver policewoman who had a twelve-year-old daughter. When Washington swung through Denver on a road trip, brewery co-owner Charlie Berger required scant convincing by Harper to direct profits from the beer toward a memorial fund to support Hollis's daughter. Berger was flattered to hear from Harper. "The fact that he was making a lot of good come from it, it's valiant. It says something about Bryce."

The Nats won four in a row to start July, and Harper aided that run by going seven-for-eighteen at the plate. He scored in each game, six times total, belted three doubles, and knocked in three runs. Tony La Russa had been watching, and he added Harper to the National League All-Star roster, replacing injured Miami slugger Giancarlo Stanton. In his Kansas City hotel room, Harper awoke to find himself on the cover of *USA Today*. Writer Bob Nightengale traced Harper's Clown Question line to Chris Sheff, a well-known Las Vegas coach. When Sheff was in the minors in 1998, he sat in a car being driven by teammate Ricky Freeman. They were cut off. "That clown just cut me off," Freeman exploded. When they pulled next to the car, a man wearing a clown suit was driving. Anyone who played for, or took a lesson from, Sheff heard a clown reference in some form. The Coyotes used it liberally in 2010.

For Harper, a much-anticipated major-league debut started becoming rich in distinction when he became the youngest position player in All-Star Game history, joining pitchers Bob Feller and Dwight Gooden as the only teenagers to play in a Midsummer Classic. As usual, Harper wasn't shy; he donned gold high-top Under Armour Highlight Spine cleats for the game. Long before the first pitch, Chipper gathered his teammates for a meeting and told them they all belonged in that clubhouse. It didn't matter if you're nineteen, he said as he smiled and pointed at Harper, "or you're forty like me; we are all equals here." For four innings at Kaufmann Stadium, Harper hung out in the dugout, often by Chipper Jones. "No matter how much fame and fortune you get, don't change your game, your mentality. Be Bryce," Jones told Harper.

Finally, the chance to start smudging those gaudy cleats arrived. Against Angels right-handed pitcher Jered Weaver, Harper led off the fifth inning and took an inside pitch on a three-two count for a free pass to first. Prince Fielder gave him a playful nudge near the base. On Buster Posey's flyout to Josh Hamilton in left, Harper tagged up and eased into second. On a David Wright bouncer, Weaver caught

Harper in a rundown between second and third. In left field, Harper lost a Mike Napoli fly ball in the lights. It fell ten feet behind Harper, and Napoli wound up on second. Harper also whiffed on a ninety-six-mph pitch from Oakland rookie Ryan Cook. The gilded slippers would not be seen again.

It barely qualified as a respite, but Harper still went home to Las Vegas. Then it was off to Miami. He dragged into the second half of the season. His batting average dropped almost every day. Against Marlins righty Ricky Nolasco on the first Sunday in August, he struck out and tomahawk-chopped his bat in half on the plate. A sliver of wood landed near Marlins catcher John Buck who, with umpire Fieldin Culbreth, stood and watched the tantrum. Nolasco shook his head. Later, Harper apologized to Buck, who told Harper not to worry about it, that when he was Harper's age he had done the same thing . . . but "in high school" and with a metal bat.

During a nine-game road trip through Houston, Phoenix, and San Francisco, Harper bottomed out by going three-for-thirty-two at the plate. All three hits were singles. His average had plummeted from .257 to .245. However, the Nationals were not built to rely on a single player; they won seven of those nine games. After his hundredth major-league game, Harper was fighting a two-month lull in which he was hitting .209.

LaRoche would see how Harper responded to a funk. The next day, August 19, Harper, in LaRoche's words, got after it. Against Mets pitcher Jeremy Hefner at Nationals Park, Harper belted his twelfth homer. He also hit a triple, which made him the first teenager in MLB history with six triples and twelve homers. Washington bumped its record to a major-league-best 74–44 by winning a thrilling extra-inning game against Atlanta on Monday, August 20. It was the first time the franchise had been thirty games over .500 since 1994, when it was the Montreal Expos. The MLB Network trumpeted its next-day broad-cast as "Harper and the Nats versus the Braves."

The phenom was about to prove he deserved such lofty billing.

Harper and the Nats lugged a five-game losing streak to Miami on Wednesday, August 29. He had not gone without a hit in back-to-back games for two weeks. Against the Marlins, he smashed his thirteenth and fourteenth home runs, both off Miami starter Jacob Turner, to ignite a run in which the Nats won twelve of fifteen games to solidify their perch atop the NL East. Harper always sat in an aisle seat, across from radio broadcaster F. P. Santangelo, on flights. Late that night, flying back to Washington, Harper was keenly aware that Mickey Mantle had slugged thirteen home runs as a teenager. Harper glanced at Santangelo on the other side of the aisle.

"I passed the Mick tonight."

Goose bumps broke out all over Santangelo. "How often do you hear that?" Santangelo beamed. "He said it with respect and reverence and maybe a little bit of astonishment, all wrapped up in one. It's something I'll remember for the rest of my life."

Santangelo would not soon forget a game against the Cubs at Nationals Park on September 5, either. Harper hit home runs off Chris Volstad and Michael Bowden to catch, and pass, Ken Griffey Jr. with his sixteenth and seventeenth homers. Harper also joined Mel Ott and Griffey as the game's only teenagers with multiple two-homer games. It fueled an impressive finish in which Harper was the game's most productive player during the final five weeks of the season, hitting .341, slugging .699, creaming ten homers, and tallying twenty-six runs. That effort earned him his second NL rookie of the month honor, for September. "When the lights are on, that boy shows up," said Nats pitcher Craig Stammen. For months, national-media lemmings had compared Angels outfielder Mike Trout, who turned twenty-one on August 7, and Harper; during that same homestretch, Trout hit .269, knocking in just nine runs, as the Angels faded from the playoff picture.

After the Nationals clinched a playoff berth, Harper and Drake LaRoche, Adam LaRoche's nine-year-old son, celebrated by spraying each other with grape juice. After they clinched the NL East, Bryce and Drake chugged apple cider as the other Nats dumped champagne and beer on each other. Harper boasted that he wanted twenty more division titles.

Based on the early returns of such a promising career, Nationals faithful could look forward to a few more division crowns. Harper hit .270 and slugged .477 in 139 games. His ninety-eight runs ranked him fifth in the National League, despite having spent his first month in Syracuse. His nine triples were eighth in his league. His twenty-two home runs placed him two behind Tony Conigliaro's superb 1964 debut on the all-time teenage chart. Harper was a main weapon for Washington, whose ninety-eight victories led the majors. His Wins Above Replacement figure of 4.9, twenty-sixth in the game, tied Harper with Jimmy Rollins of the Phillies and Fielder of the Tigers. Harper's jersey was fourth in sales, behind Jeter, Josh Hamilton, and Ichiro Suzuki. The precocious youngster helped the Nationals become the third-best road draw, with an average crowd of 33,116. Only the two New York clubs had better attendance away from home.

Boswell was reduced to backwoods slang in comparing the prodigy's season to Willie Mays, at twenty, and trying to explain Harper's exploits. "He's gone out and done tore up the whole dadgum bug-eyed NL for the entire pennant push."

The Nationals and St. Louis Cardinals split the first four games of their best-of-five playoff series. Washington's two victories were both by a run; St. Louis had steamrolled to its two wins by a combined score of 20–4. Harper had lost his groove. Trying everything from bare hands to red and white gloves, the wrestler-like eye black streaming down each cheek like he had worn at CSN, and red-tinted contact lenses, he struggled with only one hit in eighteen at bats. In Game 2, he struck out four times; a postseason golden sombrero. Even on the hit, a double, the result went pear-shaped when he was thrown out at third base trying to be greedy. When a reporter suggested that he was being anxious at the plate, Harper smirked, "Well, you should be a hitting coach."

A record crowd of 45,966 packed into Nationals Park to watch the deciding game the night of Friday, October 12. Harper began his day with a satisfying heap of Nutella pancakes in his Pentagon City condo. Against six-foot-seven right-handed pitcher Adam Wainwright in the first inning, he became the first teen to smack a postseason triple. As the first batter in the third inning, Harper tattooed a three-two Wainwright offering into the right-center bleachers. The Nats scored the game's first six runs. It was only the second postseason homer by a teenager; Andruw Jones belted the first, on October 17, 1996, a day after Harper and his family had celebrated his fourth birthday.

Trevor Kirk, parking cars at the M Resort for $9.25 an hour and about a hundred bucks in tips per shift, texted me, *ABOUT TIME!* after the home run. My mother, at home in Yorba Linda, California, texted me, *Hail Marys working. Just heard on radio in garage. So good!* When the prodigy got called up, she told me how she'd drop notes in the tin box next to the candles at church on his behalf. I said, "Uh, shouldn't you save those for important matters?" She said, "This *is* important!" Tim Chambers, nervous about imminent back surgery that would correct a loose disk that threatened to slice his sciatic nerve, rang me. "Like I said, best I ever saw!"

St. Louis oozed back into the game. In the bottom of the eighth, Kurt Suzuki slapped a two-out single off Cardinals reliever Jason Motte to score LaRoche with what looked like a valuable insurance run to give Washington a 7–5 advantage. In the top of the ninth, disaster struck. Five times, Nats reliever Drew Storen threw two-out, two-strike pitches that could have sent Washington to the National League Championship Series against the San Francisco Giants. Instead, the Cardinals quieted the District by scoring four times. Motte mopped up in the bottom of the ninth, getting Jayson Werth to fly out to right field, Harper to swing and miss at an oh-two pitch, and Ryan Zimmerman to end the game on an infield pop-up.

Chambers texted me, *REALLY? WOW . . . u just never know.*

From the head table of Donnie Roach's Paiute Golf Resort wedding reception, Bryan Harper wrote *Heartbreak* on his Twitter page.

Four hours after the Nationals' season had ended, at four thirty-nine Saturday morning, Harper sent a message to his 49,473 Twitter followers to thank them for "there" support, and to tip his cap to the Cardinals. . . . *Can't wait for next year! #NATITUDE.*

Eager to return home, Harper hopped on a flight to Las Vegas on Sunday, October 14. He celebrated his twentieth birthday with his family two days later, when he had 54,909 Twitter followers. He posted a proud-uncle photo of him feeding his infant nephew.

In its October 29, 2012 issue, *Sports Illustrated* slapped THAT'S A CROWN QUESTION, BRO on a feature about Detroit Tigers slugger Miguel Cabrera, baseball's first Triple Crown winner since Carl Yastrzemski in 1967. Harper's numbers, and words, had made deep impressions. Adam Kilgore of *The Washington Post* was so impressed by Harper, he predicted that the prodigy would win the NL Most Valuable Player award in 2013. Showtime seemed certain that Harper wound win one by the time he turned twenty-two.

Few knew Harper as well as Showtime, who had returned to the College of Southern Nevada during the summer to assist head coach Nick Garritano. Showtime was the lone CSN player or coach link to that scintillating 2010 season. Garritano and his other assistants often tapped Showtime for insight into how they approached different situations that year.

Weeks into Harper's major league career, Showtime texted him, *Proud of everything you're doing.* Harper shot back, *I want to make you guys proud. I'm playin' for all you CSN guys who helped me get here.* When Harper hit one into the upper deck of Nationals Park off Miami pitcher and CSN alum Mike Dunn on August 4, Showtime gave Harper some stick about taking "a fellow Coyote" downtown. Showtime also told Harper to take it easy on his beloved San Francisco Giants; the Nationals won five of six games against the Giants during the season. However, San Francisco provided Showtime—

whose father nearly named him Willie Mays Larimer—with his second World Series championship celebration in three years when it swept the Detroit Tigers in the Fall Classic. Soon after the Giants clinched the sweep the night of Sunday, October 28, Harper congratulated them to his 65,303 followers on Twitter: *much deserved & a great group of guys. #NLpride.*

On the warm, cloudless day Harper turned twenty, Showtime manicured the Morse Stadium infield grass between second and third base with an edge trimmer. It was the dream start to his coaching career, back where that seventeen-year-old kid started carving his path to the big leagues on a night when you could see your own breath.

"The script has been right on," Showtime said. "He's a superstar. He can handle the immense amounts of pressure, and the grinds and rigors of Major League Baseball. And he's going to continue to prove people wrong. We all should have taken the time to blink for a second, 'cause this will never happen again."

Showtime unhinged the four retired numbers, including Harper's dark blue thirty-four within a large blue circle on its white square canvas, from the outfield wall. They needed to be cleaned for the upcoming season. Showtime recalled seeing Harper alone at the end of the Nationals' dugout on television after that crushing Game 5 defeat to the Cardinals. It was a hollowness that knew no immediate solace, exactly how Showtime and the rest of the Coyotes felt in Grand Junction in 2010.

"But he'll have plenty of opportunities to have big Octobers, to get to the World Series, and carry the City of Washington to bigger and better things." Showtime squinted into the sun. "I think there's a lot more on the horizon. I think he'll continue to put up huge numbers and be the face of baseball for a long, long time."

ACKNOWLEDGMENTS

I am indebted to a host of people for moving this project from a seed of an idea to a version worthy of publication. D. J. Allen and Brian Rouff provided initial steam with a few choice words of support. Peter Feinstein led me to Brad Mendelsohn, who guided me to agent David Patterson, who steered me to editor Rob Kirkpatrick at St. Martin's. Confidant Tomas V. Mazeika provided me with invaluable counsel. That's my all-star roster.

I cannot offer enough gratitude to the College of Southern Nevada baseball team of 2010. Every player and assistant coach accepted me as if I had tried out and won a spot on the roster. Many opponents were just as patient, insightful, and open. Thank you, Bryce Harper, for your candor. I will forever think of the Coyotes, and Kenny's spicy Spanish tongue, when I see a white touring bus with dark-tinted windows.

I must also recognize Miles Davis, John Coltrane, Wes Montgomery, Dave Brubek, and many other jazz legends for providing me with the rich background that kept me in the proper writing groove.

Finally, there was the key to the project, Coach Tim Chambers. He *knew* this was historic. He *knew* the Kid would produce. He *knew* this would never happen again. Chambers, trusting me like a blood brother, set no guidelines. My sole regret was using his loo in Lamar, Colorado.

Was it worth it?

Yup.

NOTES

Prologue

Interview and correspondence sources included Tim Chambers, Scott Dysinger, Trevor Kirk, Rich Kirk, Casey Sato, Bryan Harper, Bryce Harper, Ryan Scott, Ryan Thomas, Marvin Campbell, J. Bob Thomas, Ron Harper, D. J. Whittemore, Taylor Jones; "Baseball's LeBron," by Tom Verducci; *The Glory of Their Times,* by Lawrence S. Ritter; "Harper's next step leads him to Arizona," by Adam Kilgore; and an article published in *Vegas Seven.*

Chapter One

Interview and correspondence sources included Tim Chambers, Cooper Fouts, Casey Sato, Bryce Harper, Jan Landy, Scott Dysinger, Bob Dysinger, Trevor Kirk, Rich Kirk, Greg Maddux, Ron Harper, Jim Brooks, Bryan Harper, Marvin Campbell, and Sam Thomas; *Las Vegas: A Centennial History,* by Eugene P. Moehring and Michael S. Green; "Bryce Harper SuperFractor Sale Confirmed at $12,500," by Chris Olds; *Moneyball,* by Michael Lewis; *History of Nevada,* by Russell Elliott; "Pitching like a New Man," by Bruce Anderson; "The arm that changed the Major League draft," by Jeff Passan; "Two Tough Mothers," by Charles P. Pierce; "Wave of the Future," by Tom Verducci; "The Extortionist," by Ben McGrath; "Why Scott Boras Isn't as Evil as You Think He Is," by Tommy Craggs; "High Heat," by Alan Matthews; "Likely top MLB draft pick Bryce Harper has 'growing up to do,'" by Bob Nightengale; "Harper wants to build winning team in D.C.," by Barry Svrluga and Adam Kilgore; "Washington Nationals need to sign Harper and Dunn," by Thomas Boswell; "Nationals encounter risks, rewards of dealing with Scott Boras while working to sign Bryce Harper," by Thomas Boswell; and articles in the *Las Vegas Review-Journal* and *Las Vegas Sun*.

Chapter Two

Interview and correspondence sources included Tim Chambers, Jim Brooks, Ron Harper, Bryce Harper, Scott Dysinger, Bryan Harper, Trent Cook, and Casey Sato; *Las Vegas: The Fabulous First Century,* by Thomas "Taj" Ainlay Jr. and Judy Dixon Gabaldon; *Las Vegas: A Centennial History,* by Eugene P. Moehring and Michael S. Green; *Fabulous Las Vegas in the '50s,* by Fred E. Basten and Charles Phoenix; Defense Language Institute Foreign Language Institute, 2009–2010 General Catalog; and *The Glory of Their Times,* by Lawrence S. Ritter.

Chapter Three

Interview and correspondence sources included Tim Chambers, Cooper Fouts, Bryan Harper, Glenn Ballangao, Casey Sato, Trent Cook, Trevor Kirk, Scott Dysinger, Bryce Harper, Tomo Delp, Sean Larimer, Marvin Campbell, McKenzie Chambers, Fred Parrish, Marvin Campbell Sr., Robert Cox, Marc Morse, Jim Brooks, Ron Harper, and Ryan Scott; Bryce Harper at his Nationals Park introductory press conference; "Why Teenagers Act Weird," by Sarah Mahoney; "Teen Driving," by William Triplett; "Putting Limits on Teen Drivers," by Wende Cole Henderson; "Young man hopes you'll learn from his irreversible mistake," by Melissa Rothermel; "Mom backs limits on teen drivers," by Ed Vogel and Frank Curreri; "Erin Breen, a Driving Force," by *UNLV Magazine;* "Adults' role in teen crash is probed," by Emily Richmond; "Three teens killed in Henderson car crash," by Jen Lawson and Timothy Pratt; "Drunken-Driving Deaths: Promising lives mourned," by Glenn Puit; "Road Warrior: Drunken driving nightmare provides cautionary tale," by Omar Sofradzija; "Man who bought teens beer to serve jail time," by Frank Geary and Antonio Planas; "Eye Black Used to Cut Glare, or Turn Up Spotlight," by Jere Longman; "MLB has fewer African Americans," by Bob Nightengale; "MLB All-Star Week for Jr. RBI Classic Players Around the World," by Jerry Milani; "RBI program is one big hit," by Kevin Paul Dupont; and "Where've you gone, Kurt Stillwell?" by Sandy Burgin.

Chapter Four

Interview and correspondence sources included Tim Chambers, Kevin Higgins, David Segui, Glen Evans, Steve Chatham, Jay Guest, Cooper Fouts, Bryce Harper, Josh Demello, Danny Higa, Todd Inglehart, Jeff Johnson, Jerry Reuss, and Dr. Fred Mueller; and "Lower cost of living, family ties draw Hawaiians to valley," by Lynnette Curtis.

Chapter Five

Interview and correspondence sources included Tim Chambers, Rena Chambers, Jon Hoover, Wes Johnson, Kim Chambers, Scott Dysinger, Trevor Kirk, Jino Gonzalez, and Jonathan Slack; "CCSN grows up fast . . . like its coach," by Rob Miech; "When Chambers says, 'Hi Pops,' Hoover answers," by Ron Kantowski; and "For the love of Bryce Harper: Get ready, Washington. You're about to fall head over heels for the Nationals' newest star," by Dave Sheinen.

Chapter Six

Interview and correspondence sources included Tim Chambers, Kim Chambers, Charlie Brown, Laurelie Brown, Sean Brooks, and Bryce Harper; *Sharks in the Desert: The Founding Fathers and Current Kings of Las Vegas*, by John L. Smith; "Top 10 Scandals: Gritty City," by Corey Levitan; and "Mr. Metro," by A. D. Hopkins;

Chapter Seven

Interview and correspondence sources included Tim Chambers, Steve Chatham, Diana Cox, Robert Cox, Jonathan Slack, Scott Dysinger, Bryce Harper, Bryan Harper, Trent Cook, Casey Sato, Glenn Ballangao, Marvin Campbell, Gabe Weidenaar, Ryan Scott, Ron Harper, Sheri Harper, Skip Walker, Ryan Thomas, Danny Higa, Josh Demello, Trevor Kirk, Steve Jacobucci, and Jim Brooks.

Chapter Eight

Interview and correspondence sources included Tim Chambers, Trevor Kirk, Tyler Hanks, Bryce Harper, Jim Brooks, Trent Cook, Bryan Harper, Glenn Ballangao, and D. J. Whittemore.

Chapter Nine

Interview and correspondence sources included Tim Chambers, Bryce Harper, Kevin Higgins, Donnie Roach, Marvin Campbell, Julie Roach, and Ron Kantowski; "90 Years on a Lark," by A. D. Hopkins; "Valley settlers defied the odds," by Ed Koch; "Longtime businessman Von Tobel, Jr., 96, dies," by Valerie Miller; *The Players: The Men Who Made Las Vegas*, edited by Jack E. Sheehan; *A Short History of Las Vegas*, by Barbara and Myrick Land; and "Biggest Surprises, Disappointments of Early Spring," by David Rawnsley.

Chapter Ten

Interview and correspondence sources included Tim Chambers, Al Williams, Bryce Harper, Marvin Campbell, D. G. Nelson, Dick Scott, Ryan Scott, Kristin Scott, Wes Hunt, Jay Guest, Kevin Higgins, Ray Karesky, and Cooper Fouts; *Moneyball,* by Michael Lewis, "Chase for No. 1 Pick Is 2-Man Race," by Allan Simpson; "Junior College Players on Center Stage," by Allan Simpson; "Putting the pieces back together," by Jerry Crasnick; and "A Light in the Darkness," by Pablo S. Torre.

Chapter Eleven

Interview and correspondence sources included Tim Chambers, Jay Guest, Cooper Fouts, Trevor Kirk, Marvin Campbell, Wes Hunt, Tomo Delp, Ryan Scott, and Don Cooper; and *Moneyball,* by Michael Lewis.

Chapter Twelve

Interview and correspondence sources included Tim Chambers, Donnie Roach, Gentry Croft, Marc Morse, Bryce Harper, Scott Dysinger, and Skip Walker; and "The Morse Family: Three Generations of Service," by the State Bar of Nevada.

Chapter Thirteen

Interview and correspondence sources included Tim Chambers, Bryce Harper, Steve Chatham, Kevin Higgins, Gabe Weidenaar, Pat Mahoney, Josh Demello, Tyler Hanks, Ryan Thomas, Cooper Fouts, Bryan Harper, Tomo Delp, Scott Dysinger, Donnie Roach, Casey Sato, Trent Cook, and Glen Evans; "Junior college baseball: 'Chosen One' comes to Carson," by Chris Murray; *The Mental Game of Baseball,* by H. A. Dorfman and Karl Kuehl; and "A Light in the Darkness," by Pablo S. Torre.

Chapter Fourteen

Interview and correspondence sources included Tim Chambers, Cooper Fouts, Dick Scott, Bryce Harper, Bryan Harper, Donnie Roach, Trent Cook, Casey Sato, Jim Brooks, Ray Daniels, Gabe Weidenaar, and Robert Cox; "Future Shock," by Kevin Goldstein; and articles in *The New York Times, Washington Post, Las Vegas Review-Journal, Las Vegas Sun,* MLB.com, and SI.com.

Chapter Fifteen

Interview and correspondence sources included Tim Chambers, Trent Cook, Ryan Scott, Tyler Iodence, Bryce Harper, Scott Dysinger, Marvin

Campbell, Tomo Delp, Robert Cox, Aaron Kurcz, Dave Segui, Jerry Reuss, Josh Demello, Taylor Larsen, Ryan Thomas, and Boomer Walker; *Willie Mays: The Life, the Legend,* by James S. Hirsch; and *The Boys of Summer,* by Roger Kahn.

Chapter Sixteen

Interview and correspondence sources included Tim Chambers, Cooper Fouts, Jay Guest, Kevin Higgins, Bryce Harper, Scott Dysinger, Trevor Kirk, Sam Thomas, D. J. Whittemore, and Harold Shrader; "At 17, Baseball's Next Sure Thing: Bryce Harper," by Alan Schwarz; "Bryce Harper, potential No. 1 pick in the MLB draft, faces questions about his attitude, not his ability," by Dave Sheinin; "Bryce Harper's story as unique as his bat," by Chuck Finder; and "Happy Mother's Day," by Tom Verducci.

Chapter Seventeen

Interview and correspondence sources included Tim Chambers, Glen Evans, Dustin Colbrin, Scott Dysinger, Trevor Kirk, Marvin Campbell Sr., Bryce Harper, Donnie Roach, Robert Cox, Jon Wente, Marvin Campbell Jr., Trent Cook, and Tyler Hanks; and the Chamber of Commerce of Lamar, Colorado.

Chapter Eighteen

Interview and correspondence sources included Tim Chambers, Scott Dysinger, Trevor Kirk, Bryce Harper, Michael Sato, Casey Sato, Sean Larimer, Kevin Higgins, Steve Chatham, Marvin Campbell, Cooper Fouts, Glenn Ballangao, Bryan Harper, Ryan Scott, Mary Ellen Leicht, Burke Seifrit, Ronnie Simmers, Aaron Kurcz, Marc Rardin, Glen Evans, and Brent Seifert; "The other Harper," by Patti Arnold; "Line in dirt changes Series for CSN," by Ed Graney; and "Likely top MLB draft pick Bryce Harper has 'growing up to do,'" by Bob Nightengale.

Epilogue

Interview and correspondence sources included Tim Chambers, McKenzie Chambers, J. Bob Thomas, Aaron Kurcz, Donnie Roach, Ryan Scott, Ron Harper, Bryce Harper, Marvin Campbell, Trevor Kirk, Jonathan Slack, Jeff Johnson, and Chris McKenzie; "The Devil's Doorstep: A Visit with Scott Boras," by Matt Taibbi; "Sheff out as CSN coach and athletic director," by David Schoen; "New CSN coach Garritano begins cleanup assignment," by Ed Graney; "Nationals introduce top pick Harper," by Bill Ladson; "For the love of Bryce Harper: Get ready, Washington. You're about to fall head over heels for the Nationals' newest star," by Dave Sheinin; "Bryce Harper supremely confident," by Jayson Stark; "Harper has set his goals for first spring camp," by Bill Ladson; "Bryce Harper's switch to contact lenses has him laying waste to South Atlantic League pitching," by Dave Sheinin; "Harmon Killebrew showed how a bonus baby becomes a Hall of Fame man," by Thomas Boswell; "Bryce Harper gives no reason to worry; Nationals draft pick Anthony Rendon hopefully doesn't, either," by Thomas Boswell; "Survey Finds Strasburg as MLB's Most Marketable Under 25," by Erik Swanson; "Bryce Harper promoted to Class AA Harrisburg by Washington Nationals," by Adam Kilgore; and "Harper's arrogance just what baseball needs," by Jeff Passan.

2012 Update

Interview and correspondence sources include Marvin Campbell Jr., Marvin Campbell Sr., Casey Sato, Trevor Kirk, Trent Cook, Rico Petrocelli, Tim Chambers, Danny Higa, Sean Larimer, Ryan Scott, and Marc Morse; "Chiefs pumped after second-game win; Harper homers in first-game loss," by Tom Leo; "Boy wonder Bryce Harper gets off to a nice (if chilly) start with the Syracuse Chiefs," by Bud Poliquin; "Washington Nationals' phenom Bryce Harper aims to make leap to majors now," by Associated Press; "Nationals call-up Bryce Harper, place Ryan Zimmerman on 15-day disabled list," by Amanda Comack; "Nationals promote Bryce Harper, place Ryan Zimmerman on the disabled list," by Adam Kilgore; "Is Baseball Ready For Bryce?" by Will Leitch; "Nationals vs. Dodgers: Bryce Harper dazzles, Los Angeles wins in 10," by Adam Kildore; "Bryce Harper getting respect, drawing walks already," by Adam Kilgore; "Phillies hurler Cole Hamels chose the wrong pitch to initiate rookie phenom Bryce Harper," by Tim Brown; "Bryce Harper knows how to read the unwritten rules," by Paul White; "Bryce Harper makes an immediate impact in a variety of ways for Nationals," by Thomas Boswell; "Nationals vs. Padres: Bryce Harper's first home run helps Washington overcome Sandy Leon's injury," by Adam Kilgore; "Bryce Harper loves getting booed," by Adam Kilgore; "Harper hits 1st big league HR, leads Nats to win," by Associated Press; "Morning pixels: Bryce Harper is baseball's fastest home run trotter," by Dan Steinberg; "The Phillies used extra security for Bryce Harper at Citizens Bank Park," by Adam Kilgore; "Nationals vs. Mets: Bryce Harper drives in winning run in 12th inning," by Adam Kilgore; "Nationals vs. Red Sox: Bryce Harper gets his shot, Washington completes sweep," by Adam Kilgore; "Nationals vs. Blue Jays: Bryce Harper home punctuates Washington's fifth straight win," by Adam Kilgore; "Bryce Harper trademarks 'clown question, bro': Some credit for the clown who asked it?" by *The Reliable Source;* "Bryce Harper explains why he thought the beer incident was a 'clown question'," by Sarah Kogod; "Bryce Harper replaces Giancarlo Stanton, becomes the youngest position player in All-Star Game history," by Adam Kilgore; "Is Nationals' teenage phenom baseball's next big thing?" by Bob Nightengale; "The kids are ALL-STARS," by Steve Wieberg; "All-Star Game 2012; Nationals Bryce Harper, Gio Gonzalez and Stephen Strasburg contribute to NL's 8-0 victory," by Adam Kilgore; "The Great Bryce Hype," by Rany Jazayerli; "Bryce Harper uses 'Clown Question Bro' beer to raise money for fallen policewoman in Denver," by Adam Kilgore; "Nationals vs. Mets: Bryce Harper, Ryan Zimmerman help Washington break it open in the 10th," by

Adam Kilgore; "Bryce Harper gets day off, reflects on strike-zone scuffles," by Amanda Comak; "Bryce Harper expected to get a day off after butting heads with Angel Hernandez," by Adam Kilgore; "Bryce Harper: his slump, broken bat and an apology," by James Wagner; "Nationals' Bryce Harper isn't type to stay down long," by Dan Daly; "Tommy John blasts the Strasburg shutdown plan," by Scott Boeck; "Nationals vs. Mets: Bryce Harper, Gio Gonzalez lead win over New York," by James Wagner; "Nationals vs. Braves: Washington finally wins it in the 13th inning, 5-4," by James Wagner; "Bryce Harper's wild ride," by Jerry Crasnick; "Right Makes Might," by Tom Verducci; "Derek Jeter tops jersey sales list," by Darren Rovell; "Bryce Harper has come of age when it has mattered most to the Washington Nationals," by Thomas Boswell; "Rookie strikes out four times in loss," by Nathan Fenno; "That's A Crown Question, Bro," by Michael Rosenberg; and "Bryce Harper's ridiculous 19-year-old season in perspective," by Adam Kilgore.

BIBLIOGRAPHY

Ainlay Jr., Thomas "Taj," and Judy Dixon Gabaldon. *Las Vegas: The Fabulous First Century*. Charleston: Arcadia Publishing, 2003.

Anderson, Bruce. "Pitching like a New Man." *Sports Illustrated,* June 26, 1989.

Arnold, Patti. "The other Harper: Bryan Harper shows his stuff in front of big crowd." *Grand Junction Sentinel,* June 1, 2010.

Associated Press. "Washington Nationals' phenom Bryce Harper aims to make leap to majors now." March 2, 2012.

Basten, Fred E., and Charles Phoenix. *Fabulous Las Vegas in the '50s.* Santa Monica: Angel City Press, 1999.

Boeck, Scott. "Tommy John blasts the Strasburg shutdown plan." *USA Today,* August 17, 2012.

———. "Harper hits 1st big league HR, leads Nats to win." May 15, 2012.

Boswell, Thomas. "Washington Nationals need to sign Harper and Dunn." *Washington Post,* August 12, 2010.

———. "Nationals encounter risks, rewards of dealing with Scott Boras while working to sign Bryce Harper." *Washington Post,* August 15, 2010.

———. "Harmon Killebrew showed how a bonus baby becomes a Hall of Fame man." *Washington Post,* May 18, 2011.

———."Bryce Harper gives no reason to worry; Nationals draft pick Anthony Rendon hopefully doesn't, either." *Washington Post,* June 8, 2011.

―――. "Bryce Harper makes an immediate impact in a variety of ways for Nationals." *Washington Post*, May 10, 2012.

―――. "Bryce Harper has come of age when it has mattered most to the Washington Nationals." *Washington Post*, October 2, 2012.

Brown, Tim. "Phillies hurler Cole Hamels chose the wrong pitch to initiate rookie phenom Bryce Harper." *Yahoo! Sports,* May 7, 2012.

Burgin, Sandy. "Where've you gone, Kurt Stillwell?" MLB.com, September 14, 2002.

Comack, Amanda. "Nationals call-up Bryce Harper, place Ryan Zimmerman on 15-day disabled list." *Washington Times*, April 27, 2012.

―――. "Bryce Harper gets day off, reflects on strike-zone scuffles." *Washington Times*, August 9, 2012.

Craggs, Tommy. "Why Scott Boras Isn't as Evil as You Think He Is." Deadspin, June 8, 2009.

Crasnick, Jerry. "Putting the pieces back together." ESPN.com, November 24, 2009.

―――. "Bryce Harper's wild ride." ESPN.com, October 6, 2012.

Curtis, Lynnette. "Lower cost of living, family ties draw Hawaiians to valley." *Las Vegas Review-Journal,* March 6, 2011.

Daly, Dan. "Nationals' Bryce Harper isn't type to stay down long." *Washington Times*, August 19, 2012.

Dorfman, H. A., and Karl Kuehl. *The Mental Game of Baseball: A Guide to Peak Performance.* Lanham, Md: Diamond Communications, 1995.

Dupont, Kevin Paul. "RBI program is one big hit." *Boston Globe,* April 4, 2010.

Elliott, Russell. *History of Nevada.* Lincoln: University of Nebraska Press, 1987.

Fenno, Nathan. "Rookie strikes out four times in loss." *Washington Times*, October 8, 2012.

Finder, Chuck. "Bryce Harper's story as unique as his bat." *Pittsburgh Post-Gazette,* May 30, 2010.

Geary, Frank, and Antonio Planas. "Man who bought teens beer to serve jail time." *Las Vegas Review-Journal,* May 26, 2004.

Goldstein, Kevin. "Future Shock." baseballprospectus.com, April 22, 2010.

Graney, Ed. "Line in dirt changes Series for CSN." *Las Vegas Review-Journal*, June 3, 2010.

———. "New CSN coach Garritano begins cleanup assignment." *Las Vegas Review-Journal*, November 10, 2010.

Henderson, Wende Cole. "Putting Limits on Teen Drivers." *Time*, October 15, 2006.

Heyman, Jon. "Nationals working to hire Harper's college coach as scout." SI.com, May 4, 2010.

Hirsch, James S. *Willie Mays: The Life, the Legend*. New York: Scribner, 2010.

Hopkins, A. D. "Mr. Metro." Part III: A City in Full, of The First 100 series. *Las Vegas Review-Journal*.

———. "90 Years on a Lark." Part I: The Early Years, of The First 100 series. *Las Vegas Review-Journal*.

Jazayerli, Rany. "The Great Bryce Hype." Grantland.com, June 12, 2012.

Kahn, Roger. *The Boys of Summer*. New York: Harper Perennial Modern Classics, 2006.

Kantowski, Ron. "Phenom Harper hardly a 'bad guy.'" *Las Vegas Review-Journal*, May 4, 2010.

———. "When Chambers says, 'Hi Pops,' Hoover answers." *Las Vegas Review-Journal*, June 19, 2011.

Kilgore, Adam. "Mike Rizzo scouts, meets Bryce Harper." *Washington Post*, May 3, 2010.

———. "Harper's next step leads him to Arizona." *Washington Post*, October 22, 2010.

———. "Bryce Harper promoted to Class AA Harrisburg by Washington Nationals." *Washington Post*, July 4, 2011.

———. "Nationals promote Bryce Harper, place Ryan Zimmerman on the disabled list." *Washington Post*, April 27, 2012.

———. "Nationals vs. Dodgers: Bryce Harper dazzles, Los Angeles wins in 10." *Washington Post*, April 28, 2012.

———. "Bryce Harper getting respect, drawing walks already." *Washington Post*, May 5, 2012.

———. "Bryce Harper loves getting booed." *Washington Post*, May 11, 2012.

———. "Nationals vs. Padres: Bryce Harper's first home run helps Washington overcome Sandy Leon's injury." *Washington Post*, May 14, 2012.

———. "The Phillies used extra security for Bryce Harper at Citizens Bank Park." *Washington Post*, May 22, 2012.

———. "Nationals vs. Mets: Bryce Harper drives in winning run in 12th inning." *Washington Post*, June 5, 2012.

———. "Nationals vs. Red Sox: Bryce Harper gets his shot, Washington completes sweep." *Washington Post*, June 10, 2012.

———. "Nationals vs. Blue Jays: Bryce Harper home punctuates Washington's fifth straight win." *Washington Post*, June 12, 2012.

———. "Bryce Harper uses 'Clown Question Bro' beer to raise money for fallen policewoman in Denver." *Washington Post*, June 28, 2012.

———. "Bryce Harper replaces Giancarlo Stanton, becomes the youngest position player in All-Star Game history." *Washington Post*, July 7, 2012.

———. "All-Star Game 2012; Nationals Bryce Harper, Gio Gonzalez and Stephen Strasburg contribute to NL's 8-0 victory." *Washington Post*, July 11, 2012.

———. "Nationals vs. Mets: Bryce Harper, Ryan Zimmerman help Washington break it open in the 10th." *Washington Post*, July 23, 2012.

———. "Bryce Harper expected to get a day off after butting heads with Angel Hernandez." *Washington Post*, August 9, 2012.

———. "Bryce Harper's ridiculous 19-year-old season in perspective." *Washington Post*, September 28, 2012.

Koch, Ed. "Valley settlers defied the odds." *Las Vegas Sun,* May 13, 2005.

Kogod, Sarah. "Bryce Harper explains why he thought the beer incident was a 'clown question'." *Washington Post*, July 9, 2012.

Ladson, Bill. "Taking Harper No. 1, Nats get their man." MLB.com, June 7, 2010.

———. "Nats, top pick Harper agree to five-year deal." MLB.com, August 17, 2010.

———. "Nationals introduce top pick Harper." MLB.com, August 26, 2010.

———. "Harper has set his goals for first spring camp." MLB.com, February 11, 2011.

Land, Barbara, and Myrick Land. *A Short History of Las Vegas.* Reno: University of Nevada Press, 1999.

Lawson, Jen, and Timothy Pratt. "Three teens killed in Henderson car crash." *Las Vegas Sun,* November 10, 2003.

Leitch, Will. "IS BASEBALL READY FOR BRYCE?" *GQ,* April 1, 2012.

Leo, Tom. "Chiefs pumped after second-game win; Harper homers in first-game loss." *Syracuse Post-Standard,* April 22, 2012.

Levitan, Corey. "Top 10 Scandals: Gritty City." *Las Vegas Review-Journal,* March 2, 2008.

Lewis, Michael. *Moneyball.* New York: W. W. Norton, 2004.

Longman, Jere. "Eye Black Used to Cut Glare, or Turn Up Spotlight." *New York Times,* December 3, 2006.

Mahoney, Sarah. "Why Teenagers Act Weird." *Prevention,* June 6, 2005.

Matthews, Alan. "High Heat." *Baseball America,* March 2, 2005.

McGrath, Ben. "The Extortionist." *New Yorker,* October 29, 2007.

Miech, Rob. "CCSN grows up fast . . . like its coach." *Las Vegas Sun,* May 22, 2003.

———. "Catching on Quickly." *Vegas Seven,* February 18–24, 2010.

Milani, Jerry. "MLB All-Star Week for Jr. RBI Classic Players Around the World." Major League Baseball release, June 16, 2010.

Miller, Valerie. "Longtime businessman Von Tobel, Jr., 96, dies." *Las Vegas Review-Journal,* December 31, 2009.

Moehring, Eugene P., and Michael S. Green. *Las Vegas: A Centennial History.* Reno: University of Nevada Press, 2005.

Murray, Chris. "Junior college baseball: 'Chosen One' comes to Carson." *Reno Gazette-Journal,* April 16, 2010.

Nevada, State Bar of. "The Morse Family: Three Generations of Service." www.nvbar.org/publications/NevadaLawyer, August 2003.

Nightengale, Bob. "MLB has fewer African Americans." *USA Today,* April 15, 2010.

———. "Likely top MLB draft pick Bryce Harper has 'growing up to do.' " *USA Today*, June 7, 2010.

———. "Is Nationals' teenage phenom baseball's next big thing?" *USA Today*, July 10, 2012.

Olds, Chris. "Bryce Harper SuperFractor Sale Confirmed at $12,500." The Beckett Blog, September 28, 2010. blogbeckett.wordpress.com/2010/09/28/bryce-harper-superfractor-sale-confirmed-at-12500/.

O'Reiley, Tim. "That's a wrap: Las Vegas Sands finishes condos with giant cloths." *Las Vegas Review-Journal,* June 10, 2011.

Passan, Jeff. "The arm that changed the Major League draft." Yahoo! Sports, June 5, 2006.

———. "Harper's arrogance just what baseball needs." Yahoo! Sports, June 8, 2011.

Pierce, Charles P. "Two Tough Mothers." *Sports Illustrated,* December 9, 1991.

Poliquin, Bud. "Boy wonder Bryce Harper gets off to a nice (if chilly) start with the Syracuse Chiefs." *Syracuse Post-Standard*, April 6, 2012.

Puit, Glenn. "Drunken-Driving Deaths: Promising lives mourned." *Las Vegas Review-Journal,* February 24, 2004.

Rawnsley, David. "Biggest Surprises, Disappointments of Early Spring." PGCrossChecker.com, March 25, 2010.

Reliable Source, The. "Bryce Harper trademarks 'clown question, bro': Some credit for the clown who asked it?" *Washington Post*, June 25, 2012.

———. "Morning pixels: Bryce Harper is baseball's fastest home run trotter." *Washington Post*, May 29, 2012.

Richmond, Emily. "Adults' role in teen crash is probed." *Las Vegas Sun,* November 13, 2003.

Ritter, Lawrence S. *The Glory of Their Times*. New York: Harper Perennial Modern Classics, 2010.

Rosenberg, Michael. "That's A Crown Question, Bro." *Sports Illustrated,* October 29, 2012.

Rothermel, Melissa. "Young man hopes you'll learn from his irreversible mistake," *Rebel Yell,* October 25, 2004.

Rovell, Darren. "Derek Jeter tops jersey sales list." ESPN.com, October 1, 2012.

Schoen, David. "Sheff out as CSN coach and athletic director." *Las Vegas Review-Journal,* November 3, 2010.

Schoenmann, Joe. "Wayne Newton wants to show off home, private jet, too." *Las Vegas Sun,* September 1, 2010.

Schwarz, Alan. "At 17, Baseball's Next Sure Thing: Bryce Harper." *New York Times,* May 15, 2010.

Sheehan, Jack E. *The Players: The Men Who Made Las Vegas.* Reno: University of Nevada Press, 1997.

Sheinin, Dave. "Bryce Harper, potential No. 1 pick in the MLB draft, faces questions about his attitude, not his ability." *Washington Post,* May 16, 2010.

————. "For the love of Bryce Harper: Get ready, Washington. You're about to fall head over heels for the Nationals' newest star." *Washington Post,* March 13, 2011.

————. "Bryce Harper's switch to contact lenses has him laying waste to South Atlantic League pitching." *Washington Post,* May 12, 2011.

Simpson, Allan. "Chase for No. 1 Pick Is 2-Man Race." PGCrossChecker. com, March 30, 2010.

————. "Junior College Players on Center Stage." PGCrossChecker.com, April 1, 2010.

Smith, John L. *Sharks in the Desert: The Founding Fathers and Current Kings of Las Vegas.* Fort Lee, NJ: Barricade Books, 2005.

Sofradzija, Omar. "Road Warrior: Drunken driving nightmare provides cautionary tale." *Las Vegas Review-Journal,* November 21, 2004.

Stark, Jayson. "Bryce Harper supremely confident." ESPN.com, March 1, 2011.

Svrluga, Barry, and Adam Kilgore. "Harper wants to build winning team in D.C." *Washington Post,* June 9, 2010.

Swanson, Erik. "Survey Finds Strasburg as MLB's Most Marketable Under 25." *SportsBusiness Daily,* July 20, 2010.

Taibbi, Matt. "The Devil's Doorstep: A Visit with Scott Boras." *Men's Journal,* February 23, 2009.

Torre, Pablo S. "A Light in the Darkness." *Sports Illustrated,* June 21, 2010.

Triplett, William. "Teen Driving." *CQ Researcher,* January 7, 2005.

UNLV Magazine. "Erin Breen, a Driving Force." Spring 2009.

Verducci, Tom. "Baseball's LeBron." *Sports Illustrated,* June 8, 2009.

———. "Happy Mother's Day." *Sports Illustrated,* May 17, 2010.

———. "Wave of the Future." *Sports Illustrated,* June 7, 2010.

Vogel, Ed, and Frank Curreri. "Mom backs limits on teen drivers." *Las Vegas Review-Journal,* February 18, 2005.

Wagner, James. "Bryce Harper: his slump, broken bat and an apology." *Washington Post*, August 6, 2012.

———. "Nationals vs. Mets: Bryce Harper, Gio Gonzalez lead win over New York," *Washington Post,* August 19, 2012.

———. "Nationals vs. Braves: Washington finally wins it in the 13th inning, 5-4." *Washington Post*, August 20, 2012.

Verducci, Tom. "Might Makes Right." *Sports Illustrated*, October 1, 2012.

Wargo, Buck. "Report: 2011 rebound recovery expected, but full recovery years away." *Las Vegas Sun,* June 15, 2010.

White, Paul. "Bryce Harper knows how to read the unwritten rules." *USA Today*, May 8, 2012.

Wieberg, Steve. "The kids are ALL-STARS." *USA Today*, July 10, 2012.